WOMEN, MEN AND THE GREAT WAR

▼▼▼

THIS IS THE FIRST collection of stories from the Great War to bring together writing by women and men, combatants and civilians, pacifists and propagandists, giving a broad sense of the war's cultural impact. The collection includes stories rarely if ever reprinted since they first appeared: war stories by Richard Aldington, H.D., May Sinclair, Joseph Conrad, J. M. Barrie, Radclyffe Hall, a forgotten propaganda story by Ford Madox Ford, as well as more famous works by Ernest Hemingway, Virginia Woolf, William Faulkner, Rudyard Kipling, Sapper and Katherine Mansfield.

All the pieces are complete stories, and not extracted from a longer work. With twenty-five stories in all, the collection includes biographical and literary information on each author, and an accessible introduction.

Women, Men and the Great War

▼▼▼

An anthology of stories

edited and introduced by
Trudi Tate

MANCHESTER
UNIVERSITY PRESS
Manchester and New York

distributed exclusively in the USA and Canada by St. Martin's Press

Copyright © Manchester University Press 1995

While copyright in the volume as a whole is vested in
Manchester University Press, copyright in individual chapters
belongs to their respective authors, and no chapter may be
reproduced wholly or in part without the express permission in
writing of both author and publisher.

Published by Manchester University Press
Oxford Road, Manchester M13 9NR, UK
and Room 400, 175 Fifth Avenue, New York, NY 10010, USA

Distributed exclusively in the USA and Canada
by St. Martin's Press, Inc.,
175 Fifth Avenue, New York, NY 10010, USA

British Library Cataloguing-in-Publication Data
A catalogue record is available from the British Library

Library of Congress Cataloging-in-Publication Data applied for

ISBN 0 7190 4597 5 *hardback*
ISBN 0 7190 4598 3 *paperback*✓

First published in 1995

99 98 97 96 95   10 9 8 7 6 5 4 3 2 1

Typeset in Plantin with Zapf Chancery
by Action Typesetting Ltd, Gloucester

Printed in Great Britain
by Biddles Limited, Guildford and King's Lynn

Contents

▼▼

Acknowledgements

▼▼

Permission to reprint the stories in this collection is gratefully acknowledged to the following: for 'The Case of Lieutenant Hall' by Richard Aldington, reprinted by permission of Alister Kershaw; for 'The Bowmen' by Arthur Machen, reprinted by permission of Gerald Duckworth and Co. Ltd; for 'Count Lothar's Heart' by Kay Boyle, reprinted by permission of the author and the Watkins/Loomis Agency; for 'Speed the Plough' by Mary Butts, reprinted by permission of the Estate of the Author and Carcanet Press Ltd; for 'Ear-Ring' by H.D., reprinted by permission of New Directions Publishing, New York; for 'All the Dead Pilots' by William Faulkner, reprinted by permission of Random House, New York, and Curtis Brown Ltd, London; for 'In Another Country' by Ernest Hemingway, reprinted by permission of the Hemingway Foreign Rights Trust; for 'The French Poodle' by Wyndham Lewis, copyright Wyndham Lewis and the estate of the late Mrs G. A. Wyndham Lewis by kind permission of the Wyndham Lewis Memorial Trust (a registered charity); for 'Gustav', taken from *Ashenden* by W. Somerset Maugham, reprinted by permission of Reed Consumer Books and A. P. Watt Ltd on behalf of the Royal Literary Fund; for 'Red Tape' by May Sinclair, reprinted by permission of the Estate of May Sinclair; for 'Tourty or Tourtebattre' by Gertrude Stein, reprinted by permission of David Higham Associates and the Estate of Gertrude Stein; for 'A Love Match' by Sylvia Townsend Warner, reprinted by permission of the Estate of Sylvia Townsend Warner, Random House and Chatto & Windus; for 'The Mark on the Wall' by Virginia Woolf, reprinted by permission of the Estate of Virginia Woolf and Random House UK.

Every effort has been made to contact copyright holders; the editor and publisher would be grateful for information.

Thanks are due to Jan Adams, Gillian Beer, Diana Collecott, Con Coroneos, Ian Donaldson, Maud Ellmann, Geoffrey Gilbert, Sarah Meer, Suzanne Raitt, Anita Roy, David Trotter and Caroline Zilboorg for help and advice. I would particularly like to thank Jason Edwards and Jocelyn Stitt for their valuable research assistance. The University of Edinburgh Development Trust and the School of Research and Graduate Studies in the Faculty of Arts, University of Southampton, provided support for the completion of the project which I gratefully acknowledge.

Introduction

▼▼

AROUND SEVENTY MILLION people were mobilized in the Great War; more than nine million of them died. Historians often describe it as the world's first industrial war, which drew upon advanced technology to produce unimaginable new forms of violence and suffering.[1] The Great War ended in 1918; many people rarely think about it now, yet it had a profound effect on politics, economics, and social organization, not simply in Europe, but all over the world. Much of what is happening today—including another disastrous war in Europe, in the former Yugoslavia—has its roots in this period.

The first decades of the twentieth century produced new kinds of writing as well as new kinds of warfare. Literature of the period is often deeply troubled by the traumas of the Great War and its settlement. Many writers were personally touched by the war: some were combatants, some were pacifists, many were bereaved. Rather a surprising number wrote propaganda. As Peter Buitenhuis has argued, the extent to which respected writers secretly produced propaganda—often commissioned by the Government, but published as if it were their own spontaneous work—is one of the best-kept secrets of modern literary history. J. M. Barrie, Ford Madox Ford, Rudyard Kipling, Edith Wharton and many other senior literary figures contributed to the war effort through their writing, often to the disgust of other writers—Winifred Holtby, D. H. Lawrence, Katherine Mansfield, Virginia Woolf—who opposed the war.[2]

This collection of stories attempts to represent this broad range of responses. It includes stories which draw upon different kinds of war experiences: Aldington, Ford, and Lewis were soldiers; Holtby was a member of the Women's Auxiliary Army Corps; Stein and Hemingway worked as drivers; Wharton worked for refugee relief; Maugham worked for British intelligence. Some had close relatives who served: Conrad's son, Kipling's son, H.D.'s husband, Anand's father, Mansfield's brother, Faulkner's brother.

I have also included stories written as propaganda. Many readers will consider the pieces by Barrie and Ford to be inferior examples of their work, but they raise useful questions about the relationship between fiction and propaganda, and about what constitutes a propaganda story. (The ways in which Barrie's story invokes fantasies about masculinity is quite striking in this context.) Ford is a particularly interesting war writer: thought by some of his friends to be a spy, he wrote propaganda articles and books in 1914 and 1915; in July 1915 he joined the army, partly to escape from a difficult domestic situation. He was 41, and rather eccentric—possibly something of a liability as far as the army was concerned. Later, he was to write *Parade's End*, one of the most powerful and disturbing novels of the Great War.[3] 'The Scaremonger', the story included here, was published in November 1914 in *The Bystander*, a popular magazine devoted almost entirely to patriotic stories and pictures.

Kipling, too, wrote propaganda, and was enthusiastic about the war in its early stages. However, 'Mary Postgate' (1915), the story in this collection, is arguably not a propaganda story. While it engages with the hatred and anxieties which underlie much propagandistic writing, the story uses these emotions in unexpected ways. It appears to be a story about Mary Postgate's revenge against the Germans, following the death of Wynn, the boy she has raised since childhood. Shortly after Wynn's funeral, a child in the village is killed, possibly by a German bomb. Mary finds a man she believes to be a German airman, and responsible for the bomb in the village. The man is badly injured, but Mary refuses to fetch help; instead, she waits for the man to die, apparently taking pleasure in the spectacle. Yet the ending of the story is highly ambivalent. What actually happened in the village? Is the airman's nationality clearly established? Does he exist at all, or is he a symptom of fantasy, or hysteria?[4] Who is the target of hatred in this tale? The story takes place entirely in England, away from the war zone. Yet the trauma of the war, and some of its violence, permeate the very fabric of civilian lives. Kipling's cousin, Oliver Baldwin, described it as 'the wickedest story ever written'. Not long after it was finished, Kipling's son John was killed at Loos. Kipling became much more ambivalent about the war, and devoted himself to commemorating the dead, through the Imperial War Graves Commission. The familiar phrase on hundreds of war memorials—'Their name liveth for evermore'—was Kipling's suggestion.

Another familiar image found on war memorials is the Angel of Mons. This has a curious origin. In September 1914, Arthur Machen published 'The Bowmen' (included here), a rather absurd account of St George and the bowmen of Agincourt coming to the aid of British soldiers against an overpowering force of Germans. Machen had invented the tale, but it was taken up and reprinted, much to his embarrassment, as if it were the true story of a war miracle. In the course of several retellings, 'The Bowmen' was transformed into the story of the Angels of Mons, saving the British in their hour of need. Representations of this fantasy can be found on war memorials all over Britain and the Commonwealth.[5]

'The Bowmen' tells us something about the way the war was imagined, and the kinds of fantasies it produced. Some of the stories here draw on personal experience and memories of the war; others ask questions about the very act of commemoration. What kinds of fantasies are involved in remembering the dead? Where is identification located? These questions inform Katherine Mansfield's ironic story, 'The Fly'. The central character of this story—the boss—prides himself on his ability to weep in memory of his son, killed in the war some years earlier. To what extent can mourning be sincere, the story asks, and what does it mean when someone takes pleasure in it? These are troubling questions; even more troubling is the account of the boss's cruelty towards a fly. His admiration for its fortitude seems genuine, even as he deliberately prolongs its struggle, and finally kills it. Mansfield's story investigates the ways in which disgust (as well as pleasure) can be found in repetition, in cruelty, in watching the results of one's own actions, while taking no responsibility for the consequences.[6] What does the story mean? We might interpret the fly as representing the dead son. The boss's generation started the war, and sent the son's generation off to do the actual dying (a motif found in a good deal of war writing, and especially in the trench poetry). The older men watch the younger men's struggle, genuinely admiring their courage and refusing to acknowledge their own complicity in their suffering. Men such as the boss are the survivors; they can discard the wreckage of the war, as if it were a dead fly swept into a waste-paper basket. Yet 'The Fly' is more complex than this reading suggests. Its power lies partly in the way in which the boss *identifies* with the fly, even as he causes its suffering. The fly's death represents the lost son, but it also represents a loss within the father—the loss of his own youth, perhaps, and his ability to mourn. The question of responsibility seems to evaporate in the process of identification; perhaps this is why the story is so unsettling to read. The story also suggests that identification is not always the most effective way of understanding the trauma of war; indeed, it can be an impediment to understanding, and can obscure significant historical differences.

The meaning of the Great War troubled writers for years afterwards. Some writers, such as Winifred Holtby, devoted themselves to pacifist and internationalist movements after the war. Holtby's story, 'So Handy for the Fun Fair' (1934), tells of one ordinary woman's memory of her experiences at the front, and gestures towards reconciliation with the pain of the war. A powerful account of coming to terms with loss, Holtby's story none the less lacks the edge of Mansfield's acerbic tale. The differences between the stories in this collection raise important questions about the relationship between literary form and the writing about the trauma of war. We tend to assume that the most powerful war prose is always realist, drawing upon the conventions of nineteenth-century narrative. Yet much modernist and avant-garde writing also addresses the war, often in striking and powerful ways. This collection is unusual in the way it brings together different kinds of war writing, placing realist, sentimental, and propagandist war stories alongside more experimental, modernist writings. Writers such as Butts, Faulkner, Ford, H.D., Hemingway, Lawrence, Lewis, Stein, and Woolf are known and perhaps most valued for their contributions to modernist, experimental, and avant-garde literature. Yet all these writers also had important things to say about the war. Our own knowledge of the events of the Great War often comes through literary works; indeed, literature is one of the key ways in which the war was written as history. Modernism's contribution to these processes is still inadequately understood, but it seems to me that it has had an important influence, right up to the present day, on the ways in which our culture remembers—and forgets—the Great War, and the fantasies we continue to invest in it.

One strange fantasy found in some of these stories casts the war as a source of sexual ecstasy, especially for women; we might interpret Kipling's 'Mary Postgate' or Sinclair's 'Red Tape' in these terms.[7] We also find a strain of misogyny running through a number of war stories which depict women as either uncritically excited by the war, or as agents of its trivialization (in Wharton's 'The Refugees', for example). To some extent, anxiety about the war's violence is displaced on to women, and expressed as fear or hatred of women's sexuality—an attitude expressed quite overtly by the central character in Aldington's story, 'The Case of Lieutenant Hall'. Lieutenant Hall is suffering from war neuroses, and has hallucinations about a German soldier he has killed. When someone suggests that he take leave and visit a brothel, he becomes 'furiously angry', somewhat to his own surprise. 'I said that since I had seen so many men's bodies mangled, suffering and dead, the thought of human flesh was repulsive to me', he writes in his diary. 'I said I hated the thought of women.' Women—'bloody women', Hall calls them—are blamed for men's suffering, and hated for their wholeness. Men, in this story, are spectacles of injury, mutilation, and suffering. Hall's own complicity in this process drives him into madness and eventually he kills himself. The story sets out some of the contradictions which surround gender and the war: men—who have engaged in acts of violence—sometimes blame women, who have not. Responsibility for the war is too great to bear, so it is displaced elsewhere, or negated altogether, in this case through suicide.

Anxiety about how gender is constituted in a time of industrial warfare informs a number of the stories here. We might be tempted to describe the war as a time of continual crisis; a number of critics have argued that it was certainly a period of crisis for masculinity, as large numbers of men were killed, mutilated, and driven mad in the name of a heroic masculinity.[8] But the situation—and its writing—are more complex than this.

Gender was certainly an important issue in the Great War, but we need an accurate sense of how it functioned. Almost all soldiers were men; but not all men were soldiers—far from it. The idea that half the population of Britain went off to the war is quite misleading. Even more misleading is the claim that an entire generation of men died. In fact, approximately six million British men served in the war; of these, up to one million were killed. Though the mobilization was enormous, the majority of British men were actually civilians. Furthermore, many men who went to the war never saw a battle. Front-line troops were only one part of the armed forces. In order to keep men in the trenches and on battleships or planes, there was a vast machine behind the lines, organizing food, transport and weaponry, servicing vehicles, etc. And, as Wyndham Lewis describes in *Blasting and Bombadiering* (1937), even in the front lines soldiers spent a lot of time doing nothing at all. At other times they were subject to extraordinary levels of pain and violence, mutilated in shell explosions, suffocated in gas attacks, drowned in the mud, being blown completely to pieces. Men's experience of the war ranged from intense suffering and horror, to boredom, inaction and indifference. And as societies redefined manhood in terms of soldiering, civilian men found themselves in an odd, negated position in relation to masculinity. This sometimes produced some curious anxieties in their writings (as we see in much of Lawrence, for example). But we also find that civilian men sometimes wrote extremely plausible war stories, adopting, mimicking—and also producing—the voice of a combatant masculinity (Faulkner's 'All the Dead Pilots' and Conrad's 'The Tale', for example).

What was the war's effect upon discourses of femininity? On the one hand, we find expressions of anxiety and misogyny, sometimes directed at the figures of specific women, and sometimes focused on a more general notion of 'femininity', which is often linked with the idea of someone whose body is not under threat. Some writers use women to represent the entire civilian population, and make them a target of hatred and resentment for traumatized soldiers. The war extended the horizons of many women, allowing them more mobility in the public sphere; this is celebrated by some writers and deplored by others. Like men, women occupied a range of positions in relation to the war; some supported it, others opposed it. Some were involved directly, as nurses, drivers, or workers at the front; others were involved indirectly, working in munitions and related industries. And women's writing, like men's, expresses a variety of attitudes, anxieties and fantasies about the war.

Unlike most war anthologies, this collection includes writing by women and men in roughly equal numbers. But readers will find that the writing refuses to fall into convenient categories of women's writing or men's writing. In many instances, whether a story is pro-war or anti-war, modernist or traditional in form, a tale of civilians or a tale of soldiers is at least as significant as the gender of the author.

The war permeated many aspects of civilian culture, not just at the time, but for years afterwards. We see this in the stories by Woolf and Anand. Both these pieces invoke the war only obliquely, yet they indicate how it shaped the lives of people who were geographically distant from most of its events. In 'The Mark on the Wall' (1917), the war is mentioned only briefly, referring to its effect on the newspaper. 'It's no good buying newspapers', complains one character, 'Nothing ever happens. Curse this war; God damn this war!' Reading this story today, it is easy to miss the significance of this remark. Nothing might be happening in the newspapers, but a good deal was happening in the war. In Britain, especially, the combined effects of propaganda and censorship often made newspaper reports highly inaccurate. Terrible disasters were reported as victories; casualty figures were often false; atrocity stories were invented; accounts of real suffering were suppressed. The reporting aimed to maintain (or create) civilian support for the war; stories were angled (or fabricated) to serve that end, sometimes with scant regard for the actual events. Many people commented on the hysterical tone adopted by the newspapers; some readers, such as Woolf, were also aware that the reports were by no means factually accurate. The war touched the lives of millions of people, yet none of them, whether soldier or civilian, had any reliable information about what was going on. As a result, many people became sceptical about the political processes; this was particularly troubling immediately after the war, when a broadly-based democracy was introduced into Britain for the first time.[9]

Anand's story 'The Maharaja and the Tortoise' (1944) sets up a link between the war and questions of political rights in India. A comic tale about political corruption, this story alludes in passing to the relationship between India and the colonial master which took 1.3 million Indians into the war as soldiers and labourers, and then ignored their claims for independence afterwards. The same colonial power supports the despotic maharaja after the war, his rule a blend of persuasion and coercion. In the long run, the Great War probably played a major role in the decolonizing process, weakening the European powers (and their economies) to the point that they were forced to abandon control of the countries they had colonized. Anand's brief reference to India's relationship with Britain during the Great War would have carried considerable resonance at the time it appeared, not long before independence was finally achieved. For black Americans, too, the war brought certain benefits, giving impetus to liberation movements in the United States. In other words, the effects of the war were contradictory and mixed, bringing intense suffering to millions of people, yet precipitating valuable social reforms in some countries.

In Britain, for example, the Great War led to a narrowing of the divide between classes; the rich lost some of their wealth, while the standard of living for poorer people rose significantly in terms of housing, health care, and education. In the Empire, too, results were mixed. In the short term, the British Empire expanded, as Britain claimed territories from the defunct Ottoman Empire. In the longer term, however, the war had so depleted the British economy that Britain could no longer afford to administer its colonial territories effectively, nor defend its control against local independence movements. The decolonization which occurred after the Second World War was arguably set in motion by the Great War, as was the gradual shift from Europe to the United States as the dominant world power. This shift is registered in H.D.'s enigmatic story, 'Ear-Ring' (1936). Centred around a dinner party in Greece in 1920, the story refers several times to the new explorations for oil in the former Ottoman regions—an issue which continues to exercise both Europe and the United States.

Many black soldiers fought in the Great War, especially in the armies of France and the United States. Around a quarter of a million men from French and British colonies also served as labourers, often under terrible conditions. But the experience of the war also strengthened liberation movements in colonized countries, as well as among black people in the United States. Gwendolyn Bennett's story, 'Wedding Day' (1926), is set in Paris in the years surrounding the war. The central character, Paul Watson, is a black American musician who is imprisoned for fighting with racist whites. The war provides him with an early release from prison; the story locates the war primarily in terms of racial politics, emphasizing its liberatory potential rather than its suffering. After the war, Paul seems to have gained a certain level of acceptance among white people, and he becomes engaged to a white woman. The story ends with Paul's realization that he has been exploited by his white lover, and that black rights gained in the war are at best tenuous. For all that, the story invokes the war as an agent of positive change, at least potentially. This thread of optimism is relatively rare in white writing of the post-war period, and reminds us of the complexity of the war's consequences.

Several stories engage with both the fantasies and the historical effects of the war. Radclyffe Hall's 'Miss Ogilvy Finds Herself' (1934) is a strange tale of a lesbian woman who has served in an ambulance corps, finds herself undervalued in civilian life, then lapses into a fantasy of living freely as a man in a pre-historic age. In a later edition of the collection of stories published under this title, Hall dedicated the work to all the lesbian women who had contributed to the war, and whose efforts had been ignored.

All the stories in this anthology are complete texts; none has been abridged. This allows us to explore the ways in which the war is turned into a form of history, as well as aestheticized, within the constraints of a single genre. Overall, this book attempts to give a sense of the breadth of the cultural impact of the war—an impact which can still be felt today, both in the political climate in which we live, and in the kinds of literature we produce.

Notes

1 For historical details I have drawn on the following works: J. M. Winter, *The Experience of World War I* (Oxford, Equinox, 1988); J. M. Winter, *The Great War and the British People* (London, Macmillan, 1986); Trevor Wilson, *The Myriad*

Faces of War (Oxford, Polity, 1986); Claire Tylee, *The Great War and Women's Consciousness* (London, Macmillan, 1990); Samuel Hynes, *A War Imagined* (London, The Bodley Head, 1990); Arthur Marwick, *The Deluge*, 2nd edn (London, Macmillan, 1991).

2 Other writers who wrote propaganda include Arnold Bennett, John Buchan, Arthur Conan Doyle, John Galsworthy, H. G. Wells, Mrs Humphrey Ward. Some, such as Buchan, wrote highly inaccurate reports for the newspapers, and helped to suppress information about military incompetence. Buchan was director of the Department of Information in 1917; Bennett was a director of propaganda in 1918. For a detailed and fascinating account, see Buitenhuis, *The Great War of Words* (London, Batsford, 1989).

3 *Parade's End* was published as four separate novels, 1924–28. Another war memoir, *No Enemy*, was published in 1929 (rpt New York, Ecco, 1984). For details of Ford's war experiences, see Alan Judd, *Ford Madox Ford* (London, Flamingo, 1991); Thomas Moser, *The Life in the Fiction of Ford Madox Ford* (Princeton University Press, 1980); Nora Tomlinson and Robert Green, 'Ford's Wartime Journalism', *Agenda* (1989). See also Joan Hardwick, *An Immodest Violet: The Life of Violet Hunt* (London, André Deutsch, 1990). Hunt lived with Ford for several years; their relationship ended when he went to the war.

4 See, for example, John Bayley's discussion of 'Mary Postgate', in *The Short Story* (Brighton, Harvester, 1988).

5 'The Bowmen' was first published in *The Evening News*. Many parish journals wanted to republish it; psychical journals were also interested. When Machen protested that the story was entirely his invention, it was argued that he must have received telepathic messages from soldiers who witnessed the event. The Angels of Mons version of the Bowmen story seems to have been widely believed, but, as Buitenhuis points out in *The Great War of Words*, there has never been any evidence to support the story. See also Machen's introduction to *The Bowmen and Other Legends of the War*, 2nd edn (London, Simpkin, Marshall, Hamilton, Kent and Co. Ltd, 1915).

6 For a discussion of disgust in writing of this period, see David Trotter, *The English Novel in History, 1895–1920* (London, Routledge, 1993); for a discussion of 'The Fly', see Con Coroneos, 'Flies and Violets in Mansfield', in Suzanne Raitt and Trudi Tate, eds, *Women's Fiction of the Great War* (Oxford, Oxford University Press, 1996).

7 For a discussion of women, sexuality and the Great War, see Sandra Gilbert, 'Soldier's Heart', in Sandra Gilbert and Susan Gubar, *No Man's Land*, vol. 2 (New Haven, Yale University Press, 1989). Gilbert's view is highly contentious and arguably too sweeping; for a detailed critique, see Claire Tylee, '"Maleness Run Riot": The Great War and Women's Resistance to Militarism', *Women's Studies International Forum*, 11 (1988), 199–210. For other views of women and the Great War, see Tylee's *The Great War and Women's Consciousness*; Dorothy Goldman, ed., *Women and World War I: The Written Response* (London, Macmillan, 1993); Sharon Ouditt, *Fighting Forces, Writing Women* (London, Routledge, 1993); Raitt and Tate, eds. *Women's Fiction of the Great War*.

8 See, for example, Gilbert, 'Soldier's Heart'; Elaine Showalter, *The Female Malady: Women, Madness and English Culture, 1830–1980* (London, Virago, 1987).

9 The representation of the People Act of 1918 extended the number of men who could vote, and also enfranchised some categories of women for the first time. Voting rights were not fully extended to women on equal terms with men until 1928.

▼▼▼

A Love Match

IT WAS MR PILKINGTON who brought the Tizards to Hallowby. He met them, a quiet couple, at Carnac, where he had gone for a schoolmasterly Easter holiday to look at the monoliths. After two or three meetings at a café, they invited him to their rented chalet. It was a cold, wet afternoon and a fire of pine cones crackled on the hearth. 'We collect them on our walks,' said Miss Tizard. 'It's an economy. And it gives us an object.' The words, and the formal composure of her manner, made her seem like a Frenchwoman. Afterwards, he learned that the Tizards were a Channel Island family and had spent their childhood in Jersey. The ancestry that surfaced in Miss Tizard's brisk gait and erect carriage, brown skin and compact sentences, did not show in her brother. His fair hair, his red face, his indecisive remarks, his diffident movements—as though with the rest of his body he were apologising for his stiff leg—were entirely English. He ought not, thought Mr Pilkington, to be hanging about in France. He'd done more than enough for France already. For this was in 1923 and Mr Pilkington, with every intention of preserving a historian's impartiality, was nevertheless infected by the current mood of disliking the French.

The weather continued cold and wet; there was a sameness about the granite avenues. Mr Pilkington's mind became increasingly engaged with the possibility, the desirability, the positive duty of saving that nice fellow Tizard from wasting his days in exile. He plied him with hints, with suggestions, with tactful inquiries. Beyond discovering that money was not the obstacle to return, he got no further. Tizard, poor fellow, must be under his sister's thumb. Yet it was from the sister that he got his first plain answer. 'Justin would mope if he had nothing to do.' Mr Pilkington stopped himself from commenting on the collection of pine cones as an adequate lifework. As though she had read his thought, she went on, 'There is a difference between idling in a

foreign country and being an idler in your own.' At that moment
Tizard limped into the room with crayfish bristling from his
shopping basket. 'It's begun,' he said ruefully. '*La Jeune France*
has arrived. I've just seen two young men in pink trousers with
daisy chains round their necks, riding through the town on
donkeys.' Mr Pilkington asked if this was a circus. Miss Tizard
explained that it was the new generation, and would make Carnac
a bedlam till the summer's end. 'Of course, there's a certain
amount of that sort of thing in England, too,' observed Mr Pilkington. 'But only in the South. It doesn't trouble us at Hallowby.'
As he spoke, he was conscious of playing a good card; then the
immensity of the trump he held broke upon him. He was too
excited to speak. Inviting them to dine at his hotel on the following night, he went away.

By next evening, more of *La Jeune France* had arrived, and was
mustered outside the hotel extemporising a bullfight ballet in
honour of St Cornély, patron saint of cattle and of the parish
church. Watching Tizard's look of stoically endured embarrassment Mr Pilkington announced that he had had a blow; the man
who had almost promised to become curator of the Beelby Military Museum had written to say he couldn't take up the post.
'He didn't say why. But I know why. Hallowby is too quiet for
him.'

'But I thought Hallowby had blast furnaces and strikes and all
that sort of thing,' said Tizard.

'That is Hallowby juxta Mare,' replied Mr Pilkington. 'We are
Old Hallowby. Very quiet; quite old, too. The school was founded
in 1623. We shall be having our modest tercentenary this
summer. That is why I am so put out by Dalsover's not taking up
the curatorship. I hoped to have the museum all in order. It would
have been something to visit, if it rains during the Celebrations.'
He allowed a pause.

Tizard, staring at the toothpicks, inquired, 'Is it a wet climate?'

But Mr Pilkington was the headmaster of a minor public
school, a position of command. As if the pause had not taken
place, raising his voice above the bullfight he told how fifty years
earlier Davenport Beelby, a rich man's sickly son, during a lesson
on the Battle of Minden awoke to military glory and began to
collect regimental buttons. Buttons, badges, pikes, muskets and
bayonets, shakos and helmets, despatches, newspaper cuttings,
stones from European battlefields, sand from desert campaigns—
his foolish collection grew into the lifework of a devoted eccentric
and, as such collections sometimes do, became valuable and
authoritative, though never properly catalogued. Two years ago he

had died, bequeathing the collection to his old school, with a fund sufficient for upkeep and the salary of a curator.

'I wish you'd consider coming as our curator,' said Mr Pilkington. 'I'm sure you would find it congenial. Beelby wanted an Army man. Three mornings a week would be quite enough.'

Tizard shifted his gaze from the toothpicks to the mustard jar. 'I am not an Army man,' he said. 'I just fought. Not the same thing, you know.'

Miss Tizard exclaimed, 'No! Not at all,' and changed the subject.

But later that evening she said to her brother, 'Once we were there, we shouldn't see much of him. It's a possibility.'

'Do you want to go home, Celia?'

'I think it's time we did. We were both of us born for a sober, conventional, taxpaying life, and if—'

'*Voici Noël!*' sang the passing voices. '*Voici Noël! Voici Noël, petits enfants!*'

She composed her twitching hands and folded them on her lap. 'We were young rowdies once,' he said placatingly.

A fortnight later, they were Mr Pilkington's guests at Hallowby. A list of empty houses had been compiled by Miss Robson, the secretary. All were variously suitable; each in turn was inspected by Miss Tizard and rejected. Mr Pilkington felt piqued that his offer of a post should dance attendance on the aspect of a larder or the presence of decorative tiles. Miss Tizard was a disappointment to him; he had relied on her support. Now it was the half-hearted Tizard who seemed inclined to root, while she flitted from one eligibile residence to another, appearing, as he remarked to the secretary, to expect impossibilities. Yet when she settled as categorically as a queen bee the house she chose had really nothing to be said for it. A square, squat mid-Victorian box, Newton Lodge was one of the ugliest houses in Hallowby; though a high surrounding wall with a green door in it hid the totality of its ugliness from passers-by, its hulking chimneys proclaimed what was below. It was not even well situated. It stood in a deteriorating part of the town, and was at some distance from the school buildings and the former gymnasium—Victorian also— which had been assigned to the Beelby Collection. But the house having been chosen, the curatorship was bestowed and the move made. Justin Tizard, rescued from wasting his days in exile— though too late for tercentenary celebrations—began his duties as curator by destroying a quantity of cobwebs and sending for a window-cleaner.

All through the summer holidays he worked on, sorting things into heaps, subdividing the heaps into lesser heaps. Beelby's executors must have given carte-blanche to the packers, who had acted on the principle of filling up with anything that came handy, and the unpackers had done little more than tumble things out and scatter them with notices saying 'DO NOT DISTURB'. The largest heap consisted of objects he could not account for, but unaccountably it lessened, till the day came when he could look round on tidiness. Ambition seized him. Tidiness is not enough; no one looks twice at tidiness. There must also be parade and ostentation. He bought stands, display cases, dummies for the best uniforms. Noticing a decayed wooden horse in the saddler's shop, he bought that, too; trapped, with its worser side to the wall and with a cavalry dummy astride, it made a splendid appearance. He combed plumes, shook out bearskins, polished holsters and gunstocks, oiled the demi-culverin, sieved the desert sand. At this stage, his sister came and polished with him, mended, refurbished, sewed on loose buttons. Of the two, she had more feeling for the exhibits themselves, for the discolouring glory and bloodshed they represented. It was the housewife's side that appealed to him. Sometimes, hearing him break into the whistle of a contented mind, she would look up from her work and stare at him with the unbelief of thankfulness.

Early in the autumn term, Mr Pilkington made time to visit the museum. He did not expect much and came prepared with speeches of congratulation and encouragement. They died on his lips when he saw the transformation. Instead, he asked how much the display cases had cost, and the dummies, and the horse, and how much of the upkeep fund remained after all this expenditure. He could not find fault; there was no reason to do so. He was pleased to see Tizard so well established as master in his own house. Perhaps he was also pleased that there was no reason to find fault. Though outwardly unchanged, the Tizard of Carnac appeared to have been charged with new contents—with something obstinately reckless beneath the easy-going manner, with watchfulness beneath the diffidence. But this, reflected Mr Pilkington, might well be accounted for by the startling innovations in the museum. He stayed longer than he meant, and only after leaving remembered that he had omitted to say how glad he was that Tizard had accepted the curatorship. This must be put right; he did not want to discourage the young man who had worked so hard and so efficiently, and also he must get into the way of remembering that Tizard was in fact a young man—under thirty. Somehow, one did not think of him as a young man.

Justin Tizard, newly a captain in an infantry regiment, came on leave after the battle of the Somme. His sister met the train at Victoria. There were some pigeons strutting on the platform and he was watching them when a strange woman in black came up to him, touched his shoulder, and said, 'Justin!' It was as though Celia were claiming a piece of lost luggage, he thought. She had a taxi waiting, and they drove to her flat. She asked about his health, about his journey; then she congratulated him on his captaincy. 'Practical reasons,' he said. 'My habit of not getting killed. They were bound to notice it sooner or later.' After this, they fell silent. He looked out of the window at the streets so clean and the people so busy with their own affairs. 'That's a new Bovril poster, isn't it?' he inquired. Her answer was so slow in coming that he didn't really take in whether it was yes or no.

Her flat was new, anyway. She had only been in it since their mother's remarriage. It was up a great many flights of stairs, and she spoke of moving to somewhere with a lift, now that Tim's legacy had made a rich woman of her. The room smelled of polish and flowers. There was a light-coloured rug on the floor and above this was the blackness of Celia's skirts. She was wearing black for her fiancé. The news of his death had come to her in this same room, while she was still sorting books and hanging pictures. Looking round the room, still not looking at Celia, he saw Tim's photograph on her desk. She saw his glance, and hers followed it. 'Poor Tim!' they said, both speaking at once, the timbre of their voices relating them. 'They say he was killed instantaneously,' she went on. 'I hope it's true—though I suppose they always say that.'

'I'm sure it is,' he replied. He knew that Tim had been blown to pieces. Compassion made it possible to look at her. Dressed in black, possessing these new surroundings, she seemed mature and dignified beyond her actual three years' seniority. For the first time in his life he saw her not as a sister but as an individual. But he could not see her steadily for long. There was a blur on his sight, a broth of mud and flame and frantic unknown faces and writhing entrails. When she showed him to his bedroom she stepped over mud that heaved with the bodies of men submerged in it. She had drawn the curtains. There was a bed with sheets turned back, and a bedside lamp shed a serene, unblinking light on the pillows. 'Bed!' he exclaimed, and heard the spontaneity die in his voice. 'Wonderful to see a bed!'

'And this is the bathroom. I've got everything planned. First of all, you must have a bath, lie and soak in it. And then put on these pyjamas and the dressing gown, and we will have supper.'

Left to himself, he was violently sick. Shaking with fatigue, he sat in a hot scented bath and cleaned his knees with scrupulous care, like a child. Outside was the noise of London.

The pyjamas were silk, the dressing gown was quilted and wrapped him round like a caress. In the sitting room was Celia, still a stranger, though now a stranger without a hat. There was a table sparkling with silver and crystal, smoked salmon, a bottle of champagne. It was all as she had planned it for Tim—Oh, poor Celia!

They discussed their mother's remarriage. It had been decided on with great suddenness, and appeared inexplicable. Though they refrained from saying much, their comments implied that her only reason for marrying a meat king from the Argentine was to get away from England and the war. 'There he was, at eleven in the morning, with a carnation—a foot shorter than she,' said Celia, describing the return from the registry office.

'In that case, he must be four foot three.'

'He is exactly four foot three. I stole up and measured him.'

Spoken in her imperturbable voice, this declaration struck him as immensely funny, as funny as a nursery joke. They laughed hilariously, and after this their evening went almost naturally.

Turning back after his unadorned, brotherly 'Good night, Celia,' he exclaimed, 'But where are you sleeping?'

'In here.' Before he could demur she went on, 'The sofa fits me. It would be far too short for you.'

He told her how balmily he had slept, one night behind the lines, with his head on a bag of nails.

'Exactly! That is why tonight you are going to sleep properly. In a bed.'

She heard him get into bed, heard the lamp switched off. Almost immediately she heard his breathing lengthen into slumber. Then, a few minutes later, he began to talk in his sleep.

Perhaps a scruple—the dishonourableness of being an eavesdropper, a Peeping Tom—perhaps mere craven terror, made her try not to listen. She began to read, and when she found that impossible she repeated poems she had learned at school, and when that failed she polished the silver cigarette box. But Justin's voice was raised, and the partition wall was thin, and the ghastly confidences went on and on. She could not escape them. She was dragged, a raw recruit, into battle.

In the morning she thought she would not be able to look him in the face. But he was cheerful, and so was she. She had got off from the canteen, she explained, while he was on leave; they had nothing to do but enjoy themselves. They decided to have some new experiences, so they went up the Monument. If he wants to throw himself off, she thought, I won't stop him. They looked down on London; on the curve of the Thames, the shipping, the busy lighters. They essayed how many City churches they could identify by their spires. They talked about Pepys. She would be surprised, Justin said, how many chaps carried a copy of the *Diary*, and she asked if bullets also glanced off Pepys carried in a breast pocket. So they made conversation quite successfully. And afterwards, when they had decided to go for a walk down Whitechapel High Street and lunch off winkles at a stall, many people glanced at them with kindness and sentimentality, and an old woman patted Celia's back, saying, 'God bless you, dearie! Isn't it lovely to have him home?'

Whitechapel was a good idea. The throng of people carried some of the weight of self-consciousness for them; the wind blowing up-river and the hooting of ships' sirens made them feel they were in some foreign port of call, taking a stroll till it was time to re-embark. He was less aware that she had grown strange to him, and she was momentarily able to forget the appalling stranger who had raved in her bed all night.

They dined at a restaurant, and went on to a music hall. That night he took longer to fall asleep. She had allowed herself a thread of hope, when he began to talk again. Three Justins competed, thrusting each other aside: a cold, attentive observer, a debased child, a devil bragging in hell. At intervals they were banished by a recognisable Justin interminably muttering to himself, 'Here's a sword for Toad, here's a sword for Rat, here's a sword for Mole, here's a sword for Badger.' The reiteration from that bible of their childhood would stick on the word, 'Rat'. 'Got you!' And he was off again.

The next day they went to the Zoo. The Zoo was not so effica-cious as Whitechapel. It was feeling the pinch, the animals looked shabby and dejected, many cages were empty. Two sleepless nights had made Celia's feet swell. It was pain to walk, pain to stand. She wondered how much longer she could keep it up, this 'God bless you, dearie' pretence of a lovely leave. The day accu-mulated its hours like a windlass. The load grew heavier; the windlass baulked under it, but wound on. He went to bed with the usual 'Good night, Celia'. As usual, she undressed and put on that derision of a nightdress, and wrapped herself in an eider-down and lay down to wait under the smiling gaze of Tim's photograph. She felt herself growing icy cold, couldn't remember if she had wound her watch, couldn't remember what diversion she had planned for the morrow, was walking over Richmond

Bridge in a snowstorm, when she noticed he had begun again. *She noticed*. It had come to that. Two nights of a vicarious endurance of what was being endured, had been endured, would continue to be endured by a cancelled generation, had so exhausted her that now she felt neither horror nor despair, merely a bitter acquiescence. Justin went on with his Hail Devil Rosary, and in France the guns went on and on, and the mud dried into dust and slumped back into mud again. People went down to Kent to listen to the noise of the guns: the people in Kent said that they had grown used to it, didn't hear it any longer. The icy cold sensation bored into her midriff, nailed her down in sleep.

Some outcry, some exclamation (she could not afterwards remember what it was), woke her. Before she knew what she was doing she was in the next room, trying to waken the man who lay so rigidly in her bed, who, if she could awaken him, would be Justin, her brother Justin. 'Oh, poor Justin, my poor Justin!' Throwing herself on the bed, she clasped him in her arms, lifted his head to lie against her breast, kissed his chattering lips. 'There, there!' She felt him relax, waken, drag her towards him. They rushed into the escape of love like winter-starved cattle rushing into a spring pasture.

When light came into the room, they drew a little apart and looked at each other.

'Now we've done it,' he said; and hearing the new note in his voice she replied, 'A good thing, don't you think?'

Their release left them no option. After a few hours they were not even astonished. They were mated for life, that was all—for a matter of days, so they made the most of it. At the end of his leave they parted in exaltation, he convinced that he was going off to be killed, she that she would bear his child, to which she would devote the remainder of her existence.

A little later she knew she was not pregnant.

Early in the new year Justin, still panoplied in this legendary and by now rather ludicrous charmed life, was made a major. In April, he was wounded in the leg. 'Nothing to worry about,' he wrote; 'just a few splinters. I am in bed, as peaceful as a pincushion.' Later, she heard that he had been moved to a hospital on the outskirts of London. One of the splinters had escaped notice, and gas gangrene had developed in the wound.

I shall be a peg leg, he thought. It's not decent for a peg leg to make love; even to his sister. He was ravaged with fret and behaving with perfect decorum when Celia was shown in—dressed all in leaf green, walking like an empress, smelling delicious. For a moment the leafgreen Celia was almost as much of a stranger as the Celia all in black had been. When she kissed him, he discovered that she was shaking from head to foot. 'There, there,' he said, patting her. Still holding his hand, she addressed herself to charming Nurse Painter. Nurse Painter was in favour of sisters. They weren't so much trouble, didn't upset a patient, as sweethearts or wives did—and you didn't have to be hanging round all the time, ready to shoo them off. When Celia came next day, Nurse Painter congratulated her on having done the Major no end of good. There had been a lot of pus; she liked to see a lot of pus.

They continued to give satisfaction; when Justin left hospital with a knee that would always be stiff and from time to time cause him pain, Nurse Painter's approval went with them. A sister was just what he wanted—there would be no silly excitement; and as Miss Tizard was a trifle older than the Major, there would be a restraining hand if called for. If Nurse Painter had known what lay beneath this satisfactory arrangement, it is probable that her approval would not have been seriously withdrawn. The war looked like going on for ever; the best you could hope for was a stalemate. Potatoes were unobtainable, honesty was no more, it was hate and muddle wherever you looked. If a gentleman and lady could pluck up heart enough to love and be happy—well, good luck to them!

Justin and Celia went to Oxfordshire, where they compared the dragonflies on the Windrush with the dragonflies on the Evenlode. Later, they went to France.

Beauty cannot be suborned. Never again did Justin see Celia quivering with beauty as she had done on the day she came to him in hospital. But he went on thinking she had a charming face and the most entertaining eyebrows in the world. Loving each other criminally and sincerely, they took pains to live together happily and to safeguard their happiness from injuries of their own infliction or from outside. It would have been difficult for them to be anything but inconspicuous, or to be taken for anything but a brother and sister—the kind of brother and sister of whom one says, 'It will be rather hard for her when he marries'. Their relationship, so conveniently obvious to the public eye, was equally convenient in private life, for it made them unusually intuitive about each other's feelings. Brought up to the same standard of behaviour, using the same vocabulary, they felt no need to impress each other and were not likely to be taken aback by each other's likes and dislikes. Even the fact of remembering the same foxed copy of *The Swiss Family Robinson* with the tear across the picture of the boa constrictor was a reassuring bond. During the first years in France they felt they would like to have a child—or for the sake of the other's happiness ought to have a child—and discussed the possibilities of a child put out to nurse, learning French as its native speech, and then being adopted as a postwar orphan, since it was now too late for it to be a war orphan. But however the child was dated, it would be almost certain to declare its inheritance of Grandfather Tizard's nose, and as a fruitful incest is thought even worse of than a barren one, they sensibly gave up the idea; though regretting it.

Oddly enough, after settling in Hallowby they regretted it no longer. They had a home in England, a standing and things to do. Justin had the Beelby Museum; Celia had a household. In Hallowby it was not possible to stroll out to a restaurant or to bring home puddings from the pastry cook, fillets of veal netted into bolsters by the butcher. Celia had to cook seriously, and soon found that if she was to cook meals worth eating she must go shopping too. This was just what was needed for their peace and quiet, since to be seen daily shopping saved a great deal of repetitious explanation that she and Justin could not afford to keep a servant in the house but must be content with Mrs Mugthwaite coming in three afternoons a week, and a jobbing gardener on Fridays. True, it exposed her to a certain amount of condolence and amazement from the school wives, but as they, like Mrs Mugthwaite, came only in the afternoons, she could bear with it. Soon they came more sparingly; for, as Justin pointed out, poverty is the sturdiest of all shelters, since people feel it to be rather sad and soon don't think about it, whereas her first intention of explaining that ever since her Aunt Dinah had wakened in the middle of the night to see an angered cook standing over her with a meat hatchet she had been nervous of servants sleeping under the same roof would only provoke gossip, surmise and insistent recommendations of cooks without passions. Justin was more long-sighted than Celia. She always knew what to do or say at the moment. He could look ahead, foresee dangers, and take steps to dodge them.

They did not see as much of Mr Pilkington as they had apprehended, and members of the staff were in no hurry to take up with another of Pilkington's Pets. Celia grew alarmed; if you make no friends, you become odd. She decided that they must occasionally go to church, though not too often or too enthusiastically, as it would then become odd that they did not take the Sacrament. No doubt a great many vicious church attenders took the Sacrament, and the rubric only forbids it to 'open and notorious evil-livers', which they had every intention of not being; but she could see a scruple of honour at work in Justin, so she did not labour this argument. There was a nice, stuffy pitch-pine St Cuthbert's near by, and at judicious intervals they went there for evensong—thereby renewing another bond of childhood: the pleasure of hurrying home on a cold evening to eat baked potatoes hot from the oven. How old Mr Gillespie divined from Justin's church demeanour that he was a whist player was a mystery never solved. But he divined it. He had barely saved Celia's umbrella from being blown inside out, remarking, 'You're newcomers, aren't you? You don't know the east wind at this corner,' before he was saying to Justin, 'You don't play whist, by any chance?' But probably he would have asked this of anyone not demonstrably a raving maniac, for since Colin Colbeck's death he, Miss Colbeck and Canon Pendarves were desperate for a fourth player. Canon Pendarves gave dinner parties, with a little music afterwards. Celia, driven into performance and remembering how Becky Sharp had wooed Lady Steyne by singing the religious songs of Mozart, sat down at the piano and played 'The Carmen's Whistle', one of the few things she reliably knew by heart. This audacious antiquarianism delighted the Canon, who kept her at his side for the rest of the evening, relating how he had once tried to get up a performance of Tallis's forty-part motet.

The Tizards were no longer odd. Their new friends were all considerably older than they; the middle-aged had more conscience about the war and were readier to make friends with a disabled major and his devoted maiden sister. In time, members of the staff overlooked their prejudice against Pilkington Pets and found the Tizard couple agreeable, if slightly boring.

Returning from their sober junketings Justin and Celia, safe within their brick wall, cast off their weeds of middle age, laughed, chattered and kissed with an intensified delight in their scandalous immunity from blame. They were a model couple, the most respectable couple in Hallowby, treading hand in hand the thornless path to fogydom. They began to give small dinner parties themselves. They set up a pug and a white cat. During their fifth summer in Hallowby they gave an evening party in the Beelby Museum. This dashing event almost carried them too far. It was such a success that they were begged to make an annual thing of it; and Celia was so gay, and her dress so fashionable, that she was within an inch of being thought a dangerous woman. Another party being expected of them, another had to be given. But this was a very different set-out: a children-and-parents party with a puppet show, held in St Cuthbert's Church Room, with

Canon Pendarves speaking on behalf of the Save the Children
Fund and a collection taken at the door. The collection was a
master stroke. It put the Tizards back in their place as junior
fogies—where Justin, for his part, was thankful to be. He had got
there a trifle prematurely, perhaps, being in his mid-thirties, but it
was where he intended to end his days.

He was fond of gardening, and had taken to gardening seriously, having an analysis made of the Newton Lodge soil—too
acid, as he suspected—buying phosphates and potash and lime
and kainite, treating different plots with different mixtures and
noting the results in a book. He could not dig, but he limpingly
mowed and rolled the lawn, trained climbing roses and staked
delphiniums. Within the shelter of the wall, delphiniums did
magnificently. Every year he added new varieties and when the
original border could be lengthened no further a parallel bed was
dug, with a grass walk in between. Every summer evening he
walked there, watching the various blues file off, some to darkness, some to pallor, as the growing dusk took possession of
them, while the white cat flitted about his steps like a moth.
Because one must not be wholly selfish, from time to time he
would invite a pair of chosen children to tea, cut each of them a
long delphinium lance (cutting only those which were going over,
however) and set them to play jousting matches on the lawn.
Most of them did no more than thwack, but the two little
Semples, the children of the school chaplain, fought with system,
husbanding their strokes and aiming at each other's faces. Even
when they had outgrown jousting they still came to Newton
Lodge, hunting snails, borrowing books, helping him weigh out
basic slag, addressing him as 'Justin'.

'Mary is just the age our child would have been,' remarked
Celia after one of these visits. Seeing him start at the words, she
went on, 'When you went back to be killed, and I was quite sure I
would have a baby.'

'I wouldn't stand being called Justin—if she were.'

'You might have to. They're Bright Young Things from the
cradle on, nowadays.'

By now the vogue for being a Bright Young Thing had reached
even to Hallowby, its ankles growing rather muddied and muscular on the way. It was not like Celia to prefer an inferior article,
and Justin wondered to see her tolerance of this anglicisation of
the *Jeune France* when the original movement had so exasperated
her. He hoped she wasn't mellowing; mellowness is not the food
of love. A quite contrary process, however, was at work in Celia.
At Carnac, even when accepting Pilkington as a way out of it, the

exaltation of living in defiance of social prohibitions and the absorbing manoeuvres of seeming to live in compliance with them had been stimulus enough; she had had no mercy for less serious rebels. But during the last few years the sense of sinking month by month into the acquiescence of Hallowby, eating its wholesome lotus like cabbage, conforming with the inattentiveness of habit—and aware that if she overlooked a conformity the omission would be redressed by the general conviction that Justin Tizard, though in no way exciting, was always so nice and had a sister who devoted her life to him, so nice for them both, etc. etc.—had begun to pall, and the sight of any rebellion, however puerile, however clumsy, roused up her partisanship. Since she could not shock Hallowby to its foundations, she liked to see these young creatures trying to, and wished them luck. From time to time she even made approaches to them, solicited their trust, indicated that she was ranged on their side. They accepted, confided, condescended—and dropped her.

When one is thus put back in one's place, one finds one has grown out of it, and is a misfit. Celia became conscious how greatly she disliked Hallowby society. The school people nauseated her with their cautious culture and breezy heartiness. The indigenous inhabitants were more bearable, because they were less pretentious; but they bored her. The Church, from visiting bishops down to Salvation Army cornet players, she loathed for its hypocrisy. Only in Hallowby's shabbiest quarter—in Edna Road, Gladstone Terrace and Gas Lane—could she find anyone to love. Mr Newby the fishmonger in his malodorous den; old Mrs Foe among her sallowing cabbages and bruised apples; Mr Raby, the grocer, who couldn't afford to buy new stock because he hadn't the heart to call in the money his poorer customers owed him, and so had none but the poorest customers—these people were good. Probably it was only by their goodness that they survived and had not cut their throats in despair long ago. Celia began to shop in Gas Lane. It was not a success. Much as she might love Mr Newby she loved Justin better, and when a dried haddock gave him food poisoning she had to remove her custom—since the cat wouldn't touch Newby's fish anyhow. These disheartening experiences made her dislike respectable Hallowby even more. She wanted to cast it off, as someone tossing in fever wants to cast off a blanket.

The depression began. The increase of Mr Raby's customers drove him out of business: he went bankrupt and closed the shop. Groups of unemployed men from Hallowby juxta Mare appeared in Gas Lane and Edna Road and sang at street corners—for misfortune always resorts to poor neighbourhoods for succour. People began to worry about their investments and to cut down subscriptions to such examples of conspicuous waste as the Chamber Music Society. Experts on nutrition wrote to the daily papers, pointing out the wastefulness of frying, and explaining how, by buying cheaper cuts of meat and cooking them much longer, the mothers of families on the dole would be able to provide wholesome adequate meals. Celia's uneasy goodwill and smouldering resentment found their outlet. As impetuously as she had flung herself into Justin's bed, she flung herself into relief work at Hallowby juxta Mare. Being totally inexperienced in relief work she exploded there like a nova. Her schemes were so outrageous that people in authority didn't think them worth contesting even; she was left to learn by experience, and made the most of this valuable permission. One of her early outrages was to put on a revue composed and performed by local talent. Local talent ran to the impromptu, and when it became known what scarification of local reputations could be expected, everyone wanted to hear what might be said of everyone else and Celia was able to raise the price of admission, which had been sixpence, to as much as half a guinea for the best seats. Her doings became a joke; you never knew what that woman wouldn't be up to next. Hadn't she persuaded Wilson & Beck to take on men they had turned off, because now, when half the factory stood idle, was the moment to give it a spring cleaning? Celia worked herself to the bone, and probably did a considerable amount of good, but her great service to Hallowby juxta Mare was that she made the unemployed interested in their plight instead of dulled by it, so that helpers came to her from the unemployed themselves. If she was not so deeply impressed by their goodness as she had been by the idealised goodness of Mr Newby and Mrs Foe, she was impressed by their arguments; she became political, and by 1936 she was marching in Communist demonstrations, singing:

> Twenty-five years of hunger and war
> And they call it a glorious Jubilee.

Inland Hallowby was also looking forward to the Jubilee. The school was rehearsing a curtailed version of Purcell's *King Arthur*, with Mary Semple, now home from her finishing school, coming on in a chariot to sing 'Fairest Isle'. There was to be folk dancing by Scouts and Guides, a tea for the old people, a fancy-dress procession; and to mark the occasion Mr Harvey, J.P., one of the school governors, had presented the Beelby Museum with a pair

of buckskin breeches worn by the Duke of Wellington on the field
of Talavera. 'I shall be expected to make a speech about them,'
groaned Justin. 'I think I shall hire a deputy and go away for the
day.'

Celia jumped at this. 'We'll both go away. Not just for the day
but for a fortnight. We'll go to Jersey, because you must attend the
Jubilee celebrations on your native island—a family obligation.
Representative of one of the oldest families. And if we find the
same sort of fuss going on there, we can nip over to France in the
Escudiers' boat and be quit of the whole thing. It's foolproof, it's
perfect. The only thing needed to make it perfectly perfect is to
make it a month. Justin, it's the answer.' She felt indeed that it
was the answer. For some time now, Justin had seemed distrait
and out of humour. Afraid he was unwell, she told herself he
was stale and knew that he had been neglected. An escapade
would put all right. Talavera had not been fought in vain. But she
couldn't get him to consent. She was still persuading when the
first letter arrived. It was typed and had been posted in Hallowby.
It was unsigned, and began, 'Hag.'

Reading what followed, Celia tried to hold on to her first
impression that the writer was some person in Hallowby juxta
Mare. 'You think you're sitting pretty, don't you? You think no
one has found you out.' She had made many enemies there; this
must come from one of them. Several times she had been accused
of misappropriating funds. Yes, that was it: '... and keep such a
tight hold on him.' But why *him*? It was as though two letters lay
on the flimsy page—the letter she was bent on reading and the
letter that lay beneath and glared through it. It was a letter about
her relations with Justin that she tore into bits and dropped in the
wastepaper basket as he came down to breakfast.

She could hardly contain her impatience to get the bits out
again, stick them on a backing sheet, make sure. Nothing is ever
quite what it first was; the letter was viler, but it was also feebler.
It struck her as amateurish.

The letter that came two days later was equally vile but better
composed; the writer must be getting his or her hand in. A third
was positively elegant. Vexatiously, there was no hint of a demand
for hush money. Had there been, Celia could have called in the
police, who would have set those ritual springes into which blackmailers—at any rate, blackmailers one reads of in newspapers—walk so artlessly. But the letters did not blackmail, did
not even threaten. They stated that what the writer knew was
common knowledge. After two letters, one on the heels of the
other, which taunted Celia with being ugly, ageing and sexually

ridiculous—letters that ripped through her self-control and made her cry with mortification—the writer returned to the theme of common knowledge and concluded with an 'It may interest you to hear that the following know all about your loathsome performances' and a list of half a dozen Hallowby names. Further letters laconically listed more names. From the outset, Celia had decided to keep all this to herself, and still held to the decision; but she hoped she wouldn't begin to talk in her sleep. There was less chance of this, as by now she was sleeping scarcely at all.

It was a Sunday morning and she and Justin were spraying roses for greenfly when Justin said, 'Puss, what are you concealing?' She syringed Mme Alfred Carrière so violently that the jet bowed the rose, went beyond it, and deluged a robin. Justin took the syringe out of her hand and repeated the question.

Looking at him, she saw his face was drawn with woe. 'No, no, it's nothing like that,' she exclaimed. 'I'm perfectly well. It's just that some poisen-pen imbecile ...'

When he had read through the letters, he said thoughtfully, 'I'd like to wring that little bitch's neck.'

'Yes, it is some woman or other, isn't it? I felt sure of that.'

'Some woman or other? It's Mary Semple.

'That pretty little Mary Semple?'

'That pretty little Mary Semple. Give me the letters. I'll soon settle her.' He looked at his watch. 'No, I can't settle her yet. She'll still be in church.'

'But I don't understand why.'

'You do, really.'

'Justin! Have you been carrying on with Mary Semple?'

'No, I wouldn't say that. She's got white eyelashes. But ever since she came home Mary Semple has been doing all she could to carry on with me. There I was in the Beelby, you see, like a bull at the stake. No one comes near the place now; I was at her mercy. And in she tripped, and talked about the old days, telling me her little troubles, showing me poems, pitying me for my hard lot. I tried to cool her down, I tried to taper it off. But she was bent on rape, and one morning I lost all patience, told her she bored me and that if she came again I'd empty the fire bucket over her. She wept and wailed, and I paid no attention, and when there was silence I looked cautiously round and she was gone. And a day or so after'—he looked at the mended letter—'yes, a couple of days after, she sat her down to take it out of you.'

'But, Justin—how did she know about us?'

'No fire without smoke, I suppose. I dare say she overheard her parents cheering each other along the way with Christian surmises. Anyhow, children nowadays are brought up on that sort of useful knowledge.'

'No fire without smoke,' she repeated. 'And what about those lists?'

'Put in to make your flesh creep, most likely. Even if they do know, they weren't informed at a public meeting. Respectable individuals are too wary about libel and slander to raise their respectable voices individually. It's like that motet Pendarves used to talk about, when he could never manage to get them all there at once. Extraordinary ambitions people have! Fancy wanting to hear forty singers simultaneously yelling different tunes.'

'It can be done. There was a performance at Newcastle—he was dead by then. But, Justin—'

'That will do, Celia. I am now going off to settle Mary Semple.'

'How will you manage to see her alone?'

'I shall enter her father's dwelling. Mary will manage the rest.'

The savagery of these last words frightened her. She had not heard that note in his voice since he cried out in his sleep. She watched him limp from the room as though she were watching an incalculable stranger. A moment later he reappeared, took her hand, and kissed it. 'Don't worry, Puss. If need be, we'll fly the country.'

Whatever danger might lie ahead, it was the thought of the danger escaped that made her tremble. If she had gone on concealing those letters—and she had considered it her right and duty to do so—a wedge would have been driven between her and Justin, bruising the tissue of their love, invisibly fissuring them, as a wedge of ice does in the living tree. And thus a scandal about their incest would have found them without any spontaneity of reaction and distracted by the discovery of how long she had been arrogating to herself a thing that concerned them both. 'Here and now,' she exclaimed, 'I give up being an elder sister who knows best.' Justin, on his way to the Semples', was muttering to himself, 'Damn and blast it, why couldn't she have told me sooner? If she had it would all be over by now.' It did not occur to him to blame himself for a lack of openness. This did not occur to Celia, either. It was Justin's constancy that mattered, not his fidelity—which was his own business.

When he reappeared, washed and brushed and ready for lunch, and told her there would be no more billets-doux from Mary, it was with merely tactical curiosity that she asked, 'Did you have to bribe her?' And as he did not answer at once, she went on to ask, 'Would you like potted shrimps or mulligatawny? There's both.'

They did not have to fly the country. Mary Semple disposed of the rest of her feelings by quarrelling with everyone in the cast of *King Arthur* and singing 'Fairest Isle' with such venom that her hearers felt their blood run cold, and afterwards remarked that stage fright had made her sing out of tune. The people listed by Mary as cognisant showed no more interest in the Tizards than before. The tradesmen continued to deliver. Not a cold shoulder was turned. But on that Sunday morning the balance between Justin and Celia had shifted, and never returned to its former adjustment. Both of them were aware of this, so neither of them referred to it, though at first Celia's abdication made her rather insistent that Justin should know best, make decisions, assert his authority. Justin asserted his authority by knowing what decisions could be postponed till the moment when there was no need to make them at all. Though he did not dislike responsibility, he was not going to be a slave to it. Celia's abdication also released elements in her character which till then had been penned back by her habit of common sense and efficiency. She became slightly frivolous, forgetful and timid. She read novels before lunch, abandoned all social conscience about bores, mislaid bills, took second helpings of *risotto* and mashed potatoes and began to put on weight. She lost her aplomb as a driver and had one or two small accidents. She discovered the delights of needing to be taken away for pick-me-up holidays. Mrs Mugthwaite, observing all this, knew it was the Change, and felt sorry for poor Mr Tizard; the Change wasn't a thing that a brother should be expected to deal with. From time to time, Justin and Celia discussed leaving Hallowby and going to live somewhere away from the east-coast climate and the east wind at the corner by St Cuthbert's, but they put off moving, because the two animals had grown old, were set in their ways, and would be happier dying in their own home. The pug died just before the Munich crisis, the cat lived on into the war.

So did Mr Pilkington, who died from overwork two months before the first air raid on Hallowby juxta Mare justified his insistence on constructing an air-raid shelter under the school playing fields. This first raid was concentrated on the ironworks, and did considerable damage. All next day, inland Hallowby heard the growl of demolition explosives. In the second raid, the defences were better organised. The enemy bombers were driven off their target before they could finish their mission. Two were brought down out to sea. A third, twisting inland, jettisoned its remaining bombs on and around Hallowby. One dropped in Gas Lane, another just across the road from Newton Lodge. The blast brought down the roof and dislodged a chimney stack. The rescue workers, turning the light of their torches here and there, noting the usual disparities between the havocked and the unharmed, the fireplace blown out, the portrait smiling above it, followed the trail of bricks and rubble upstairs and into a bedroom whose door slanted from its hinges. A cold air met them; looking up, they saw the sky. The floor was deep in rubble; bits of broken masonry, clots of brickwork, stood up from it like rocks on a beach. A dark bulk crouched on the hearth, and was part of the chimney stack, and a torrent of slates had fallen on the bed, crushing the two bodies that lay there.

The wavering torchlights wandered over the spectacle. There was a silence. Then young Foe spoke out. 'He must have come in to comfort her. That's my opinion.' The others concurred. Silently, they disentangled Justin and Celia, and wrapped them in separate tarpaulin sheets. No word of what they had found got out. Foe's hypothesis was accepted by the coroner and became truth.

▼▼

All the Dead Pilots

I

IN THE PICTURES, the snapshots hurriedly made, a little faded, a little dog-eared with the thirteen years, they swagger a little. Lean, hard, in their brass-and-leather martial harness, posed standing beside or leaning upon the esoteric shapes of wire and wood and canvas in which they flew without parachutes, they too have an esoteric look; a look not exactly human, like that of some dim and threatful apotheosis of the race seen for an instant in the glare of a thunderclap and then forever gone.

Because they are dead, all the old pilots, dead on the eleventh of November, 1918. When you see modern photographs of them, the recent pictures made beside the recent shapes of steel and canvas with the new cowlings and engines and slotted wings, they look a little outlandish: the lean young men who once swaggered. They look lost, baffled. In this saxophone age of flying they look as out of place as, a little thick about the waist, in the sober business suits of thirty and thirty-five and perhaps more than that, they would look among the saxophones and miniature brass bowlers of a night club orchestra. Because they are dead too, who had learned to respect that whose respect in turn their hardness had commanded before there were welded center sections and parachutes and ships that would not spin. That's why they watch the saxophone girls and boys with slipstream-proof lipstick and aeronautical flasks piling up the saxophone crates in private driveways and on golf greens, with the quick sympathy and the bafflement too. 'My gad,' one of them—ack emma, warrant officer pilot, captain and M.C. in turn—said to me once; 'if you can treat a crate that way, why do you want to fly at all?'

But they are all dead now. They are thick men now, a little thick about the waist from sitting behind desks, and maybe not so good at it, with wives and children in suburban homes almost paid out, with gardens in which they putter in the long evenings after the 5:15 is in, and perhaps not so good at that either: the hard, lean

men who swaggered hard and drank hard because they had found
that being dead was not as quiet as they had heard it would be.
That's why this story is composite: a series of brief glares in
which, instantaneous and without depth or perspective, there
stood into sight the portent and the threat of what the race could
bear and become, in an instant between dark and dark.

II

In 1918 I was at Wing Headquarters, trying to get used to a
mechanical leg, where, among other things, I had the censoring of
mail from all squadrons in the Wing. The job itself wasn't bad,
since it gave me spare time to experiment with a synchronized
camera on which I was working. But the opening and reading of
the letters, the scrawled, brief pages of transparent and honorable
lies to mothers and sweethearts, in the script and spelling of
schoolboys. But a war is such a big thing, and it takes so long. I
suppose they who run them (I dont mean the staffs, but whoever
or whatever it is that controls events) do get bored now and then.
And it's when you get bored that you turn petty, play horse.

So now and then I would go up to a Camel squadron behind
Amiens and talk with the gunnery sergeant about the synchro-
nization of the machine guns. This was Spoomer's squadron. His
uncle was the corps commander, the K.G., and so Spoomer, with
his Guards' Captaincy, had also got in turn a Mons Star, a
D.S.O., and now a pursuit squadron of single seaters, though the
third barnacle on his tunic was still the single wing of an observer.

In 1914 he was in Sandhurst: a big, ruddy-colored chap with
china eyes, and I like to think of his uncle sending for him when
the news got out, the good news. Probably at the uncle's club (the
uncle was a brigadier then, just recalled hurriedly from Indian
service) and the two of them opposite one another across the
mahogany, with the newsboys crying in the street, and the general
saying, 'By gad, it will be the making of the Army. Pass the wine,
sir.'

I daresay the general was put out, not to say outraged, when
he finally realized that neither the Hun nor the Home Office
intended running this war like the Army wanted it run. Anyway,
Spoomer had already gone out to Mons and come back with his
Star (though Ffollansbye said that the general sent Spoomer
out to get the Star, since it was going to be one decoration you
had to be on hand to get) before the uncle got him transferred
to his staff, where Spoomer could get his D.S.O. Then perhaps
the uncle sent him out again to tap the stream where it came to

surface. Or maybe Spoomer went on his own this time. I like to think so. I like to think that he did it through pro patria, even though I know that no man deserves praise for courage or opprobrium for cowardice, since there are situations in which any man will show either of them. But he went out, and came back a year later with his observer's wing and a dog almost as large as a calf.

That was in 1917, when he and Sartoris first came together, collided. Sartoris was an American, from a plantation at Mississippi, where they grew grain and Negroes, or the Negroes grew the grain—something. Sartoris had a working vocabulary of perhaps two hundred words, and I daresay to tell where and how and why he lived was beyond him, save that he lived in the plantation with his great-aunt and his grandfather. He came through Canada in 1916, and he was at Pool. Ffollansbye told me about it. It seems that Sartoris had a girl in London, one of those three-day wives and three-year widows. That's the bad thing about war. They—the Sartorises and such—didn't die until 1918, some of them. But the girls, the women, they died on the fourth of August, 1914.

So Sartoris had a girl. Ffollansbye said they called her Kitchener, 'because she had such a mob of soldiers.' He said they didn't know if Sartoris knew this or not, but that anyway for a while Kitchener—Kit—appeared to have ditched them all for Sartoris. They would be seen anywhere and any time together, then Ffollansbye told me how he found Sartoris alone and quite drunk one evening in a restaurant. Ffollansbye told how he had already heard that Kit and Spoomer had gone off somewhere together about two days ago. He said that Sartoris was sitting there, drinking himself blind, waiting for Spoomer to come in. He said he finally got Sartoris into a cab and sent him to the aerodrome. It was about dawn then, and Sartoris got a captain's tunic from someone's kit, and a woman's garter from someone else's kit, perhaps his own, and pinned the garter on the tunic like a barnacle ribbon. Then he went and waked a corporal who was an ex-professional boxer and with whom Sartoris would put on the gloves now and then, and made the corporal put on the tunic over his underclothes. 'Namesh Spoomer,' Sartoris told the corporal. 'Cap'm Spoomer'; swaying and prodding at the garter with his finger. 'Distinguish Sheries Thighs,' Sartoris said. Then he and the corporal in the borrowed tunic, with his woolen underwear showing beneath, stood there in the dawn, swinging at one another with their naked fists.

III

You'd think that when a war had got you into it, it would let you be. That it wouldn't play horse with you. But maybe it wasn't that. Maybe it was because the three of them, Spoomer and Sartoris and the dog, were so humorless about it. Maybe a humorless person is an unflagging challenge to them above the thunder and the alarms. Anyway, one afternoon—it was in the spring, just before Cambrai fell—I went up to the Camel aerodrome to see the gunnery sergeant, and I saw Sartoris for the first time. They had given the squadron to Spoomer and the dog the year before, and the first thing they did was to send Sartoris out to it.

The afternoon patrol was out, and the rest of the people were gone too, to Amiens I suppose, and the aerodrome was deserted. The sergeant and I were sitting on two empty petrol tins in the hangar door when I saw a man thrust his head out the door of the officers' mess and look both ways along the line, his air a little furtive and very alert. It was Sartoris, and he was looking for the dog.

'The dog?' I said. Then the sergeant told me, this too composite, out of his own observation and the observation of the entire enlisted personnel exchanged and compared over the mess tables or over pipes at night: that terrible and omniscient inquisition of those in an inferior station.

When Spoomer left the aerodrome, he would lock the dog up somewhere. He would have to lock it up in a different place each time, because Sartoris would hunt until he found it, and let it out. It appeared to be a dog of intelligence, because if Spoomer had only gone down to Wing or somewhere on business, the dog would stay at home, spending the interval grubbing in the refuse bin behind the men's mess, to which it was addicted in preference to that of the officers. But if Spoomer had gone to Amiens, the dog would depart up the Amiens road immediately on being freed, to return later with Spoomer in the squadron car.

'Why does Mr. Sartoris let it out?' I said. 'Do you mean that Captain Spoomer objects to the dog eating kitchen refuse?'

But the sergeant was not listening. His head was craned around the door, and we watched Sartoris. He had emerged from the mess and he now approached the hangar at the end of the line, his air still alert, still purposeful. He entered the hanger. 'That seems a rather childish business for a grown man,' I said.

The sergeant looked at me. Then he quit looking at me. 'He wants to know if Captain Spoomer went to Amiens or not.'

After a while I said, 'Oh. A young lady. Is that it?'

He didn't look at me. 'You might call her a young lady. I suppose they have young ladies in this country.'

I thought about that for a while. Sartoris emerged from the first hangar and entered the second one. 'I wonder if there are any young ladies any more anywhere,' I said.

'Perhaps you are right, sir. War is hard on women.'

'What about this one?' I said. 'Who is she?'

He told me. They ran an estaminet, a 'bit of a pub' he called it—an old harridan of a woman, and the girl. A little place on a back street, where officers did not go. Perhaps that was why Sartoris and Spoomer created such a furore in that circle. I gathered from the sergeant that the contest between the squadron commander and one of his greenest cubs was the object of general interest and the subject of the warmest conversation and even betting among the enlisted element of the whole sector of French and British troops. 'Being officers and all,' he said.

'They frightened the soldiers off, did they?' I said, 'Is that it?' The sergeant did not look at me. 'Were there many soldiers to frighten off?'

'I suppose you know these young women,' the sergeant said. 'This war and all.'

And that's who the girl was. What the girl was. The sergeant said that the girl and the old woman were not even related. He told me how Sartoris bought her things—clothes, and jewelry; the sort of jewelry you might buy in Amiens, probably. Or maybe in a canteen, because Sartoris was not much more than twenty. I saw some of the letters which he wrote to his great-aunt back home, letters that a third-form lad in Harrow could have written, perhaps bettered. It seemed that Spoomer did not make the girl any presents. 'Maybe because he is a captain,' the sergeant said. 'Or maybe because of them ribbons he dont have to.'

'Maybe so,' I said.

And that was the girl, the girl who, in the centime jewelry which Sartoris gave her, dispensed beer and wine to British and French privates in an Amiens back street, and because of whom Spoomer used his rank to betray Sartoris with her by keeping Sartoris at the aerodrome on special duties, locking up the dog to hide from Sartoris what he had done. And Sartoris taking what revenge he could by letting out the dog in order that it might grub in the refuse of plebeian food.

He entered the hangar in which the sergeant and I were: a tall lad with pale eyes in a face that could be either merry or surly, and quite humorless. He looked at me. 'Hello,' he said.

'Hello,' I said. The sergeant made to get up.

'Carry on,' Sartoris said. 'I dont want anything.' He went on to the rear of the hangar. It was cluttered with petrol drums and empty packing cases and such. He was utterly without self-consciousness, utterly without shame of his childish business.

The dog was in one of the packing cases. It emerged, huge, of a napped, tawny color; Ffollansbye had told me that, save for Spoomer's wing and his Mons Star and his D.S.O., he and the dog looked alike. It quitted the hangar without haste, giving me a brief, sidelong glance. We watched it go on and disappear around the corner of the men's mess. Then Sartoris turned and went back to the officers' mess and also disappeared.

Shortly afterward, the afternoon patrol came in. While the machines were coming up to the line, the squadron car turned onto the aerodrome and stopped at the officers' mess and Spoomer got out. 'Watch him,' the sergeant said. 'He'll try to do it like he wasn't watching himself, noticing himself.'

He came along the hangars, big, hulking, in green golf stockings. He did not see me until he was turning into the hangar. He paused; it was almost imperceptible, then he entered, giving me a brief, sidelong glance. 'How do,' he said in a high, fretful, level voice. The sergeant had risen. I had never seen Spoomer even glance toward the rear, toward the overturned packing case, yet he had stopped. 'Sergeant,' he said.

'Sir,' the sergeant said.

'Sergeant,' Spoomer said. 'Have those timers come up yet?'

'Yes, sir. They came up two weeks ago. They're all in use now, sir.'

'Quite so. Quite so.' He turned; again he gave me a brief, sidelong glance, and went on down the hangar line, not fast. He disappeared. 'Watch him, now,' the sergeant said. 'He wont go over there until he thinks we have quit watching him.'

We watched. Then he came into sight again, crossing toward the men's mess, walking briskly now. He disappeared beyond the corner. A moment later he emerged, dragging the huge, inert beast by the scruff of its neck. 'You mustn't ear that stuff,' he said. 'That's for soldiers.'

IV

I didn't know at the time what happend next. Sartoris didn't tell me until later, afterward. Perhaps up to that time he had not anything more than instinct and circumstantial evidence to tell him that he was being betrayed: evidence such as being given by

Spoomer some duty not in his province at all and which would keep him on the aerodrome for the afternoon, then finding and freeing the hidden dog and watching it vanish up the Amiens road at its clumsy hand gallop.

But something happened. All I could learn at the time was, that one afternoon Sartoris found the dog and watched it depart for Amiens. Then he violated his orders, borrowed a motor bike and went to Amiens too. Two hours later the dog returned and repaired to the kitchen door of the men's mess, and a short time after that, Sartoris himself returned on a lorry (they were already evacuating Amiens) laden with household effects and driven by a French soldier in a peasant's smock. The motor bike was on the lorry too, pretty well beyond repair. The soldier told how Sartoris had driven the bike full speed into a ditch, trying to run down the dog.

But nobody knew just what had happened, at the time. But I had imagined the scene, before he told me. I imagined him there, in that bit of a room full of French soldiers, and the old woman (she could read pips, no doubt; ribbons, anyway) barring him from the door to the living quarters. I can imagine him, furious, baffled, inarticulate (he knew no French) standing head and shoulders above the French people whom he could not under-stand and that he believed were laughing at him. 'That was it,' he told me. 'Laughing at me behind their faces, about a woman. Me knowing that he was up there, and them knowing I knew that if I busted in and dragged him out and bashed his head off, I'd not only be cashiered, I'd be clinked for life for having infringed the articles of alliance by invading foreign property without warrant or something.'

Then he returned to the aerodrome and met the dog on the road and tried to run it down. The dog came on home, and Spoomer returned, and he was just dragging it by the scruff of the neck from the refuse bin behind the men's mess, when the after-noon patrol came in. They had gone out six and come back five, and the leader jumped down from his machine before it had stopped rolling. He had a bloody rag about his right hand and he ran toward Spoomer stooped above the passive and stiff-legged dog. 'By gad,' he said, 'they have got Cambrai!'

Spoomer did not look up. 'Who have?'

'Jerry has, by gad!'

'Well, by gad,' Spoomer said, 'Come along, now. I have told you about that muck.'

A man like that is invulnerable. When Sartoris and I talked for the first time, I started to tell him that. But then I learned that

Sartoris was invincible too. We talked, that first time. 'I tried to get him to let me teach him to fly a Camel,' Sartoris said. 'I will teach him for nothing. I will tear out the cockpit and rig the duals myself, for nothing.'

'Why?' I said. 'What for?'

'Or anything. I will let him choose it. He can take an S.E. if he wants to, and I will take an Ak.W. or even a Fee and I will run him clean out of the sky in four minutes. I will run him so far into the ground he will have to stand on his head to swallow.'

We talked twice: that first time, and the last time. 'Well you did better than that,' I said the last time we talked.

He had hardly any teeth left then, and he couldn't talk very well, who had never been able to talk much, who lived and died with maybe two hundred words. 'Better than what?' he said.

'You said before that you would run him clean out of the sky. You didn't do that; you did better: you have run him clean off the continent of Europe.'

V

I think I said that he was invulnerable too. November 11, 1918, couldn't kill him, couldn't leave him growing a little thicker each year behind an office desk, with what had once been hard and lean and immediate grown a little dim, a little baffled, and betrayed, because by that day he had been dead almost six months.

He was killed in July, but we talked that second time, that other time before that. This last time was a week after the patrol had come in and told that Cambrai had fallen, a week after we heard the shells falling in Amiens. He told me about it himself, through his missing teeth. The whole squadron went out together. He left his flight as soon as they reached the broken front, and flew back to Amiens with a bottle of brandy in his overall leg. Amiens was being evacuated, the roads full of lorries and carts of household goods, and ambulances from the Base hospital, and the city and its immediate territory was now interdict.

He landed in a short meadow. He said there was an old woman working in a field beyond the canal (he said she was still there when he returned an hour later, stooping stubbornly among the green rows, beneath the moist spring air shaken at slow and monstrous intervals by the sound of shells falling in the city) and a light ambulance stopped halfway in the roadside ditch.

He went to the ambulance. The engine was still running. The driver was a young man in spectacles. He looked like a student, and he was dead drunk, half sprawled out of the cab. Sartoris had a drink from his own bottle and tried to rouse the driver, in vain. Then he had another drink (I imagine that he was pretty well along himself by then; he told me how only that morning, when Spoomer had gone off in the car and he had found the dog and watched it take the Amiens road, how he had tried to get the operations officer to let him off patrol and how the operations officer had told him that La Fayette awaited him on the Santerre plateau) and tumbled the driver back into the ambulance and drove on to Amiens himself.

He said the French corporal was drinking from a bottle in a doorway when he passed and stopped the ambulance before the estaminet. The door was locked. He finished his brandy bottle and he broke the estaminet door in by diving at it as they do in American football. Then he was inside. The place was empty, the benches and tables overturned and the shelves empty of bottles, and he said that at first he could not remember what it was he had come for, so he thought it must be a drink. He found a bottle of wine under the bar and broke the neck off against the edge of the bar, and he told how he stood there, looking at himself in the mirror behind the bar, trying to think what it was he had come to do. 'I looked pretty wild,' he said.

Then the first shell fell. I can imagine it: he standing there in that quiet, peaceful, redolent, devastated room, with the bashed-in door and the musing and waiting city beyond it, and then that slow, unhurried, reverberant sound coming down upon the thick air of spring like a hand laid without haste on the damp silence; he told how dust or sand or plaster, something, sifted somewhere, whispering down in a faint hiss, and how a big, lean cat came up over the bar without a sound and flowed down to the floor and vanished like dirty quicksilver.

Then he saw the closed door behind the bar and he remembered what he had come for. He went around the bar. He expected this door to be locked too, and he grasped the knob and heaved back with all his might. It wasn't locked. He said it came back into the shelves with a sound like a pistol, jerking him off his feet. 'My head hit the bar,' he said. 'Maybe I was a little groggy after that.'

Anyway, he was holding himself up in the door, looking down at the old woman. She was sitting on the bottom stair, her apron over her head, rocking back and forth. He said that the apron was quite clean, moving back and forth like a piston, and he standing in the door, drooling a little at the mouth. 'Madame,' he said. The old woman rocked back and forth. He propped himself carefully and leaned and touched her shoulder. ''Toinette,' he said. 'Où est-elle, 'Toinette?' That was probably all the French he knew; that, with *vin* added to his 196 English words, composed his vocabulary.

Again the old woman did not answer. She rocked back and forth like a wound-up toy. He stepped carefully over her and mounted the stair. There was a second door at the head of the stair. He stopped before it, listening. His throat filled with a hot, salty liquid. He spat it, drooling; his throat filled again. This door was unlocked also. He entered the room quietly. It contained a table, on which lay a khaki cap with the bronze crest of the Flying Corps, and as he stood drooling in the door, the dog heaved up from the corner furthest from the window, and while he and the dog looked at one another above the cap, the sound of the second shell came dull and monstrous into the room, stirring the limp curtains before the window.

As he circled the table the dog moved too, keeping the table between them, watching him. He was trying to move quietly, yet he struck the table in passing (perhaps while watching the dog) and he told how, when he reached the opposite door and stood beside it, holding his breath, drooling, he could hear the silence in the next room. Then a voice said:

'Maman?'

He kicked the locked door, then he dived at it, again like the American football, and through it, door and all. The girl screamed. But he said he never saw her, never saw anyone. He just heard her scream as he went into the room on all-fours. It was a bedroom; one corner was filled by a huge wardrobe with double doors. The wardrobe was closed, and the room appeared to be empty. He didn't go the wardrobe. He said he just stood there on his hands and knees, drooling, like a cow, listening to the dying reverberation of the third shell, watching the curtains on the window blow once into the room as though to a breath.

He got up. 'I was still groggy,' he said. 'And I guess that brandy and the wine had kind of got joggled up inside me.' I daresay they had. There was a chair. Upon it lay a pair of slacks, neatly folded, a tunic with an observer's wing and two ribbons, an ordnance belt. While he stood looking down at the chair, the fourth shell came.

He gathered up the garments. The chair toppled over and he kicked it aside and lurched along the wall to the broken door and entered the first room, taking the cap from the table as he passed. The dog was gone.

He entered the passage. The old woman still sat on the bottom step, her apron over her head, rocking back and forth. He stood at the top of the stair, holding himself up, waiting to spit. Then beneath him a voice said: 'Que faites-vous en haut?'

He looked down upon the raised moustached face of the French corporal whom he had passed in the street drinking from the bottle. For a time they looked at one another. Then the corporal said, 'Descendez,' making a peremptory gesture with his arm. Clasping the garments in one hand, Sartoris put the other hand on the stair rail and vaulted over it.

The corporal jumped aside. Sartoris plunged past him and into the wall, banging his head hollowly again. As he got to his feet and turned, the corporal kicked at him, striking for his pelvis. The corporal kicked him again. Sartoris knocked the corporal down, where he lay on his back in his clumsy overcoat, tugging at his pocket and snapping his boot at Sartoris' groin. Then the corporal freed his hand and shot point-blank at Sartoris with a short-barreled pistol.

Sartoris sprang upon him before he could shoot again, trampling the pistol hand. He said he could feel the man's bones through his boot, and that the corporal began to scream like a woman behind his brigand's moustaches. That was what made it funny, Sartoris said: that noise coming out of a pair of moustaches like a Gilbert and Sullivan pirate. So he said he stopped it by holding the corporal up with one hand and hitting him on the chin with the other until the noise stopped. He said that the old woman had not ceased to rock back and forth under her starched apron. 'Like she might have dressed up to get ready to be sacked and ravaged,' he said.

He gathered up the garments. In the bar he had another pull at the bottle, looking at himself in the mirror. Then he saw that he was bleeding at the mouth. He said he didn't know if he had bitten his tongue when he jumped over the stair rail or if he had cut his mouth with the broken bottle neck. He emptied the bottle and flung it to the floor.

He said he didn't know then what he intended to do. He said he didn't realize it even when he had dragged the unconscious driver out of the ambulance and was dressing him in Captain Spoomer's slacks and cap and ribboned tunic, and tumbled him back into the ambulance.

He remembered seeing a dusty inkstand behind the bar. He sought and found in his overalls a bit of paper, a bill rendered him eight months ago by a London tailor, and, leaning on the bar, drooling and spitting, he printed on the back of the bill Captain Spoomer's name and squadron number and aerodrome, and put the paper into the tunic pocket beneath the ribbon and the wing, and drove back to where he had left his aeroplane.

There was an Anzac battalion resting in the ditch beside the road. He left the ambulance and the sleeping passenger with them, and four of them helped him to start his engine, and held the wings for his tight take-off.

Then he was back at the front. He said he did not remember getting there at all; he said the last thing he remembered was the old woman in the field beneath him, then suddenly he was in a barrage, low enough to feel the concussed air between the ground and his wings, and to distinguish the faces of troops. He said he didn't know what troops they were, theirs or ours, but that he strafed them anyway. 'Because I never heard of a man on the ground getting hurt by an aeroplane,' he said. 'Yes, I did; I'll take that back. There was a farmer back in Canada plowing in the middle of a thousand-acre field and a cadet crashed on top of him.'

Then he returned home. They told at the aerodrome that he flew between two hangars in a slow roll, so that they could see the valve stems in both wheels, and that he ran his wheels across the aerodrome and took off again. The gunnery sergeant told me that he climbed vertically until he stalled, and that he held the Camel mushing on its back. 'He was watching the dog,' the sergeant said. 'It had been home about an hour and it was behind the men's mess, grubbing in the refuse bin.' He said that Sartoris dived at the dog and then looped, making two turns of an upward spin, coming off on one wing and still upside down. Then the sergeant said that he probably did not set back the air valve, because at a hundred feet the engine conked, and upside down Sartoris cut the tops out of the only two poplar trees they had left.

The sergeant said they ran then, toward the gout of dust and the mess of wire and wood. Before they reached it, he said the dog came trotting out from behind the men's mess. He said the dog got there first and that they saw Sartoris on his hands and knees, vomiting, while the dog watched him. Then the dog approached and sniffed tentatively at the vomit and Sartoris got up and balanced himself and kicked it, weakly but with savage and earnest purpose.

VI

The ambulance driver, in Spoomer's uniform, was sent back to the aerodrome by the Anzac major. They put him to bed, where he was still sleeping when the brigadier and the Wing

Commander came up that afternoon. They were still there when an ox cart turned onto the aerodrome and stopped, with, sitting on a wire cage containing chickens, Spoomer in a woman's skirt and a knitted shawl. The next day Spoomer returned to England. We learned that he was to be a temporary colonel at ground school.

'The dog will like that, anyway,' I said.

'The dog?' Sartoris said.

'The food will be better there,' I said.

'Oh,' Sartoris said. They had reduced him to second lieutenant, for dereliction of duty by entering a forbidden zone with government property and leaving it unguarded, and he had been transferred to another squadron, to the one which even the B.E. people called the Laundry.

This was the day before he left. He had no front teeth at all now, and he apologized for the way he talked, who had never really talked with an intact mouth. 'The joke is,' he said, 'it's another Camel squadron. I have to laugh.'

'Laugh?' I said.

'Oh, I can ride them. I can sit there with the gun out and keep the wings level now and then. But I can't fly Camels. You have to land a Camel by setting the air valve and flying it into the ground. Then you count ten, and if you have not crashed, you level off. And if you can get up and walk away, you have made a good landing. And if they can use the crate again, you are an ace. But that's not the joke.'

'What's not?'

'The Camels. The joke is, this is a night-flying squadron. I suppose they are all in town and they dont get back until after dark to fly them. They're sending me to a night-flying squadron. That's why I have to laugh.'

'I would laugh,' I said. 'Isn't there something you can do about it?'

'Sure. Just keep that air valve set right and not crash. Not wash out and have those wing flares explode. I've got that beat, I'll just stay up all night, pop the flares and sit down after sunrise. That's why I have to laugh, see. I cant fly Camels in the daytime, even. And they dont know it.'

'Well, anyway, you did better than you promised,' I said. 'You have run him off the continent of Europe.'

'Yes,' he said. 'I sure have to laugh. He's got to go back to England, where all the men are gone. All those women, and not a man between fourteen and eighty to help him. I have to laugh.'

VII

When July came, I was still in the Wing office, still trying to get used to my mechanical leg by sitting at a table equipped with a paper cutter, a pot of glue and one of red ink, and laden with the meager, thin, here soiled and here clean envelopes that came down in periodical batches—envelopes addressed to cities and hamlets and sometimes less than hamlets, about England—when one day I came upon two addressed to the same person in America: a letter and a parcel. I took the letter first. It had neither location nor date:

Dear Aunt Jenny

Yes I got the socks Elnora knitted. They fit all right because I gave them to my batman he said they fit all right. Yes I like it here better than where I was these are good guys here except these damn Camels. I am all right about going to church we dont always have church. Sometimes they have it for the ak emmas because I reckon a ak emma needs it but usually I am pretty busy Sunday but I go enough I reckon. Tell Elnora much oblige for the socks they fit all right but maybe you better not tell her I gave them away. Tell Isom and the other niggers hello and Grandfather tell him I got the money all right but war is expensive as hell.

Johnny

But then, the Malbroucks dont make the wars, anyway. I suppose it takes too many words to make a war. Maybe that's why.

The package was addressed like the letter, to Mrs Virginia Sartoris, Jefferson, Mississippi, U.S.A., and I thought, What in the world would it ever occur to him to send to her? I could not imagine him choosing a gift for a woman in a foreign country; choosing one of those trifles which some men can choose with a kind of infallible tact. His would be, if he thought to send anything at all, a section of crank shaft or maybe a handful of wrist pins salvaged from a Hun crash. So I opened the package. Then I sat there, looking at the contents.

It contained an addressed envelope, a few dog-eared papers, a wrist watch whose strap was stiff with some dark dried liquid, a pair of goggles without any glass in one lens, a silver belt buckle with a monogram. That was all.

So I didn't need to read the letter. I didn't have to look at the contents of the package, but I wanted to. I didn't want to read the letter, but I had to.

—Squadron, R.A.F., France.
5th July, 1918.

Dear Madam,

I have to tell you that your son was killed on yesterday morning. He was shot down while in pursuit of duty over the enemy lines. Not due to carelessness or lack of skill. He was a good man. The E.A. outnumbered your son and had more height and speed which is our misfortune but no fault of the Government which would give us better machines if they had them which is no satisfaction to you. Another of ours, Mr R. Kyerling 1000 feet below could not get up there since your son spent much time in the hangar and had a new engine in his machine last week. Your son took fire in ten seconds Mr Kyerling said and jumped from your son's machine since he was side slipping safely until the E.A. shot away his stabiliser and controls and he began to spin. I am very sad to send you these sad tidings though it may be a comfort to you that he was buried by a minister. His other effects sent you later.

I am, madam, and etc.
C. Kaye Major

He was buried in the cemetary just north of Saint Vaast since we hope it will not be shelled again since we hope it will be over soon by our padre since there were just two Camels and seven E.A. and so it was on our side by that time.

C.K. Mjr.

The other papers were letters, from his great-aunt, not many and not long. I dont know why he had kept them. But he had. Maybe he just forgot them, like he had the bill from the London tailor he had found in his overalls in Amiens that day in the spring.

... let those foreign women alone. I lived through a war myself and I know how women act in war, even with Yankees. And a good-for-nothing hellion like you ...

And this:

... we think it's about time you came home. Your grandfather is getting old, and it don't look like they will ever get done fighting over there. So you come on home. The Yankees are in it now. Let them fight if they want to. It's their war. It's not ours.

And that's all. That's it. The courage, the recklessness, call it what you will, is the flash, the instant of sublimation; then flick! the old darkness again. That's why. It's too strong for steady diet.

And if it were a steady diet, it would not be a flash, a glare. And so, being momentary, it can be preserved and prolonged only on paper: a picture, a few written words that any match, a minute and harmless flame that any child can engender, can obliterate in an instant. A one-inch sliver of sulphur-tipped wood is longer than memory or grief; a flame no larger than a sixpence is fiercer than courage or despair.

MARY BUTTS

▼▼▼

Speed the Plough

H E LAY IN BED, lax and staring, and obscure images rose and hung before him, dissolved, reshaped. His great illness passed from him. It left him too faint for any sequence of thought. He lay still, without memory, without hope. Such concrete impressions as came to him were sensuous and centred round the women of the hospital. They distressed him. They were not like the Kirchner girls in the worn *Sketch* he fingered all day. La Coquetterie d'une Ange. One need not know French to understand Coquetterie, and Ange was an easy guess. He stared at the neat counterpane. A tall freckled girl with draggled red hair banged down a cup of cocoa and strode away.

Coquetterie, mannequin, lingerie, and all one could say in English was underwear. He flicked over the pages of the battered *Sketch*, and then looked at the little nurse touching her lips with carmine.

'Georgette,' he murmured sleepily, 'crêpe georgette.'

He would always be lame. For years his nerves would rise and quiver and knot themselves, and project loathsome images. But he had a fine body, and his soldiering had set his shoulders and hardened his hands and arms.

'Get him back on to the land,' the doctors said.

The smells in the ward began to assail him, interlacing spirals of odour, subtle but distinct. Disinfectant and distemper, the homely smell of blankets, the faint tang of blood, and then a sour draught from the third bed where a man had been sick.

He crept down under the clothes. Their associations rather than their textures were abhorrent to him, they reminded him of evil noises ... the crackle of starched aprons, clashing plates, unmodulated sounds. Georgette would never wear harsh things like that. She would wear ... beautiful things with names ... velours and organdie, and that faint windy stuff aerophane.

He drowsed back to France, and saw in the sky great aeroplanes dipping and swerving, or holding on their line of steady flight like a travelling eye of God. The wisps of cloud that trailed a moment behind them were not more delicate than her dress....

'What he wants, doctor, to my mind, is rousing. There he lies all day in a dream. He must have been a strong man once. No, we don't know what he was. Something out of doors I should think. He lies there with that precious Kirchner album, never a word to say.'

The doctor nodded.

He lay very still. The presence of the matron made him writhe like the remembered scream of metal upon metal. Her large hands concealed bones that would snap. He lay like a rabbit in its form, and fright showed his dull gums between his drawn-back lips.

Weeks passed. Then one day he got up and saw himself in a glass. He was not surprised. It was all as he had known it must be. He could not go back to the old life. It seemed to him that he would soil its loveliness. Its exotics would shrivel and tarnish as he limped by. 'Light things, and winged, and holy' they fluttered past him, crêpe velours, crêpe de Chine, organdie, aerophane, georgette.... He had dropped his stick ... there was no one to wash his dirty hands.... The red-haired nurse found him crying, and took him back to bed.

For two months longer he laboured under their kindness and wasted under their placidity. He brooded, realizing with pitiful want of clarity that there were unstable delicate things by which he might be cured. He found a ritual and a litany. Dressed in vertical black, he bore on his outstretched arms, huge bales of wound stuffs. With a turn of the wrist he would unwrap them, and they would fall from him rayed like some terrestrial star. The Kirchner album supplied the rest. He named the girls, Suzanne and Verveine, Ambre and Desti, and ranged them about him. Then he would undress them, and dress them again in immaculate fabrics. While he did that he could not speak to them because his mouth would be barred with pins.

The doctors found him weaker.

Several of the nurses were pretty. That was not what he wanted. Their fresh skins irritated him. Somewhere there must still be women whose skins were lustrous with powder, and whose eyes were shadowed with violet from an ivory box. The brisk provincial women passed through his ward visiting from bed to bed. In their homely clothes there was an echo of the lovely fashions of *mondaines*, buttons on a skirt where a slit should have been, a shirt cut to the collar bone whose opening should have sprung from the hollow between the breasts.

Months passed. The fabric of his dream hardened into a shell for his spirit. He remained passive under the hospital care.

They sent him down to a farm on a brilliant March day.

His starved nerves devoured the air and sunlight. If the winds parched, they braced him, and when the snow fell it buried his memories clean. Because she had worn a real musquash coat, and carried a brocade satchel he had half-believed the expensive woman who had sat by his bed, and talked about the worth and the beauty of a life at the plough's tail. Of course he might not be able to plough because of his poor leg ... but there was always the milking ... or pigs ... or he might thatch....

Unfamiliarity gave his world a certain interest. He fluttered the farmer's wife. Nothing came to trouble the continuity of his dream. The sheen on the new grass, the expanse of sky, now heavy as marble, now luminous; the embroidery that a bare tree makes against the sky, the iridescent scum on a village pond, these were his remembrancers, the assurance of his realities. Beside them a cow was an obscene vision of the night.

Too lame to plough or to go far afield, it seemed as though his fate must overtake him among the horned beasts. So far he had ignored them. At the afternoon milking he had been an onlooker, then a tentative operator. Unfortunately the farmer recognized a born milkman. At five o'clock next morning they would go out together to the byres.

At dawn the air was like a sheet of glass; behind it one great star glittered. Dimmed by a transparent shutter, the hard new light poured into the world. A stillness so keen that it seemed the crystallization of speed hung over the farm. From the kitchen chimney rose a feather of smoke, vertical, delicate, light as a plume on Gaby's head. As he stamped out into the yard in his gaiters and corduroys he thought of the similitude and his mouth twisted.

In the yard the straw rose in yellow bales out of the brown dung pools. Each straw was brocaded with frost, and the thin ice crackled under his boots. 'Diamanté,' he said at last, 'that's it.'

On a high shoulder of down above the house, a flock of sheep were gathered like a puffy mat of irregular design. The continual bleating, the tang of the iron bell, gave coherence to the tranquillity of that Artemisian dawn. A hound let loose from the manor by some early groom passed menacing over the soundless grass. A cock upon the pigsty wall tore the air with his screams. He stopped outside the byre now moaning with restless life. The cock brought memories. 'Chanticleer, they called him, like that play once ...'

He remembered how he had once stood outside the window of a famous shop and thrilled at a placard.... 'In twenty-four hours M. Lewis arrives from Paris with the Chanticleer toque.' It had been a stage hit, of course, one hadn't done business with it, but O God! the London women whose wide skirts rose with the wind till they bore them down the street like ships. He remembered a phrase he had heard once, a 'scented gale'. They were like that. The open door of the cow-shed steamed with the rankness that had driven out from life.... Inside were twenty female animals waiting to be milked.

He went in to the warm reeking dark.

He squatted on the greasy milking stool, spoke softly to his beast, and tugged away. The hot milk spurted out into the pail, an amazing substance, pure, and thick with bubbles. Its contact with caked hides and steaming straw sickened him. The gentle beast rubbed her head against her back and stared. He left the stall and her warm breath. The light was gaining. He could see rows of huge buttocks shifting uneasily. From two places, he heard the milk squirting in the pails. He turned to it again, and milked one beast and another, stripping each clean.

The warm milk whose beauty had pleased began to nauseate him. There was a difference in nature between that winking, pearling flow and the pale decency of a Lyons' tea jug. So this was where it all started. Dimly he realized that this was where most of life started, indifferent of any later phase. 'Little bits of fluff,' Rosalba and all the Kirchner tribe ... was Polaire only a cow ... or Delysia? ... The light had now the full measure of day. A wind that tasted delicately of shingle and the turf flew to meet him. The mat on the down shoulder was now a dissolving view of ambulating mushrooms.

'Yes, my son,' the farmer was saying, 'you just stay here where you're well off, and go on milking for me. I know a born milkman when I see one, and I don't mind telling you you're it. I believe you could milk a bull if you were so inclined....'

He sat silent, overwhelmed by the disarming kindness.

'See how the beasts take to you,' the voice went on. 'That old cow she's a terror, and I heard you soothing her down till she was pleasant as yon cat. It's dairy work you were cut out for.... There's a bull coming round this forenoon ... pedigree ... cost me a bit. You come along.'

As yet they did not work him very hard, he would have time to think. He dodged his obligations towards the bull, and walked over to an upland field. He swept away the snow from under a thorn bush, folded his coat beneath him, and lit a cigarette.

'And I stopped, and I looked, and I listened.' Yes, that was it. and about time too. For a while he whistled slowly Robey's masterpiece.

He had to settle with his sense of decency. It was all very well. These things might have to happen. The prospect of a milkless, meatless London impressed him as inconvenient. Still most of that stuff came from abroad, by sea. That was what the blockade was for. 'I've got to get away from this. I never thought of this before, and I don't like it. I've been jockeyed into it somehow, and I don't like it. It's dirty, yes dirty, like a man being sick. In London we're civilized....'

A gull floated in from the sea, and up the valley where the horses steamed at the spring ploughing.

'A bit of it may be all right, it's getting near that does one in. There aren't any women here. They're animals. Even those girls they call the squire's daughters. I never saw such boots.... They'd say that things were for use, and in London they're for show.... Give me the good old show....' He stopped to dream. He was in a vast circular gallery so precipitous that standing one felt impelled to reel over and sprawl down into the stalls half a mile below. Some comedian had left the stage. Two gold-laced men were changing the numbers on either side. The orchestra played again, something that had no common tune. Then there swung on to the stage a woman plumed and violent, wrapped in leopard skin and cloth-of-gold. Sometimes she stepped like a young horse, sometimes she moved with the easy trailing of a snake. She did nothing that was not trivial, yet she invested every moment with a significance whose memory was rapture.

Quintessence was the word he wanted. He said ... 'There's a lot of use in shows.'

Then he got up stiffly, and walked down the steep track to the farm, still whistling.

When the work was over he went out again. Before the pub, at the door marked 'hotel', a car was standing, a green car with glossy panels and a monogram, cushioned inside with grey and starred with silver. A chauffeur, symphonic also in green and bright buttons, was cranking her up. Perched upon the radiator was a naked silver girl. A woman came out of the inn. She wore white furs swathed over deep blue. Her feet flashed in their glossy boots. She wore a god in green jade and rose. Her gloves were rich and thick, like moulded ivory.

'Joy riding,' said a shepherd, and trudged on, but he stood ravished. It was not all dead then, the fine delicate life that had been the substance of his dream. Rare it might be, and decried, but it endured. The car's low humming died away, phantom-like he saw it in the darkling lane, a shell enclosing a pearl, the quintessence of cities, the perfection of the world.

He had heard her voice. 'I think we'll be getting back now.' She was going back to London. He went into the bar and asked the landlady who she was.

'Sort of actress,' the landlord said. And then, 'the war ought to have stopped that sort of thing.'

'Why, what's the harm?'

'Spending the money that ought to go to beating those bloody Germans.'

'All the same her sort brings custom,' the wife had said.

He drank his beer and went out into the pure cold evening. It was six o'clock by the old time, and the radiance was unnatural.

He walked down the damp lane, pale between the hedgerows. It widened and skirted a pond covered with vivid slime.

'And that was all they had to say about her....'

He hated them. A cart came storming up the hill, a compelling noise, grinding wheels and creaking shafts and jingling harness; hard breathing, and the rough voice of the carter to his beast.

At the pond the horse pulled up to breathe, his coat steamed, the carter leaned on the shaft.

'Some pull that.'

'Aye, so it be.' He noticed for the first time the essential difference in their speech.

Carter and horse went up the hill. He lit another cigarette.

Something had happened to him, resolving his mind of all doubts. He saw the tail lights of a car drawing through the vast outskirts of a city. An infinite fine line went out from it and drew him also. That tail lamp was his star. Within the car a girl lay rapt, insolent, a cigarette at her lips.

He dreamed. Dark gathered. Then he noticed that something luminous was coming towards him. Down the hollow lane white patches were moving, irregular, but in sequence, patches that seemed to his dulled ears to move silently, and to eyes trained to traffic extraordinarily slow. The sun had passed. The shadow of the hill overhung the valley. The pale light above intensified its menace. The straggling patches, like the cups of snow the downs still held in every hollow, made down the lane to the pond's edge. It was very cold. From there no lighted windows showed. Only the tip of his cigarette was crimson as in Piccadilly.

With the sound of a charging beast, a song burst from him, as, soundless, each snowy patch slid from the land on to the mirrored back of the pond. He began to shout out loud.

Some lame, some tame, some game for anything, some like a
  stand-up fight,
Some stay abed in the morning, and some stay out all night.
Have you seen the ducks go by, go a-rolling home?
Feeling very glad and spry, have you seen them roam?
There's mamma duck, papa duck, the grand old drake,
Leading away, what a noise they make.
Have you heard them quack, have you heard them quack, have you
  seen those ducks go by?
Have you seen the ducks go by, go a-rolling home? ...

The way back to the farm his voice answered Lee White's, and
the Vaudeville chorus sustained them. At the farm door they
forsook him. He had to be coherent to the farmer. He sought
inspiration. It came. He played with the latch, and then walked
into the kitchen, lyrical....

'And I stopped, and I looked, and I left.'

A month later found him on his knees, vertical in black cloth,
and grey trousers, and exquisite bow tie. A roll of Lyons brocade,
silver, and peach, was pliant between his fingers as the teats of a
cow. Inside it a girl stood frowning down upon him.

Despair was on her face, and on the faces of the attendant
women.

'But if you can't get me the lace to go with it, what am I to
wear?'

'I am sorry, madame.... Indeed we have done all that is possible. It seems that it is not to be had. I can assure madame that we
have done our best.' He rose and appealed to the women. His
conviction touched them all.

'Madame, anything that we can do ...'

The lovely girl frowned on them, and kicked at her half-pinned
draperies.

'When the war starts interfering with my clothes,' she said, 'the
war goes under....'

His eyes kindled.

WINIFRED HOLTBY

▼▼

So Handy for the Fun Fair

I'D NEVER MEANT to go back. What is done, is done, I say; but when I pulled off that double for twenty quid, I said to Jim, 'I'll give your three a treat this time.'

We've all got our faults; none knows better than I do. But taking it by and large, I couldn't have picked up a nicer family round Huddersfield. It hasn't been all jam for them, either, with a stepmother and her children messing about the house, just when they thought they were through with that sort of thing. Not that you ever are, really.

Well, Charlie had read somewhere about a Week-end Bank Holiday Excursion to Boulogne, and nothing would satisfy him but they must go—all three of them. But Milly, being just married and expecting, wouldn't travel, and Jim said he wasn't going to have Edna gadding off to foreign parts alone with Charlie, though she's eighteen and has been three years in the haberdashery at Hanson's, and isn't the sort you'd take liberties with. So in the end, I had to go to keep them out of mischief, and Jim's sister Lizzie came to mind the children.

I can't think now why I'd never told them about having been in France before. It's funny, isn't it? Partly, I suppose, it was because of Jim. I hadn't married him to make his life a misery, and I never yet met a man who didn't hate a woman to have gone one better on him, even if only by seeing active service with the Waacs while he was an indispensable in the Cloth Trade.

And then, of course, when you've three stepchildren to start with, and four of your own, with twins too, there's not much time for talking about your past life. 'Live for to-day'—that's always been my motto. And when Charlie told me how educational it was to go abroad, and how French the French were, and all that sort of thing, I just let him talk on. Young people seem to think no one has ever lived before them.

They might have been right too. When the boat turned to back into Boulogne Harbour, and I saw the striped tents on the shore, and the trams and flowers and the girls on the quay in their bright summer dresses, I could have sworn I'd never set eyes on the place.

We had a good time too, I will say, what with the shops and the cafés, and tram rides to Wimereux and a two-bob tour round the sights, and the Casino. I won fifty francs there. That's ten shillings. Always one of the winners I am. Lucky at cards, unlucky in love, they say—oh, well!

It was Edna who wanted the bus ride to Le Touquet. She was mad to tell the other girls in Hanson's she'd seen the posh hotel where the Prince of Wales stays, and the society beauties with their painted toe-nails. And the funny part was, I might never have known we'd even been near Calette (my view from the window being blocked by a fat Frenchwoman, all bust and bundles), but the bus broke down outside the village, and there we were, with two hours to wait for the next one, or a three-mile walk into Etaples to take the tram there.

Some of the passengers were quite upset; but I say the thing to do with a holiday is to enjoy it, no matter what happens.

We all got out, and Edna began arguing the point with that nice French boy, Gaston, from the pension. Quite vexed with her, I was; for though she's a good girl and pretty enough, she's often a bit stiff and silly with boys. Sex antagonism they call it nowadays. Sex, my eye, *I* say, and I was backing up Gaston, because few things are more broadening to the mind than being made love to in a foreign language, and what Edna wants is broadening.

So at first I didn't recognise the place.

How should I? It wasn't as if I'd been expecting it. I didn't know the buses from Boulogne to Le Touquet would go that way. There weren't any when I was in Calette. Then the village had changed—red brick houses, garage, petrol pumps and all that. It might have been just anywhere—and us walking up the street in a crowd together, grumbling because we should be late at Le Touquet.

Then, suddenly, we came upon the Fun Fair.

Every one stopped.

I? It was the queerest turn I've ever had.

This was Calette—and then again, it wasn't.

There was the little lake beyond the village, and the pine trees in a fringe along the sand dune; there was the farm we used to call the Manor House, where we went for oeufs and chips on evenings off duty. There was the hill above the church where our camp had been.

It was Calette all right, and no mistake.

But instead of huts and dumps and bundles of wire every-where, here were caravans and stalls and steam horses, swing-boats hitting the sky, the girls squealing, the lads joking, and the curé, black as a crow in his old cassock, grinning as though he'd swallowed sixpence.

The same curé.

'Why, it's like Feast Day,' Charlie said.

And Lily Dawson, who was with our lot, cried: 'Come on! Let's have some fun here till the next bus turns up.'

Edna didn't want to. She said swing-boats were common. She wanted to see the Casino at Le Touquet. 'I hate crowds,' she said. 'Smelly peasants.'

I knew Gaston was dying to take her round with him and understood enough English to hurt his feelings, so I said, 'Well, there's one thing about the French. They do know how to enjoy themselves. Give a Frenchman a couple of chairs, a bottle of wine and a cracked gramophone, and he's got night-life going in two minutes. You take Edna round and show her the sights a bit, young fellow.'

At first they wouldn't go. Edna pretended she was afraid, and Charlie said that he didn't like to leave me. 'This isn't Cleethorpes, Ma,' he said. 'What if they run away with you?' And I saw they thought that an old woman like me was long past fun fairs.

I'd never known anything could be so queer. For here was Calette—that I'd last seen so different, with the mud and the camps, and the ambulance trains and all that—now gone gay. And here was I, standing beside the lake, with those young people treating me as though I were ninety in the shade—I who had been—

Not that I blame them. When you're well past forty and have lost your figure as I lost mine after Maudie and the twins, it's no use pretending you are what you have been.

And there was the party from the bus well away among the stalls and side shows, screaming out French to each other, more like sea-birds than human beings, and the Indians who guarded the tent for the pig-faced lady watching with sad brown faces as though we were the savages and they the Christians who'd paid to see the sights.

And the chance that one of those old fat farmers might be François....

So then I couldn't bear it. I had to get away a bit till I knew where I was more.

So I gave a wink, and said: 'Don't you worry about me. I'm going to mouse round a bit on my own until the bus comes. And if a nice old farmer with a beard asks me to have a drink with him, maybe I'll say no, and maybe I won't!' And off I went, leaving them all together—Edna and Gaston, Charlie and Lily Dawson.

Edna and Charlie think I'm awful sometimes. But they'll never know how much disapproving of my way of talk has improved their own. Being shocked is sometimes as good an education as college, I say.

So I strolled round the lake towards the Manor House, trying to make up my mind just what I did feel.

It's no good pretending you don't forget the war nowadays, sometimes for months together; and when I *have* remembered, many's the time when, in spite of everything, I've wished I was back again.

Of course, there were the air-raids, and the cold and the mud, and being sorry about the poor young fellows; and the work I suppose was hard enough, though it beats me to remember what we did now.

But don't talk to me about its being a hard life for women in the army.

Why, there was that year before Maudie went to school, when I had the twins crawling about the kitchen, and Frank on the way, and Jim came home one night to say they were going on half-time at the mill—well, I had something to think about then, I can tell you.

And in the war, we were young.

It's all very well talking like Mrs. Fox, who's a Christian Scientist, and says that the Body's an Illusion. An illusion that weighs thirteen stone takes some forgetting. And it's not as if I couldn't remember what it was like to be light upon your feet.

I was chambermaid at the Hotel Majestic at Scarborough when the war began, and it doesn't take a girl half an hour to find out whether she's pretty or not in the hotel world.

No harm, mind you. But I will say that for the boys—they were good to me, especially the young officers doing themselves well on their last leave. I felt I had the world in my pocket those days.

And I used to tease them because of the bombardment and say that I'd been under fire first.

It wasn't till 1917 that Ginger Ferroll tried to cut his throat in the top bathroom, and I let myself in and got the razor from him, and made him sit down and be sensible. He didn't want to go back, poor devil. And I chaffed him, and said, 'Don't you fret, lad. I'll join the Waacs and get out to France, and we'll have a jolly good time together!' And he said, 'Not you. You girls don't care for anything but getting all the dough you can out of us.' And that put me on my mettle.

So I joined up, and what with having had hotel experience and not being so young as some, and knowing how to behave when I'd a mind to, I was assistant hostel forewoman at Folkestone before you could say Jack Robinson, and drafted out to France first thing in 1918. But I never heard what happened to Ginger Ferroll.

You know—I don't want another war and people killing each other, and Frankie mebbe losing his eyesight, but it's no use pretending I didn't enjoy the army.

Having been in the hotel line, I was used to numbers and rules, and being up to time and all that. As for work, I'd been on my legs from half-past five in the morning till after midnight during the summer season what with parties going early and parties coming late, and pekinese to be fed in the pantry, and baths at all hours. In the army it was twice as free and easy—and no fear of a week's notice.

But it wasn't only that.

Back there in Calette I knew there'd been more in it than sing-songs after roll-call and seeing a new country.

I can't remember Boulogne, except it rained there, and we waited about all day in a sort of hostel. Then they packed us into a goods van and left us to it.

That journey! Were we tired? Oh, no! It's only a rumour. Shut up and stuck in a siding while train after train went past us, and some whose first night it was in France thought it might well be their last, for we'd be suffocated before we arrived anywhere. It was nearly morning before they let us out again. No wonder I thought Calette was miles from Boulogne.

The queer part was, we didn't really grumble. We took it all as gospel. Winning the war. That's what we thought we were doing, lugging our kit up the dark hill from the village, and tumbling into bed in a great hut like a warehouse.

Next morning Mrs. Brooks, the administrator—our officer like—had us all up in the messroom. Plump little bit she was, like a pouter pigeon, buttoned tight into her tunic and her cap over one eye. And she gave us a jaw about our duty, and not disgracing the King's uniform, and not speaking to officers nor Paris-plaging with the signallers, nor walking in the woods with the Australians. But all that, she gave us to think, was neither here nor there. The really black sin—that if we committed we'd be sent home, and no excuses taken—was fraternising with the French. You bet I listened. I wasn't going to be sent home—not likely. But I was shocked in a way, I don't mind telling you. Fraternising with Froggies? With all those nice khaki lads about? Not likely! That's what I thought. Life's comic.

But it looked as though I was to see the Froggies, anyway.

First day I were there, old Brooks sent me down with Lloyd, the stores clerk, to get her eggs and butter at a French farm. Army rations weren't good enough for that lady. Every day, it would be fresh milk or vegetables or a chicken, and we had to fetch them in twos, because of the Moral Danger—what ho!

Well, I was game. I put on my hat and turned up my collar, and went forth to war, ready for anything.

The farm was a bit back from the main street, and like nothing I'd ever seen outside a pig-sty. There were mud plaster walls all round a sort of fold-yard, with straw and pigs and God knows what in the middle, and a low one-storied house facing on to it, with hens running in and out of the door, and a couple of tow-haired brats and an old idiot drooling and gibbering at us from the stable.

Once inside, the place was clean enough, I will say that, with a sanded floor and open fireplace. Madame Haudiquet always had a big pan with some sort of mess for the pigs stewing over it. And there was a square table with yellow oil-cloth under the lamp, and a door opening out into the bedroom showing the high, feather bed with the white counterpane.

But bare. Skinned to the bone; that's how I felt it. Not a crock, not a plant, not a cushion, nor a nice enlarged photo; not a thing in the place that you could do without except a treadle machine that had been Marie's *dot* when she married. It's no wonder the French think so much about beds, when they never make a room for themselves fit to sit in.

Talk about home life. The gloom of that place fairly hit you in the face when you went into it. Outside, on that first day, it was sunny. A bright, windy morning after the fog and rain. Inside it wasn't so much dark as dismal. I stood blinking like a fool on the doorstep, while Lloyd called out to old Madame, 'Hallo, Ma! No *poulet* to-day. Just *oeufs* and *lait*, please. *Tout de suite* and the tooter the sweeter!'

And in came François, hopping on his crutch from the dairy, and said, 'Good-morning, mees. Is there something I can do for you?'

And from that moment it was all over with me. Talk about moral danger—well.

He was good-looking, of course; but it wasn't that, quite. I'd seen some nice boys at the Hotel Majestic.

And it wasn't that he said anything—though he *could* talk. Politics, the war, places, books—all that stuff.

That first time we stood there staring at each other, while Lloyd went on gassing about her eggs and butter. Only when we went, the young man offered to carry the basket, and Lloyd said, 'That's queer. He's never done that before. Perhaps he's getting sweet on me.' And began to giggle. So I asked who he was, and she told me he was the son of the house, who had been wounded, and Madame was as mean as a mouse-trap, but the milk was the cleanest in the district, and François speaking English made it easier. The villagers said there was a curse on the family.

Well, curse or no curse, French or English, I knew well enough that François Haudiquet was the man for me.

Mind you, it was days before we ever said anything but so many eggs and so much butter, and please and thank you; but one day the orderly with me wanted some stuff from the café— cigarettes or something—and keen as I was to keep the rules, I let her go. Besides, I knew by that time I wanted to talk to François more than anything, and two was company, even in that kitchen.

Old Madame was there as usual, glowering at us out of her little pig's eyes, as though I was going to pinch the butter. But she went out to get the eggs herself, and François and I were left alone together. The first time alone, and not a word to say.

Then down came the storm—crash, on to the shutters, and the hailstones dancing like bounce-ball on the pavé. Madame came back with the eggs, and I thanked her and took my basket and looked out into the weather. And I must say, the more I looked the less I liked it.

Then François said, 'It is bad time, eh?' You know how the French talk. Bad time—*mauvais temps*. 'Perhaps you wait a little.'

I expect I said something saucy. I was always one for answering back in those days. And he laughed.

That roused them. Goodness knows, I'd heard plenty of laughter in my time. We always were larking about in our family. But François looked as though he'd raised the devil, and the old woman stared, and the old man came mumbling and grumbling in from the downstairs bedroom, and Marie draped and draggled in, gawping as though the roof had fallen. God knows what they thought. But I knew I wanted to be out of that bedlam at the double.

Then François asked, 'Perhaps mademoiselle would prefer an umbrella?' They had one of those big black cotton affairs in the corner.

But I told him I was a soldier, and soldiers could not carry umbrellas, as he must know, being a soldier too.

I can't tell you how he started when I said that—as though no one had ever troubled before to notice what he was—except a child of the devil and all that rot. I might have given him a thousand pounds. Not that he said much.

Come to think of it, I never was with him more than half an hour at the outside together, and always those others in and out of the kitchen.

But bit by bit, I got the story from him. You see, he'd been the bright boy of the family, scholarships at the village school and so on. And they all meant to make a priest of him, and sent him to some college.

I've never been one for religion. A short life and a gay one, that's my motto. But François wasn't the sort to take life easy. The more he knew about things, the more they worried him, sitting up all hours to find out if God existed, till at last he had to say he was an agnostic or atheist, or whatever it is they call it. And then the fat was in the fire.

He had to leave off learning to be a priest, though they said he still could be a schoolmaster. But when he came home to tell his family, the old man had a sort of fit—a stroke, I should say—and has never been right in the head since. So François had to stay at home to run the farm, and a fine time they all gave him, with his mother telling him it was all his fault, and the priest saying the curse of God was on him, and all his plans in ruins. But worst of it all, he said, were the church bells, calling and calling him, and the feeling he couldn't go to Mass, because he was a heretic. I think the war came as a relief to him. No one could have wanted to stay in that house. Then in 1915 he was wounded—all down the left side, leg off at the knee and five operations. Oh, they put him through it! And when he came out of hospital, it was back to the farm again, and all the old wretched business—with the pain from his bad leg added. They blamed him for his father's queerness, and for Marie's husband being killed—yes, and for the war too. 'All due to the wickedness of these unbelieving times,' the curé used to say. Can you beat it? And when the pain kept him awake at nights, he'd ask himself whether, maybe, it wasn't all his fault, and whether he had a right to make so many people miserable 'for a matter of conscience....' Matter of conscience!

So you see, he'd never had any fun—not ever. No fun fair for François, I thought, looking down at the crowd by the lake and the steam horses.

Hot it was, and the Manor House closed up now. I tried to ask a lad if it was turned back to a farm, but he couldn't understand me.

There used to be a short cut up to the road by the railway, and I found it again, remembering how the primroses used to flower even among that trampled mess and wire.

That was a spring—1918.

Made for love, if there hadn't been a war on. Daffodils in the woods behind the sandhills—like sunlight under the trees, they were. The girls gathered hats full on off-duty days to take in to the hospitals. Some of them did other things there too. 'Walking in the woods' we called it. Oh, well, you're only young once.

And I'd fallen in love, no doubt about it. I, who could have had any lad round the camp, and that officer—I've forgotten his name now—making what are called advances every time I went to the Q.M. Stores. I, who they'd called the Beauty Queen of Calette. I'd gone in right off the deep end over a crippled Froggie.

Of course, it seems mad now the way we acted, or rather didn't act, as you might say. But there was a war on. And you could never explain to Edna, or young Charlie, what a difference that made.

All day long you'd hear the thud, thud, thud, of the guns. And every week fresh rumours came about the Germans, how they'd got us on the run and were breaking through at Arras or Amiens, or somewhere. And often we looked along the road expecting to see them come in their grey uniforms, marching up to murder us.

And at nights, we had the Raids.

So for ten minutes a day my life was François Haudiquet, hobbling about on his crutch down at the farm, and for the rest it was the war and the camp, and army. (Did I say I'd been made hostel forewoman?) I'd never known before what it would be like, putting the new draft through their paces, and polishing them up before they were went off to other places.

I enjoyed it.

I liked giving orders.

I liked making them march decently.

'Squad, 'shun! Right turn! By the left, wheel! Eyes right.' What the devil was it we used to shout, marching them from the station?

Talk about fools! I was one then, I could tell you. Too keen on the army and then not keen enough, maybe.

For I wouldn't risk my job going with François. I, who could have cured him of his devils, I let him look at me with those great eyes of his, and sometimes sit for a while, behind the cow-shed, and make him laugh at himself and all his fancies.

But always I was busy, always getting back to the camp and all that.

Until that day when I wasn't busy enough.

It was the beginning of May, and I was tired. For over a month we'd had our nights' rest broken. When they weren't raiding us, they were raiding Etaples, and that kept us awake if it did nothing worse. It made some of the girls jumpy, and all of us cross. As for old Brooks, she thrived upon it, I will say that for her. Nothing spoiled her appetite—not a nerve in her body.

One morning I was off down to the Haudiquets as usual when she spotted me. 'Clark,' she called. I can remember it as well as if it was yesterday. I turned back and saluted—had to. And she asked me what I was doing, and when she found out that I was still going myself to fetch her stuff, even though it wasn't properly speaking my job any longer, she didn't half give it me. Bad organisation—inefficiency—slackness—Lord knows what she didn't say.

And I stood 'Yes, ma'aming' and 'No, ma'aming' with black rage in my heart. But she had to let me go that morning, because she'd ordered a chicken and the Colonel was coming to lunch, and no other girl was about just then to fetch it, except a new orderly she couldn't let go alone.

At the farm I told the orderly to wait in the kitchen and keep an eye on Madame. I had, I said, to go and choose a duck or something. I made François come out with me into the cow-shed.

Funny. To this day I can smell that mixture of turnips and cow dirt and sour milk and hay there.

And when I got him to myself, I just lammed into him. I was going to be taken off this job, I said, and it was all his fault. If he had chosen to be an Englishman instead of a Froggie we could have had fun together. All the other girls had boys they went about with, who took them to tea in Etaples or concerts at the Y.M. hut. But I had to go creeping and crawling, and never seeing him except in front of his old mother, and we were young and life was passing, and why couldn't he have fallen in love with some one else instead of me and left me free to go with boys of my own kind?

I can't remember all of it. It seems crazy now, just crazy. But I'd been in love with him for weeks, and I was tired and everything seemed against me, and I lost my temper.

I've seen a thing or two in my day, but I've never forgotten the way he took my hands and held me off at arms' length, and said, stern as a judge: 'What do you mean? When have I harmed you, ever?' And I cried out that he had made me love him and it wasn't fair.

And then I don't remember.

I know that at one time he dropped his crutch and took me into his arms and kissed me. And then it came upon me that this was all that mattered. What did I care for the war or for the army? This was where I belonged. Let them discharge me!

And I told him not to go down that night to the estaminet, where he usually sat with old Ma Creuset, but I would get out, after roll-call or before—it didn't matter—and if he'd wait for me in the cow-shed, I'd show him whether I loved him or not—I promised. We would walk in the woods together.

And so I left him. The last thing I did for him was to pick up his crutch and hand it to him, and run out to tell the orderly that the duck was too skinny and we must go at once. As we went through the yard, I saw him leaning on his crutch against the door-post.

Back at camp, old Ma Brooks sent for me. I went not caring if she ordered me never to go near the Haudiquets again.

But it was to say that Reynolds, the forewoman whose place I had taken when she was sent to Abbeville, had been wounded in an air-raid.

'The girls are having a stiff time there,' she told me. 'Sleeping out at night in Creçy Forest, and all that. You took her place well here, Clark,' she said. 'Between ourselves, I don't care how you amuse yourself in private. What we want now are girls who can keep their heads and keep their spirits up, and not give way during emergencies.' She didn't care how I amused myself in private! And I'd wasted all those months—that was all I thought—until I heard her saying: 'So pack your kit at once and report in the orderly room at twelve-thirty. You are taking seven draft girls, two cooks, two general domestics and three baker-esses, down with you to Abbeville. And you're staying there in place of Reynolds. It's a stiff job, but I'm paying you a high compliment in sending you.'

Mind you, I couldn't stand that woman. A bitch if ever there was one. Hard-faced. Greedy.

But she gave orders. There was a war on. 'With our backs to the wall.' What was it they had told us? 'And believing in the justice of our cause, each one of us must fight on to the end.'

I believed nothing, except that I loved François.

But in half an hour, with my kit in a suit-case, I was marching seven women to the orderly room.

'Squad, 'shun! Sal-ute! Left turn! Quick march!'

We were off down to the station—off to Abbeville.

Would you believe it?

The Civic Quarter Library
www.leedsmet.ac.uk/lis/lss

Borrowed

Customer   Cairns, Tammy Claire Jane (M

                                    Due Date

1 Soldier heroes : B   29/9/2011,23:59
1705185554

2 Women, men and the   29/9/2011,23:59
1701707737

3 The pity of war   29/9/2011,23:59
1702774611

4 Blighty : British   29/9/2011,23:59
1701575756

                    19.09.2011 16:19:55

For renewals telephone (0113) 812 6161
        Thank you and see you soon

It wasn't till we were quite half-way to Abbeville that I realised I'd sent no message back to François.

I wrote a note and gave it to the driver. I wrote from Abbeville another line and posted it. I told him I was sorry I'd kept him waiting; but at least he could get free and come to me. He wasn't under army orders, like what I was. It wasn't so far from Calette to Abbeville. I swore I loved him, and should love him always.

But he never answered. I waited and wrote and waited, and wrote and waited. I thought of him sitting there in the kitchen that Tuesday evening, with old Madame driving him mad, chewing the fat at him, and Marie whining and those two kids bellowing, and the old man drooling over his coffee.

I thought of that red-haired Lloyd setting her cap at him, when she went to the farm for *oeufs* and *poulets*.

I thought of all the French girls in the village—for he was a good-looking chap for all his misery.

And then I told myself he'd never waited. After all, had he said a word to me? All the chances he'd had, and never a whisper. It was I who'd made the running, thrown myself at his head, putting ideas into it that never came there natural. Why, he'd nearly been a priest, and in France priests don't have women—or so they say. And I remembered what the French said we Waacs were. I'd only behaved just as they thought we all did.

So after the third time, I didn't write again.

And that's the last I'd ever heard of François.

But when Bert came along, making no bones about what he wanted, married man and all, I let him have it. And after the war, there was Chris and Bill and Larry; and the queer thing is, I've never felt cheap with one of them. I still feel a good woman as you might say—a good wife too, I've been to poor old Jim. And the only man I feel ashamed about is François—who never but once even kissed me. It's the things you don't do, not the things you do, you feel most sorry for. That's why I've always tried to give Charlie and Edna and Millie and my own four a good time.

And I'd never meant to go back to Calette, never.

But seeing that I was here, I thought I might just as well have a look at the farm again, and perhaps see François.

It would be queer to see him again and ask him if he remembered me; though I know what I am, and I know what I was then. So I thought, 'Perhaps I won't say anything—just see him.'

It wasn't till I'd gone right up the village street and back again, I realised I couldn't find the farm again.

The place was as dumb as the grave and as hot as what comes

after. Only a few hens clucking about, and the dust blowing, and the tunes from the steam horses. Not a soul about; they'd all gone down to the Fun Fair.

Then at last I recognised the estaminet. It had been renamed the 'Café de la Victoire,' but there was old Ma Creuset all right, set in the doorway, too fat and too rheumaticky to go gadding. I knew the bottles of sweets in the window, and the round table with the red oil-cloth on it, and the sort of sideboard affair with polished glasses.

So in I walked, bold as brass, saying, 'Hallo, Ma Creuset!' And she gawped like a hen at me knowing her name.

Not a word of English could she remember, and my French wasn't too bright, but Boulogne had brought back a few words.

So I was able to ask, '*Ou est la famille Haudiquet?*'

'Haudiquet? Haudiquet?' You know how the French twist their tongues round a name so that a Christian can hardly say it.

'*Dans la guerre,*' I said. 'They had a farm, *une ferme, oeufs—lait. Poulets.*'

'*La Guerre, Haudiquet, une ferme, oh, oui, oui, oui!*' she cried and set off jabbering.

'François?' I pushed in. 'Oui, François aussi.' And then a whole lot of French, then, '*Vengeance de Dieu.*' I recognised that. 'Vengeance of God.' That's what they were always saying.

And suddenly after all these years I knew it was more important to me to know what had happened to François than anything else in the world. I got hold of Ma Creuset's hands, and cried, '*Ou est-il?*' I knew that. I'd asked Madame Haudiquet that. Dozens of times, I'd shouted out '*Ou est-il?*'

And then I heard her say something about an église.

I knew what that meant. Église. Church. The church down the village street over the railway line above the Fun Fair.

And off I went to that church as though cops were after me.

My! It was hot, the pavement like an oven shelf, and the streets fairly dancing. I could hear the organ from the steam horses grinding out its old tune:

> *Après la guerre fini*
> *Tous les anglais partis,*
> *Tum, tum, tum, tum, te-tay,*
> *Beaucoup petits bébés.*

That was what they used to sing when we were in Calette. But there were no babies this time. Maude and the twins and Frankie are blue-eyed like me and Jim. I've often wondered what it would have been like to have a brown-eyed baby with black hair like François.

By the time I got to the church, I knew what sort of a fool I was.

Of course, it wasn't this church. Old Ma Creuset meant he'd turned a priest again—gone back to the Church—the Église—because of the vengeance of God upon his family.

And there was I, who underneath everything had fretted for him all these years, and now nearly killed myself dashing off to the nearest churchyard, stuck like a fool among the marble angels and crosses, and all those messy wire flowers the French seem to think so much of, and what with the heat and the hurry and the upset, I came all over queer like. A sort of heart-attack. I haven't got the figure for running these days.

So down I sat, even though it was on the steps of the War Memorial, and called myself all manner of born idiots. For now I was sure of what had happened. François hadn't been missing me. Oh, dear, no—I'd shocked him. Made myself cheap. Thought myself the world's wonder—like those old maids Gracie Fields sings about. I'd kidded myself finely over François—yes, and over Bert and all the others. A harlot. A cheap woman. Throwing myself at their heads because I couldn't bear not to give a man a bit of pleasure, when it was so easy, and life so short, and chance never comes twice down the same road.

The organ by the lake had changed its tune now.

'Chocolate Soldier Waltz—My Hero'—that's what they were playing. My hero! Yes—me for a bonnie heroine. Sold, I'd been. Sickened one man of women, driven him back into the Church for safety; cried myself dry over him, night after night, and all the time—oh, sold, I felt! Even though I'd guessed this was what might have happened. Sold, and sick and stupid.

I suppose I must have shut my eyes a minute, because when I opened them, I still thought I was dreaming. I was staring hard at a white slab on the other side of the pathway, and on the white in black letters I read his name, 'Haudiquet.'

I looked and blinked, and looked again. Then I got up—I'm a bit short-sighted—and this is what I read. I read till I learned it by heart, and wrote it down, and asked young Gaston next day to translate it, just to be quite certain:

Ici reposent
les corps de la famille
Haudiquet—
tous tués par un obus
d'un aviateur allemand,

le 11 mai, 1918.
Louis François Haudiquet, agé 69 ans
Marie Joséphine, son épouse, agée 65 ans
Marie Latour, veuve de Félix Latour, leur fille, agée 25 ans
François Joseph, leur fils, agé 25 ans.
Qu'ils reposent en paix.

It was May 11 when I went to Abbeville, and on May 11 François had been killed.

So that was why he had never written.

He'd been at home—that's how the Germans got him.

So he had waited for me. And I hadn't come. And now he'd never know what had kept me from him.

He hadn't let me down. I had let him down. For if I'd come, if we'd walked in the woods together, he wouldn't have been back there when the bomb fell. He'd have been away with me and safe and happy.

Oh, he'd been let down nicely.

It wouldn't bear thinking of. It wouldn't bear thinking of.

But I stood thinking—me, a married woman with four children, and Charlie and Edna down there at the Fun Fair. I stood in the churchyard crying over a French farmer, who'd been dead these fifteen years, as though he'd been killed yesterday.

But the steam horses gave two sharp sort of hoots then—like a factory whistle, and the tune changed again. And I saw by the clock the bus would be round in twenty minutes; and I'd better go back and look after my young people.

For what's past is past, and they'd be waiting for me. You can't help the dead, and no use to blame the living.

And it came to me there that in a way I'd been right first time. God had got François in the end. He'd meant him for a priest and if I'd had him, I should always have had to fight against religion. I'd have stood up to any woman those days; but I doubt if I could have beaten all that business about being a priest, and sin and hell and devils. Just as François couldn't beat the army and taking orders.

It was too much for me. It's always been too much. I came down from that churchyard not knowing whether to be glad or sorry—whether I'd found out that by going to Abbeville and obeying orders I'd killed my François—or whether perhaps I'd saved him. But I hadn't disgusted him, because he'd waited. At least before he died he knew I'd loved him, and even to a man in love with God, that must be something.

So back I went, there being naught else for it, and found Edna in the swing boats, her hair blowing, smiling at Gaston, pretty as a picture. And Charlie was buying sweets for Lily Dawson, and the crowds were shouting and larking, gay as ever.

They saw me after a bit, and said, 'Hallo, Ma! Did you have a good time? Did you get off with a Frenchman?' And I said: 'Don't ask impertinent questions. What d'you take me for? Do you think a good-looking young woman like me couldn't click in a crowd like this if I wanted?'

And they all screamed with laughing. And Edna teased poor Gaston, and said, 'Yes. It *would* be a French bus to break down on the way to Le Touquet!' And he, so happy-like and pleased with every one, said, 'Break down, yes. Very bad, yes. But so—what you call?—so handy for the Fun Fair!'

KATHERINE MANSFIELD

▼▼▼

The Fly

'Y'ARE VERY SNUG in here,' piped old Mr. Woodifield, and he peered out of the great, green-leather armchair by his friend the boss's desk as a baby peers out of its pram. His talk was over; it was time for him to be off. But he did not want to go. Since he had retired, since his ... stroke, the wife and the girls kept him boxed up in the house every day of the week except Tuesday. On Tuesday he was dressed and brushed and allowed to cut back to the City for the day. Though what he did there the wife and girls couldn't imagine. Made a nuisance of himself to his friends, they supposed.... Well, perhaps so. All the same, we cling to our last pleasures as the tree clings to its last leaves. So there sat old Woodifield, smoking a cigar and staring almost greedily at the boss, who rolled in his office chair, stout, rosy, five years older than he, and still going strong, still at the helm. It did one good to see him.

Wistfully, admiringly, the old voice added, 'It's snug in here, ur n my word!'

'Yes, it's comfortable enough,' agreed the boss, and he flipped the *Financial Times* with a paper-knife. As a matter of fact he was proud of his room; he liked to have it admired, especially by old Woodifield. It gave him a feeling of deep, solid satisfaction to be planted there in the midst of it in full view of that frail old figure in the muffler.

'I've had it done up lately,' he explained, as he had explained for the past—how many?—weeks. 'New carpet,' and he pointed to the bright red carpet with a pattern of large white rings. 'New furniture,' and he nodded towards the massive bookcase and the table with legs like twisted treacle. 'Electric heating!' He waved almost exultantly towards the five transparent, pearly sausages glowing so softly in the tilted copper pan.

But he did not draw old Woodifield's attention to the photograph over the table of a grave-looking boy in uniform standing in one of those spectral photographers' parks with photographers' storm-clouds behind him. It was not new. It had been there for over six years.

'There was something I wanted to tell you,' said old Woodifield, and his eyes grew dim remembering. 'Now what was it? I had it in my mind when I started out this morning.' His hands began to tremble, and patches of red showed above his beard.

Poor old chap, he's on his last pins, thought the boss. And, feeling kindly, he winked at the old man, and said jokingly, 'I tell you what. I've got a little drop of something here that'll do you good before you go out into the cold again. It's beautiful stuff. It wouldn't hurt a child.' He took a key off his watch-chain, unlocked a cupboard below his desk, and drew forth a dark, squat bottle. 'That's the medicine,' said he. 'And the man from whom I got it told me on the strict Q.T. it came from the cellars at Windsor Castle.'

Old Woodifield's mouth fell open at the sight. He couldn't have looked more surprised if the boss had produced a rabbit.

'It's whisky, ain't it?' he piped feebly.

The boss turned the bottle and lovingly showed him the label. Whisky it was.

'D'you know,' said he, peering up at the boss wonderingly, 'they won't let me touch it at home.' And he looked as though he was going to cry.

'Ah, that's where we know a bit more than the ladies,' cried the boss, swooping across for two tumblers that stood on the table with the water-bottle, and pouring a generous finger into each. 'Drink it down. It'll do you good. And don't put any water with it. It's sacrilege to tamper with stuff like this. Ah!' He tossed off his, pulled out his handkerchief, hastily wiped his moustaches, and cocked an eye at old Woodifield, who was rolling his in his chaps.

The old man swallowed, was silent a moment, and then said faintly, 'It's nutty!'

But it warmed him; it crept into his chill old brain—he remembered.

'That was it,' he said, heaving himself out of his chair. 'I thought you'd like to know. The girls were in Belgium last week having a look at poor Reggie's grave, and they happened to come across your boy's. They're quite near each other, it seems.'

Old Woodifield paused, but the boss made no reply. Only a quiver in his eyelids showed that he heard.

'The girls were delighted with the way the place is kept,' piped the old voice. 'Beautifully looked after. Couldn't be better if they were at home. You've not been across, have yer?'

'No, no!' For various reasons the boss had not been across.

'There's miles of it,' quavered old Woodifield, 'and it's all as neat as a garden. Flowers growing on all the graves. Nice broad paths.' It was plain from his voice how much he liked a nice broad path.

The pause came again. Then the old man brightened wonderfully.

'D'you know what the hotel made the girls pay for a pot of jam?' he piped. 'Ten francs! Robbery, I call it. It was a little pot, so Gertrude says, no bigger than a half-crown. And she hadn't taken more than a spoonful when they charged her ten francs. Gertrude brought the pot away with her to teach 'em a lesson. Quite right, too; it's trading on our feelings. They think because we're over there having a look round we're ready to pay anything. That's what it is.' And he turned towards the door.

'Quite right, quite right!' cried the boss, though what was quite right he hadn't the least idea. He came round by his desk, followed the shuffling footsteps to the door, and saw the old fellow out. Woodifield was gone.

For a long moment the boss stayed, staring at nothing, while the grey-haired office messenger, watching him, dodged in and out of his cubby-hole like a dog that expects to be taken for a run. Then: 'I'll see nobody for half an hour, Macey,' said the boss. 'Understand? Nobody at all.'

'Very good, sir.'

The door shut, the firm heavy steps recrossed the bright carpet, the fat body plumped down in the spring chair, and leaning forward, the boss covered his face with his hands. He wanted, he intended, he had arranged to weep....

It had been a terrible shock to him when old Woodifield sprang that remark upon him about the boy's grave. It was exactly as though the earth had opened and he had seen the boy lying there with Woodifield's girls staring down at him. For it was strange. Although over six years had passed away, the boss never thought of the boy except as lying unchanged, unblemished in his uniform, asleep for ever. 'My son!' groaned the boss. But no tears came yet. In the past, in the first months and even years after the boy's death, he had only to say those words to be overcome by such grief that nothing short of a violent fit of weeping could relieve him. Time, he had declared then, he had told everybody, could make no difference. Other men perhaps might recover, might live their loss down, but not he. How was it possible? His boy was an only son. Ever since his birth the boss had worked at building up this business for him; it had no other meaning if it was not for the boy. Life itself had come to have no other meaning. How on earth could he have slaved, denied himself, kept going all those years without the promise for ever before him of the boy's stepping into his shoes and carrying on where he left off?

And that promise had been so near being fulfilled. The boy had been in the office learning the ropes for a year before the war. Every morning they had started off together; they had come back by the same train. And what congratulations he had received as the boy's father! No wonder; he had taken to it marvellously. As to his popularity with the staff, every man jack of them down to old Macey couldn't make enough of the boy. And he wasn't in the least spoilt. No, he was just his bright natural self, with the right word for everybody, with that boyish look and his habit of saying, 'Simply splendid!'

But all that was over and done with as though it never had been. The day had come when Macey had handed him the telegram that brought the whole place crashing about his head. 'Deeply regret to inform you ...' And he had left the office a broken man, with his life in ruins.

Six years ago, six years.... How quickly time passed! It might have happened yesterday. The boss took his hands from his face; he was puzzled. Something seemed to be wrong with him. He wasn't feeling as he wanted to feel. He decided to get up and have a look at the boy's photograph. But it wasn't a favourite photograph of his; the expression was unnatural. It was cold, even stern-looking. The boy had never looked like that.

At that moment the boss noticed that a fly had fallen into his broad inkpot, and was trying feebly but desperately to clamber out again. Help! Help! said those struggling legs. But the sides of the inkpot were wet and slippery; it fell back again and began to swim. The boss took up a pen, picked the fly out of the ink, and shook it on to a piece of blotting-paper. For a fraction of a second it lay still on the dark patch that oozed round it. Then the front legs waved, took hold, and, pulling its small, sodden body up, it began the immense task of cleaning the ink from its wings. Over and under, over and under, went a leg along a wing as the stone goes over and under the scythe. Then there was a pause, while the fly, seeming to stand on the tips of its toes, tried to expand first one wing and then the other. It succeeded at last, and, sitting down, it began, like a minute cat, to clean its face. Now one could imagine that the little front legs rubbed against each other lightly, joyfully. The horrible danger was over; it had escaped; it was ready for life again.

But just then the boss had an idea. He plunged his pen back into the ink, leaned his thick wrist on the blotting-paper, and as the fly tried its wings down came a great heavy blot. What would it make of that? What indeed! The little beggar seemed absolutely cowed, stunned, and afraid to move because of what would happen next. But then, as if painfully, it dragged itself forward. The front legs waved, caught hold, and, more slowly this time, the task began from the beginning.

He's a plucky little devil, thought the boss, and he felt a real admiration for the fly's courage. That was the way to tackle things; that was the right spirit. Never say die; it was only a question of ... But the fly had again finished its laborious task, and the boss had just time to refill his pen, to shake fair and square on the new-cleaned body yet another dark drop. What about it this time? A painful moment of suspense followed. But behold, the front legs were again waving; the boss felt a rush of relief. He leaned over the fly and said to it tenderly, 'You artful little b...' And he actually had the brilliant notion of breathing on it to help the drying process. All the same, there was something timid and weak about its efforts now, and the boss decided that this time should be the last, as he dipped the pen deep into the inkpot.

It was. The last blot fell on the soaked blotting-paper, and the draggled fly lay in it and did not stir. The back legs were stuck to the body; the front legs were not to be seen.

'Come on,' said the boss. 'Look sharp!' And he stirred it with his pen—in vain. Nothing happened or was likely to happen. The fly was dead.

The boss lifted the corpse on the end of the paper-knife and flung it into the waste-paper basket. But such a grinding feeling of wretchedness seized him that he felt positively frightened. He started forward and pressed the bell for Macey.

'Bring me some fresh blotting-paper,' he said sternly, 'and look sharp about it.' And while the old dog padded away he fell to wondering what it was he had been thinking about before. What was it? It was ... He took out his handkerchief and passed it inside his collar. For the life of him he could not remember.

GERTRUDE STEIN

▼▼

Tourty or Tourtebattre

A Story of the Great War

TOURTEBATTRE came to visit us in the court he said he heard Americans were in town and he came to see us and we said what is your name and what americans have you known and we said we would go to see him and we did not and we did not give him anything.

Then when we went out to see the hospital we did not take him anything. We asked to see him. Then when the new things came we did take a package to him and we did not see him but he came and called on us to thank us and we were out.

Reflections

If I must reflect I reflect upon Ann Veronica. This is not what is intended. Mrs. Tourtebattre. Of this we know nothing.

Can we reflect one for another.

Profit and loss is three twenty five never two seventy five.

Yes that is the very easy force, decidedly not.

Then Tourtebattre used to come all the time and then he used to tell us how old he was when he was asked and he took sugar in his coffee as it was given to him. He was not too old to be a father he was thirty seven and he had three children and he told us that he liked to turn a phrase.

China. Whenever he went to the colonies his sister was hurt in an automobile accident. This did not mean that she suffered.

Some one thought she was killed. Will you please put that in.

His father's watch, his wife gave all his most precious belongings to a man who did not belong to the town he said he belonged to. We did not know the truth of this.

Reflections

We should not color our hero with his wife's misdeeds. Because you see he may be a religion instead of a talker. Little bones have to come out of his hand for action this was after his wound. A good deal.

He was wounded in the attack in April right near where he was always going to visit his wife and he saw the church tower and then he was immediately evacuated to an american hospital where every one was very American and very kind and Miss Bell tried to talk french to him and amuse him but overcome with her difficulties with the french language she retired which made him say she was very nice and these stories that he told to us you told to Sister Cecile which did not please her and she said we must come and hear from every one else the stories they all told of the kindness they had received in the American hospital before they came to her and she said to them what did the major do, and they said he played ball. He did. And you too and all of them said, no sister but you were wounded in an attack. We were both wounded, said the soldier.

Reflections

Reflections on Sister Cecile lead us to believe that she did not reflect about Friday but about the book in which she often wrote. We were curious. She wrote this note. This is it. Name life, wife, deed, wound, weather, food, devotion, and expression.

What did he ask for.

Why I don't know.

Why don't you know.

I don't call that making literature at all.

What has he asked for.

I call literature telling a story as it happens.

Facts of life make literature.

I can always feel rightly about that.

We obtained beads for him and our own pictures in it.

Dear pictures of us.

We can tell anything over.

We gave him colored beads and he made them with paper that he bought himself of two different colors into frames that we sent with our pictures to our cousins and our papas in America.

Can we say it.

We cannot.

Now.

Then he told us about his wife and his child.

He does not say anything about them now.

Some immediate provision was necessary.

We said in English these are the facts which we are bringing to your memory.

What is capitol.

He told us of bead buttons and black and white. He answered her back very brightly.

He is a man.

Reflections

What were the reflections.

Have we undertaken too much.

What is the name of his wife.

They were lost. We did not look forward. We did not think much. How long would he stay. Our reflections really came later.

The first thing we heard from her was that the woman was not staying and had left her new address.

How do you do.

We did not look her up.

Her mother and her mother.

Can you think why Marguerite did not wish Jenny Picard to remain longer.

Because she stole.

Not really.

Yes indeed. Little things.

This will never do.

And then.

I said we must go to see her.

And you said we will see.

One night, no one day she called with her mother.

Who was very good looking.

She was very good looking.

And the little boy.

Can you think of the little boy.

They both said that they were not polite.

But they were.

Reflections can come already.

We believed her reasons were real reasons.

Who is always right.

Not she nor her eleven sisters.

No one knew who was kind to her.

What is kindness.

Kindness is being soft or good and has nothing to do with amiable. Albert is kind and good.

And their wives.

Can you tell the difference between wives and children.
Queen Victoria and Queen Victoria.
They made you jump.
And I said the mother you said the mother. I did not remember the mother was in Paris but you did.

RICHARD ALDINGTON

▼▼▼

The Case of Lieutenant Hall
Extracts from a Diary

12TH NOVEMBER 1918. 'The War is over.' I never thought
I should live to write these words. We were told about 7
A.M. Surprisingly little enthusiasm, but the men are fed up
beyond human endurance. About 9 I was amazed to hear heavy
artillery fire from the north. At first, we thought the Armistice
news was simply another latrine rumour, and that the war was
still on; afterwards I was told that the Canadians made a last hour
attack. I celebrated the Armistice by sleeping most of the day in
my billet. We are all worn out. After dark the R.S.M. came and
asked permission for the men to fire off Verey lights and S.O.S.
rockets as fireworks. The C.O. said 'Yes,' and told me to go and
see no damage was done. It was pitch dark, but the whole Division seemed to be shooting off lights and rockets, once signals of
deadly peril and suffering, now mere harmless fireworks. Some
merry lads of another unit started throwing Mills bombs, to the
terror of the civilians. (There'll be a row about that. Don't they
know there's a peace on?) The S.M. fired a Verey light, which
back-fired and nearly blew my head off. I told him firmly that I
never had a fancy for being killed, particularly when the war was
over. Afterwards, I walked in the ghostly shades of the garden
behind B.H.Q. The darkness was friendly, the silence almost
divine. For a long time I stood looking at the stars, very dim
among thin clouds. My feelings were too confused and profound
for expression. If I could interpret that miraculous silence! As
Villiers said, one needs four orchestras to do it.

Did not sleep very well, probably because I slept so long during
the day. But I was, and am, still very tired, and glad to rest. I feel
rather anxious about the future.

22nd November 1918. We are not going to Germany after all. Last
night at dinner the C.O. gave the quietus to a hydra of rumours
by telling us that we are to garrison a part of Belgium. The C.O. is

going on leave, and Major Shanks will be in temporary command. This is bad news for me, since Shanks is a detestable fellow, and he and I get on badly. We are always rowing in Mess. If it weren't for the C.O. I should apply to go back to the Company. There is very little work for Intelligence Officers now.

I wonder how much longer we shall be kept out here? All the talk is of demobilisation, and the men are becoming extremely restive. I treat my little band of Observers very gingerly. We hear we are to become schoolmasters, and lecture to the troops on arithmetic and geography. The W.O. undoubtedly believes in getting its money's worth out of the infantry subaltern.

I worry greatly about demobilisation, and what I shall do when I get free. Woke up in a sweat last night, dreaming I was in the line, and couldn't get to sleep again.

27th November 1918. Here we are in our new quarters. The C.O.—good fellow that he is—put off his leave to march us over and see us installed. He leaves to-morrow, and may not return. But he has arranged with the Adjutant that I am to leave as soon as my papers come through.

The place we are billeted in is most dreary, a long, straggling, dirty village in flat, desolate fields. The inhabitants resent having troops billeted on them, and the men are (rightly) dissatisfied with the filthy and wretched accommodation. I rode over ahead of the Battalion to see that all billets were ready. I have quite a decent bed in a cottage kept by a very clean woman with a little boy. I gave them some white bread, which the little boy had never tasted before. He thought it was cake. I don't know why this upset me, but it did. The misery of these people, the misery of this flat wintry land, lies on us all.

I had a rotten dream last night—those four Boches on the Somme. God! I wish that hadn't happened, or that I could forget it.

2nd December 1918. The C.O. has gone on leave, and that imbecile Shanks is in command. The first thing he did was to call an officers' conference, and tell us that the Battalion was getting far too slack. Discipline must be tightened up! That, when the troops are madly fretting to be demobilised, and all sorts of rumours of mutinies are flying about!

To-day Shanks had a Battalion parade at 8.30. Some of the billets are a mile and a half away from the parade ground, which meant that the men had to get up far earlier than usual. It was bitterly cold, and he kept us there nearly two hours. The men shivered in the ranks, and three fainted. Shanks inspected every man minutely, and strafed like a lunatic. Then he made a most tactful speech to the troops. Told them this was not Peace, only an Armistice (as it is technically), and that the Germans might start the war again at any moment—a silly lie. He also said that we should not have won the war until we 'make Germany pay,' and that it would take at least forty years to collect the indemnities! The troops are frantic about it. I hear the Company Commanders have decided to go very easy with the men. I certainly shall. We don't want a mutiny.

10th December 1918. Row with Shanks in Mess last night. I have returned to the Company in consequence. Much more comfortable humanly, but their Mess is a long way from my billet. Shanks got on this eternal business of Making Germany Pay. I asked him if he thought we fought for money, and he flew into a temper and called me a Bolshie. I said it was men like him who made Bolshies, and he got purple in the face with rage. I turned aside and began talking to the Doc., who said—rather tactlessly under the circumstances—that there is great unrest in England. I said I felt sure there would be enormous trouble with Labour. Shanks heard me, and said rudely that I and other Bolshie agitators ought to be shot. I thereupon left the Mess, and this morning asked the Adjutant for permission to return to the Company. No news of my papers. It is all extremely worrying. I don't know what I shall do in England, but at present all I want is to get shot of the Army. Of course, they can't demobilise five million men in a week, but they seem to delight in prolonging the torments of the P.B.I. What is the sense of keeping us week after week in these dismal surroundings? The 'classes' for the men are a wash-out. They are very peeved at being given dictation and sums to do.

I have slept very badly this past week.

26th December 1918. The C.O. is back—thank God—but I remain with the Company. He says nothing, but the Battalion notices the change in command. Several days this past month I feared Shanks would cause a mutiny. The swine's going on leave, and every one profoundly hopes never to see him again.

On Christmas Day there was a dinner for the officers of the Brigade, turkey and champagne. Shanks got drunk, and revolted everybody by getting up unsteadily and proposing: 'The health of the Dead.' The Brigadier, who had accepted other toasts from him, ignored this; and Jackson, sitting besides Shanks, pulled him down into his chair. Shanks, who toadies to the

Brigadier disgustingly, shut up for the rest of the evening. I thought it a dismal party. Nobody really believes in the war or cares who won it.

My papers have not come, and I am beginning to despair. Everybody seems to be jumpy and disgusted. Stanton, commanding 'B,' has amazed everybody by saying he is going to take Holy Orders. He is a hard-bitten war officer, and some people thought, and think, it is simply a dodge to get early demobilisation. I don't believe it. I know Stanton intimately, and he told me some time ago that he received the revelation of God the day after the Armistice. He is a simple-minded man, and mistook his psychological processes, *i.e.* he thought his relief at the end of the war was God. But if it comforts him—why not? The poor devil had his genitals hopelessly mutilated at Passchendaele—it's a wonder he's alive.

I'm getting very worried about myself. I sleep very little, and pass the hours in a constant apprehension of some undefined horror or calamity. I can't settle to anything. It is all complicated with almost nightly dreams—horrible—of those Boches.

12th January 1919. The whole countryside is now deep under snow, and it is horribly cold. We have practically no fuel, except a little coal-dust which is utterly useless. In the Mess we sit and chatter with cold round a stove which is only kept alight by frantic efforts on the part of the orderly. The snow is too deep for walking, and parades are a farce. The men suffer less than we do in some respects, because they can sit round the kitchen fires of the peasants, which etiquette forbids us to do. There is no coal to be bought, so we are going to buy and cut down some trees—if any can be found in this barren waste. We hear that the German prisoners are properly fed and warmed in huts, and at the same time we hear of further threats of mutiny among our own men. I am not surprised, if they are treated as we are. The Battalion is slowly dissolving as men are demobbed, but those left behind are getting almost frantic with impatience. We hear that the boys of nineteen are to be drafted to Divisions on the Rhine, and that 12 officers will be required to volunteer for service there. The Orderly Room had twelve names within an hour—some, officers who funk returning to civilian life; others, who will do anything to get away from here. It is too cold to write any more—my fingers are frozen.

13th January 1919. Another utterly dreary day—cold grey sky, a wind that seems to sweep acute particles of steel against the bare skin, and a landscape deep in snow. In the Mess we have long futile discussions. Interesting to see how we are beginning to shed military prejudice, and to take on civilian prejudice in our relations. For instance, the first officer to be demobbed was a young Jew in 'A' Company, who was a perfect wash-out in the line, and treated by everybody accordingly. Then it was discovered that his father had made a fortune out of war material, and an order came that he was to be demobbed immediately. They sent a car over from Division for him. We watched him depart almost in awe, and he waved a patronising farewell.

Stanton has gone, and I am now very lonely. I spend much of the time lying fully clothed in bed for warmth, and brooding. It would be better if I did something, but what on earth is there to do? The nearest town is seven miles away, and we subalterns are allowed no transport at all. Even if we had horses it would be cruelty to ride them in this frost.

15th January 1919. Last night I had a curious experience. The moon rose in a clear frosty sky, and as I lay in bed waiting for my servant to warn me for dinner, I watched it through the frost patterns on the window. I thought it looked like a face, a yellow dead man's face swollen with corruption. Suddenly it seemed to me that this moon-face was the face of one of the men—I can't write the old insult 'Boche' any longer—I killed on the Somme. The most awful feeling of sick terror and apprehension went through me—infinitely worse than waiting to go over the top. I felt all the hairs creep on my skull, and I almost screamed aloud. I broke out in a cold perspiration, which was also a horrible experience in itself. What I should have done I don't know if my servant hadn't come in.

For the first time in months I got drunk in Mess, not so drunk that I fell about or even talked too wildly, but drunker than the others realised. I stayed as late as I could, and then got Connely to walk back to my billet with me. I felt I couldn't stand that horrible moon-face alone. But to my surprise it was gone. The moon was high in the sky, very clear and small and silvery. I slept like a log, but have a rotten headache this morning. I am terrified of moon-rise this evening, but I know I shall have to look.

I tried to conceal it from myself, but after the shock of last night, I've got to face the fact that my nerves are in a perfectly rotten state. Somehow or other I shall have to pull myself together. The scene of those four men I killed haunts me waking and sleeping. I can't get rid of it.

You remember where it was? Yes, where it was? Why did I do it,

O God, why did I do it? It was in 1916 in a trench near Trônes
Wood. I was leading bayonet man as we were clearing out a
trench, and I'd got a traverse in front of the others. I must have
been quite mad. The man behind me threw a bomb, and I rushed
round the traverse as soon as it burst. I came on four Germans.
They dropped their rifles, threw up their arms, and yelled
'Kamerad.' They were helpless before me, and I—God pity me!—
I shot three of them, and bayoneted the fourth in the back as he
tried to run. He screamed as he fell, rolled over, and looked at me
with an awful expression of loathing, hatred, and reproach. I
gazed at him in horror, shaking all over, with the rifle falling from
my hands. That instant the platoon sergeant rushed into the bay,
clapped me on the shoulder, shouting: 'Good lad! Well done,
indeed!' I dropped my rifle. He shouted: 'Pick up your hipe, and
come on, there's more of the bastards round here.' Of course, he
thought I had killed the men in fight—they were lying· on the
rifles they had dropped. Men shoved past me in the trench. I was
violently sick. When I recovered, the sergeant was patting me on
the back, and he gave me some rum to drink. I took my rifle and
went on with him—we had won the trench. The face of the bayoneted man still glared horror and hatred at me as I stepped over
his body.

The C.O. publicly congratulated me, and I got the M.M. and a
recommendation for a commission.

16th January 1919. Last evening I drew my curtains at sunset,
and lay in bed brooding for hours and hours until my servant
came. I couldn't bear that moon looking in on me. I never felt so
depressed in my life. It is obvious, now I look honestly at the
future, that I have nothing to live for or hope. I've been longing to
get away from the Army, but what on earth am I to do in civilian
life? As far as I can see from the orders of demobilisation, all
England wants are miners and agricultural workers, and men
whose families have plenty of money. (They released an officer of
nineteen yesterday—his parents have 'influence.') How much
better it would have been if I'd been killed on the Somme. But no.
I purchased my life by murdering four helpless men and, like a
coward, pretended I had killed them in fair fight....

When I opened the cottage door to walk down to the Mess, I
saw that ghastly moon-face glaring at me. It had just that same
look of hatred and loathing. Hell! It's ghastly. For a moment I
was frozen quite motionless, with my hair rising on my head, and
that filthy cold sweat on my face. Then I turned and ran like
mad, slipping and stumbling on the frozen snow. I rushed into

the Mess, and they all looked at me in surprise:

'What's up? What's the matter?'

I managed to pull myself together then, and said:

'Oh, nothing. It's so bloody cold I ran along to get a bit warm before dinner.'

I was shivering all over, but my face was covered with sweat. Connely said:

'Well, you seem to have succeeded. You're in a hell of a sweat.'

I pretended I was hot and sat near the door, though I was really chilled through. Connely gave me some vermouth to drink, and my hand shook so much I spilt half of it on my tunic. I pretended I had been for a long run, and that I was still shaking with the exertion. I felt rotten all through dinner, and I noticed they looked at me in a queer way.

After Mess, I left early. Connely got up, and said he'd come with me—for which I was grateful. I took one glance at the moon—it still was that dreadful face, but smaller and more malignant. I looked on the ground all the way. Going along, Connely said:

'Are you feeling ill, old man?'

'No. Why?'

'Oh, nothing much. Only, the last few days we've been thinking you look seedy and very worried about something. Is anything wrong?'

I tried to laugh it off:

'I'm as fit as a fiddle, old boy. But it's hellish boring to hang about here day after day, with nothing to do, and damn-all in the way of amusement.'

'Yes, I know. But honestly, Hall, you do look rather ill, and you were positively ghastly when you rushed into Mess to-night.'

'Was I? Yes, I was awfully cold.'

'You said you were too hot.'

Luckily we then reached the cottage door. I said:

'Well, good-night, old man. Thanks for coming along.'

'Good-night.'

I ran in and shut the door quickly so as not to see the face. Of course, that damned servant had opened my curtains. I shut my eyes tight, groped my way across the room, and drew them close, close.

17th January 1919. Yesterday morning (the 16th) I felt so rotten that I sent my servant with a chit to the Company Commander, asking to be excused parade. I lay in bed all day, and my servant brought my meals. They were horribly cold, but I didn't mind. I

just felt I couldn't face the world. I tried to read, but couldn't—
just lay there brooding.

I got up for first parade to-day, and after breakfast was told to
report to the Orderly Room. I saw the C.O. who was very nice,
but questioned me closely. I told him there was nothing wrong,
but that perhaps the extreme cold coupled with the lack of fuel
had injured my health a little. He said:

'But we had much worse times in the line.'

'Yes, sir, but then we were under the stress of fighting. Now
that's over, we feel the strain a bit.'

'You're sure there's nothing on your mind?'

'Oh no, sir. I'm only a bit worried about the delay in my demobilisation. I want to get back to work.'

He looked at me hard, and asked me if I had any work to do. I
said yes, that the man who had signed the application for my
release would give me work. This was a lie, but I feel I must get
away from the Army and this ceaseless brooding—and the terrible
face. Finally the C.O. said:

'Well, I want the M.O. to have a look at you. Go along to his
billet now, will you?'

I saluted and left. I was afraid the M.O. would question me,
and perhaps find out the secret, but fortunately he only sounded
me, took my pulse, looked at my tongue, and said:

'M'm. Bit run down. Don't overdo it, and take three months'
rest when you're demobbed. Cheer-o.'

Take three months' rest! And on what?

Thank God it's cloudy to-night.

18th January 1919. I got rather drunk again last night, and slept
well until about four in the morning. Then I dreamed I was in a
gas attack, and couldn't get my mask on. I woke up and found I
had got the clothes over my head and was half stifled. Then I lay
awake miserably thinking over old miseries—the Somme, Arras,
Passchendaele, the utter weariness of it all—and gazing blankly at
a blank future. I was glad when it was time to get up for first
parade.

Connely came along to my billet about three this afternoon,
and talked the usual out-worn topics for a time. Then he said:

'By the bye, Hall, there's an order that each Company is to
send an officer for two days' leave to Lille. We think you ought to
go from our Company. You'll get a change, you can stay at the
officers' club, and'—here he giggled rather self-consciously—
'there's a lot of "red-lamps" in Lille, you know.'

I don't know why, but this made me furiously angry. I told him they could shove their bloody leave he knew where. I said that since I had seen so many men's bodies mangled, suffering and dead, the thought of human flesh was repulsive to me. I said I hated the thought of women. I almost yelled at him:

'I don't want your bloody whores! I don't want ever to touch a bloody woman. Didn't they urge us into that hell, and do their best to keep us there? Look at Stanton, with his genitals mangled, becoming a bloody parson—poor devil. Women? Pah!'

Connely looked a little scared and surprised:

'Steady on, old man. Why so violent? After all, think of young What's-his-name in the A.S.C., who came and lunched with us— you know, the fellow who was so cheery because he was going home to get married on a hundred a year.'

'Yes—A.S.C. We're P.B.I. Yes, get married on a hundred a year, condemn some infatuated female to an eternity of drudgery, and get her with kids to come out and be slaughtered in their turn. I tell you, Connely, we all ought to submit to castration rather than beget children to be exploited and murdered like the men lying out there....'

Then I did an idiotic thing, which makes me burn with shame to remember. I threw myself on the bed and cried. Connely was very decent about it. He came and patted me on the shoulder, and said:

'That's all right, old man, I understand. Don't you worry. I'll go to Lille. And—I won't mention this to any one.'

Then he went away.

I begin to be afraid of myself. The sleeplessness, constant dreams of being in the line, the haunting of those men I murdered, the moon-face, then flying into such a rage about nothing, and crying like a silly girl. Christ! I wish I could get out of it all.

20th January 1919. 'Nothing to report,' as we used to send back from the line. I've had practically no sleep for two days, and feel rotten. When I do fall alseep, I immediately wake up in horror, with a vision of that face of loathing and hatred threatening me. I believe that man meant to haunt me when he died. I feel his presence, his dreadful, decayed, loathsome presence in the room. Last night I had a feeling he was standing there, invisible, watching me suffer with a dreadful revengeful glee.

Funny thing—this morning I got out my revolver to see how it would feel to hold it against my head and perhaps end everything, and I found the bullets had been taken out. I questioned my servant, and he knew nothing about it. Connely perhaps? He doesn't know I have twenty rounds in my pouch.

The cold is frightful. Lots of the men are being demobilised now. I begin to think I am doomed to Shanks's forty years' watch on the Rhine.

27th January 1919. I've felt too wretched to write anything in this diary for a week. The same old tale—sleeplessness, boredom, worry, a sort of agony of contrition over the whole war, and my dastardly share in it.

But to-day comes good news. I am demobilised, and leave here on the morning of the 29th!

I should be happy if it were not that the murdered German—the bayoneted one—seems never to leave me now. I caught him gazing at me over the dinner-table last night. The others were amazed because I jumped out of my chair, and yelled: 'Go away! Go away! Don't torture me!' I apologised to the Mess President, and went straight back to my billet. Thank God, I'm going, and haven't to face them much longer. I really must pull myself together.

31st January 1919. I am writing this in a vilely cold tent at the Base Camp, waiting for orders to proceed to England. Opposite me, I can see some German prisoners laughing and talking round a glowing stove in a hut. It looks really as if the W.O. particularly wishes to insult us in every way possible. We T.G. officers are treated more contemptuously than the men—the men can mutiny, we can't. I suppose we could, but they know we won't. In these last two years the whole war (which was to purify every one's morals) has resolved itself into the most abject devil-take-the-hindmost scramble for safety. The demobilisation is if anything slightly worse. I'd never have got away from the Battalion if they hadn't thought I was going to have a nervous breakdown, and therefore wanted to get rid of me. As for the cant which is being talked in England ... Well, we're helpless victims of the cowardice, greed, and gullibility of man and womankind, escpecially womankind. God, how I hate the women, especially those who 'gave' so willingly!

Rotten journey down here, but I'm told everybody who is too poor or too unimportant to be given a car has the same experience. However, it's a great deal to be on the move towards freedom, and away from the ghastly Belgian landscape.

I started off early on the morning of the 29th in the Company Mess cart. We had a devil of a job getting through the snow—there was a heavy fall—and I had to help the driver shove the cart through the drifts. About eleven, I got to the town which is rail-head for our Division, and my valise was dumped at a huge empty house, which is the officers' club. The place was swarming with subalterns, none of whom I knew. I could get no food, so ate my iron rations, and then walked about the town. It has a very fine Romanesque cathedral, with only two shell-holes in the apse. There is a wonderful carved screen—a juba I think they call it—in front of the chancel. I spent a very happy hour looking round the building—a reminder that there might be something else in the world beside blood, death, horror, mud, greed, money, money, money. When I think of the crimes of those who sent us to hell and kept us there, my own awful crime seems less unbearable. I understood Stanton—reject the world and live in prayer with the ideal. Unfortunately, I thought the head of the Christ looked like the bayoneted man. Perhaps I was wrong.

After dark a lot of the fellows started off for 'red lamps.' I opened my valise, which was thrown with others on the bare boards of an unfurnished room, and got down into kip. I was awakened by some of the others coming in, and did not get to sleep again. However, I lay on my side with my eyes shut and listened to their talk—mostly about the 'red lamp' girls, and then what they would do in Blighty. They all seemed to be engaged to girls in England—foul. I was awake most of the night, listening to their heavy breathing, snores, and mutterings. Most of them seem to have awful dreams of the war. Their breathing would change to a snore, then to a groan which would become quite dreadful in its agony, and then abruptly stop as the man woke up. I felt deep pity for them—nervous wrecks before they're thirty.

Next morning we were roused at five and given tea and more iron rations. Marched a huge column of men to the station, and entrained in cattle-trucks. We were all entrained by eight, but the train did not start until after one. We crawled through Belgium in the afternoon twilight, ghastly over that dead landscape of snow. I have not felt such cold since the winter of '16. We crawled on with various long halts throughout the night, trying to keep ourselves warm over a brazier. About dawn we got to a station which had been in the old line—smashed to pieces. There we dumped the frost-bite cases, and got some hot soup. The shattered trees and broken buildings were all covered with the thickest hoar frost I have ever seen—more like snow. Everything glittered coldly in the early sunlight. It was late last night when we got here, handed over the men, and were told to look for places in the tents of the officers' camp. The other fellows in this tent are very decent, but furious at the way they are treated. To-day we went out and spent

a lot of francs on a meal in a civilian restaurant—we all felt
starved. I have got chilblains and a headache which started about
a week ago and never stops. I wish I could do something about it.
The German is very persistent these days. He came down the line
with us, and I see him standing by the tent entrance, gazing at me
steadfastly and with implacable hatred.

Later: I have just heard that I leave for England to-morrow
morning.

1st March 1919. This diary has been neglected for a month. It has
been very strange, returning to England, civilian life and ways,
after the tremendous physical and moral efforts of the past years.
I am confused, tired, and miserable. The perpetual headache, the
sleeplessness, the nightmares, and that infernal German—I can
feel him behind me now, but I won't look round.

All this existence in London seems most unreal. What gave a
false appearance of reality to our life in the line was that we were
not—at least directly—merely slaves of the economic idea. We
were slaves of the military idea. Our purpose, the purpose
imposed on us, was to kill, not to make profits. No doubt, the
military idea now is eventually the slave of the economic idea—
military force is only the last weapon of commercial competition.
But that is all covered over with decorations such as Honour,
Country, Glory, Duty, and the like. It takes a little shrewdness to
see that the people who own the land and the factories also run
the Army. The Army is Tweedledee pretending to be Tweedledum,
with a very big DUM! But I believe the apparent escape from the
economic idea accounts for much of the enthusiasm with which
people rushed into the war. (Of course, a lot of the first rush of
heroes were unemployed who wanted food—odd to bargain your
life for a few ill-cooked meals and a bad suit of clothes.) Personally I cannot see life either as 'your King and Country need you,'
i.e. getting killed to further the material aims of people who
manipulate these gross symbols—nor can I see it merely as
'paying one's own way.' At present it costs a great deal to pay
one's own way. I imagine prices will remain high until the demobilised soldiers and munition workers have spent all—and that
isn't much individually—they got out of the war. When their
money has finally reached its destiny (*i.e.* the pockets of the War-
makers) it will be 'invested,' prices will decline, and there will be
plenty of unemployment.

Even now, it is difficult for ex-soldiers to get employment.
Many of us are in a rotten state, and quite unfit to perform those
actions which would enable us to 'pay our way.' We are not an

economically sound proposition, and it is too much to expect that industry (always so heavily burdened, as the *Times* says) should carry more than a small proportion of the war duds. I'm one of the lucky ones—three pounds a week as a temporary clerk in Whitehall. The Colonel who interviewed me in the first instance was very nice. He asked particulars of my service, looked up my record, congratulated me on my murders, and said:

'Have you any influence?'

'No, sir.'

'Don't you know any one in—er—a position of importance, who would give you a recommendation to—er—some respectable firm?'

'I'm afraid not, sir.'

'Well, we'll do the best we can for you. Leave your name and address, and I'll communicate with you.'

I started on my job to-day. I don't like it.

2nd March 1919. Yesterday I meant to write down the circumstances of demobilisation, the last day in the Army, but got diverted somehow. I find it very difficult to think consecutively these days....

There were about fifteen officers and three thousand men on the boat. We landed at Dover, and with some difficulty got the men—who were very restive and impatient—into column, and marched them through an indifferent town, up a long steep hill, to some huts behind the castle. I had never seen the castle at close quarters before—it has fine architectural qualities. We hung round the huts for two or three hours, queuing up for our 'tickets.' The officers got theirs quickly, and while the men we had brought were still waiting, we were sent off to march an earlier batch to the train. Each officer had about five hundred men, and they marched anyhow, yelling insults. I managed to get the front ranks of my lot singing, and soon they all joined in. At the station, I stood to one side and watched them march to the train where the N.C.O.'s took charge of them. Most of them shouted to me: 'Good luck, sir, good-bye!' And I shouted back: 'Good luck, good-bye.' That was the triumphal return we were promised. When the last of my lot had gone by, I turned and walked to the officers' compartment—a civilian again.

3rd March 1919. To-day I received the document granting me a commission, with the King's signature in facsimile at the bottom—a proud heirloom to hand down to my posterity, I don't think.

God! I wish I could get out of it all. I'm sick of putting down all the old miseries here. If I could sleep at night without horrid nightmares of the German I might be able to endure it—even the fatuous struggle with documents at the office. But I'm as fed up with life as we all were with the war. I bought a Shakespeare to-day, and the first words I read were Mercutio's: 'They have made worm's meat of me.' Very true, and clever of Shakespeare to foresee it.

7th March 1919. Of course, I tell myself it's all nerves, but that German is certainly a curious phenomenon. I ought to write about it to some of those experts who collect ghosts. It may be a delusion, but it's real enough to me. I don't see how I can go on living with the constant haunting of that spectral face. If I walk up to it, the damn thing disappears; I turn around, and there it is on the other side of the room. When I read or write I can *feel* it behind me. I keep the electric light on all night now, even when I fall asleep—it's awful to wake up in the dark.

15th March 1919. I found my service revolver was rusty and still muddy around the butt. I'd like to tick my servant off for leaving it so dirty. I cleaned it very carefully, and found myself almost wishing I was going up the line again. After all, that's the only thing I know how to do, and the only place where I could forget everything. We made a damned silly mistake in being so eager to get back—the lucky ones are out there under six feet of French mud, God bless it. I saw a play the other night making fun of the demobilised officer who couldn't shake down to civilian life. A damned nice sense of humour that playwright has. You tell men for years they're heroes, saving the nation, and making the world safe for everybody—and then you sneer at them because in two months they don't immediately become efficient and obsequious commercial travellers! I'd like to kick that fellow where he keeps his intelligence, *i.e.* in his backside.

20th March 1919. I keep my revolver under my pillow at nights. These weapons of destruction are the only beautiful things in the modern world.

21st March 1919. A significant anniversary! I've had no sleep for three nights now. Every time I fall into a doze the German comes and presses his decaying face against mine. God in hell, it's horrible! I can't stand it.

The following item of news appeared in several newspapers:

'A Coroner's Inquest was held yesterday on the body of Henry William Hall (26) who was found dead in bed on the morning of 22nd March. He had shot himself through the head with a service revolver. In accepting the Jury's Verdict of "Suicide while of Unsound Mind," the Coroner remarked that it seemed a pity this young man should have taken his life in the bloom and vigour of his youth. The deceased had been given a good post in Whitehall, but he (the Coroner) understood that he was dissatisfied with his lot. The Coroner felt it his duty to utter a warning to young men now returning to civilian life. They must realise that a high standard of conduct is expected of those who had the honour to serve their country in the field. They must also realise that they had no right to expect that they should drop into easy jobs, or that they could all keep up the standard of extravagant living they had been accustomed to in the Army. They must realise that the civilian population had gone without necessities to give them comforts, and it was about time they realised that the boot is on the other foot. While paying every tribute to the Heroism of Our Glorious Troops, he did think that it was about time these young men came to their senses, realised that life is not all sky-larking, and settled down to do a little honest work.'

H.D.

▼▼

Ear-Ring

SOMEONE HAD BOUGHT her with two diamonds and she carried that implication with her, as heads, self-consciously and a shade too indifferently, did not turn towards her. One sensed her coming (it was the same, last night) but having had two nights of exactly this same entrance, Madelon Thorpe felt slightly immunized against it. She thought, this is my third night in Athens. Madelon measured time by those diamonds, they stressed something, were other than they appeared (don't look at her), were shriek-marks obviously, were paper-weights, set at two corners of the billowing fabric of her perception of this ball-room, dining-room of the *Hôtel Acropole et Angleterre*, embossed in gold letters on the menu. Madelon measured time by those stones; I have been here three days, I sailed from the port of London to the port of Athens; it must be now, nearly a month since we left. One had to hold on to something.

Archie Rowe was their guest, Eleanor's guest that is, I am Eleanor Eddington's guest. If only Eleanor wouldn't hunch forward so (she thought of her as 'Eleanor' in this milieu, rather than 'E.E.' or 'Edd,' as she had learned to call her). If only Eleanor wouldn't leave everything to me. Archie Rowe, half-Greek, had the most fantastic ideas of how people from London should act. Here, everyone knew everything. Dare she ask about the diamonds? He would make no obvious comment. She must wait patiently. The diamonds were cutting into circles of small-talk; compact, magnetic centres, grouped about small tables, and, at intervals, larger tables, by some law of common gravitation, gravitated from them. They might be divided in everything, upper, lower and middle parties, royalists and Venizelists, but by some unwritten pact, transcending the mere manifestoes of kings and emperors, they were banded together against this; this not too attractive, not too un-attractive visitor from beyond the Black Sea. Though almost all were visitors, they revolved in their

various circles (small tables and larger, set at intervals), away, at
least, from this. In their incredible disparities and antipathies,
social, racial and political, they were held together by one thing—
their aloofness from the diamonds.

The diamonds, rather than the woman who wore them, sought
recognition. Or were the diamonds arrogant in their indifference,
did they, by some occult power, drive these human entities to
shun them? Archie Rowe would have their history. They might
have been gouged out, *en passant*, from a royal diadem, or,
equally, they might have been filched from some sacrosanct
Byzantine shrine. Or, even more astonishingly, they might have
been the exact and peculiar property of the taller partner, a stolid
bulk of broadcloth that followed the satin sheath, above which
rose a head, a catastrophe, pale and cut-off and un-related to the
body, swathed in black, beneath it. The head was, in no way,
remarkable. Madelon (not looking at it) remembered it from last
night, from the night before last. The shoulders and the head were
a marble cast, Clyte, set on a black stand; this head would revolve,
if the base were edged slightly to left, to right. Almost, one felt,
the bulkier attendant, who might be equally a butler or a grand-
duke, was curator of this questionable treasure—a not very good
head, done in inferior marble, of a second-rate Clyte. The hair,
loose above the temples, was of no special period; late Edwardian
might suggest it. The black velvet band, at the throat, suggested a
crack in the bust that had not been adequately mended. Altogether, the thing was not worth looking at; an unwritten yet
overstressed social law decreed, moreover, that one should not
look.

The diamonds were, unquestionably, out of all proportion, but it
couldn't be just that. Archie Rowe, assuredly, had chapter and
verse up his sleeve. The pair drawn, so to speak, in the wake of
those stones, might be anybody. But where everybody was somebody, and all non-relatedly and extravagantly individual, how did
it happen that these two, dressed in black, correct in all their attitudes, attracted this sort of implied and negative attention? The
waiters had left a narrow gangway. But between their row and
that other set of tables, shoved, in intimate irregularity, against a
dark maroon curtain, ran Lethe or Styx. Was it just the diamonds
did it? Whose were they? Who had worn them? They were searchlights. Revolving lights, from a squat lighthouse, cut across small
tables and larger tables, all of whose personal individualities were
magnetized to this one point, their supreme indifference. Whatever they might whisper furtively, hiding a cough, as it were,

behind a napkin, be sure it was not diamonds. Did Madelon imagine it? It seemed the negation of their impression, was focussing it all in her direction. She would be fused herself, to a common centre (if she did not dodge their influence, like these others) and be burnt up by them.

But this was ridiculous. She was giving them undue value. There was so much else to think of. Talk ran high; no matter how decorous the undertone, one felt there was some high voltage, some high-explosive power, about the simplest utterance. One almost saw glitter of epigram, running like a magnesium flare from table to table; large table-circles and smaller circles, seemed to repeat collective messages, in different languages. There was incredible babel of tongues; each cut across the other, French, English, English-French, French-English. Occasionally, there was an unpredictable guttural undertone; somewhere, just beneath them, must be the Dutch ambassador, for Archie Rowe was saying, 'Miss Eddington, there's a dance to-morrow at the Dutch Legation, do you care for dancing?'

Talk about anything but the diamonds. The woman was about to sit down. Certainly, I don't know what it's all about, but someone must look at her. It makes it too important that no one should look. Almost, as if mesmerized by the diamonds, Madelon looked up. There was nothing new in this sight. The black, rather heavy, broad-cloth shoulders of the male partner, were, as usual, inclined slightly as he waited for his companion to be seated. The black satin sheath was without wrinkle or fold, as if an expert lady's maid had, just this moment, run an iron across it. The sheath wrinkled in parallel lines, as a knee bent slightly. The owner of the diamonds shoved a knee round the edge of the table, finding a foot-hold, the other side of Lethe. Across Styx, she flung out a smile.

Nobody answered the smile. The petroleum magnate, just above the diamonds, went on talking to his secretary. She always wore the same hat. From time to time, she affectedly dipped its forward-set willow-plume across her eyes, and as affectedly, flung it back. She and the wife of the military attaché from Washington, always wore their hats. Petroleum and attaché sat above Eleanor, Archie Rowe and Madelon; almost at their elbow, the other side, sat England talking French to somebody, with morose almond eyes, who might be Persian. A girl, alone at a table, had been pointed out, at lunch time, as relief-committee back from Serbia. Dutch a bit lower down, and another guttural. Beyond, was the edge of no-man's-land, people even Archie Rowe couldn't find time to bow to. And all talking and no one talking, she felt certain, about diamonds. Eleanor, at last, realizing that mischief might be done here and Archie Rowe might be annoyed, was now patiently staring at them. Madelon, having all but smiled at the diamond, now in question, thought she might as well say something. She formed a question, with half-open lips, which Archie fearfully interrupted, 'Ah—' as he let slide his shallow soup-spoon, he turned sideways to take the wine-list from the waiter, and breathed rather than whispered, 'fabulous Wr-ussians.'

They must be that, certainly.

What Russian was not fabulous, who had escaped a red revolution by way of a black sea, moreover, complete with diamonds? There was no other possible Russian in this hotel, perhaps not in the whole world. Say 'Russian' and you say 'fabulous.' Archie had told them nothing. He seemed to sense everything, separately, from the two sides of his face, like a fish.

The diamonds diminished. One was cut off by the pink lamp-shade; identical lamps were set on all their tables. The diamond hung, glittering in space, against the dark maroon curtain. It was laid vertical on dark velvet, like a diamond in a show-case, reversing the common-places of mere gravity. It should fall down or they should fall down or they should fall up. War dizziness and late London war and a trip, but three days finished, on a winter sea, from the port of London to the port of Athens, made all this feasible. Everything, in this back-water, left by the high-tide of events, went round in concentric circles. Only the diamond remained static, it was the centre of a mystical circle, a problem out of geometry. The upside-down museum-case held a head, now she thought of it, guillotined by a narrow bank of black-velvet (French revolution, Russian revolution); it seemed the only reality in the surcharged atmosphere of a room, where everything might, at any moment, slip over the edge of nothing into nowhere. Hold on to something. Archie was naming various notables to Eleanor, indicating their whereabouts, with an inclination of a shoulder or almost imperceptible jerk of an elbow. He covered even these slightest of indiscretions, by side-talk in Greek to a waiter; his words, now as she attended to them, seemed to merge into the syllables of that pair, across the narrow aisle. Russian and modern Greek—was there so much to choose between them?

Where there were so many questions to be asked, why not stick, as everyone else seemed bent on ignoring it, to the most obvious? Where did the diamonds come from? People, even Russians, even in nineteen-twenty, didn't go about, even in Athens, wearing jewels, like roc's eggs, in their ears.

Madelon said a number to herself, thought 'nineteen-twenty,' and already, the hard fact of four decisive numbers in a row (1–9–2–0) had jerked her into some feasible contact with these others. She repeated the number to herself, across the laboured witticisms of Archie Rowe, at the expense of the late head of the British school of Athens. The discreet jibe was carefully calculated to reach the ears of the present head of the school, who was, Archie had earlier informed them, the owner of the somewhat coffin-like, somewhat something-in-the-diplomatic set of shoulders, two tables beyond them, to his left. Was this arrangement of tables carefully calculated, or were they all dumped down, anywhere? Certainly, it would be assumed that they, personally, were above the salt but, then, how did those particular Russians happen to have snaffled that desirable corner table? Or was it all chance? There did seem, it is true, a sort of loose logic in the arrangement of their neighbours, this side of the aisle. They were all, so to speak, English-speaking, a mixed, to be sure, bag, but differentiated somehow from Balkans, Russians, native Greeks, visiting Roumanians; the inhabitants of the lower half of the room were frankly indefinable. The Russians with the diamonds seemed to be the high-water mark of the Balkan tide-wave. Nineteen-twenty, Madelon repeated, like some abracadabra (1–9–2–0), a charm to make this snap into some proportion. I am in Athens, she said to herself, and this is nineteen-twenty; she repeated it like a telephone number.

Now, as she said to herself, it took form, Madelon found she had something else to hold to, beside diamonds. One, nine, two, O. Write it in a row, like a sum from the baby-arithmetic, or write it, with dashes in between, like a Morse-code signal. It was some sort of signal. Everything in the world had gone down, in a vortex of babel-tongues, long since. This was a whirl-pool in a back-wash, something, in miniature, of what that had been. It was a relic; already, in nineteen-twenty, pre-war. Pre merry-widow, at that.

The crowd looked, for all its casual appearance, like a carefully arranged curtain for an opera-bouffe finale. But it is something quite different; really, she thought, it is chemisty, it is pure geometry. They were a fabulous mixture, altogether, in a test-tube (that hotel ball-room). Little tables and larger seemed to seethe, each with its particular alchemic property. The diamonds were two radium-points of something indissoluble, where everything else was seething. The rest of the mixture, vibrated away, in chemical disapprobation, would have nothing to do with them. *'Prophilia?'* asked Archie Rowe, with a slightly quizzical inflection, as if to remind her where she was, dragging her back from diamonds.

'Oh yes,' she said quickly, 'thank you so much. I like it so much.' She had said all this before, she knew exactly what she would say, she knew he would say, 'Do you like the *retsinato?*' Even before he spoke the word, she knew he was going to ask if they liked the resinous Greek wine, as if she were thinking for him, for herself. It was a common-place question, here, and it had a common-place answer, yet as she said it, she seemed to have been saying it over and over, all her life, with no interim, of boats and ports, and blue hyacinths in a basket, at Gibraltar. She knew she had to say it, so she said it, 'It takes *time* to get used to it. It has a special sort of *tang*, hasn't it? I mean, after one *has* got used to it,' etcetera. She was saying it for Eleanor. Why didn't Eleanor speak up, say her own lines? She drags me into this startling milieu and just leaves me to flounder in it. 'Petroleum,' said Eleanor.

Archie Rowe had an infallible, Levant perception of all the shades of everything that didn't matter. Or did petroleum matter? There were wells here, drills there, claims somewhere other ... the Standard-oil people. She let Eleanor get on with it, while she tried to detach herself from them, by listening-in, on her own, to the actual petroleum, in person at her shoulder. What would he say about it?

It was not that the voice was so specifically 'American,' though it was that. It was the quality of the tone, rather than the words or the accent, that seemed to vibrate in a different atmosphere, or in a different *lack* of atmosphere, would perhaps be more explicit. They bored into the thick Balkan air like one of his own steam-drills. Steam-drill of his accent, made vacuum about it. Each word fell precisely, with a mechanical tip-tap, like words written on a machine. Almost, visibly, a ribbon ticked in the air between them. Madelon listened-in to this arid, not unpleasant voice that somehow, for all its constructed integrity, spelt destruction. It destroyed this thick air, laden with cross-currents and counter-currents of diplomatic suavity, like a truck piled high with dynamite, veering suddenly into a *mardi-gras* carnival. Respecting it, Madelon yet turned with a new vision to the almond-eyed Levant who might, with all his apparent futility, be something true-Persian, out of an art collection. With all his dreary, rather oiled Levant-like stupidity, there was a suggestion, as of a garden;

minute, flat roses twined over a trellis, his non-communicable eyes looked inward. Spice-jasmine might not exactly express anything about him. It was a sensation, maybe a false sensation, but spare me from the steam-drill. I'd rather rot with Omar.

I know this rotting with Omar is quite wrong and Athens is the last place to say it, but spare me from the steam-drill. Nevertheless, she continued to follow the tick-tick in the air, with a sort of fascination of desperation. No wonder the world fears this hundred-per-cent American; we must be loyal to it. It deflates Archie Rowe, for one thing, and values the studied negligence and would-be aristocratic insolence of his expensively acquired manner, at its worth. It manages to put in its place, the not unmusical low drawl, that is the head of the British school of Athens, speaking French, with that explicit sort of accent, to the sallow complexioned Levant, who might be Persian. Persians and Greeks. The petroleum-king said nothing actively destructive, but what he said demolished everything. No *léger-de-main* of the unconscious or sheer conscious ingenuity, could really, ever (could it?) link Sparta up with oil-wells and the Hellespont with steam-drills? Archie was speaking of these same things, but in a slightly superior manner, now, to Eleanor. Archie would consider it beneath his dignity to refer to Xerxes, Thucydides or what not; he ignored the surface values of antiquity. Not so the petroleum magnate. He peppered his discourse with them. Yet his phrases suggested a thumbed text-book, rather than reality, either spiritual or economic. He was discussing an excursion with the secretary, whose slightly weary intonation vaguely suggested Boston. Delphi, he was explaining, was quite out of the question, the road was broken, or flooded or taken over by brigands. Anyhow, they couldn't get to Delphi. He might charter some sort of tramp to take them to Aegina. She should see Eleusis ... Marathon ... a tablet set up to the thousand slain at Thermopylae, or was it at Château Therry?

Xerxes—Salamas—Woodrow Wilson—the Ulysses-bow of the last Geneva conference—the Achilles heel of something or somebody or other—a dump of supplies, left by a battleship that hadn't managed to get to Constantinople—this was all so much old iron, scrap-iron, to be disposed of. But not to be annihilated just like that, dynamited to nothing; O, no! There were waste products to be utilized, the very thoughts, one felt, of Socrates still gave off their utilitarian by-product. The slender, intellectualized fingers were manipulating, well in anticipation of dessert, the long, slender cigar. He was already waiting for his cigar. For a moment, that pair of apparently ill-assorted Americans, who yet vibrated to something (for all her tenderly, weary Boston manner) in common, seemed more astonishing than any mere flagrant white Russians, escaping by way of a black sea, from a red peril. The white Russians were apparently doomed. How long would they hold out? Probably, just as long as they could accrue credit, or attain merit, from the diamonds.

She had got it down to dollars and diamonds. (One must hold on to something.) The mid-West by way of Wall Street voice, ruled lines on paper, neat columns of debit and loss and fractional margins. Say one, nine, two, O, and link it up to something. Anything, everything else here, fluttered in and out of the dimensions, in and out of history, destroyed the most simple time-values, brought pre-war into some perspective but by way of things forgotten or relegated to an attic, with old copies of Floradora. The old-copy-book with lines, ruled in precise fours, and the thumbed score of Floradora were resurrected here, and here, of all places. History repeated itself in white-Russian coiffures, out of a smart show-case of the late nineties. Have we come to Athens for this?

Dollars and diamonds, at least, punctuated all this; the only feasible and solid points of reality were, yet, the most unreal. The white Russians depended on that most mystical value, a value set by some Levant merchant on two diamonds, on their lives exactly. Wall-street might totter, at any moment, like a too-high wall of bricks, come tumbling down and Liberty fall, with a splash, to rust in the north river. Liberty? Wasn't that just the thing that had held the show together? *Acropole et Angleterre*, she read again under her breath, pretending to scan the menu. But that combination was impossible.

Not so impossible. Wasn't there Lord Byron by the Zappeon Garden, wasn't there Timon of Athens … Maid of Athens … why not? There was no tracking down reality, through poetry, or was it the *Prophilia*? I've not had more than two glasses. Archie tilts the bottle toward me as I finger the stem of my glass, an almost empty crystal goblet in which I might see anything. Hold on to some reality. What then, is reality? Diamonds? Petroleum? White wine, certainly, with a name, *Prophilia*. She wanted to ask Archie Rowe about the other wines here. But, as he was still outlining, in a slightly self-deprecatory manner, pronunciation of modern Greek for Eleanor, she let her mind slide off this suave, too-subtle layer and slip back to the uncompromisingly pitched voice that was now holding forth to the secretary, likewise on Greek etymology. His was more practical, explicit; it applied equally to Woodrow Wilson and to Pericles. Autocracy, he was explaining to the slightly (one felt) supercilious secretary, was the rule of the few, democracy (ah, there we are) of the many. There was plutocracy as well (he must know all about that), demos, he said was their state, a deme. O, the United States of Pericles, yes certainly. It was a new light on that past. Demos, a deme, our state, the English county, or the French province (he knows everything). Archie was now holding forth, rather more from the autocratic level, on a little 'do' at Oxford. How long would Eleanor conceal the barb that was on the verge of being let fly? Madelon would have been interested in hearing Archie Rowe's paternal grandfather's history, an Englishman of the Gladstone and the seven-isles' tradition. Archie would probably consider it 'not done' to be too serious about the old Ionian controversy. Madelon would be sure to approach the subject from exactly the wrong angle. She was tired of the arid vibration of the magnate. Did one come here to Athens to learn facts, with a mid-west accent, from the back of the dictionary, over Greek white-wine? How could she reach Archie, before Eleanor let her barb fly? If she said something definitely to do with nineteen-twenty, she might make a *lié*. She said, *lié, liaison, heptanésos*.

She breathed *heptanésos*, under her breath, no use saying it out aloud. It meant the seven islands, but she didn't dare pronounce it. She deliberately shut out the arid mid-west voice, that went on talking about democracy. She thought, democracy, a deme, daemon, diamond. She thanked Archie Rowe, yes a drop more, but (archly) no more—how exactly did you pronounce it? *Prophilia*, the Greek word looked so exciting, written like that, in Greek letters, on the bottle. He said she was quaint, managing, curiously, to insert a *w* between the syllables, breaking up the word in syllables and managing (how did he do it?) to insinuate his overworked lisping *w* somewhere. He asked them if they had any other special preference for Greek wine, he himself preferred French always, the implication being that they had made a social blunder, or not? She answered, anyway, with no hesitation, exalted by the sound and delight of it, *Mavrodaphne*. She had no idea of what it was like, she said, had only seen the word printed, and the look of it made her quite drunk. 'O, old *'daphne*,' he dismissed it.

But now they were on the subject of grapes, couldn't he talk about them? She wanted to ask him about their different vineyards, about red, black and white grapes, some sort of dwarf-grape, she had heard mentioned somewhere, that someone said was not the usual currant. Grapes ripened specifically flavoured, she had been told, on the rock-slopes of Achaea, and wasn't that (hadn't he told them earlier) his nome? Demos, a deme, nomos, a state or wasn't it? There were the white mulberry trees and black. Did they make wine from the berries? Silkworms? These were the things that mattered. But Archie Rowe would go on impressing himself and the neighbouring tables, about someobdy-or-other at Oxford who had been sent down, or sent up (did they know him?) not turning his slant fish-eyes, but drawing their attention, by a flutter of an eyebrow, to another excellency or other who had entered. The wife of the American military attaché was by far the best dressed woman in the room. She wore a bundle of violets, at her waist. She sat a little too self-consciously erect, 'quaint,' as Archie would have put it, as her arm bent awkwardly to the suave formality, as that excellency bent to brush her fingers. She was young, happy, pretty, no doubt superlatively tactful, but she creaked, just a little, in her social joints.

Someone, not visible, the other side of the attaché, was saying in another near-Boston voice (another petroleum secretary?) that they were all like that, tiresome, and she was sure that Allie shouldn't be hurt about it. Would her mother please tell Allie (dear child) that they were all like that? Why shouldn't she do a little digging? Poor little thing, it showed a suitable interest, didn't it? And with that pathetic little pen-knife, saved over, so touching, from her school pencil-box, at home. That really was the last touch. Who was it had pounced on her? And from what excavation trench, exactly? She'd have something to say to them (tell Allie) ... This famous Allie was no doubt, the leggy child she had brushed against, on the stairs, taking two at a time, gallantly, till she saw some grown-up coming. Allie was now, apparently, upstairs, sleeping.

One looked through one eye of Archie Rowe and out of the other. He had two eyes, for a Chelsea art-ball, painted over a sallow, pink, English-Levant face. His mother drew far away. One could not visualize a pure Greek mother for this. She lived at Patras. They must stop at Patras, he said, on their way up the Corinthian Gulf. He wanted them to see all the 'beawty spots,' Corfu certainly. They awaited, while a bodiless, pseudo-French confection, of sorts, was shoved between their shoulders.

The young wife of the American military attaché was obviously very popular. The clear hyacinth-pink and wedgewood-blue and primrose-yellow of the gowns she had worn, with suitable accessories, these three nights to dinner, made Madelon think of the paper-dolls she had cut out, as a child, with a bouquet or a parasol or a basket to match each individual costume. It was as if these notable frocks were flimsy things to dress a doll in. The fabulous Russian had only one frock obviously. The clothes of the English group were weathered and a bit old-fashioned, apparently, by choice. The paper-doll brought the backs of coloured magazines into focus. Who would have expected that here? Wasn't it enough to cope with history in its magnified and heroic dimensions, without bringing in an apple-blossom paper-doll, who could never have been Marie Antoinette? People, here, were all out of art-collections. Why, this doll?

Even Archie here, for instance, as he turned the other fish-side, in possible recognition of yet another 'celeb-wity,' was almost out of an Egyptian room, albeit, in a provincial and not very good collection. He was second-rate but authentic. His dinner-jacket was too perfect. His hands were podgy but sensitive, he was not, in the least, what he most affected, English. There was, now, the tuning-up of an orchestra—did Archie say, Hungarian?—from a gallery. Music lifted the floor and the tables with it, to a blue-danube period-waltz. They were whirled high, and dropped, as down the shaft of a lift, by the whirl-wind bow of the leader, who shook dark hair forward, to greet applause, over a balcony. It was only the preliminary bars, to show what they could do. Now he began in earnest.

They sometimes cleared the tables, Rowe said, toward midnight, did Miss Eddington dance? Eleanor shot a shocked 'certainly not' at Archie, who retired, like a turtle, into his dinner-jacket. There was a pronounced flutter of heightened conversation, as they drew near coffee. Would they like it in the lounge? Eleanor snapped 'no' to him. It was all going to be too difficult with Eleanor.

A single violin cut a swallow-wing pattern through the air, and she would be transported with it, if she were not careful. Even to think '*heptanésos*, seven-isles,' was too much. She could not yet afford to try her own wings, float above this heavy laden atmosphere, herself hover above clouds of cigarette-smoke—incense? —toward this near sky. Perhaps they were right to shut out what was so real.

There was a slice of that Turkish-delight that Rowe had been talking about, on the edge of a small plate. A tiny coffee-cup held too-black coffee, but she ought by now—after all of three days— to be used to it. She looked at the semi-transparent slab of thick sweet, powdered with soft sugar. 'Is this that honey-and-sesame *loukoumi* you spoke of,' she asked Rowe, though it couldn't possibly be anything else, 'do have one of my cigarettes,' managing a little stage-business, on the side, for Eleanor was being tiresome. Obviously, Eleanor wanted Archie Rowe to go home, but obviously, he couldn't do that quite yet. 'Do they put dope in these things?' What now, had she said to him? The honey-and-sesame tasted, to the tongue, like soothing syrup or a cough-drop, it was strangely aromatic, in an unknown dimension. It was Keats—what was it—all that mixture of syrup-steeped fruits and peel and candied citron. It was things in jars, on a shelf, in an old-fashioned country store; opium? Poppy-seed. The room went round and with it, the Russian diamonds. It's getting too hot here.

It was no hotter than it had been. Outside, lay a street, lined with fern-shaped trees that dropped red berries. Across the street, shallow steps led down into a garden, a winter square, where already a few orange-trees promised an early blossom. Under smoke and silver olives, two bronze deer stood alert. She had walked that morning in the garden of the king, *kepos basilikos*, they called it. She had hesitated before entrances to little churches that were set, squat, like bee-hives, facing the newer thoroughfare. She had smelt that invidious incense that yet had not drawn her in, to worship. She had turned off the market, into the street of Pan, to face three such squat churches, Soter, Stephen and Simon, was it? Impressions mellowed by time, yet remained distinct. Now she was losing something. She was beginning to sag toward Lethe; where there was so much to remember, why not forget? Or was it the hint, back of her mind, of poppies?

She must say something. The only thing that vied, in clarity, with debit and credit and the idea of numbers ruled on paper, was a fight of silver, that was yet a violin, that, with all its exaggerated and emotionally timed rise and fall, swept over their heads, out to the bluer aether. With it, as she watched it, were those sharply defined impressions of columns, cut against blue, against violet, against deep-violet, against purple, as the sun sank beyond Lycabettos. Lycabettos rose like a ship, about to set sail, Hymettus rested, like a ship in harbour. Only the Acropolis remained static, itself a harbour, an island above a city, a city set on a hill, an idea, that, in all its eternal and remote dimension, still cut patterns in the race mind, the human consciousness, now murky with din and battle, as that violin's rhythm and sway, cut pattern across fumes of countless cigarettes, the dreary reiteration of a thousand diplomats. She must hold on a little longer.

Rowe was, at last, trying to placate Eleanor, frankly, with comparative Greek pronunciations. O, but keep him, keep him away from Homer. Why should I keep him away from Homer?

Why not listen to what he may say? O, don't, don't listen to
Archie Rowe making the right comparisons, soothing down the
intensity of the classics, devitalising, as he had been expensively
taught to do, his mother's racial heritage. Keep Archie Rowe off
this, at any price. Say anything. She found herself pronouncing in
a rapt voice—he will think I am quite mad,—'Ah, the Acropolis.'
Now what would she do about it? There was nothing to do about
it, but keep on.

Her words fluttered into the thing they had avoided all that
evening. She had broken a taboo, it was not 'done' to talk about
Ionian columns against violet, in Athens, in nineteen-twenty. She
listened to the violin, lost its silver pattern, say something. Eleanor
would not help her, was delighted that she was caught. A net drew
over her mood, the silver flash of her own wit must save her. But
her words fell, too late, between them, annihilated diplomacies,
space, time and distance, 'It's smaller than anyone could think.
It's smaller and colder. It's frozen. It's alive. It's more alive than
anything living to-day. It's far and cold, like a flower frozen under
white ice. It is white ice, and white fire. It has never been ruined,
for it has never been built. It's in a state of building.' Archie Rowe
was gazing at her, as if pointedly, by inference, to avoid what must
be evident. This lady wasn't used to Greek wine, even their light
Prophilia went to her head, or was she quite mad? 'It's like a flower
seen frozen in a crystal. It's even more luminous than anything,
anyone yet saw; someone dreamed it ... in a crystal.'

Nothing mattered, now that she had said this. She was burning
with that fanatic fervour that leads eccentric, middle-aged dere-
licts to stand up, on a tub, at Hyde Park Corner and hold forth
about the millenium. She was holding forth and she didn't care
who saw it. Then she remembered Eleanor. Archie Rowe is her
guest, I am the guest of Eleanor. Now, how could she retrieve it?
Anything was better than this, this fervour about the Parthenon in
Athens. She leaned over swiftly, in a moment annihilated her
social blunder by one, only a shade less flagrant, yet still permis-
sible. She actually whispered, '*those diamonds*.'

He looked at her, as if he hadn't seen her, then as if he saw her.
He didn't say anything, there was nothing to say. Of course, he
had chapter and verse up his sleeve, but he wouldn't divulge the
secret. Mrs.—ah—Thorpe, wasn't (he was now quite certain)—
ah—quite one of us. He turned to Eleanor.

But now she was free.

Madelon looked at the girl frankly, but now saw her as something,
again different. But what she saw her as, she could not yet say.

Was the Russian woman doomed, by some law deeper than the social law of gossips and of diplomats? Were rigorous laws functioning here, laws far older than the Norman Conqueror, the authentic county inheritance of the head of the British school, at work here? Was there some vein of mystery, some occult knowledge that they all shared? Was mid-west right to ignore Salamis, except as a stepping-stone to oil wells, and was little Allie (upstairs sleeping) protected and forewarned, when some authorised academic snob purloined her pen-knife from her? Could they, even to-day, dig too deep? Was it wise to penetrate below a surface that the British school so carefully kept in its place, that an opera-bouffe royal family had the wit and courage to ignore, that Archie Rowe, with a mother from Achaea, went to Oxford expensively, to forget? They should have ordered French wine, certainly, *Bordeaux*; *Hock* even.

Last night, the night before, after a three weeks' broken and exciting voyage, had been stepping-stones (Salamis, to oil wells) to this night. To-night was different, To-night, she was whirled into the whirl-pool in a back-water, the scum of little tables was lifted high, they were all flung out and back into unpredictable dimensions. Was it merely the *Prophilia*? Did poppy juice distil all this, from a sugar-sweet, sugar-coated bit of sticky sweetmeat? Black coffee took off the taste of sugar-coated sugar, but something lingered, a suspicion, a taste in another direction. O no, it wasn't opium, Archie had laughed at them. What was it, if it wasn't opium?

The walls lifted and fell to the tune of a blue-danube epoch. *Mavrodaphne* was a word to beware, even *Prophilia* might conjure, who knows what, from the floor. Who knows what might rise, like a ball-room Mephistopheles out of this floor? Here, anything might happen. The voices of the Americans, who were departing in a cluster, cut its zip-pattern into the blue-danube. The British school was speaking English casually, now, to an acquaintance, who had risen to join his table. Waiters less astutely, balanced trays and swept crumbs off tables, less ostentatiously. There was a pause, like a breath drawn. Diamonds.

It was all there. A secret that she hadn't striven to solve, that she had dismissed as unworthy of solution, the way they began to draw things, in cut-off triangles and the way they superimposed things, in the new painting. In London, that hadn't come true, quite to her, but she saw now, what the eccentric new-art sought for. She wanted to shout to Eleanor, Eleanor Eddington, E.E. or Edd as she had learned to call her; she wanted to snatch the core of herself out of Madelon Thorpe, Madd as Eleanor called her, she wanted something, unrelated to time, related to infinity to communicate with something unrelated to time, related to infinity. Make that correspondence and nothing else matters, you may dismiss Archie Rowe and the head-waiter and the breakfast butler upstairs (who would mistake her for Eleanor) in a breath. You related time-out-of-time, to time-in-time and you get snatches of each, in bits of jagged-off triangles. In your mind, you have a sort of tube, like their nursery kaleidoscope, all the colours are there, violet, violets of Hymettus, ultra-violet and sea-purple; you say *Mavrodaphne* and you get drunk, she had told Archie, like that. *Prophilia* was something different. It was the sharp edge of a cut-off triangle, that must be the one facet of that diamond. That must be each facet of a diamond that was a new way of thinking. Everything dissolved in the chemistry of this post-war, Balkan dining-room, in the *Hôtel Acropole et Angleterre*, but this thing. A new way of looking at things ...

Don't look at the diamond. Eleanor is shuffling her feet and I'll have to wait till Rowe, tediously, takes leave before, upstairs, I can burst into this new layer, this new discovery, before I can tell Edd, or E.E., as I have learned to call her, how she can paint pictures like that. This is the new music. Everything seems unrelated yet diametrically related, as you slant one facet of a diamond into another set of values.

MULK RAJ ANAND

▼▼▼

The Maharaja and the Tortoise

OF ALL THE ANCIENT (and, of course, noble) princely houses which have succeeded in preserving, by natural and artificial means, the continuity of their blood stream through the ages, the line of the Maharajas of Udhampur, of the Suraj-Bansi Clan who claim their descent from the Sun, by way of the God-King Rama, is the most ancient and most noble.

They are proud and warlike chieftains whose chivalry is a byword in Indian homes, whose jewels and diamonds and rubies and sapphires and elephants are coveted by all the shopgirls of Europe, and whose splendid contributions in men, money and materials to the British Raj, in bringing law and order to India, have been recognized by the Sarkar through treaties which appoint them the guardians of millions of the poor, and by the grant to them of various titles, certificates and scrolls.

Besides being confirmed a 'Descendant of the Sun' by special decree of the Government of India, on the death of his revered father Maharaja Gulab Singh and on his accession to the ancestral throne, His Highness Maharajadhiraj Sir Ganga Singh Bahadur was made Knight Commander of the Star of India (2nd class) for his services as an orderly to His Majesty the King-Emperor at the Coronation Durbar at Delhi. And he was awarded a salute of twenty-one guns for supplying a whole brigade of sappers and miners and for his valiant services in the field and at home during the War. The Hindu University of Hathras had conferred on him the honorary degree of Doctor of Laws for contributing lavishly to its funds and several women's clubs in America, and the Honourable Society of Haberdashers of the United Kingdom had elected him an honorary member. Besides these a long list of chosen letters of the Latin, Arabic and Sanskrit alphabets had accrued to his name during the years.

Be it said to the credit of His Highness that though he was gracious enough to accept all these honours, and had indeed in his younger days been eager enough to seek them, the superabundance of these titles, mostly couched in Angrezi speech which he did not understand, seemed to him irrelevant in his mature years, except as the necessary adjuncts of a modern existence, like the patent-leather shoes, and the eighteen-carat gold watch studded with diamonds, which he wore on special occasions with the ceremonial robes of the ancient and princely house of Udhampur.

For, in spite of his loyalty and devotion to the British Crown and his consequent assumption of the privileges that this devotion and loyalty brought in their train, His Highness had never really accepted the suzerainty of the dirty, beef-eating race of which even the Kings were used to wiping their bottoms with paper. He was a strict Hindu and, being true to the great traditions of his house and conscious that its eminence among the princely houses was founded more on the spiritual than the temporal power associated with his ancestors, he valued only one title, 'Descendant of the Sun', and did not care for the other decorations.

In fact, as he grew in age, he had been inclined to care less and less for the things of this world and more and more for the things of the spirit. But, since the habits which he had cultivated in his hot-headed youth, and the responsibilities of his position as the head of his state did not altogether conduce to renunciation, he had compromised and accepted the appurtenances of a modern existence at the same time as he sought to deepen his faith in the invisible, ethereal God and to cast off the false cloak of the flesh.

Now, as every one knows, even the greatest saints and prophets of this world have found it difficult to achieve the ideal of complete detachment or non-attachment. The Lord Buddha who preached the cessation of all desire in order to rid the world of suffering died of meat-poisoning. And Jesus wept in vain. And Lao Tze suffered from pangs of bad conscience about his love of the world, and the gout.

It is not to be wondered at, therefore, if His Highness Maharaja Sir Ganga Singh failed in the pursuit of God. For this evil iron age imposes certain limits even on the most heroic sons of India! Hedged in between a diabolical Sarkar, whose real feelings about him were difficult to discover in spite of his intimacy with the Political Resident, Sir Francis Wimperley, and a people who were always clamouring for something or other, His Highness was in a doubly difficult position in realizing the great spiritual ideals of his inheritance.

The catastrophe which led to his disillusionment is one of the most important miracles of religious history in the world and has

become a legend to all true followers of the faith, besides being
the greatest spiritual crisis in the annals of Rajasthan since the
Johur, the last sacrifice by the Rajputs when they were besieged in
the hill fort of Chitore by the lusty slave King of Delhi, Ala-ud-
din, and since the performance of Suttee by Queen Padmani, who
burned herself with her female companions rather than yield to
the conqueror.

It so happened that as Maharaja Sir Ganga Singh reached the
age of forty and felt he was getting old he sought the advice of
Pandit Ram Prashad, who was both the High Priest and the
Prime Minister of Udhampur, to prepare an easy passage for his
journey to the next world.

Pandit Ram Prashad, a clever little lawyer who had been able to
maintain his position in the state for seven years—a longer term
of office than had been enjoyed by any other Vizier, because he
was superior in cunning to all the other courtiers—advised His
Highness that, according to the holy books, on the appearance of
every full moon, he should donate his weight in gold to the
priests, entertain seven hundred of them to a feast in the palace
and take to prayer, mentioning the name of God three hundred
and seventy-five times on the rosary after offering oblations every
morning to his ancestor, the Sun, seated in the lotus seat by the
edge of the Ganges. If this ritual was not followed, said the
Pandit, His Highness was in grave danger because, the access to
heaven apart, he would have prolonged illnesses, as the planets
Saturn and Venus were daily clashing in the scroll of his horo-
scope.

As the palace of the Maharaja of Udhampur was situated on
the edge of the desert of Rajputana, and the River Ganges flowed
about a hundred and fifty miles away up north, His Highness was
hard put to it to understand how he could offer oblations to the
Sun sitting by the Ganges water. But Pandit Ram Prashad had a
more agile mind than His Highness, or, for that matter, anyone
else in Udhampur. He immediately called Sardar Bahadur Singh,
a contractor who paid the best commissions, and arranged the
construction of a tank which was to be filled from the River
Ganges by means of a pipe-line all the way from Hardwar, where
the holy river first enters the plains from the hills. The cost was to
be a meagre hundred and eighty lakhs. And he presented this plan
to His Highness.

Needless to say, money was no consideration to His Highness
Maharaja Sir Ganga Singh, as every one knew that he had given a
hundred lakhs to the Sarkar during the war and had spent forty
lakhs on a fleet of Packards which broke their axles on the rutted,

unpaved tracks of Udhampur and lay rusting in the stables. So that when Pandit Ram Prashad laid the scheme before His Highness he nodded assent even as his bleary eyes, yellowed by the smoke of opium, closed in a half-sleep and he sank deeper into the cow-tailed cushions, the carved silver handle of the long tube of his hubble-bubble dropping from his hand.

There is a sacred belief in India in a system of government called the Ram Raj. According to this the monarch is regarded as the father-mother of a happy family, which not only includes the male and female members of the royal household but even the dirty, ragged, lice-ridden common people of the kingdom. Since it was said in Udhampur that all the Rajputs from the Maharaja-dhiraj downwards were cousins who once belonged to the same clan, caste and race, the belief in Ram Raj in this state was most intense. But though the kinship on which this belief was founded was not too obvious during those resplendent feasts which were held in honour of visiting officials at the palace, it appeared on other occasions, especially at times of national emergency when the people were asked to give up their own occupations and help to increase the prestige of their spiritual and temporal head by dedicating themselves to some duty in the service of the state.

When the plan of building a tank by the palace and connecting it by a pipe-line to the Ganges, was conceived in order to enable His Highness to offer oblations and prayers to his ancestor the Sun, all the manhood, as well as the womanhood and even the childhood, of Udhampur was conscripted to help in the building and earn the blessings that would indirectly accrue to them through the Maharaja's realization of easy access to heaven.

Though there were some in Udhampur who thought the scheme fantastic, others believed that the Maharaja, who had once spoiled his religion by crossing the black waters and shaking hands with people who ate cow's flesh, and by whoring and drinking, was now returning in his old age to the right path. And they accepted a mere pittance from the contractor and willingly worked day and night, sweating and straining, with the thousand names of God on their thirsty lips and the roots of wild plants in their bellies, to complete the work.

It did not take many months before the long line from Hardwar to Udhampur was laid and a beautiful square tank built, connecting the palace by means of three steps with the holy water.

With that large-heartedness which was characteristic of His Highness's family, capable of the uttermost hatred for the enemy and the tenderest solicitude for those who had won favour, the Maharaja had all those who had pooh-poohed the plan of constructing the tank flogged and banished, and all those who had helped in preparing the conditions through which he was to perform the prescribed ceremonies feasted. And there was some weeping in Udhampur, but also much rejoicing; and, as always happens on such occasions, the shouting and the laughter drowned the tears.

For a few days after these celebrations His Highness could not start practising the prescribed ritual of offering prayers and oblations to the father Sun, from whom he was descended, because it seemed difficult, after the feasts which were held on the auspicious occasion of opening the tank, to settle down to the serious business of praying every morning, especially as His Highness had never been an early riser, and also because he was not feeling too well after the effect on his liver of rich food during the banquets.

When a number of digestive powders had restored his liver somewhat, the Maharaja developed gout in his left foot, and that made it difficult for him to stir from the velvet cow-tailed cushions on which he reclined, swathed in bandages and Kashmir shawls.

This enforced delay in search of the kingdom of heaven fortunately gave His Highness time for some heart-searching as a preliminary to the prayers which he was soon going to undertake.

He asked himself whether the favourite young Rani, who had come in the palanquin sent by a prince of Nepal on the inception of the project for building the tank, was not right when she insisted that he should have his proud beard, which spread in two different directions at the chin, shaved off. Did it really make him look old? And was it a fact that the Angrezi log considered a man young at sixty? If what General Bhola Singh, the Commander-in-chief of his army, had told him was true, that by taking a paste made of the powdered flesh of a male bear's organs one could rejuvenate oneself and even become the father of a child, then he had only to set his hunters searching for game and not despair or feel old at forty.... Why impose on himself the duty of offering oblations and saying prayers, anyhow, when one could easily get the priests to repeat the holy verses for a little money, or even get them to say that the feasting of a thousand priests or the bestowal of gifts to a shrine could ensure one's salvation? He had never learnt any sacred verses and formulas and, after all, what was he to say to the Sun if, indeed, he did go down to the tank at dawn and throw water skywards? The longer he reclined on the cushions and the more his gout pained him, the more such doubts and misgivings assailed him. And he twisted his beard between the forefinger and thumb of his left hand as he rested his head on his right. But a good mixture of opium and tobacco in the chilm of his hubble-bubble dispelled every thought and he succeeded in postponing the awkward decision for days on end.

But, for some curious reason, Pandit Ram Prashad kept on plaguing the Maharaja with inquiries about when His Highness was going to begin saying the prescribed prayers. Besides the clashing of the planets Saturn and Venus in His Highness's horo-scope, said the Prime Minister, the construction of the tank and the pipe-line from Hardwar had almost emptied the State trea-sury. The only way of collecting new taxes from the peasantry was by sedulously persuading them to believe that His Highness's prayers would bring merit to the whole kingdom, as the prayers of no other person could. The fellow was so persistent that he nearly bit off the Maharaja's ears by his constant bullying and nagging. And he absolutely refused to point any other way of securing the advantages of heaven, although previously he had prescribed the feasting of seven hundred priests in every emergency as a way of getting out of the more arduous sacrifices.

The Maharaja's pretences about his indisposition, his igno-rance of the sacred verses, etcetera, were met by the argument that by attaining purity of heart he would attain good health. And since His Highness could not confess that the real reason for his lack of pious zeal was that he wanted to have one last fling before he regarded himself as an old spent man, fit only for the mumbling of prayers, he found himself in a corner.

One day, indeed, he burst into a regal rage and declared that it was not necessary for him, the Descendant of the Sun, to pray in order to be taken into favour by his ancestors, and that no dog of a Brahmin could force him to renounce life at the age of forty.

But Pandit Ram Prashad respectfully assured him that if, after spending all the revenue of his state, he did not devote himself entirely to religion, and if he, the Prime Minister, was not given a free hand to rule the state in the best interests of the praja, he would have to declare the treasury bankrupt and beg the British Sarkar to force His Highness to abdicate and appoint a court of wards.

The Maharaja had no option but to submit to this threat. However, he sought a few days' grace from the Prime Minister on the plea that he wanted to learn the words of the *Gayatri*, the hymn to the Sun, before he started to pray, but really in an attempt to evade the ordeal should something happen in the meantime to make that possible.

Pandit Ram Prashad appointed a priest to come and help His Highness to memorize the *Gayatri*. And His Highness had perforce to listen to the recitation hundreds of times. Long before he had learnt the whole thing by heart he pretended that he knew it, as it was the only way he could keep the Prime Minister's abominable nominee away from the palace.

And at length the day was appointed when the Maharaja was to begin worship on the edge of the tank and to bring merit to himself and his subjects.

With the beating of drums, the blowing of conches, the striking of cymbals and gongs and the tolling of bells, His Highness rose at dawn from the side of his favourite consort and, with his feet swathed in bandages, for he still suffered from gout, he limped down the three steps which led from the balcony of his Diwan to the edge of the tank, where Pandit Ram Prashad and the other courtiers, priests and people had preceded him.

The eastern sky was colouring with a rosy flush as the refulgent visage of the Sun, the ancestor of Maharaja Sir Ganga Singh, showed up over the rim of the hills beyond the desert.

The whole congregation dipped themselves for a ceremonial bath in the sacred water. Pandit Ram Prashad, in his capacity of High Priest of the kingdom, then led the prayers.

The Prime Minister and the other priests would lift the holy water from the third step of the tank in their upturned palms and, showing it to the Sun, pour it before them to the accompaniment of the *Gayatri*.

The Maharaja followed them rather dreamily, as his eyes did not seem to have quenched their sleep during the night.

After the recitation of mantras was over, the congregation sat down in the lotus seat on the lowest step of the tank to repeat parts of the *Bhagvad Gita* and to contemplate the vision of God in their souls with closed eyes, as is prescribed by the rules of Hindu ritualistic worship.

His Highness was afraid that if he closed his eyes tight to contemplate God he might fall asleep and tumble into the water. So he had to be vigilant if only to keep himself balanced in his seat. As he kept opening his eyes and shutting them he saw what appeared to be a piece of round green moss floating among the flower-petals and the rice which had been copiously sprinkled by the congregation during the singing of the hymns.

The continual hum of the prayers recited by the priests became monotonous, and His Highness, catching himself half asleep, deliberately opened his eyes and scanned the landscape. Millions of his devout subjects, who had helped to construct the pond, were gathered all round, apparently happy to be sharing in this communion which he had graced by his presence.

Feeling that he might be observed he bent his head. The curious piece of moss had now floated near to his bandaged feet, as if drawn by the dirty-looking green potion showing through the bandages which the barber of the palace had wrapped round his feet. His Highness could not move his hands to throw away the scum as he held them in the prescribed posture like the opening petals of the lotus flower on his knees. And yet he did not want the scum to stick to his gouty feet. He dared not move his body at all lest Pandit Ram Prashad should rebuke him for inattention afterwards. And yet he felt he must do something about it. In his panic he thought he could stir the scum away with a slight move- ment of his feet without attracting the attention of any member of the congregation or the priests....

With one brisk little movement he stirred his left foot in the water and closed his eyes, sure that if he did not see himself do this no one else would.

But there was a sharp shooting pain near the big toe of his foot and he lifted his lids with a dazed look of horror in his eyes.

A little piece of pale brown flesh floated before him and a stream of blood was spurting from the bandages between his toes like a miniature fountain.

'A tortoise! A tortoise!' the priests shouted, and drew back with upraised hands and scurrying legs.

'The tortoise has bitten off the Maharaja's toe!' a courtier shouted, lifting the piece of flesh from where it was sinking behind the disappearing tortoise.

'Murder! murder!' shouted another courtier.

'Blood!' shouted a third.

'Keep quiet! keep quiet!' shrieked His Highness, as he felt half afraid that the Prime Minister would rebuke him for ruining the ceremony by this unseemly behaviour and the millions of his subjects might regard this inauspicious accident as the harbinger of more trouble to come.

But the frightened priests and the cowardly courtiers fled up the palace steps. And cries of Ram! Ram! Hari! Hari! arose from the throngs of people on the other sides of the tank. For every one now believed from the pandemonium at the three steps that some evil had befallen the Maharaja.

With a resurgence of princely pride His Highness stood where he was and, though his face twitched and he went pale all over, he waved his arms in the gesture which signifies the casting of a blessing, in order to assure the people that he could maintain his composure even when his courtiers flew in a panic.

At this instant his own astonishment at his calm filled him with a greater degree of princely pride and he confronted Pandit Ram Prashad, the Prime Minister, who stood on the first step casting the shadow of his presence on the Maharaja, with an accusing stare in his eyes.

'Catch that swine! Catch that robber who has run away with my big toe!' the Maharaja shouted. 'Don't stand there looking at me! It is your infernal advice which has led to this.... I shall break your head if you cannot catch the culprit and bring it to justice!'

And, shaking his hands at the Prime Minister, glaring at the retreating figures, shouting, cursing, moaning and whimpering, he limped up the three steps, fainted, and fell face downwards on the marble floor.

The women of the Zenana came weeping up to the balcony and there was mourning in the palace as well as in the capital, as if the Maharaja were dead or dying.

But with a dauntlessness deriving from the Himalayan blood in her veins, the favourite Rani took His Highness in hand: she issued a proclamation to the people under her own name, giving a full account of the accident, and assuring the populace that the Maharaja was well on the way to recovery and would soon see that the perpetrators of the attempt on his life were brought to justice.

The Prime Minister now realized that his attempt to wrest control of His Highness's earthly kingdom by pointing out to him the advantages of the kingdom of heaven had failed. And recalling how even in the moment of his direst pain, when he had been bitten by the tortoise, the Maharaja had kept calm while he and the other courtiers had fled to safety up the steps, he now felt afraid of the weak, opium-eating monarch whom he had thought as wax in his hand to twist as he liked. He did not know what kind of retribution the Rajput in His Highness would demand from him if he didn't produce the culprit tortoise. And yet what could you do to a reptile to revenge yourself? Have it killed? But there would surely be no satisfaction in that, as most of the water creatures had cold blood anyhow. Apart from the Maharaja's words before he fainted, however, the favourite Queen's behaviour was menacing.

He forthwith ordered the fishermen of the village to lay their nets and catch the tortoise which had bitten off the big toe of His Highness's right foot, and he offered the prize of a rupee to the man who would produce the reptile dead or five rupees to the man who would produce it alive.

It was not long that this prize remained unearned. For during the very next hour fishermen brought several tortoises, dead and alive, in baskets to the Prime Minister, who was hard put to it to discover which was the tortoise that had bitten off the toe of His Highness's right foot. And, for a moment, he was perplexed. But with that genius for inventing stratagems which is the secret of diplomacy, he had all the tortoises but one thrown back into the tank, and then he went to His Highness's presence, bowed obsequiously, and said: 'Your Highness's orders have been carried out. The tortoise has been caught. Would your Highness give the necessary command?'

Maharaja Sir Ganga Singh's princely pride, fanned by his favourite consort's care, had crystallized into a stubborn sense of hurt dignity. His Highness shouted to the Prime Minister:

'Bring this biti-chod tortoise before the Court and let it be tried before me and let a just punishment be meted out to it and all the other culprits! ...'

It seemed a ridiculous thing for the Maharaja to want to try a tortoise in his court. But the Prime Minister was used to the strange and absurd whims of His Highness. He kept cool and had the tortoise brought into the court.

On seeing the reptile waving its head in the basket, His Highness ground his teeth in fury and, foaming at the mouth, exclaimed:

'Bring it up here so that I may trample upon it with the foot which it has disabled!'

'Sire,' the Prime Minister advised, 'it has sharp, knife-like teeth, and may bite off the whole of your royal foot.'

This restrained His Highness from taking the law into his own hands immediately. But he pompously proclaimed:

'We, Ganga Singh, Maharajadhiraj of Udhampur, scion of the Suraj-Bansi Clan, constitute ourselves as the supreme Judge of this court as well as plaintiff and prosecutor in this case. Let whosoever dares to come to the defence of this infamous tortoise, who bit our toe, speak in its defence. But be assured that if the guilt be proved against the said tortoise, then both the reptiles—the said tortoise and its counsel—shall be beheaded instantaneously in our presence.'

The redness in His Highness's eyes, as well as the cracked fury of his stentorian utterance, was obviously an attempt to imitate the violent and grandiloquent manner of public prosecutors in the fascist states which he had visited during his last European tour. The Prime Minister came forward and said: 'I shall defend the culprit.'

There were whispers of pity, remorse and joy in the hall, as the noblemen, the courtiers, and the servants were sure that the bleeding, bandaged toe of His Highness was the surest proof of the guilt of the tortoise, and would, in being proved, involve difficulties for the Prime Minister since he had the temerity to defend the reptile.

'Acha then, proceed, you, dog of a Brahmin,' the Maharaja roared, confirming the worst fears of the audience, his anger taking force from the pain in his foot.

'You are my father-mother,' said the wily Ram Prashad without being ruffled by the Maharaja's abuse, 'as you are father-mother of the people of this land. But I have been responsible for encouraging your Highness to have this tank constructed, and I have a plea to make.'

'Make it then!' said the Majaraja.

'Sire!' began the Prime Minister, adopting the familiar and timeworn method of flattery: 'Your Highness is a scion of the Sun and, therefore, the greatest and the mightiest Prince in the land. Your counsel is heard in far lands and your fame has spread into the farthest corners of the world, even in the lands of perpetual ice and snow where you have travelled. But Your Highness may be pleased to know that, according to the holy books, it is a sin to kill a Brahmin, and punishable by the consignment of the killer to twenty cold hells. Therefore I am free from attack from the highest as well as the lowest of the land.'

Having secured immunity for himself with the aid of Manu's four thousand years old code, which is recognized in part by the Government of India and of course as a whole in the native states, he proceeded to apply his peculiar religious-forensic knowledge to the defence of the tortoise.

'As for this reptile, the sages of old prophesied that the God Vishnu would be born in the iron age in the form of a tortoise and would be transported through an underground passage to a tank specially built for it by a Descendant of the Sun. And that, by the sacrifice of a toe of the said Descendant, the world would get the first sign that the God Vishnu, the antecedent of the Sun, had come to live in the old land of Rajasthan again. After that event the old ideal of Ram Raj, of a perfect kingdom, would be realized in the state....'

And he further stated that if His Highness would recognize this sign, and forgive those whom he considered his enemies, he would have the gift of a son and heir born to him by his youngest Queen and get a safe passage to heaven into the bargain. Otherwise, he said, a lifelong curse would descend upon the Maharaja:

he would be made to abdicate and the Suraj-Bansi Clan would die out for ever.

'Incarnation of Vishnu!' mocked a courtier who had ambitions to the post of Prime Minister and therefore hated Pandit Ram Prashad and saw through his machinations. 'Incarnation of the devil! That tortoise has disabled His Highness for life and it is made out to be the vehicle of God!'

His Highness's vanity was flattered by the Prime Minister's explanation. But, driven almost crazy by the pain of his injured foot, he sweated and blew hot whiffs of breath as he rolled about in a frenzy of indecision on the cushions on which he leaned.

'I have fulfilled my mission in warning you of the portents,' said Ram Prashad to make up His Highness's mind for him.

'What proof is there,' said the courtier who was the rival of the Prime Minister, 'that this is the tortoise which is, of all the tortoises in the tank, the incarnation of Vishnu?'

'What proof is there,' parried the Prime Minister, 'that this is the tortoise which bit off the toe of His Highness's right foot?'

The Maharaja seemed to be overcome by the Prime Minister's logic.

'To be sure Pandit Ram Prashad seems right,' he said, scratching his beard. 'For the portents as he described them tally with the legend that God appears to every scion of the Suraj-Bansi Clan.'

'But, Sire!' said the enemy of the Prime Minister, 'what proof is there that the miracle would happen in this manner? Where are the holy books which lay it down?'

'Pandit Ram Prashad is a holy Bramin apart from being a vizier,' said one of the partisans of the Prime Minister.

And there was a way of words, an exchange of fiery glances, and tempers threatened to rise, and were controlled only by the state of His Highness's health.

'What judgment should I pass in the circumstances, Panditji?' asked His Highness reverently of the Prime Minister.

'I would suggest that you order this tortoise to be taken back to the River Ganges whence it came,' said the Prime Minister, 'so that if, as I say, it is the incarnation of the God Vishnu, it will come back and manifest itself again.'

That course of action appealed to His Highness's way of thinking. If it was really the God Vishnu it would come back and do something to reveal itself, though he would not like it to do so in quite the same way as the last time; and if it was only a tortoise this would be the best way of getting rid of the nuisance and yet to save face after all the brave words he had used and been unable to act upon. His Highness therefore delivered judgment accordingly.

In the law reports of Udhampur state published by His Highness's Government, in emulation of the practice of England, where justice is mainly custom and precedent, the sentence reads as follows:

'We, Sir Ganga Singh, Maharajadhiraj of Udhampur, scion of the Suraj-Bansi Clan, Knight Commander of the Star of India (2nd class), etc., order that the tortoise in the palace tank, which is suspected of being either an arch-criminal or the incarnation of the God Vishnu, be exiled to the River Ganges for a year, so that it can prove its authenticity by a miracle of divine will,' etc.

During that year a tortoise bit off the five fingers of a washerwoman who was cleaning clothes by the tank, and a Son of God was born to the favourite Rani.

At the instance of the Prime Minister, His Highness the Maharaja declared a public holiday to celebrate the latter event. And every one believed that the God Vishnu had become incarnate in the old Maharaja and that Ram Raj had come to Udhampur, that it had become a perfect state.

▼▼▼

In Another Country

IN THE FALL the war was always there, but we did not go to it any more. It was cold in the fall in Milan and the dark came very early. Then the electric lights came on, and it was pleasant along the streets looking in the windows. There was much game hanging outside the shops, and the snow powdered in the fur of the foxes and the wind blew their tails. The deer hung stiff and heavy and empty, and small birds blew in the wind and the wind turned their feathers. It was a cold fall and the wind came down from the mountains.

We were all at the hospital every afternoon, and there were different ways of walking across the town through the dusk to the hospital. Two of the ways were alongside canals, but they were long. Always, though, you crossed a bridge across a canal to enter the hospital. There was a choice of three bridges. On one of them a woman sold roasted chestnuts. It was warm, standing in front of her charcoal fire, and the chestnuts were warm afterward in your pocket. The hospital was very old and very beautiful, and you entered through a gate and walked across a courtyard and out of a gate on the other side. There were usually funerals starting from the courtyard. Beyond the old hospital were the new brick pavilions, and there we met every afternoon and were all very polite and interested in what was the matter, and sat in the machines that were to make so much difference.

The doctor came up to the machine where I was sitting and said: 'What did you like best to do before the war? Did you practise a sport?'

I said: 'Yes, football.'

'Good,' he said. 'You will be able to play football again better than ever.'

My knee did not bend and the leg dropped straight from the knee to the ankle without a calf, and the machine was to bend the knee and make it move as in riding a tricycle. But it did not bend yet, and instead the machine lurched when it came to the bending part. The doctor said: 'That will all pass. You are a fortunate young man. You will play football again like a champion.'

In the next machine was a major who had a little hand like a baby's. He winked at me when the doctor examined his hand, which was between two leather straps that bounded up and down and flapped the stiff fingers, and said: 'And will I too play football, captain-doctor?' He had been a very great fencer and, before the war, the greatest fencer in Italy.

The doctor went to his office in the back room and brought a photograph which showed a hand that had been withered almost as small as the major's, before it had taken a machine course, and after was a little larger. The major held the photograph with his good hand and looked at it very carefully. 'A wound?' he asked.

'An industrial accident,' the doctor said.

'Very interesting, very interesting,' the major said, and handed it back to the doctor.

'You have confidence?'

'No,' said the major.

There were three boys who came each day who were about the same age I was. They were all three from Milan, and one of them was to be a lawyer, and one was to be a painter, and one had intended to be a soldier, and after we were finished with the machines, sometimes we walked back together to the Café Cova, which was next door to the Scala. We walked the short way through the communist quarter because we were four together. The people hated us because we were officers, and from a wine-shop someone would call out, 'A basso gli ufficiali!' as we passed. Another boy who walked with us sometimes and made us five wore a black silk handkerchief across his face because he had no nose then and his face was to be rebuilt. He had gone out to the front from the military academy and been wounded within an hour after he had gone into the front line for the first time. They rebuilt his face, but he came from a very old family and they could never get the nose exactly right. He went to South America and worked in a bank. But this was a long time ago, and then we did not any of us know how it was going to be afterward. We only knew that there was always the war, but that we were not going to it any more.

We all had the same medals, except the boy with the black silk bandage across his face, and he had not been at the front long enough to get any medals. The tall boy with a very pale face who was to be a lawyer had been a lieutenant of Arditi and had three medals of the sort we each had only one of. He had lived a very long time with death and was a little detached. We were all a little detached, and there was nothing that held us together except that we met every afternoon at the hospital. Although, as we walked to the Cova through the tough part of town, walking in the dark, with light and singing coming out of the wine-shops, and sometimes having to walk into the street when the men and women would crowd together on the sidewalk so that we would have had to jostle them to get by, we felt held together by there being something that had happened that they, the people who disliked us, did not understand.

We ourselves all understood the Cova, where it was rich and warm and not too brightly lighted, and noisy and smoky at certain hours, and there were always girls at the tables and the illustrated papers on a rack on the wall. The girls at the Cova were very patriotic, and I found that the most patriotic people in Italy were the café girls—and I believe they are still patriotic.

The boys at first were very polite about my medals and asked me what I had done to get them. I showed them the papers, which were written in very beautiful language and full of *fratellanza* and *abnegazione*, but which really said, with the adjectives removed, that I had been given the medals because I was an American. After that their manner changed a little towards me, although I was their friend against outsiders. I was a friend, but I was never really one of them after they had read the citations, because it had been different with them and they had done very different things to get their medals. I had been wounded, it was true; but we all knew that being wounded, after all, was really an accident. I was never ashamed of the ribbons, though, and sometimes, after the cocktail hour, I would imagine myself having done all the things they had done to get their medals; but walking home at night through the empty streets with the cold wind and all the shops closed, trying to keep near the street lights, I knew that I would never have done such things, and I was very much afraid to die, and often lay in bed at night by myself, afraid to die and wondering how I would be when I went back to the front again.

The three with the medals were like hunting-hawks; and I was not a hawk, although I might seem a hawk to those who have never hunted; they, the three, knew better and so we drifted apart. But I stayed good friends with the boy who had been wounded his first day at the front, because he would never know how he would have turned out; so he could never be accepted either, and I liked him because I thought perhaps he would not have turned out to be a hawk either.

The major, who had been the great fencer, did not believe in bravery, and spent much time while we sat in the machines correcting my grammar. He had complimented me on how I spoke Italian, and we talked together very easily. One day I had said that Italian seemed such an easy langauge to me that I could not take a great interest in it; everything was so easy to say. 'Ah, yes,' the major said. 'Why, then, do you not take up the use of grammar?' So we took up the use of grammar, and soon Italian was such a difficult language that I was afraid to talk to him until I had the grammar straight in my mind.

The major came very regularly to the hospital. I do not think he ever missed a day, although I am sure he did not believe in the machines. There was a time when none of us believed in the machines, and one day the major said it was all nonsense. The machines were new then and it was we who were to prove them. It was an idiotic idea, he said, 'a theory, like another.' I had not learned my grammar, and he said I was a stupid impossible disgrace, and he was a fool to have bothered with me. He was a small man and he sat straight up in his chair with his right hand thrust into the machine and looked straight ahead at the wall while the straps thumped up and down with his fingers in them.

'What will you do when the war is over if it is over?' he asked me. 'Speak grammatically!'

'I will go to the States.'

'Are you married?'

'No, but I hope to be.'

'The more of a fool you are,' he said. He seemed very angry. 'A man must not marry.'

'Why, signor maggiore?'

'Don't call me "signor maggiore".'

'Why must not a man marry?'

'He cannot marry. He cannot marry,' he said angrily. 'If he is to lose everything, he should not place himself in a position to lose that. He should not place himself in a position to lose. He should find things he cannot lose.'

He spoke very angrily and bitterly, and looked straight ahead while he talked.

'But why should he necessarily lose it?'

'He'll lose it,' the major said. He was looking at the wall. Then he looked down at the machine and jerked his little hand out from between the straps and slapped it hard against his thigh. 'He'll lose it,' he almost shouted. 'Don't argue with me!' Then he called to the attendant who ran the machines. 'Come and turn this damned thing off.'

He went back into the other room for the light treatment and the massage. Then I heard him ask the doctor if he might use his telephone and he shut the door. When he came back into the room, I was sitting in another machine. He was wearing his cape and had his cap on, and he came directly towards my machine and put his arm on my shoulder.

'I am so sorry,' he said, and patted me on the shoulder with his good hand. 'I would not be rude. My wife has just died. You must forgive me.'

'Oh—' I said, feeling sick for him. 'I am *so* sorry.'

He stood there biting his lower lip. 'It is very difficult,' he said. 'I cannot resign myself.'

He looked straight past me and out through the window. Then he began to cry. 'I am utterly unable to resign myself,' he said and choked. And then crying, his head up, looking at nothing, carrying himself straight and soldierly, with tears on both his cheeks and biting his lips, he walked past the machines and out of the door.

The doctor told me that the major's wife, who was very young and whom he had not married until he was definitely invalided out of the war, had died of pneumonia. She had been sick only a few days. No one expected her to die. The major did not come to the hospital for three days. Then he came at the usual hour, wearing a black band on the sleeve of his uniform. When he came back, there were large framed photographs around the wall, of all sorts of wounds before and after they had been cured by the machines. In front of the machine the major used were three photographs of hands like his that were completely restored. I do not know where the doctor got them. I always understood we were the first to use the machines. The photographs did not make much difference to the major because he only looked out of the window.

▼▼

Miss Ogilvy Finds Herself

1

MISS OGILVY STOOD on the quay at Calais and surveyed the disbanding of her Unit, the Unit that together with the coming of war had completely altered the complexion of her life, at all events for three years.

Miss Ogilvy's thin, pale lips were set sternly and her forehead was puckered in an effort of attention, in an effort to memorise every small detail of every old war-weary battered motor on whose side still appeared the merciful emblem that had set Miss Ogilvy free.

Miss Ogilvy's mind was jerking a little, trying to regain its accustomed balance, trying to readjust itself quickly to this sudden and paralysing change. Her tall, awkward body with its queer look of strength, its broad, flat bosom and thick legs and ankles, as though in response to her jerking mind, moved uneasily, rocking backwards and forwards. She had this trick of rocking on her feet in moments of controlled agitation. As usual, her hands were thrust deep into her pockets, they seldom seemed to come out of her pockets unless it were to light a cigarette, and as though she were still standing firm under fire while the wounded were placed in her ambulances, she suddenly straddled her legs very slightly and lifted her head and listened. She was standing firm under fire at that moment, the fire of a desperate regret.

Some girls came towards her, young, tired-looking creatures whose eyes were too bright from long strain and excitement. They had all been members of that glorious Unit, and they still wore the queer little forage-caps and the short, clumsy tunics of the French Militaire. They still slouched in walking and smoked Caporals in emulation of the Poilus. Like their founder and leader these girls were all English, but like her they had chosen to serve England's ally, fearlessly thrusting right up to the trenches in search of the wounded and dying. They had seen some fine things in the course of three years, not the least fine of which was the cold, hard-faced woman who commanding, domineering, even hectoring at times, had yet been possessed of so dauntless a courage and of so insistent a vitality that it vitalised the whole Unit.

'It's rotten!' Miss Ogilvy heard someone saying. 'It's rotten, this breaking up of our Unit!' And the high, rather childish voice of the speaker sounded perilously near to tears.

Miss Ogilvy looked at the girl almost gently, and it seemed, for a moment, as though some deep feeling were about to find expression in words. But Miss Ogilvy's feelings had been held in abeyance so long that they seldom dared become vocal, so she merely said 'Oh?' on a rising inflection—her method of checking emotion.

They were swinging the ambulance cars in mid-air, those of them that were destined to go back to England, swinging them up like sacks of potatoes, then lowering them with much clanging of chains to the deck of the waiting steamer. The porters were shoving and shouting and quarrelling, pausing now and again to make meaningless gestures; while a pompous official was becoming quite angry as he pointed at Miss Ogilvy's own special car—it annoyed him, it was bulky and difficult to move.

'Bon Dieu! Mais dépêchez-vous donc!' he bawled, as though he were bullying the motor.

Then Miss Ogilvy's heart gave a sudden, thick thud to see this undignified, pitiful ending; and she turned and patted the gallant old car as though she were patting a well-beloved horse, as though she would say: 'Yes, I know how it feels—never mind, we'll go down together.'

2

Miss Ogilvy sat in the railway carriage on her way from Dover to London. The soft English landscape sped smoothly past: small homesteads, small churches, small pastures, small lanes with small hedges; all small like England itself, all small like Miss Ogilvy's future. And sitting there still arrayed in her tunic, with her forage-cap resting on her knees, she was conscious of a sense of complete frustration; thinking less of those glorious years at the Front and of all that had gone to the making of her, than of all that had gone to the marring of her from the days of her earliest childhood.

She saw herself as a queer little girl, aggressive and awkward because of her shyness; a queer little girl who loathed sisters and dolls, preferring the stable-boys as companions, preferring to play with footballs and tops, and occasional catapults. She saw herself climbing the tallest beech trees, arrayed in old breeches illicitly come by. She remembered insisting with tears and some temper that her real name was William and not Wilhelmina. All these childish pretences and illusions she remembered, and the bitterness that came after. For Miss Ogilvy had found as her life went on that in this world it is better to be one with the herd, that the world has no wish to understand those who cannot conform to its stereotyped pattern. True enough in her youth she had gloried in her strength, lifting weights, swinging clubs and developing muscles, but presently this had grown irksome to her; it had seemed to lead nowhere, she being a woman, and then as her mother had often protested: muscles looked so appalling in evening dress—a young girl ought not to have muscles.

Miss Ogilvy's relation to the opposite sex was unusual and at that time added much to her worries, for no less than three men had wished to propose, to the genuine amazement of the world and her mother. Miss Ogilvy's instinct made her like and trust men for whom she had a pronounced fellow-feeling; she would always have chosen them as her friends and companions in preference to girls or women; she would dearly have loved to share in their sports, their business, their ideals and their wide-flung interests. But men had not wanted her, except the three who had found in her strangeness a definite attraction, and those would-be suitors she had actually feared, regarding them with aversion. Towards young girls and women she was shy and respectful, apologetic and sometimes admiring. But their fads and their foibles, none of which she could share, while amusing her very often in secret, set her outside the sphere of their intimate lives, so that in the end she must blaze a lone trail through the difficulties of her nature.

'I can't understand you,' her mother had said, 'you're a very odd creature—now when I was your age ...'

And her daughter had nodded, feeling sympathetic. There were two younger girls who also gave trouble, though in their case the trouble was fighting for husbands who were scarce enough even in those days. It was finally decided, at Miss Ogilvy's request, to allow her to leave the field clear for her sisters. She would remain in the country with her father when the others went up for the Season.

Followed long, uneventful years spent in sport, while Sarah and Fanny toiled, sweated and gambled in the matrimonial market. Neither ever succeeded in netting a husband, and when the Squire died leaving very little money, Miss Ogilvy found to her great surprise that they looked upon her as a brother. They had so often jibed at her in the past, that at first she could scarcely believe her senses, but before very long it became all too real: she it was who must straighten out endless muddles, who must make the dreary arrangements for the move, who must find a cheap but genteel house in London and, once there, who must cope with the family accounts which she only, it seemed, could balance.

It would be: 'You might see to that, Wilhelmina; you write, you've got such a good head for business.' Or: 'I wish you'd go down and explain to that man that we really can't pay his account till next quarter.' Or: 'This money for the grocer is five shillings short. Do run over my sum, Wilhelmina.'

Her mother, grown feeble, discovered in this daughter a staff upon which she could lean with safety. Miss Ogilvy genuinely loved her mother, and was therefore quite prepared to be leaned on; but when Sarah and Fanny began to lean too with the full weight of endless neurotic symptoms incubated in resentful virginity, Miss Ogilvy found herself staggering a little. For Sarah and Fanny were grown hard to bear, with their mania for telling their symptoms to doctors, with their unstable nerves and their acrid tongues and the secret dislike they now felt for their mother. Indeed, when old Mrs. Ogilvy died, she was unmourned except by her eldest daughter who actually felt a void in her life—the unforeseen void that the ailing and weak will not infrequently leave behind them.

At about this time an aunt also died, bequeathing her fortune to her niece Wilhelmina who, however, was too weary to gird up her loins and set forth in search of exciting adventure—all she did was to move her protesting sisters to a little estate she had purchased in Surrey. This experiment was only a partial success, for Miss Ogilvy failed to make friends of her neighbours; thus at fifty-five she had grown rather dour, as is often the way with shy, lonely people.

When the war came she had just begun settling down—people do settle down in their fifty-sixth year—she was feeling quite glad that her hair was grey, that the garden took up so much of her time, that, in fact, the beat of her blood was slowing. But all this was changed when war was declared; on that day Miss Ogilvy's pulses throbbed wildly.

'My God! If only I were a man!' she burst out, as she glared at Sarah and Fanny, 'if only I had been born a man!' Something in her was feeling deeply defrauded.

Sarah and Fanny were soon knitting socks and mittens and mufflers and Jaeger trench-helmets. Other ladies were busily working at depots, making swabs at the Squire's, or splints at the Parson's; but Miss Ogilvy scowled and did none of these things— she was not at all like other ladies.

For nearly twelve months she worried officials with a view to getting a job out in France—not in their way but in hers, and that was the trouble. She wished to go up to the front-line trenches, she wished to be actually under fire, she informed the harassed officials.

To all her enquiries she received the same answer: 'We regret that we cannot accept your offer.' But once thoroughly roused she was hard to subdue, for her shyness had left her as though by magic.

Sarah and Fanny shrugged angular shoulders: 'There's plenty of work here at home,' they remarked, 'though of course it's not quite so melodramatic!'

'Oh ... ?' queried their sister on a rising note of impatience—and she promptly cut off her hair: 'That'll jar them!' she thought with satisfaction.

Then she went up to London, formed her admirable unit and finally got it accepted by the French, despite renewed opposition.

In London she had found herself quite at her ease, for many another of her kind was in London doing excellent work for the nation. It was really surprising how many cropped heads had suddenly appeared as it were out of space; how many Miss Ogilvies, losing their shyness, had come forward asserting their right to serve, asserting their claim to attention.

There followed those turbulent years at the front, full of courage and hardship and high endeavour; and during those years Miss Ogilvy forgot the bad joke that Nature seemed to have played her. She was given the rank of a French lieutenant and she lived in a kind of blissful illusion; appalling reality lay on all sides and yet she managed to live in illusion. She was competent, fearless, devoted and untiring. What then? Could any man hope to do better? She was nearly fifty-eight, yet she walked with a stride, and at times she even swaggered a little.

Poor Miss Ogilvy sitting so glumly in the train with her manly trench-boots and her forage-cap! Poor all the Miss Ogilvies back from the war with their tunics, their trench-boots, and their childish illusions! Wars come and wars go but the world does not change: it will always forget an indebtedness which it thinks it expedient not to remember.

3

When Miss Ogilvy returned to her home in Surrey it was only to find that her sisters were ailing from the usual imaginary causes, and this to a woman who had seen the real thing was intolerable, so that she looked with distaste at Sarah and then at Fanny. Fanny was certainly not prepossessing, she was suffering from a spurious attack of hay fever.

'Stop sneezing!' commanded Miss Ogilvy, in the voice that had so much impressed the Unit. But as Fanny was not in the least impressed, she naturally went on sneezing.

Miss Ogilvy's desk was piled mountain-high with endless tiresome letters and papers: circulars, bills, months-old correspondence, the gardener's accounts, an agent's report on some fields that required land-draining. She seated herself before this collection; then she sighed, it all seemed so absurdly trivial.

'Will you let your hair grow again?' Fanny enquired ... she and Sarah had followed her into the study. 'I'm certain the Vicar would be glad if you did.'

'Oh?' murmured Miss Ogilvy, rather too blandly.

'Wilhelmina!'

'Yes?'

'You will do it, won't you?'

'Do what?'

'Let your hair grow; we all wish you would.'

'Why should I?'

'Oh, well, it will look less odd, especially now that the war is over—in a small place like this people notice such things.'

'I entirely agree with Fanny,' announced Sarah.

Sarah had become very self-assertive, no doubt through having mismanaged the estate during the years of her sister's absence. They had quite a heated dispute one morning over the south herbaceous border.

'Whose garden is this?' Miss Ogilvy asked sharply. 'I insist on auricula-eyed sweet-williams! I even took the trouble to write from France, but it seems that my letter has been ignored.'

'Don't shout,' rebuked Sarah, 'you're not in France now!'

Miss Ogilvy could gladly have boxed her ears: 'I only wish to God I were,' she muttered.

Another dispute followed close on its heels, and this time it happened to be over the dinner. Sarah and Fanny were living on weeds—at least that was the way Miss Ogilvy put it.

'We've become vegetarians,' Sarah said grandly.

'You've become two damn tiresome cranks!' snapped their sister.

Now it never had been Miss Ogilvy's way to indulge in acid recriminations, but somehow, these days, she forgot to say: 'Oh?' quite so often as expediency demanded. It may have been Fanny's perpetual sneezing that had got on her nerves; or it may have been Sarah, or the gardener, or the Vicar, or even the canary; though it really did not matter very much what it was just so long as she found a convenient peg upon which to hang her growing irritation.

'This won't do at all,' Miss Ogilvy thought sternly, 'life's not worth so much fuss, I must pull myself together.' But it seemed this was easier said than done; not a day passed without her losing her temper and that over some trifle: 'No, this won't do at all—it just mustn't be,' she thought sternly.

Everyone pitied Sarah and Fanny: 'Such a dreadful, violent old thing,' said the neighbours.

But Sarah and Fanny had their revenge: 'Poor darling, it's shell-shock, you know,' they murmured.

Thus Miss Ogilvy's prowess was whittled away until she herself was beginning to doubt it. Had she ever been that courageous person who had faced death in France with such perfect composure? Had she ever stood tranquilly under fire, without turning a hair, while she issued her orders? Had she ever been treated with marked respect? She herself was beginning to doubt it.

Sometimes she would see an old member of the Unit, a girl who, more faithful to her than the others, would take the trouble to run down to Surrey. These visits, however, were seldom enlivening.

'Oh, well ... here we are ...' Miss Ogilvy would mutter.

But one day the girl smiled and shook her blond head: 'I'm not—I'm going to be married.'

Strange thoughts had come to Miss Ogilvy, unbidden, thoughts that had stayed for many an hour after the girl's departure. Alone in her study she had suddenly shivered, feeling a sense of complete desolation. With cold hands she had lighted a cigarette.

'I must be ill or something,' she had mused, as she stared at her trembling fingers.

After this she would sometimes cry out in her sleep, living over in dreams God knows what emotions; returning, maybe, to the battlefields of France. Her hair turned snow-white; it was not unbecoming yet she fretted about it.

'I'm growing very old,' she would sigh as she brushed her thick mop before the glass; and then she would peer at her wrinkles.

For now that it had happened she hated being old; it no longer appeared such an easy solution of those difficulties that had always beset her. And this she resented most bitterly, so that she became the prey of self-pity, and of other undesirable states in which the body will torment the mind, and the mind, in its turn, the body. Then Miss Ogilvy straightened her ageing back, in spite of the fact that of late it had ached with muscular rheumatism, and she faced herself squarely and came to a resolve.

'I'm off!' she announced abruptly one day; and that evening she packed her kit-bag.

4

Near the south coast of Devon there exists a small island that is still very little known to the world, but which, nevertheless, can boast an hotel; the only building upon it. Miss Ogilvy had chosen this place quite at random, it was marked on her map by scarcely more than a dot, but somehow she had liked the look of that dot and had set forth alone to explore it.

She found herself standing on the mainland one morning looking at a vague blur of green through the mist, a vague blur of green that rose out of the Channel like a tidal wave suddenly suspended. Miss Ogilvy was filled with a sense of adventure; she had not felt like this since the ending of the war.

'I was right to come here, very right indeed. I'm going to shake off all my troubles,' she decided.

A fisherman's boat was parting the mist, and before it was properly beached, in she bundled.

'I hope they're expecting me?' she said gaily.

'They du be expecting you,' the man answered.

The sea, which is generally rough off that coast, was indulging itself in an oily ground-swell; the broad, glossy swells struck the side of the boat, then broke and sprayed over Miss Ogilvy's ankles.

The fisherman grinned: 'Feeling all right?' he queried. 'It du be tiresome most times about these parts.' But the mist had suddenly drifted away and Miss Ogilvy was staring wide-eyed at the island.

She saw a long shoal of jagged black rocks, and between them the curve of a small sloping beach, and above that the lift of the island itself, and above that again, blue heaven. Near the beach stood the little two-storied hotel which was thatched, and built entirely of timber; for the rest she could make out no signs of life apart from a host of white seagulls.

Then Miss Ogilvy said a curious thing. She said: 'On the south-west side of that place there was once a cave—a very large cave. I remember that it was some way from the sea.'

'There du be a cave still,' the fisherman told her, 'but it's just above highwater level.'

'A-ah,' murmured Miss Ogilvy thoughtfully, as though to herself; then she looked embarrassed.

The little hotel proved both comfortable and clean, the hostess both pleasant and comely. Miss Ogilvy started unpacking her bag, changed her mind and went for a stroll round the island. The island was covered with turf and thistles and traversed by narrow green paths thick with daisies. It had four rock-bound coves of which the south-western was by far the most difficult of access. For just here the island descended abruptly as though it were hurtling down to the water; and just here the shale was most treacherous and the tide-swept rocks most aggressively pointed. Here it was that the seagulls, grown fearless of man by reason of his absurd limitations, built their nests on the ledges and reared countless young who multiplied, in their turn, every season. Yes, and here it was that Miss Ogilvy, greatly marvelling, stood and stared across at a cave; much too near the crumbling edge for her safety, but by now completely indifferent to caution.

'I remember ... I remember ...' she kept repeating. Then: 'That's all very well, but what do I remember?'

She was conscious of somehow remembering all wrong, of her memory being distorted and coloured—perhaps by the endless things she had seen since her eyes had last rested upon that cave. This worried her sorely, far more than the fact that she should be remembering the cave at all, she who had never set foot on the island before that actual morning. Indeed, except for the sense of wrongness when she struggled to piece her memories together, she was steeped in a very profound contentment which surged over her spirit, wave upon wave.

'It's extremely odd,' pondered Miss Ogilvy. Then she laughed, so pleased did she feel with its oddness.

5

That night after supper she talked to her hostess who was only too glad, it seemed, to be questioned. She owned the whole island and was proud of the fact, as she very well might be, decided her boarder. Some curious things had been found on the island, according to comely Mrs. Nanceskivel: bronze arrow-heads, pieces of ancient stone celts; and once they had dug up a man's skull and thigh-bone—this had happened while they were sinking a well. Would Miss Ogilvy care to have a look at the bones? They were kept in a cupboard in the scullery.

Miss Ogilvy nodded.

'Then I'll fetch him this moment,' said Mrs. Nanceskivel, briskly.

In less than two minutes she was back with the box that

contained those poor remnants of a man, and Miss Ogilvy, who had risen from her chair, was gazing down at those remnants. As she did so her mouth was sternly compressed, but her face and her neck flushed darkly.

Mrs. Nanceskivel was pointing to the skull: 'Look, miss, he was killed,' she remarked rather proudly, 'and they tell me that the axe that killed him was bronze. He's thousands and thousands of years old, they tell me. Our local doctor knows a lot about such things and he wants me to send these bones to an expert; they ought to belong to the Nation, he says. But I know what would happen, they'd come digging up my island, and I won't have people digging up my island, I've got enough worry with the rabbits as it is.' But Miss Ogilvy could no longer hear the words for the pounding of the blood in her temples.

She was filled with a sudden, inexplicable fury against the innocent Mrs. Nanceskivel: 'You ... *you* ...' she began, then checked herself, fearful of what she might say to the woman.

For her sense of outrage was overwhelming as she stared at those bones that were kept in the scullery; moreover, she knew how such men had been buried, which made the outrage seem all the more shameful. They had buried such men in deep, well-dug pits surmounted by four stout stones at their corners—four stout stones there had been and a covering stone. And all this Miss Ogilvy knew as by instinct, having no concrete knowledge on which to draw. But she knew it right down in the depths of her soul, and she hated Mrs. Nanceskivel.

And now she was swept by another emotion that was even more strange and more devastating: such a grief as she had not conceived could exist; a terrible unassuageable grief, without hope, without respite, without palliation, so that with something akin to despair she touched the long gash in the skull. Then her eyes, that had never wept since her childhood, filled slowly with large, hot, difficult tears. She must blink very hard, then close her eyelids, turn away from the lamp and say rather loudly:

'Thanks, Mrs. Nanceskivel. It's past eleven—I think I'll be going upstairs.'

6

Miss Ogilvy closed the door of her bedroom, after which she stood quite still to consider: 'Is it shell-shock?' she muttered incredulously. 'I wonder, can it be shell-shock?'

She began to pace slowly about the room, smoking a Caporal. As usual her hands were deep in her pockets; she could feel small, familiar things in those pockets and she gripped them, glad of their presence. Then all of a sudden she was terribly tired, so tired that she flung herself down on the bed, unable to stand any longer.

She thought that she lay there struggling to reason, that her eyes were closed in the painful effort, and that as she closed them she continued to puff the inevitable cigarette. At least that was what she thought at one moment—the next, she was out in a sunset evening, and a large red sun was sinking slowly to the rim of a distant sea.

Miss Ogilvy knew that she was herself, that is to say she was conscious of her being, and yet she was not Miss Ogilvy at all, nor had she a memory of her. All that she now saw was very familiar, all that she now did was what she should do, and all that she now was seemed perfectly natural. Indeed, she did not think of these things; there seemed no reason for thinking about them.

She was walking with bare feet on turf that felt springy and was greatly enjoying the sensation; she had always enjoyed it, ever since as an infant she had learned to crawl on this turf. On either hand stretched rolling green uplands, while at her back she knew that there were forests; but in front, far away, lay the gleam of the sea towards which the big sun was sinking. The air was cool and intensely still, with never so much as a ripple or bird-song. It was wonderfully pure—one might almost say young—but Miss Ogilvy thought of it merely as air. Having always breathed it she took it for granted, as she took the soft turf and the uplands.

She pictured herself as immensely tall; she was feeling immensely tall at that moment. As a matter of fact she was five feet eight which, however, was quite a considerable height when compared to that of her fellow-tribesmen. She was wearing a single garment of pelts which came to her knees and left her arms sleeveless. Her arms and her legs, which were closely tattooed with blue zig-zag lines, were extremely hairy. From a leathern thong twisted about her waist there hung a clumsily made stone weapon, a celt, which in spite of its clumsiness was strongly hafted and useful for killing.

Miss Ogilvy wanted to shout aloud from a glorious sense of physical well-being, but instead she picked up a heavy, round stone which she hurled with great force at some distant rocks.

'Good! Strong!' she exclaimed. 'See how far it goes!'

'Yes, strong. There is no one so strong as you. You are surely the strongest man in our tribe,' replied her little companion.

Miss Ogilvy glanced at this little companion and rejoiced that they two were alone together. The girl at her side had a smooth

brownish skin, oblique black eyes and short, sturdy limbs. Miss
Ogilvy marvelled because of her beauty. She also was wearing a
single garment of pelts, new pelts, she had made it that morning.
She had stitched at it diligently for hours with short lengths of gut
and her best bone needle. A strand of black hair hung over her
bosom, and this she was constantly stroking and fondling; then
she lifted the strand and examined her hair.

'Pretty,' she remarked with childish complacence.

'Pretty,' echoed the young man at her side.

'For you,' she told him, 'all of me is for you and none other. For
you this body has ripened.'

He shook back his own coarse hair from his eyes; he had sad
brown eyes like those of a monkey. For the rest he was lean and
steel-strong of loin, broad of chest, and with features not too
uncomely. His prominent cheekbones were set rather high, his
nose was blunt, his jaw somewhat bestial; but his mouth, though
full-lipped, contradicted his jaw, being very gentle and sweet in
expression. And now he smiled, showing big, square, white teeth.

'You ... woman,' he murmured contentedly, and the sound
seemed to come from the depths of his being.

His speech was slow and lacking in words when it came to
expressing a vital emotion, so one word must suffice and this he
now spoke, and the word that he spoke had a number of meanings. It meant: 'Little spring of exceedingly pure water.' It meant:
'Hut of peace for a man after battle.' It meant: 'Ripe red berry
sweet to the taste.' It meant: 'Happy small home of future generations.' All these things he must try to express by a word, and
because of their loving she understood him.

They paused, and lifting her up he kissed her. Then he rubbed
his large shaggy head on her shoulder; and when he released her
she knelt at his feet.

'My master; blood of my body,' she whispered. For with her
it was different, love had taught her love's speech, so that she
might turn her heart into sounds that her primitive tongue could
utter.

After she had pressed her lips to his hands, and her cheek to his
hairy and powerful forearm, she stood up and they gazed at the
setting sun, but with bowed heads, gazing under their lids,
because this was very sacred.

A couple of mating bears padded towards them from a thicket,
and the female rose to her haunches. But the man drew his celt
and menaced the beast, so that she dropped down noiselessly and
fled, and her mate also fled, for here was the power that few dared
to withstand by day or by night, on the uplands or in the forests.

And now from across to the left where a river would presently lose itself in the marshes, came a rhythmical thudding, as a herd of red deer with wide nostrils and starting eyes thundered past, disturbed in their drinking by the bears.

After this the evening returned to its silence, and the spell of its silence descended on the lovers, so that each felt very much alone, yet withal more closely united to the other. But the man became restless under that spell, and he suddenly laughed; then grasping the woman he tossed her above his head and caught her. This he did many times for his own amusement and because he knew that his strength gave her joy. In this manner they played together for a while, he with his strength and she with her weakness. And they cried out, and made many guttural sounds which were meaningless save only to themselves. And the tunic of pelts slipped down from her breasts, and her two little breasts were pear-shaped.

Presently, he grew tired of their playing, and he pointed towards a cluster of huts and earthworks that lay to the eastward. The smoke from these huts rose in thick straight lines, bending neither to right nor left in its rising, and the thought of sweet burning rushes and brushwood touched his consciousness, making him feel sentimental.

'Smoke,' he said.

And she answered: 'Blue smoke.'

He nodded: 'Yes, blue smoke—home.'

Then she said: 'I have ground much corn since the full moon. My stones are too smooth. You make me new stones.'

'All you have need of, I make,' he told her.

She stole closer to him, taking his hand: 'My father is still a black cloud full of thunder. He thinks that you wish to be head of our tribe in his place, because he is now very old. He must not hear of these meetings of ours, if he did I think he would beat me!'

So he asked her: 'Are you unhappy, small berry?'

But at this she smiled: 'What is being unhappy? I do not know what that means any more.'

'I do not either,' he answered.

Then as though some invisible force had drawn him, his body swung round and he stared at the forests where they lay and darkened, fold upon fold; and his eyes dilated with wonder and terror, and he moved his head quickly from side to side as a wild thing will do that is held between bars and whose mind is pitifully bewildered.

'Water!' he cried hoarsely, 'great water—look, look! Over there.

This land is surrounded by water!'

'What water?' she questioned.

He answered: 'The sea.' And he covered his face with his hands.

'Not so,' she consoled, 'big forests, good hunting. Big forests in which you hunt boar and aurochs. No sea over there but only the trees.'

He took his trembling hands from his face: 'You are right ... only trees,' he said dully.

But now his face had grown heavy and brooding and he started to speak of a thing that oppressed him: 'The Roundheaded-ones, they are devils,' he growled, while his bushy black brows met over his eyes, and when this happened it changed his expression which became a little sub-human.

'No matter,' she protested, for she saw that he forgot her and she wished him to think and talk only of love. 'No matter. My father laughs at your fears. Are we not friends with the Round-headed-ones? We are friends, so why should we fear them?'

'Our forts, very old, very weak,' he went on, 'and the Round-headed-ones have terrible weapons. Their weapons are not made of good stone like ours, but of some dark, devilish substance.'

'What of that?' she said lightly. 'They would fight on our side, so why need we trouble about their weapons?'

But he looked away, not appearing to hear her. 'We must barter all, all for their celts and arrows and spears, and then we must learn their secret. They lust after our women, they lust after our lands. We must barter all, all for their sly brown celts.'

'Me ... bartered?' she queried, very sure of his answer otherwise she had not dared to say this.

'The Roundheaded-ones may destroy my tribe and yet I will not part with you,' he told her. Then he spoke very gravely: 'But I think they desire to slay us, and me they will try to slay first because they well know how much I mistrust them—they have seen my eyes fixed many times on their camps.'

She cried: 'I will bite out the throats of these people if they so much as scratch your skin!'

And at this his mood changed and he roared with amusement: 'You ... woman!' he roared. 'Little foolish white teeth. Your teeth were made for nibbling wild cherries, not for tearing the throats of the Roundheaded-ones!'

'Thoughts of war always make me afraid,' she whimpered, still wishing him to talk about love.

He turned his sorrowful eyes upon her, the eyes that were sad even when he was merry, and although his mind was often obtuse, yet he clearly perceived how it was with her then. And his blood caught fire from the flame in her blood, so that he strained her against his body.

'You ... mine ...' he stammered.

'Love,' she said, trembling, 'this is love.'

And he answered: 'Love.'

Then their faces grew melancholy for a moment, because dimly, very dimly in their dawning souls, they were conscious of a longing for something more vast than this earthly passion could compass.

Presently, he lifted her like a child and carried her quickly southward and westward till they came to a place where a gentle descent led down to a marshy valley. Far away, at the line where the marshes ended, they discerned the misty line of the sea; but the sea and the marshes were become as one substance, merging, blending, folding together; and since they were lovers they also would be one, even as the sea and the marshes.

And now they had reached the mouth of a cave that was set in the quiet hillside. There was bright green verdure beside the cave, and a number of small, pink, thick-stemmed flowers that when they were crushed smelt of spices. And within the cave there was bracken newly gathered and heaped together for a bed; while beyond, from some rocks, came a low liquid sound as a spring dripped out through a crevice. Abruptly, he set the girl on her feet, and she knew that the days of her innocence were over. And she thought of the anxious virgin soil that was rent and sown to bring forth fruit in season, and she gave a quick little gasp of fear:

'No ... no ...' she gasped. For, divining his need, she was weak with the longing to be possessed, yet the terror of love lay heavy upon her. 'No ... no ...' she gasped.

But he caught her wrist and she felt the great strength of his rough, gnarled fingers, the great strength of the urge that leapt in his loins, and again she must give that quick gasp of fear, the while she clung close to him lest he should spare her.

The twilight was engulfed and possessed by darkness, which in turn was transfigured by the moonrise, which in turn was fulfilled and consumed by dawn. A mighty eagle soared up from his eyrie, cleaving the air with his masterful wings, and beneath him from the rushes that harboured their nests, rose other great birds, crying loudly. Then the heavy-horned elks appeared on the uplands, bending their burdened heads to the sod; while beyond in the forests the fierce wild aurochs stamped as they bellowed their love songs.

But within the dim cave the lord of these creatures had put by his weapon and his instinct for slaying. And he lay there defenceless with tenderness, thinking no longer of death but of life as he murmured the word that had so many meanings. That meant: 'Little spring of exceedingly pure water.' That meant: 'Hut of peace for a man after battle.' That meant: 'Ripe red berry sweet to the taste.' That meant: 'Happy small home of future generations.'

7

They found Miss Ogilvy the next morning; the fisherman saw her and climbed to the ledge. She was sitting at the mouth of the cave. She was dead, with her hands thrust deep into her pockets.

GWENDOLYN BENNETT

▼▼

Wedding Day

HIS NAME was Paul Watson and as he shambled down rue Pigalle he might have been any other Negro of enormous height and size. But as I have said, his name was Paul Watson. Passing him on the street, you might not have known or cared who he was, but any one of the residents about the great Montmartre district of Paris could have told you who he was as well as many interesting bits of his personal history.

He had come to Paris in the days before colored jazz bands were the style. Back home he had been a prize fighter. In the days when Joe Gans was in his glory Paul was following the ring, too. He didn't have that fine way about him that Gans had and for that reason luck seemed to go against him. When he was in the ring he was like a mad bull, especially if his opponent was a white man. In those days there wasn't any sympathy or nicety about the ring and so pretty soon all the ringmasters got down on Paul and he found it pretty hard to get a bout with anyone. Then it was that he worked his way across the Atlantic Ocean on a big liner—in the days before colored jazz bands were the style in Paris.

Things flowed along smoothly for the first few years with Paul's working here and there in the unfrequented places of Paris. On the side he used to give boxing lessons to aspiring youths or gymnastic young women. At that time he was working so steadily that he had little chance to find out what was going on around Paris. Pretty soon, however, he grew to be known among the trainers and managers began to fix up bouts for him. After one or two successful bouts a little fame began to come into being for him. So it was that after one of the prize-fights, a colored fellow came to his dressing room to congratulate him on his success as well as invite him to go to Montmartre to meet 'the boys.'

Paul had a way about him and seemed to get on with the colored fellows who lived in Montmartre and when the first

Negro jazz band played in a tiny Parisian cafe Paul was among them playing the banjo. Those first years were without event so far as Paul was concerned. The members of that first band often say now that they wonder how it was that nothing happened during those first seven years, for it was generally known how great was Paul's hatred for American white people. I suppose the tranquility in the light of what happened afterwards was due to the fact that the cafe in which they worked was one in which mostly French people drank and danced and then too, that was before there were so many Americans visiting Paris. However, everyone had heard Paul speak of his intense hatred of American white folks. It only took two Benedictines to make him start talking about what he would do to the first 'Yank' that called him 'nigger.' But the seven years came to an end and Paul Watson went to work in a larger cafe with a larger band, patronized almost solely by Americans.

I've heard almost every Negro in Montmartre tell about the night that a drunken Kentuckian came into the cafe where Paul was playing and said:

'Look heah, Bruther, what you all doin' ovah heah?'

'None ya bizness. And looka here, I ain't your brother, see?'

'Jack, do you heah that nigger talkin' lak that tah me?'

As he said this, he turned to speak to his companion. I have often wished that I had been there to have seen the thing happen myself. Every tale I have heard about it was different and yet there was something of truth in each of them. Perhaps the nearest one can come to the truth is by saying that Paul beat up about four full-sized white men that night besides doing a great deal of damage to the furniture about the cafe. I couldn't tell you just what did happen. Some of the fellows say that Paul seized the nearest table and mowed down men right and left, others say he took a bottle, then again the story runs that a chair was the instrument of his fury. At any rate, that started Paul Watson on his siege against the American white person who brings his native prejudices into the life of Paris.

It is a verity that Paul was the 'black terror.' The last syllable of the word, nigger, never passed the lips of a white man without the quick reflex action of Paul's arm and fist to the speaker's jaw. He paid for more glassware and cafe furnishings in the course of the next few years than is easily imaginable. And yet, there was something likeable about Paul. Perhaps that's the reason that he stood in so well with the policemen of the neighborhood. Always some divine power seemed to intervene in his behalf and he was excused after the payment of a small fine with advice about his future conduct. Finally, there came the night when in a frenzy he shot the two American sailors.

They had not died from the wounds he had given them hence his sentence had not been one of death but rather a long term of imprisonment. It was a pitiable sight to see Paul sitting in the corner of his cell with his great body hunched almost double. He seldom talked and when he did his words were interspersed with oaths about the lowness of 'crackers.' Then the World War came.

It seems strange that anything so horrible as that wholesale slaughter could bring about any good and yet there was something of a smoothing quality about even its baseness. There has never been such equality before or since such as that which the World War brought. Rich men fought by the side of paupers; poets swapped yarns with dry-goods salesmen, while Jews and Christians ate corned beef out of the same tin. Along with the general leveling influence came France's pardon of her prisoners in order that they might enter the army. Paul Watson became free and a French soldier. Because he was strong and had innate daring in his heart he was placed in the aerial squad and cited many times for bravery. The close of the war gave him his place in French society as a hero. With only a memory of the war and an ugly scar on his left cheek he took up his old life.

His firm resolutions about American white people still remained intact and many chance encounters that followed the war are told from lip to lip proving that the war and his previous imprisonment had changed him little. He was the same Paul Watson to Montmartre as he shambled up rue Pigalle.

Rue Pigalle in the early evening has a sombre beauty—gray as are most Paris streets and other-worldish. To those who know the district it is the Harlem of Paris and rue Pigalle is its dusky Seventh Avenue. Most of the colored musicians that furnish Parisians and their visitors with entertainment live somewhere in the neighborhood of rue Pigalle. Some time during every day each of these musicians makes a point of passing through rue Pigalle. Little wonder that almost any day will find Paul Watson going his shuffling way up the same street.

He reached the corner of rue de la Bruyere and with sure instinct his feet stopped. Without half thinking he turned into 'the Pit.' Its full name is The Flea Pit. If you should ask one of the musicians why it was so called, he would answer you to the effect that it was called 'the pit' because all the 'fleas' hang out there. If you did not get the full import of this explanation, he would go further and say that there were always 'spades' in the pit and they were as thick as fleas. Unless you could understand this latter attempt at clarity you could not fully grasp what the Flea-Pit means to the Negro musicians in Montmartre. It is a tiny cafe of the genus that is called *bistro* in France. Here the fiddle players, saxophone blowers, drum-beaters and ivory ticklers gather at four in the afternoon for a porto or a game of billiards. Here the cabaret entertainers and supper musicians meet at one o'clock at night or thereafter for a whiskey and soda, or more billiards. Occasional sandwiches and a 'quiet game' also play their parts in the popularity of the place. After a season or two it becomes a settled fact just what time you may catch so-and-so at the famous 'Pit.'

The musicians were very fond of Paul and took particular delight in teasing him. He was one of the chosen few that all of the musicians conceded as being 'regular.' It was the pet joke of the habitues of the cafe that Paul never bothered with girls. They always said that he could beat up ten men but was scared to death of one woman.

'Say fellow, when ya goin' a get hooked up?'

'Can't say, Bo. Ain't so much on skirts.'

'Man alive, ya don't know what you're missin'—somebody little and cute telling ya sweet things in your ear. Paris is full of women folks.'

'I ain't much on 'em all the same. Then too, they're all white.'

'What's it to ya? This ain't America.'

'Can't help that. Get this—I'm collud, see? I ain't got nothing for no white meat to do. If a woman eva called me nigger I'd have to kill her, that's all!'

'You for it, son. I can't give you a thing on this Mr. Jefferson Lawd way of lookin' at women.'

'Oh, tain't that. I guess they're all right for those that wants 'em. Not me!'

'Oh you ain't so forty. You'll fall like all the other spades I've ever seen. Your kind falls hardest.'

And so Paul went his way—alone. He smoked and drank with the fellows and sat for hours in the Montmartre cafes and never knew the companionship of a woman. Then one night after his work he was walking along the street in his queer shuffling way when a woman stepped up to his side.

'Voulez vous.'

'Naw, gowan away from here.'

'Oh, you speak English, don't you?'

'You an 'merican woman?'

'Used to be 'fore I went on the stage and got stranded over here.'

'Well, get away from here. I don't like your kind!'

'Aw, Buddy, don't say that. I ain't prejudiced like some fool women.'

'You don't know who I am, do you? I'm Paul Watson and I hate American white folks, see?'

He pushed her aside and went on walking alone. He hadn't gone far when she caught up to him and said with sobs in her voice:—

'Oh, Lordy, please don't hate me 'cause I was born white and an American. I ain't got a sou to my name and all the men pass me by cause I ain't spruced up. Now you come along and won't look at me cause I'm white.'

Paul strode along with her clinging to his arm. He tried to shake her off several times but there was no use. She clung all the more desperately to him. He looked down at her frail body shaken with sobs, and something caught at his heart. Before he knew what he was doing he had said:—

'Naw, I ain't that mean. I'll get you some grub. Quit your cryin'. Don't like seein' women folks cry.'

It was the talk of Montmartre. Paul Watson takes a woman to Gavarnni's every night for dinner. He comes to the Flea Pit less frequently, thus giving the other musicians plenty of opportunity to discuss him.

'How times do change. Paul, the woman-hater, has a Jane now.'

'You ain't said nothing, fella. That ain't all. She's white and an 'merican, too.'

'That's the way with these spades. They beat up all the white men they can lay their hands on but as soon as a gang of golden hair with blue eyes rubs up close to them they forget all they ever said about hatin' white folks.'

'Guess he thinks that skirt's gone on him. Dumb fool!'

'Don' be no chineeman. That old gag don' fit for Paul. He cain't understand it no more'n we can. Says he jess can't help himself, everytime she looks up into his eyes and asks him does he love her. They sure are happy together. Paul's goin' to marry her, too. At first she kept saying that she didn't want to get married cause she wasn't the marrying kind and all that talk. Paul jus' laid down the law to her and told her he never would live with no woman without being married to her. Then she began to tell him all about her past life. He told her he didn't care nothing about what she used to be jus' so long as they loved each other now. Guess they'll make it.'

'Yeah, Paul told me the same tale last night. He's sure gone on her all right.'

'They're gettin' tied up next Sunday. So glad it's not me. Don't trust these American dames. Me for the Frenchies.'

'She ain't so worse for looks, Bud. Now that he's been furnishing the green for the rags.'

'Yeah, but I don't see no reason for the wedding bells. She was right—she ain't the marrying kind.'

... and so Montmartre talked. In every cafe where the Negro musicians congregated Paul Watson was the topic for conversation. He had suddenly fallen from his place as bronze God to almost less than the dust.

The morning sun made queer patterns on Paul's sleeping face. He grimaced several times in his slumber, then finally half-opened his eyes. After a succession of dream-laden blinks he gave a great yawn, and rubbing his eyes, looked at the open window through which the sun shone brightly. His first conscious thought was that this was the bride's day and that bright sunshine prophesied happiness for the bride throughout her married life. His first impulse was to settle back into the covers and think drowsily about Mary and the queer twists life brings about, as is the wont of most bridegrooms on their last morning of bachelorhood. He put this impulse aside in favor of dressing quickly and rushing downstairs to telephone to Mary to say 'happy wedding day' to her.

One huge foot slipped into a worn bedroom slipper and then the other dragged painfully out of the warm bed were the courageous beginnings of his bridal toilet. With a look of triumph he put on his new gray suit that he had ordered from an English tailor. He carefully pulled a taffeta tie into place beneath his chin, noting as he looked at his face in the mirror that the scar he had received in the army was very ugly—funny, marrying an ugly man like him.

French telephones are such human faults. After trying for about fifteen minutes to get Central 32.01 he decided that he might as well walk around to Mary's hotel to give his greeting as to stand there in the lobby of his own, wasting his time. He debated this in his mind a great deal. They were to be married at four o'clock. It was eleven now and it did seem a shame not to let her have a minute or two by herself. As he went walking down the street towards her hotel he laughed to think of how one always cogitates over doing something and finally does the thing he wanted to in the beginning anyway.

Mud on his nice gray suit that the English tailor had made for him. Damn—gray suit—what did he have a gray suit on for, anyway. Folks with black faces shouldn't wear gray suits. Gawd, but it was funny that time when he beat up that cracker at the Periquet. Fool couldn't shut his mouth he was so surprised. Crackers—damn 'em—he was one nigger that wasn't 'fraid of 'em. Wouldn't he have a hell of a time if he went back to America where black was black. Wasn't white nowhere, black wasn't. What was that thought he was trying to get ahold of—bumping around in his head—something he started to think about but couldn't remember it somehow.

The shrill whistle that is typical of the French subway pierced its way into his thoughts. Subway—why was he in the subway—he didn't want to go any place. He heard doors slamming and saw the blue uniforms of the conductors swinging on to the cars as the trains began to pull out of the station. With one or two strides he reached the last coach as it began to move up the platform. A bit out of breath he stood inside the train and looking down at what he had in his hand he saw that it was a tiny pink ticket. A first class ticket in a second class coach. The idea set him to laughing. Everyone in the car turned and eyed him, but that did not bother him. Wonder what stop he'd get off—funny how these French said descend when they meant get off—funny he couldn't pick up French—been here so long. First class ticket in a second class coach!—that was one on him. Wedding day today, and that damn letter from Mary. How'd she say it now, 'just couldn't go through with it,' white women just don't marry colored men, and she was a street woman, too. Why couldn't she have told him flat that she was just getting back on her feet at his expense. Funny that first class ticket he bought, wish he could see Mary—him a-going there to wish her 'happy wedding day,' too. Wonder what that French woman was looking at him so hard for? Guess it was the mud.

D. H. LAWRENCE

▼▼

Monkey Nuts

AT FIRST JOE THOUGHT the job O.K. He was loading hay on the trucks, along with Albert, the corporal. The two men were pleasantly billetted in a cottage not far from the station: they were their own masters, for Joe never thought of Albert as a master. And the little sidings of the tiny village station was as pleasant a place as you could wish for. On one side, beyond the line, stretched the woods: on the other, the near side, across a green smooth field red houses were dotted among flowering apple trees. The weather being sunny, work being easy, Albert, a real good pal, what life could be better! After Flanders, it was heaven itself.

Albert, the corporal, was a clean-shaven, shrewd-looking fellow of about forty. He seemed to think his one aim in life was to be full of fun and nonsense. In repose, his face looked a little withered, old. He was a very good pal to Joe, steady, decent and grave under all his 'mischief'; for his mischief was only his laborious way of skirting his own ennui.

Joe was much younger than Albert—only twenty-three. He was a tallish, quiet youth, pleasant looking. He was of a slightly better class than his corporal, more personable. Careful about his appearance, he shaved every day. 'I haven't got much of a face,' said Albert. 'If I was to shave every day like you, Joe, I should have none.'

There was plenty of life in the little goods-yard: three porter youths, a continual come and go of farm wagons bringing hay, wagons with timber from the woods, coal carts loading at the trucks. The black coal seemed to make the place sleepier, hotter. Round the big white gate the station-master's children played and his white chickens walked, whilst the station-master himself, a young man getting too fat, helped his wife to peg out the washing on the clothes line in the meadow.

The great boat-shaped wagons came up from Playcross with

the hay. At first the farm-men waggoned it. On the third day one of the land-girls appeared with the first load, drawing to a standstill easily at the head of her two great horses. She was a buxom girl, young, in linen overalls and gaiters. Her face was ruddy, she had large blue eyes.

'Now that's the waggoner for us, boys,' said the corporal loudly.

'Whoa!' she said to her horses; and then to the corporal: 'Which boys do you mean?'

'We are the pick of the bunch. That's Joe, my pal. Don't you let on that my name's Albert,' said the corporal to his private. 'I'm the corporal.'

'And I'm Miss Stokes,' said the land-girl coolly, 'if that's all the boys you are.'

'You know you couldn't want more, Miss Stokes,' said Albert politely. Joe, who was bare-headed, whose grey flannel sleeves were rolled up to the elbow, and whose shirt was open at the breast, looked modestly aside as if he had no part in the affair.

'Are you on this job regular, then?' said the corporal to Miss Stokes.

'I don't know for sure,' she said, pushing a piece of hair under her hat, and attending to her splendid horses.

'Oh, make it a certainty,' said Albert.

She did not reply. She turned and looked over the two men coolly. She was pretty, moderately blonde, with crisp hair, a good skin, and large blue eyes. She was strong, too, and the work went on leisurely and easily.

'Now!' said the corporal, stopping as usual to look round, 'pleasant company makes work a pleasure—don't hurry it, boys.' He stood on the truck surveying the world. That was one of his great and absorbing occupations: to stand and look out on things in general. Joe, also standing on the truck, also turned round to look what was to be seen. But he could not become blankly absorbed, as Albert could.

Miss Stokes watched the two men from under her broad felt hat. She had seen hundreds of Alberts, khaki soldiers standing in loose attitudes, absorbed in watching nothing in particular. She had seen also a good many Joes, quiet, good-looking young soldiers with half-averted faces. But there was something in the turn of Joe's head, and something in his quiet, tender-looking form, young and fresh—which attracted her eye. As she watched him closely from below, he turned as if he felt her, and his dark-blue eyes met her straight, light-blue gaze. He faltered and turned aside again and looked as if he were going to fall off the truck. A slight flush mounted under the girl's full, ruddy face. She liked him.

Always, after this, when she came into the sidings with her team, it was Joe she looked for. She acknowledged to herself that she was sweet on him. But Albert did all the talking. He was so full of fun and nonsense. Joe was a very shy bird, very brief and remote in his answers. Miss Stokes was driven to indulge in repartee with Albert, but she fixed her magnetic attention on the younger fellow. Joe would talk with Albert, and laugh at his jokes. But Miss Stokes could get little out of him. She had to depend on her silent forces. They were more effective than might be imagined.

Suddenly, on Saturday afternoon, at about two o'clock, Joe received a bolt from the blue—a telegram: 'Meet me Belbury Station 6.00 P.M. to-day. M. S.' He knew at once who M. S. was. His heart melted, he felt weak as if he had had a blow.

'What's the trouble, boy?' asked Albert anxiously.

'No—no trouble—it's to meet somebody.' Joe lifted his dark-blue eyes in confusion towards his corporal.

'Meet somebody!' repeated the corporal, watching his young pal with keen blue eyes. 'It's all right, then; nothing wrong?'

'No—nothing wrong. I'm not going,' said Joe.

Albert was old and shrewd enough to see that nothing more should be said before the housewife. He also saw that Joe did not want to take him into confidence. So he held his peace, though he was piqued.

The two soldiers went into town, smartened up. Albert knew a fair number of the boys round about; there would be plenty of gossip in the market-place, plenty of lounging in groups on the Bath Road, watching the Saturday evening shoppers. Then a modest drink or two, and the movies. They passed an agreeable, casual, nothing-in-particular evening, with which Joe was quite satisfied. He thought of Belbury Station, and of M. S. waiting there. He had not the faintest intention of meeting her. And he had not the faintest intention of telling Albert.

And yet, when the two men were in their bedroom, half undressed, Joe suddenly held out the telegram to his corporal, saying: 'What d'you think of that?'

Albert was just unbuttoning his braces. He desisted, took the telegram form, and turned towards the candle to read it.

'*Meet me Belbury Station 6.00 p.m. to-day. M. S.*,' he read, *sotto voce*. His face took on its fun-and-nonsense look.

'Who's M. S.?' he asked, looking shrewdly at Joe.

'You know as well as I do,' said Joe, non-committal.

'*M. S.*,' repeated Albert. 'Blamed if I know, boy. Is it a woman?'

The conversation was carried on in tiny voices, for fear of disturbing the householders.

'I don't know,' said Joe, turning. He looked full at Albert, the two men looked straight into each other's eyes. There was a lurking grin in each of them.

'Well, I'm—*blamed*!' said Albert at last, throwing the telegram down emphatically on the bed.

'Wha—at?' said Joe, grinning rather sheepishly, his eyes clouded none the less.

Albert sat on the bed and proceeded to undress, nodding his head with mock gravity all the while. Joe watched him foolishly.

'What?' he repeated faintly.

Albert looked up at him with a knowing look.

'If that isn't coming it quick, boy!' he said. 'What the blazes! What ha' you bin doing?'

'Nothing!' said Joe.

Albert slowly shook his head as he sat on the side of the bed.

'Don't happen to me when *I've* bin doin' nothing,' he said. And he proceeded to pull off his stockings.

Joe turned away, looking at himself in the mirror as he unbuttoned his tunic.

'You didn't want to keep the appointment?' Albert asked, in a changed voice, from the bedside.

Joe did not answer for a moment. Then he said:

'I made no appointment.'

'I'm not saying you did, boy. Don't be nasty about it. I mean you didn't want to answer the—unknown person's summons—shall I put it that way?'

'No,' said Joe.

'What was the deterring motive?' asked Albert, who was now lying on his back in bed.

'Oh,' said Joe, suddenly looking round rather haughtily. 'I didn't want to.' He had a well-balanced head, and could take on a sudden distant bearing.

'Didn't want to—didn't cotton on, like. Well—*they be artful, the women*—' he mimicked his landlord. 'Come on into bed, boy. Don't loiter about as if you'd lost something.'

Albert turned over, to sleep.

On Monday Miss Stokes turned up as usual, striding beside her team. Her 'whoa!' was resonant and challenging, she looked up at the truck as her steeds came to a standstill. Joe had turned aside, and had his face averted from her. She glanced him over—save for his slender succulent tenderness she would have despised him. She sized him up in a steady look. Then she turned to Albert, who was looking down at her and smiling in his mischievous turn. She knew his aspects by now. She looked straight back at him, though her eyes were hot. He saluted her.

'Beautiful morning, Miss Stokes.'

'Very!' she replied.

'Handsome is as handsome looks,' said Albert.

Which produced no response.

'Now, Joe, come on here,' said the corporal. 'Don't keep the ladies waiting—it's the sign of a weak heart.'

Joe turned, and the work began. Nothing more was said for the time being. As the week went on all parties became more comfortable. Joe remained silent, averted, neutral, a little on his dignity. Miss Stokes was off-hand and masterful. Albert was full of mischief.

The great theme was a circus, which was coming to the market town on the following Saturday.

'You'll go to the circus, Miss Stokes?' said Albert.

'I may go. Are you going?'

'Certainly. Give us the pleasure of escorting you.'

'No, thanks.'

'That's what I call a flat refusal—what, Joe? You don't mean that you have no liking for our company, Miss Stokes?'

'Oh, I don't know,' said Miss Stokes. 'How many are there of you?'

'Only me and Joe.'

'Oh, is that all?' she said, satirically.

Albert was a little nonplussed.

'Isn't that enough for you?' he asked.

'Too many by half,' blurted out Joe, jeeringly, in a sudden fit of uncouth rudeness that made both the others stare.

'Oh, I'll stand out of the way, boy, if that's it,' said Albert to Joe. Then he turned mischievously to Miss Stokes. 'He wants to know what M. stands for,' he said, confidentially.

'Monkeys,' she replied, turning to her horses.

'What's M. S.?' said Albert.

'Monkey-nuts,' she retorted, leading off her team.

Albert looked after her a little discomfited. Joe had flushed dark, and cursed Albert in his heart.

On the Saturday afternoon the two soldiers took the train into town. They would have to walk home. They had tea at six o'clock, and lounged about till half-past seven. The circus was in a meadow near the river—a great red-and-white striped tent.

Caravans stood at the side. A great crowd of people was gathered round the ticket-caravan.

Inside the tent the lamps were lighted, shining on a ring of faces, a great circular bank of faces round the green grassy centre. Along with some comrades, the two soldiers packed themselves on a thin plank seat, rather high. They were delighted with the flaring lights, the wild effect. But the circus performance did not affect them deeply. They admired the lady in black velvet with rose-purple legs who leapt so neatly on to the galloping horse; they watched the feats of strength, and laughed at the clown. But they felt a little patronising, they missed the sensational drama of the cinema.

Half-way through the performance Joe was electrified to see the face of Miss Stokes not very far from him. There she was, in her khaki and her felt hat, as usual; he pretended not to see her. She was laughing at the clown; she also pretended not to see him. It was a blow to him, and it made him angry. He would not even mention it to Albert. Least said, soonest mended. He liked to believe she had not seen him. But he knew, fatally, that she had.

When they came out it was nearly eleven o'clock; a lovely night, with a moon and tall, dark, noble trees: a magnificent May night. Joe and Albert laughed and chaffed with the boys. Joe looked round frequently to see if he were safe from Miss Stokes. It seemed so.

But there were six miles to walk home. At last the two soldiers set off, swinging their canes. The road was white between tall hedges, other stragglers were passing out of the town towards the villages; the air was full of pleased excitement.

They were drawing near to the village when they saw a dark figure ahead. Joe's heart sank with pure fear. It was a figure wheeling a bicycle; a land girl; Miss Stokes. Albert was ready with his nonsense. Miss Stokes had a puncture.

'Let me wheel the rattler,' said Albert.

'Thank you,' said Miss Stokes. 'You *are* kind.'

'Oh, I'd be kinder than that, if you'd show me how,' said Albert.

'Are you sure?' said Miss Stokes.

'Doubt my words?' said Albert. 'That's cruel of you, Miss Stokes.'

Miss Stokes walked between them, close to Joe.

'Have you been to the circus?' she asked him.

'Yes,' he replied, mildly.

'Have *you* been?' Albert asked her.

'Yes. I didn't see you,' she replied.

'What!—you say so! Didn't see us! Didn't think us worth looking at,' began Albert. 'Aren't I as handsome as the clown, now? And you didn't as much as glance in our direction? I call it a downright oversight.'

'I never *saw* you,' reiterated Miss Stokes. 'I didn't know you saw me.'

'That makes it worse,' said Albert.

The road passed through a belt a dark pine-wood. The village, and the branch road, was very near. Miss Stokes put out her fingers and felt for Joe's hand as it swung at his side. To say he was staggered is to put it mildly. Yet he allowed her softly to clasp his fingers for a few moments. But he was a mortified youth.

At the cross-road they stopped—Miss Stokes should turn off. She had another mile to go.

'You'll let us see you home,' said Albert.

'Do me a kindness,' she said. 'Put my bike in your shed, and take it to Baker's on Monday, will you?'

'I'll sit up all night and mend it for you, if you like.'

'No thanks. And Joe and I'll walk on.'

'Oh—ho! Oh—ho!' sang Albert. 'Joe! Joe! What do you say to that, now, boy? Aren't you in luck's way? And I get the bloomin' old bike for my pal. Consider it again, Miss Stokes.'

Joe turned aside his face, and did not speak.

'Oh, well! I wheel the grid, do I? I leave you, boy—'

'I'm not keen on going any further,' barked out Joe, in an uncouth voice. 'She bain't my choice.'

The girl stood silent, and watched the two men.

'There now!' said Albert. 'Think o' that! If it was *me* now—' But he was uncomfortable. 'Well, Miss Stokes, have me,' he added.

Miss Stokes stood quite still, neither moved nor spoke. And so the three remained for some time at the lane end. At last Joe began kicking the ground—then he suddenly lifted his face. At that moment Miss Stokes was at his side. She put her arm delicately round his waist.

'Seems I'm the one extra, don't you think?' Albert inquired of the high bland moon.

Joe had dropped his head and did not answer. Miss Stokes stood with her arm lightly round his waist. Albert bowed, saluted, and bade good-night. He walked away, leaving the two standing.

Miss Stokes put a light pressure on Joe's waist, and drew him down the road. They walked in silence. The night was full of scent—wild cherry, the first bluebells. Still they walked in silence. A nightingale was singing. They approached nearer and nearer,

till they stood close by his dark bush. The powerful notes sounded
from the cover, almost like flashes of light—then the interval of
silence—then the moaning notes, almost like a dog faintly
howling, followed by the long, rich trill, and flashing notes. Then
a short silence again.

Miss Stokes turned at last to Joe. She looked up at him, and in
the moonlight he saw her faintly smiling. He felt maddened, but
helpless. Her arm was round his waist, she drew him closely to
her with a soft pressure that made all his bones rotten.

Meanwhile Albert was waiting at home. He put on his overcoat,
for the fire was out, and he had had malarial fever. He looked
fitfully at the *Daily Mirror* and the *Daily Sketch*, but he saw
nothing. It seemed a long time. He began to yawn widely, even to
nod. At last Joe came in.

Albert looked at him keenly. The young man's brow was black,
his face sullen.

'All right, boy?' asked Albert.

Joe merely grunted for a reply. There was nothing more to be
got out of him. So they went to bed.

Next day Joe was silent, sullen. Albert could make nothing of
him. He proposed a walk after tea.

'I'm going somewhere,' said Joe.

'Where—Monkey-nuts?' asked the corporal. But Joe's brow
only became darker.

So the days went by. Almost every evening Joe went off alone,
returning late. He was sullen, taciturn and had a hang-dog look, a
curious way of dropping his head and looking dangerously from
under his brows. And he and Albert did not get on so well any
more with one another. For all his fun and nonsense, Albert was
really irritable, soon made angry. And Joe's stand-offish sulkiness
and complete lack of confidence riled him, got on his nerves. His
fun and nonsense took a biting, sarcastic turn, at which Joe's eyes
glittered occasionally, though the young man turned unheeding
aside. Then again Joe would be full of odd, whimsical fun,
outshining Albert himself.

Miss Stokes still came to the station with the wain: Monkey-
nuts, Albert called her, though not to her face. For she was very
clear and good-looking, almost she seemed to gleam. And Albert
was a tiny bit afraid of her. She very rarely addressed Joe whilst
the hay-loading was going on, and that young man always turned
his back to her. He seemed thinner, and his limber figure looked
more slouching. But still it had the tender, attractive appearance,
especially from behind. His tanned face, a little thinned and darkened, took a handsome, slightly sinister look.

'Come on, Joe!' the corporal urged sharply one day. 'What're you doing, boy? Looking for beetles on the bank?'

Joe turned round swiftly, almost menacing, to work.

'He's a different fellow these days, Miss Stokes,' said Albert to the young woman. 'What's got him? Is it Monkey-nuts that don't suit him, do you think?'

'Choked with chaff, more like,' she retorted. 'It's as bad as feeding a threshing machine, to have to listen to some folks.'

'As bad as what?' said Albert. 'You don't mean *me*, do you, Miss Stokes?'

'No,' she cried. 'I don't mean you.'

Joe's face became dark red during these sallies, but he said nothing. He would eye the young woman curiously, as she swung so easily at the work, and he had some of the look of a dog which is going to bite.

Albert, with his nerves on edge, began to find the strain rather severe. The next Saturday evening, when Joe came in more black-browed than ever, he watched him, determined to have it out with him.

When the boy went upstairs to bed, the corporal followed him. He closed the door behind him carefully, sat on the bed and watched the younger man undressing. And for once he spoke in a natural voice, neither chaffing nor commanding.

'What's gone wrong, boy?'

Joe stopped a moment as if he had been shot. Then he went on unwinding his puttees, and did not answer or look up.

'You can hear, can't you?' said Albert, nettled.

'Yes, I can hear,' said Joe, stooping over his puttees till his face was purple.

'Then why don't you answer?'

Joe sat up. He gave a long, sideways look at the corporal. Then he lifted his eyes and stared at a crack in the ceiling.

The corporal watched these movements shrewdly.

'And *then* what?' he asked, ironically.

Again Joe turned and stared him in the face. The corporal smiled very slightly, but kindly.

'There'll be murder done one of these days,' said Joe, in a quiet unimpassioned voice.

'So long as it's by daylight—' replied Albert. Then he went over, sat down by Joe, put his hand on his shoulder affectionately, and continued, 'What is it, boy? What's gone wrong? You can trust me, can't you?'

Joe turned and looked curiously at the face so near to his.

'It's nothing, that's all,' he said laconically.

Albert frowned.

'Then who's going to be murdered?—and who's going to do the murdering?—me or you—which is it, boy?' He smiled gently at the stupid youth, looking straight at him all the while, into his eyes. Gradually the stupid, hunted, glowering look died out of Joe's eyes. He turned his head aside, gently, as one rousing from a spell.

'I don't want her,' he said, with fierce resentment.

'Then you needn't have her,' said Albert. 'What do you go for, boy?'

But it wasn't as simple as all that. Joe made no remark.

'She's a smart-looking girl. What's wrong with her, my boy? I should have thought you were a lucky chap, myself.'

'I don't want 'er,' Joe barked, with ferocity and resentment.

'Then tell her so and have done,' said Albert. He waited awhile. There was no response. 'Why don't you?' he added.

'Because I don't,' confessed Joe, sulkily.

Albert pondered—rubbed his head.

'You're too soft-hearted, that's where it is, boy. You want your mettle dipping in cold water, to temper it. You're too soft-hearted—'

He laid his arm affectionately across the shoulders of the younger man. Joe seemed to yield a little towards him.

'When are you going to see her again?' Albert asked. For a long time there was no answer.

'When is it, boy?' persisted the softened voice of the corporal.

'To-morrow,' confessed Joe.

'Then let me go,' said Albert. 'Let me go, will you?'

The morrow was Sunday, a sunny day, but a cold evening. The sky was grey, the new foliage very green, but the air was chill and depressing. Albert walked briskly down the white road towards Beeley. He crossed a larch plantation, and followed a narrow by-road, where blue speedwell flowers fell from the banks into the dust. He walked swinging his cane, with mixed sensations. Then having gone a certain length, he turned and began to walk in the opposite direction.

So he saw a young woman approaching him. She was wearing a wide hat of grey straw, and a loose, swinging dress of nigger-grey velvet. She walked with slow inevitability. Albert faltered a little as he approached her. Then he saluted her, and his roguish, slightly withered skin flushed. She was staring straight into his face.

He fell in by her side, saying impudently:

'Not so nice for a walk as it was, is it?'

She only stared at him. He looked back at her.

'You've seen me before, you know,' he said, grinning slightly. 'Perhaps you never noticed me. Oh, I'm quite nice looking, in a quiet way, you know. What—?'

But Miss Stokes did not speak: she only stared with large, icy blue eyes at him. He became self-conscious, lifted up his chin, walked with his nose in the air, and whistled at random. So they went down the quiet, deserted grey lane. He was whistling the air: 'I'm Gilbert, the filbert, the colonel of the nuts.'

At last she found her voice:

'Where's Joe?'

'He thought you'd like a change: they say variety's the salt of life—that's why I'm mostly in pickle.'

'Where is he?'

'Am I my brother's keeper? He's gone his own ways.'

'Where?'

'Nay, how am I to know? Not so far but he'll be back for supper.'

She stopped in the middle of the lane. He stopped facing her.

'Where's Joe?' she asked.

He struck a careless attitude, looked down the road this way and that, lifted his eyebrows, pushed his khaki cap on one side, and answered:

'He is not conducting the service to-night: he asked me if I'd officiate.'

'Why hasn't he come?'

'Didn't want to, I expect. *I* wanted to.'

She stared him up and down, and he felt uncomfortable in his spine, but maintained his air of nonchalance. Then she turned slowly on her heel, and started to walk back. The corporal went at her side.

'You're not going back, are you?' he pleaded. 'Why, me and you, we should get on like a house on fire.'

She took no heed, but walked on. He went uncomfortably at her side, making his funny remarks from time to time. But she was as if stone deaf. He glanced at her, and to his dismay saw the tears running down her cheeks. He stopped suddenly, and pushed back his cap.

'I say, you know—' he began.

But she was walking on like an automaton, and he had to hurry after her.

She never spoke to him. At the gate of her farm she walked straight in, as if he were not there. He watched her disappear. Then he turned on his heel, cursing silently, puzzled, lifting off his cap to scratch his head.

That night, when they were in bed, he remarked:

'Say, Joe, boy; strikes me you're well-off without Monkey-nuts. Gord love us, beans ain't in it.'

So they slept in amity. But they waited with some anxiety for the morrow.

It was a cold morning, a grey sky shifting in a cold wind, and threatening rain. They watched the wagon come up the road and through the yard gates. Miss Stokes was with her team as usual; her 'Whoa!' rang out like a war-whoop.

She faced up at the truck where the two men stood.

'Joe!' she called, to the averted figure which stood up in the wind.

'What?' he turned unwillingly.

She made a queer movement, lifting her head slightly in a sipping, half-inviting, half-commanding gesture. And Joe was crouching already to jump off the truck to obey her, when Albert put his hand on his shoulder.

'Half a minute, boy! Where are you off? Work's work, and nuts is nuts. You stop here.'

Joe slowly straightened himself.

'Joe?' came the woman's clear call from below.

Again Joe looked at her. But Albert's hand was on his shoulder, detaining him. He stood half averted, with his tail between his legs.

'Take your hand off him, you!' said Miss Stokes.

'Yes, Major,' retorted Albert satirically.

She stood and watched.

'Joe!' Her voice rang for the third time.

Joe turned and looked at her, and a slow, jeering smile gathered on his face.

'Monkey-nuts!' he replied, in a tone mocking her call.

She turned white—dead white. The men thought she would fall. Albert began yelling to the porters up the line to come and help with the load. He could yell like any non-commissioned officer upon occasion.

Some way or other the wagon was unloaded, the girl was gone. Joe and his corporal looked at one another and smiled slowly. But they had a weight on their minds, they were afraid.

They were reassured, however, when they found that Miss Stokes came no more with the hay. As far as they were concerned, she had vanished into oblivion. And Joe felt more relieved even than he had felt when he heard the firing cease, after the news had come that the armistice was signed.

Virginia Woolf

▼▼

The Mark on the Wall

PERHAPS IT WAS the middle of January in the present year that I first looked up and saw the mark on the wall. In order to fix a date it is necessary to remember what one saw. So now I think of the fire; the steady film of yellow light upon the page of my book; the three chrysanthemums in the round glass bowl on the mantelpiece. Yes, it must have been the winter time, and we had just finished our tea, for I remember that I was smoking a cigarette when I looked up and saw the mark on the wall for the first time. I looked up through the smoke of my cigarette and my eye lodged for a moment upon the burning coals, and that old fancy of the crimson flag flapping from the castle tower came into my mind, and I thought of the cavalcade of red knights riding up the side of the black rock. Rather to my relief the sight of the mark interrupted the fancy, for it is an old fancy, an automatic fancy, made as a child perhaps. The mark was a small round mark, black upon the white wall, about six or seven inches above the mantelpiece.

How readily our thoughts swarm upon a new object, lifting it a little way, as ants carry a blade of straw so feverishly, and then leave it.... If that mark was made by a nail, it can't have been for a picture, it must have been for a miniature—the miniature of a lady with white powdered curls, powder-dusted cheeks, and lips like red carnations. A fraud of course, for the people who had this house before us would have chosen pictures in that way—an old picture for an old room. That is the sort of people they were— very interesting people, and I think of them so often, in such queer places, because one will never see them again, never know what happened next. They wanted to leave this house because they wanted to change their style of furniture, so he said, and he was in process of saying that in his opinion art should have ideas behind it when we were torn asunder, as one is torn from the old lady about to pour out tea and the young man about to hit the tennis ball in the back garden of the suburban villa as one rushes past in the train.

But for that mark, I'm not sure about it; I don't believe it was made by a nail after all; it's too big, too round, for that. I might get up, but if I got up and looked at it, ten to one I shouldn't be able to say for certain; because once a thing's done, no one ever knows how it happened. Oh! dear me, the mystery of life; the inaccuracy of thought! The ignorance of humanity! To show how very little control of our possessions we have—what an accidental affair this living is after all our civilization—let me just count over a few of the things lost in one lifetime, beginning, for that seems always the most mysterious of losses—what cat would gnaw, what rat would nibble—three pale blue canisters of bookbinding tools? Then there were the bird cages, the iron hoops, the steel skates, the Queen Anne coal-scuttle, the bagatelle board, the hand organ—all gone, and jewels, too. Opals and emeralds, they lie about the roots of turnips. What a scraping paring affair it is to be sure! The wonder is that I've any clothes on my back, that I sit surrounded by solid furniture at this moment. Why, if one wants to compare life to anything, one must liken it to being blown through the Tube at fifty miles an hour—landing at the other end without a single hairpin in one's hair! Shot out at the feet of God entirely naked! Tumbling head over heels in the asphodel meadows like brown paper parcels pitched down a shoot in the post office! With one's hair flying back like the tail of a race-horse. Yes, that seems to express the rapidity of life, the perpetual waste and repair; all so casual, all so haphazard....

But after life. The slow pulling down of thick green stalks so that the cup of the flower, as it turns over, deluges one with purple and red light. Why, after all, should one not be born there as one is born here, helpless, speechless, unable to focus one's eyesight, groping at the roots of the grass, at the toes of the Giants? As for saying which are trees, and which are men and women, or whether there are such things, that one won't be in a condition to do for fifty years or so. There will be nothing but spaces of light and dark, intersected by thick stalks, and rather higher up perhaps, rose-shaped blots of an indistinct colour—dim pinks and blues—which will, as time goes on, become more definite, become—I don't know what....

And yet that mark on the wall is not a hole at all. It may even be caused by some round black substance, such as a small rose leaf, left over from the summer, and I, not being a very vigilant housekeeper—look at the dust on the mantelpiece, for example, the dust which, so they say, buried Troy three times over, only fragments of pots utterly refusing annihilation, as one can believe.

The tree outside the window taps very gently on the pane.... I want to think quietly, calmly, spaciously, never to be interrupted, never to have to rise from my chair, to slip easily from one thing to another, without any sense of hostility, or obstacle. I want to sink deeper and deeper, away from the surface, with its hard separate facts. To steady myself, let me catch hold of the first idea that passes.... Shakespeare.... Well, he will do as well as another. A man who sat himself solidly in an arm-chair, and looked into the fire, so—A shower of ideas fell perpetually from some very high Heaven down through his mind. He leant his forehead on his hand, and people, looking in through the open door—for this scene is supposed to take place on a summer's evening—But how dull this is, this historical fiction! It doesn't interest me at all. I wish I could hit upon a pleasant track of thought, a track indirectly reflecting credit upon myself, for those are the pleasantest thoughts, and very frequent even in the minds of modest mouse-coloured people, who believe genuinely that they dislike to hear their own praises. They are not thoughts directly praising oneself; that is the beauty of them; they are thoughts like this:

'And then I came into the room. They were discussing botany. I said how I'd seen a flower growing on a dust heap on the site of an old house in Kingsway. The seed, I said, must have been sown in the reign of Charles the First. What flowers grew in the reign of Charles the First?' I asked—(but I don't remember the answer). Tall flowers with purple tassels to them perhaps. And so it goes on. All the time I'm dressing up the figure of myself in my own mind, lovingly, stealthily, not openly adoring it, for if I did that, I should catch myself out, and stretch my hand at once for a book in self-protection. Indeed, it is curious how instinctively one protects the image of oneself from idolatry or any other handling that could make it ridiculous, or too unlike the original to be believed in any longer. Or is it not so very curious after all? It is a matter of great importance. Supposing the looking-glass smashes, the image disappears, and the romantic figure with the green of forest depths all about it is there no longer, but only that shell of a person which is seen by other people—what an airless, shallow, bald, prominent world it becomes! A world not to be lived in. As we face each other in omnibuses and underground railways we are looking into the mirror; that accounts for the vagueness, the gleam of glassiness, in our eyes. And the novelists in future will realize more and more the importance of these reflections, for of course there is not one reflection but an almost infinite number;

those are the depths they will explore, those the phantoms they will pursue, leaving the description of reality more and more out of their stories, taking a knowledge of it for granted, as the Greeks did and Shakespeare perhaps—but these generalizations are very worthless. The military sound of the word is enough. It recalls leading articles, cabinet ministers—a whole class of things indeed which, as a child, one thought the thing itself, the standard thing, the real thing, from which one could not depart save at the risk of nameless damnation. Generalizations bring back somehow Sunday in London, Sunday afternoon walks, Sunday luncheons, and also ways of speaking of the dead, clothes, and habits—like the habit of sitting all together in one room until a certain hour, although nobody liked it. There was a rule for everything. The rule for tablecloths at that particular period was that they should be made of tapestry with little yellow compartments marked upon them, such as you may see in photographs of the carpets in the corridors of the royal palaces. Tablecloths of a different kind were not real tablecloths. How shocking, and yet how wonderful it was to discover that these real things, Sunday luncheons, Sunday walks, country houses, and tablecloths were not entirely real, were indeed half phantoms, and the damnation which visited the disbeliever in them was only a sense of illegitimate freedom. What now takes the place of those things I wonder, those real standard things? Men perhaps, should you be a woman; the masculine point of view which governs our lives, which sets the standard, which established Whitaker's Table of Precedency, which has become, I suppose, since the war, half a phantom to many men and women, which soon, one may hope, will be laughed into the dustbin where the phantoms go, the mahogany sideboards and the Landseer prints, Gods and Devils, Hell and so forth, leaving us all with an intoxicating sense of illegitimate freedom—if freedom exists....

In certain lights that mark on the wall seems actually to project from the wall. Nor is it entirely circular. I cannot be sure, but it seems to cast a perceptible shadow, suggesting that if I ran my finger down that strip of the wall it would, at a certain point, mount and descend a small tumulus, a smooth tumulus like those barrows on the South Downs which are, they say, either tombs or camps. Of the two I should prefer them to be tombs, desiring melancholy like most English people, and finding it natural at the end of a walk to think of the bones stretched beneath the turf.... There must be some book about it. Some antiquary must have dug up those bones and given them a name.... What sort of a man is an antiquary, I wonder? Retired

Colonels for the most part, I daresay, leading parties of aged
labourers to the top here, examining clods of earth and stone,
and getting into correspondence with the neighbouring clergy,
which, being opened at breakfast time, gives them a feeling of
importance, and the comparison of arrow-heads necessitates
cross-country journeys to the county towns, an agreeable necessity both to them and to their elderly wives, who wish to make
plum jam or to clean out the study, and have every reason for
keeping that great question of the camp or the tomb in perpetual suspension, while the Colonel himself feels agreeably
philosophic in accumulating evidence on both sides of the question. It is true that he does finally incline to believe in the camp;
and, being opposed, indites a pamphlet which he is about to read
at the quarterly meeting of the local society when a stroke lays
him low, and his last conscious thoughts are not of wife or child,
but of the camp and that arrow-head there, which is now in the
case at the local museum, together with the foot of a Chinese
murderess, a handful of Elizabethan nails, a great many Tudor
clay pipes, a piece of Roman pottery, and the wineglass that
Nelson drank out of—proving I really don't know what.

No, no, nothing is proved, nothing is known. And if I were to
get up at this very moment and ascertain that the mark on the
wall is really—what shall we say?—the head of a gigantic old nail,
driven in two hundred years ago, which has now, owing to the
patient attrition of many generations of housemaids, revealed its
head above the coat of paint, and is taking its first view of modern
life in the sight of a white-walled fire-lit room, what should I
gain?—Knowledge? Matter for further speculation? I can think
sitting still as well as standing up. And what is knowledge? What
are our learned men save the descendants of witches and hermits
who crouched in caves and in woods brewing herbs, interrogating
shrew-mice and writing down the language of the stars? And the
less we honour them as our superstitions dwindle and our respect
for beauty and health of mind increases.... Yes, one could imagine
a very pleasant world. A quiet, spacious world, with the flowers so
red and blue in the open fields. A world without professors or
specialists or house-keepers with the profiles of policemen, a
world which one could slice with one's thought as a fish slices the
water with his fin, grazing the stems of the water-lilies, hanging
suspended over nests of white sea eggs.... How peaceful it is
down here, rooted in the centre of the world and gazing up
through the grey waters, with their sudden gleams of light, and
their reflections—if it were not for Whitaker's Almanack—if it
were not for the Table of Precedency!

I must jump up and see for myself what that mark on the wall really is—a nail, a rose-leaf, a crack in the wood?

Here is nature once more at her old game of self-preservation. This train of thought, she perceives, is threatening mere waste of energy, even some collision with reality, for who will ever be able to lift a finger against Whitaker's Table of Precedency? The Archbishop of Canterbury is followed by the Lord High Chancellor; the Lord High Chancellor is followed by the Archbishop of York. Everybody follows somebody, such is the philosophy of Whitaker; and the great thing is to know who follows whom. Whitaker knows, and let that, so Nature counsels, comfort you, instead of enraging you; and if you can't be comforted, if you must shatter this hour of peace, think of the mark on the wall.

I understand Nature's game—her prompting to take action as a way of ending any thought that threatens to excite or to pain. Hence, I suppose, comes our slight contempt for men of action— men, we assume, who don't think. Still, there's no harm in putting a full stop to one's disagreeable thoughts by looking at a mark on the wall.

Indeed, now that I have fixed my eyes upon it, I feel that I have grasped a plank in the sea; I feel a satisfying sense of reality which at once turns the two Archbishops and the Lord High Chancellor to the shadows of shades. Here is something definite, something real. Thus, waking from a midnight dream of horror, one hastily turns on the light and lies quiescent, worshipping the chest of drawers, worshipping solidity, worshipping reality, worshipping the impersonal world which is a proof of some existence other than ours. That is what one wants to be sure of.... Wood is a pleasant thing to think about. It comes from a tree; and trees grow, and we don't know how they grow. For years and years they grow, without paying any attention to us, in meadows, in forests, and by the side of rivers—all things one likes to think about. The cows swish their tails beneath them on hot afternoons; they paint rivers so green that when a moorhen dives one expects to see its feathers all green when it comes up again. I like to think of the fish balanced against the stream like flags blown out; and of water-beetles slowly raising domes of mud upon the bed of the river. I like to think of the tree itself: first the close dry sensation of being wood; then the grinding of the storm; then the slow, delicious ooze of sap. I like to think of it, too, on winter's nights standing in the empty field with all leaves close-furled, nothing tender exposed to the iron bullets of the moon, a naked mast upon an earth that goes tumbling, tumbling, all night long. The song of birds must sound very loud and strange in June; and how cold the feet of insects must feel upon it, as they make laborious progresses up the creases of the bark, or sun themselves upon the thin green awning of the leaves, and look straight in front of them with diamond-cut red eyes.... One by one the fibres snap beneath the immense cold pressure of the earth, then the last storm comes and, falling, the highest branches drive deep into the ground again. Even so, life isn't done with; there are a million patient, watchful lives still for a tree, all over the world, in bedrooms, in ships, on the pavement, lining rooms, where men and women sit after tea, smoking cigarettes. It is full of peaceful thoughts, happy thoughts, this tree. I should like to take each one separately—but something is getting in the way.... Where was I? What has it all been about? A tree? A river? The Downs? Whitaker's Almanack? The fields of asphodel? I can't remember a thing. Everything's moving, falling, slipping, vanishing.... There is a vast upheaval of matter. Someone is standing over me and saying:

'I'm going out to buy a newspaper.'

'Yes?'

'Though it's no good buying newspapers.... Nothing ever happens. Curse this war; God damn this war! ... All the same, I don't see why we should have a snail on our wall.'

Ah, the mark on the wall! It was a snail.

▼▼

The French Poodle

I WAS REMINDED of another man's fate when I saw Peter yesterday, in khaki, with his dog. The dog appeared rather confused by Peter's newly resumed uniform. It fell in behind other people in khaki: even when keeping in orderly proximity to its master, it followed a certain indifference or contempt.— Peter's destiny had nothing sultry in its lines: his dog was a suburban appendage. It was the khaki and the dog brought me to the other story.

It appears the following things happened to a man called Rob Cairn, during a long sick-leave. The time was between July and October 1915. I can tell the story with genuine completeness: for James Fraser, the man he saw most of then, told it to me with a great wealth of friendly savagery.

Rob Cairn was drifting about London in mufti, by no means well, and full of anxiety, the result of his ill-health and the shock he had received at finding himself blown into the air and painted yellow by the unavoidable shell. His tenure on earth seemed inse-cure, and he could not accustom himself to the idea of insecurity. When the shell came he had not bounded gracefully and coldly up, but with a clumsy dismay. His spirit, that spirit that should have been winged for the life of a soldier, and ready fiercely to take flight into the unknown, strong for other lives, was also grub-bily attached to the earth. It, like his body, was not graceful in its fearlessness, nor resilient, nor young. All the minutiæ of existence mesmerised it. It could not disport itself genially in independence of surrounding objects and ideas. Even as a boy he had never been able to learn to dive: hardly to swim. Yet he was a big red-headed chap that those who measure men by redness and by size would have considered fairly imposing as a physical specimen. It requires almost a professional colour-matcher, as a matter of fact, to discriminate between the different reds: and then the various constitutional conditions they imply is a separate discovery.

Cairn, then, was arrested in a vague but troublesome maze of discomfort and ill-health: his sick leave, after he had left the hospital, lasted some time. As an officer, therefore more responsible, he had more latitude. He was an architect. He went to his office every day for an hour or two. But he was haunted by the necessity to return once more to the trench-life with which he had been for some weeks mesmerically disconnected, and which he felt was another element, with which he had only become acquainted in a sudden dream. This element of malignant and monotonous missiles, which worried less or more, sleeplessness and misery, now appeared to him in its true colours. They were hard, poisonous and flamboyant. A fatiguing sonority, an empty and pretentious energy: something about it all like the rhetoric of a former age, revolted him. It all seemed incredibly old and superannuated. Should he go back and get killed it would be as though the dead of a century ago were striking him down. Cairn must have been a fairly brave man, considering all things, before his tossing. It was now with him rather sullen neurasthenia at the thought of recommencing, than anything else: renewed monotonous actions and events, and fear not of death but of being played with too much.

James Fraser, his partner, who because of heart-trouble had been unable to join the Army, heard all this from his friend, and cursed 'the whole business' of bloodshed in sympathy with the recriminating soldier.

'I'm sure there's something wrong, Rob. How do you feel exactly; physically, I mean? What can happen to a man inside who is blown up in the air? What do the doctors exactly say?'

'They can find nothing. I don't believe there is anything. But I don't feel at all well. It's something in my brain, rather, that's dislocated: cracked, I think, sometimes. I shall never be any good out there again.'

He read a great deal, chiefly Natural History. The lives of animals seemed to have a great fascination for his stolid, faithful thoughts. When he got an idea he stuck to it with unconscious devotion. He was a good friend to his ideas.

One of the principal notions to which he became attached at this time was that human beings suffered in every way from the absence of animal life around them. Pigs, horses, buffalos, snakes, birds, goats: the majority of men living in towns were deprived of this rich animal neighbourhood. The sanity of direct animal processes: the example suggested constantly by the equilibrium of these various cousins of ours, with their snouts and their wings: the steady and soothing brotherhood of their bodies; this environment appeared necessary to human beings.

'Few men and many animals!' as he said to Fraser, blinking dogmatically and heavily, light red eyelashes falling with a look of modesty at the base of eyes always seeming a little dazzled by the reds all round them. 'That's what I should like; rather than *men* and nothing else. It is bad for men to beat and kill each other. When there are no patient backs of beasts to receive their blows men turn them more towards their fellows. Irruptions of the hunting instinct are common in cities. Irruptions of all instincts are common and inevitable in modern life, among human swarms. Men have taken to the air; they are fighting there almost before they can fly. Man is losing his significance.'

Fraser had an objection to make.

'You suggest the absence of animals—Did not men in every time kill and beat one another?'

Cairn twisted as it were archly in his chair.

'Men loved each other better formerly; and—they at least killed other animals as well. I have never killed any animal; never a bird; not a mouse; not knowingly an insect; but I have killed men.'

He said this staring hard at his friend, as though he might be able to discover the meaning of this fact in his face.

'And I did not mind killing men,' he proceeded. 'I hardly knew what killing meant.'

'You do now?' his delighted partner asked him.

Rob looked at him with suspicion.

'No; possibly because I have never killed anyone I could see properly.'

'Yes; your gunner's scalps are very abstract. But, again, I do not see what you mean. Do you think that a butcher, because of his familiarity with the shambles, would have more compunction in killing a man?'

'No. But it would do him no harm to kill a man or anything else, of course. Then he's a professional murderer.'

'But why did you never kill birds?' Fraser asked him with uninterested persistence.

'I should have if I'd lived among them.—Do you think men would eat each other if there were no succulent animals left?'

'Very likely.' Fraser laughed in accordance with the notion. 'They might possibly at all events eat all the ugly women!'

Rob Cairn discussed these things with a persistent and often mildly indignant solemnity. The trenches had scarred his mind. Swarms of minute self-preservative and active thoughts moved in the furrows. Little bombs of irritable logic appeared whirling up from these grave clefts and exploded around his uneasy partner. Fraser wondered if Cairn would be able to take up his place in the business again, if nothing happened to him, as usefully as he had occupied it before the war. He seemed queer and was not able at the office to concentrate his mind on anything for more than a few minutes.

As to the war, his ideas appeared quite confusedly stagnant. He wondered, arguing along the same lines of the incompleteness of modern life, whether the savagery we arrive at were better than the savagery we come from.

'Since we must be savage, is not a real savage better than a sham one?'

'Must we be savage?' Fraser would ask.

'This "great war" is the beginning of a period, far from being a war-that-will-end-war, take my word for it.'

So Cairn was a tired man, and his fancy set out on a pilgrimage to some patriarchal plain. He had done his eight months' sprint, and was exhausted. His bounce into the air had shaken him out of his dream. He was awake and harshly anxious and reflective.

It was at this point that he bought his French poodle.

In answer to an advertisement in two papers for a fairly large dog, a lady at Guildford answered that she had such an animal to sell. The lady brought the dog to his flat in a street off Theobalds Road, and he immediately bought it. He was very shy with it at first. He was conscious of not being its first love, and attempted to bribe it into forgetfulness of its former master by giving it a great deal to eat. It shortly vomited in his sitting-room. It howled a great deal at first.

But the dog soon settled down to novel life. Cairn became excessively fond of it. He abused a man in the street who insulted it. It was a large fat and placid brute that received Rob's caresses with obedient steadiness, occasionally darting friendship back at him. As he held it against his legs Cairn felt a deep attachment for this warm bag of blood and bone, whose love was undiluted habit and an uncomplicated magnetism. It recognised his friendliness in spasms of servile good nature, as absent-minded as its instincts.

Cairn noted all the modes of its nature with a delighted care. Its hunger enthralled him; its ramping gruff enthusiasm at the prospect of the streets filled him with an almost Slavic lyricism and glee. He was calm in the midst of its hysteria; but there was a contented pathos in his quietness. Its adventures with other dogs he followed with indulgence. The amazing physical catholicism of its taste he felt was a just reproach to his fastidiousness and maturity. It would have approached a rhinoceros with amorous proposals, were it not for elementary prudence.

He called his dog Carp. He loved him like a brother. But it is not at all sure that in the end Carp did not take the place that some lady should have occupied in his heart, as many of the attachments of men for girls seem a sentiment sprung up in the absence of a dog. Cairn had had one sweetheart; but after several years of going about together she had seemed so funny to him— she had seemed settling down like an old barge into some obscure and too personal human groove—that he had jerked himself away. The war had put the finishing touch to their estrangement.

'Dolly's lurch is becoming more pronounced,' was his Monday morning's bulletin at the office. She appeared to remain an incredible time on each foot, while her body swung round. In following her out of the restaurant he felt that she was doing a sort of lugubrious cake-walk. He could hardly help getting into step. She became more dogmatic every minute: and rheumatism made her knuckles like so many dull and obstinate little faces.

'You're getting tired of her at last.' Fraser advised him to take advantage of his mood and to say good-bye to her.

He had done so and had regretted it ever since. He felt superstitious about this parting: he regarded her in this conjuncture, as a mascot abandoned. He blamed his partner and the war for this. Somehow his partner and the war were closely connected. In many ways he found them identified—a confused target for his resentment. When he found himself cursing the war he found himself disliking his partner so much the *next* minute that it seemed the *same* minute. Fraser did not approve of Carp, either: although Carp appeared to like Fraser better than he did his own master. Cairn noticed this, and his humour did not improve. Towards the end they did not see him so much at the office as formerly. Once or twice a week he put in an appearance, rather primed with criticism of the conduct of the business in his absence. Then he turned up one day in khaki again: he was going back to the Front in a couple of days. Fraser and he got on better than they had done of late. He was much more open and good-humoured, and had seemingly recovered his old personality entirely. This may have been due somewhat to his friend's sentimental spurt of pleasantness under the circumstances.

'What are you going to do with Carp?'

When Fraser asked him this he seemed confused.

'I hadn't thought about that—.'

They did not say anything, and there was the illusion of sudden groping out of sight.

'Are you going to take him to the Front?' Fraser suggested, and laughed impatiently.

'No, he might get shot there,' Cairn replied, screwing up his nose, and recovering his good humour, apparently. 'I must give him away.'

Fraser knew how fond he was of the dog, and attributed his awkwardness to his dislike at the notion of parting from it.

'Let me keep it for you,' he said, generously.

'No, thanks. I'll get rid of it.'

Fraser saw his partner on the following day at their office. The next thing that he heard was that Cairn was ill in bed, and that his return to France would have to be again postponed. On going to his friend's flat he crossed at the door two men carrying out a small box. The charwoman was very mysterious. He asked what the box was.

'It's the dog,' she replied.

'Is he sold then?' Fraser asked.

'No. 'E's dead.'

He looked at her melodramatically unconcerned and bloated face for a moment.

Rob Cairn was alone in his bedroom. He was very exhausted, and faintly bad-tempered.

'What's up? Have you had a relapse?'

'Yes—something: I'm not well.'

'Can I do anything for you?'

Cairn was lying on his back and hardly looked at his visitor.

'No, thanks. Listen.' He turned towards Fraser, and his face became long and dulled with excitement. 'Listen to this. You know Carp, the dog? I killed it yesterday.—I shot it with a revolver; but I aimed too low. It nearly screamed the place down.—Poor brute!—You know—'

He suddenly lurched round, face downwards, flattened in his arm, and sobbed in a deep howling way, that reminded Fraser of a dog.

When he looked up his face was a scared and bitter mask.

'What a coward I am! Poor beast! Poor—. How could I—'

'Nonsense, Rob! You're not yourself. You know you're not yourself! Have you seen a doctor? Don't worry about this—.'

'I'm only glad of one thing. I *know* I shall pay for it. That thought is the only one that quiets me. I know as surely as I am lying here that my hour is fixed! I have killed my best living luck. Not that I wanted the luck! God, no! I care little enough what happens to me! But that poor beast!—'

'Damn you and your mascots! You are the slave of any poodle—!'

Fraser remembered his detestable lady-love, and the perpetual threat of an idiotic marriage.

The doctor came into the room.—He told me that he fancied more had happened between Cairn and Carp, at the dog's death, than his friend had cared to tell him. Cairn was another fortnight in London, then went to France. Two weeks after that he was killed. He understood the mechanism of his destiny better than his partner.

EDITH WHARTON

▼▼

The Refugees

I

ON THE 8th of September, 1914, Charlie Durand stood help-lessly blinking through his spectacles at the throng of fugitives which the Folkestone train had just poured out upon the platform of Charing Cross.

He was aware of a faint haze on the spectacles which he usually kept clear of the slightest smirch. It had been too prolonged, too abominable, too soul-searching, the slow torture of his hours of travel with the stricken multitude in which he had found himself entangled on the pier at Boulogne.

Charlie Durand, Professor of Romance Languages in a western University, had been spending the first weeks of a hard-earned Sabbatical holiday in wandering through Flanders and Belgium, and on the fatal second of August had found himself at Louvain, whose University, a year or two previously, had honoured him with a degree.

On the advice of the American consul he had left Belgium at once, and, deeply disturbed by the dislocation of his plans, had carried his shaken nerves to a lost corner of Normandy, where he had spent the ensuing weeks in trying to think the war would soon be over.

It was not that he was naturally hard or aloof about it, or wanted to be; but the whole business was so contrary to his conception of the universe, and his fagged mind, at the moment, was so incapable of prompt readjustment, that he needed time to steady himself. Besides, his conscience told him that his first duty was to get back unimpaired to the task which just enabled him to keep a mother and two sisters above want. His few weeks on the continent had cost much more than he had expected, and most of his remaining francs had gone to the various appeals for funds that penetrated even to his lost corner; and he decided that the prudent course (now that everybody said the war was certainly going to last till November) would be to slip over to

cheap lodgings in London, and bury his nose in the British
Museum.

This decision, as it chanced, had coincided with the annihilation of Louvain and Malines. News of the rapid German advance
had not reached him; but at Boulogne he found himself caught in
the central eddy of fugitives, tossed about among them like one of
themselves, pitched on the boat with them, dealt with compas-
sionately but firmly by the fagged officials at Folkestone, jammed
into a cranny of the endless train, had chocolate and buns thrust
on him by ministering angels with high heeels and powdered
noses, and shyly passed these refreshments on to the fifteen dazed
fellow-travellers packed into his compartment.

His first impulse was to turn back and fly the sight at any cost.
But his luggage had already passed out of his keeping, and he had
not the courage to forsake it. Moreover, a slight congenital lameness made flight in such circumstances almost impossible. So
after a fugitive had come down heavily on his lame foot he
resigned himself to keeping in the main current and letting it
sweep him onto the boat.

Once on board, he had hastened to isolate himself behind a
funnel, in an airless corner reeking of oil and steam, while the
refugees, abandoned to unanimous seasickness, became for the
time an indistinguishable animal welter. But the run to London
had brought him into closer contact with them. It was impossible
to sit for three mortal hours with an unclaimed little boy on one's
lap, opposite a stony-faced woman holding a baby that never
stopped crying, and not give them something more than what
remained of one's chocolate and buns. The woman with the child
was bad enough; though perhaps less perversely moving than the
little blonde thing with long soiled gloves who kept staring
straight ahead and moaning: 'My furs—oh, my furs.' But worst of
all was the old man at the other end of the compartment: the
motionless old man in a frayed suit of professorial black, with a
face like a sallow bust on a bracket in a university library.

It was the face of Durand's own class and of his own profession, and it struck him as something not to be contemplated
without dire results to his nervous system. He was glad the old
man did not speak to him, but only waved away with a silent bow
the sandwich he offered; and glad that he himself was protected
by a slight stammer (which agitation always increased) from any
attempt at sustained conversation with the others. But in spite of
these safeguards the run to London was dreadful.

On the platform at Charing Cross he stood motionless, trying
to protect his lame leg and yet to take up as little room as

possible, while he waited for the tide to flow by and canalize itself. There was no way in which he could help the doomed wretches: he kept repeating that without its affording him the least relief. He had given away his last available penny, keeping barely enough to pay for a few frugal weeks in certain lodgings he knew of off Bedford Square; and he could do nothing for the moment but take up as little space as possible till a break in the crowd should let him hobble through to freedom. But that might not be for another hour; and meanwhile, helplessly, he gazed at the scene through misty spectacles.

The refugees were spread out about him in a stagnant mass, through which, over which, almost, there squeezed, darted, skimmed and criss-crossed the light battalions of the benevolent. People with badges were everywhere, philanthropists of both sexes and all ages, sorting, directing, exhorting, contradicting, saying 'Wee, wee,' and 'Oh, no,' and 'This way, please—oh, dear, what *is* "this way" in French?', and 'I beg your pardon, but that bed-warmer belongs to *my* old woman'; and industriously adding, by all the means known to philanthropy, to the distress and bewilderment of their victims.

Durand saw the old Professor who had travelled with him slip by alone, as if protected by his silent dignity. He saw other faces that held benevolence at bay. One or two erect old women with smooth hair and neat black bonnets gave him a sharper pang than the drooping and dishevelled; and he watched, with positive anguish, a mother pausing to straighten her little boy's collar. But what on earth could one do for any one of them?

Suddenly he was aware of a frightened touch on his arm.

'Oh, Monsieur, je vous en prie, venez! *Do* come!'

The voice was a reedy pipe, the face that of a little elderly lady so dry and diaphanous that she reminded him, in her limp dust-coloured garments, of a last year's moth shaken out of the curtains of an empty room.

'Je vous en *prie*,' she repeated, with a plaintive stress on the last word. Her intonation was not exactly French; he supposed it was some variety of provincial Belgian, and wondered why it sounded so unlike anything he had been hearing. Her face was as wild as anything so small and domesticated could be. Tears were running down her cheeks, and the hand on his sleeve twitched in its cotton glove.

'Mais oui—mais oui,' he found himself reassuring her. Her look of anxiety disappeared, and as he drew the cotton glove through his arm the tears seemed to be absorbed into her pale wrinkles.

'So many of them obviously want to be left alone; here's one who wants to be looked after,' he thought to himself, with a whimsical satisfaction in the discovery, as he yielded to the pull on his arm.

He was of a retiring nature, and compassion, far from making him expansive, usually contracted his faculties to the point of cowardice; but the scenes he had traversed were so far beyond any former vision of human wretchedness that all the defences of his gentle egotism had broken down, and he found himself suddenly happy, and almost proud, at having been singled out as a rescuer. He understood the passionate wish of all the rescuers to secure a refugee and carry him or her away in triumph against all competitors; and while his agile mind made a rapid sum in division his grasp tightened on the little old lady's arm, and he muttered to himself: 'They shan't take her from me if I have to live on dry bread.'

With a victim on his arm—and one who looked the part so touchingly—it was easier to insinuate his way through the crowd, and he fended off all the attempts of fair highwaymen to snatch his prize from him with an energy in which the prize ably seconded him.

'No, no, *no!*' she repeated, in mild piping English, tightening her clutch as he tightened his; and presently he discovered that she had noticed his lameness, and with her free hand was making soft defensive dabs at the backs and ribs that blocked their advance.

'You're lame, too—did *they* do it?' she whispered, falling into French again; and he said, chivalrously: 'Oh, yes—but it wasn't their fault...'

'The savages! I shall *never* feel in that way about them—though it's noble of you,' she murmured; and the inconsequence of this ferocity toward her fellow-sufferers struck him as refreshingly feminine. Like most shy men he was dazzled by unreasonable women.

'Are you in very great pain?' she continued, as they reached the street.

'Oh no—not at all. I bet you won't... The trouble is—' he broke off, confronted by an unforeseen difficulty.

'What *is* your trouble?' she sighed, leaning her little head toward him.

'Why—I—the fact is, I don't know London ... or England ... *jamais été,*' he confessed, merging the two languages in a vain effort at fluency.

'But of course—why should you? Only trust me...'

'Ah, you *do* know it, then?' What luck to have found a refugee who could take care of him! He vowed her half his worldly goods on the spot.

She was busy signalling a hansom, and did not answer.

'Is all this your luggage?' A porter had followed him with it. He felt that he ought to have been asking her for hers, but dared not, fearing a tragic answer. He supposed she had been able to bring away nothing but her threadbare cloak, and the little knobbly bag that had been prodding his ribs ever since they had linked arms.

'How lucky to have been able to save so much!' she sighed, as his bags and boxes were hoisted to the hansom.

'Yes—in such a fight,' he agreed; and wondered if she were a little flighty as she added: 'I suppose you didn't bring your mattress? Not that it matters in the very least. Quick, get in!' she shrieked out, pushing him past her into the hansom, and adding, as she scrambled in and snapped the doors shut: 'My sister-in-law ... she's so grasping ... I don't want her to see us...' She pushed up the lid, and cried out a name unfamiliar to her companion, but to which horse and driver instantly responded.

Durand sank back without speaking. He was bewildered and disconcerted, and her last words had shocked him. 'My sister-in-law ... she's so grasping...' The refugees, then, poor souls, were torn by the same family jealousies as more prosperous mortals. Affliction was supposed to soften, but apparently in such monstrous doses it had the opposite effect. He had noticed, on the journey, symptoms of this reciprocal distrust among the herded creatures. It was no doubt natural ... but he wished his little refugee had not betrayed the weakness.

The thought of the victim they were deserting (perhaps as helpless and destitute as his own waif) brought a protest to his stammering tongue.

'Ought—oughtn't we to take your sister-in-law with us? Hadn't we better turn back?'

'For Caroline? Oh, no, non, *no!*' She screamed it in every tongue. 'Cher monsieur, please! She's sure to have her own ... such heaps of them...'

Ah—it was jealousy, then; jealousy of the more favoured sister-in-law, who was no doubt younger and handsomer, and had been fought over by rival rescuers, while she, poor pet, had had to single one out for herself. Well, Durand felt he would not have exchanged her for a beauty—so frail, fluttered, plaintive did she seem, so small a vessel to contain so great a woe.

Suddenly it struck him that it was *she* who had given the order to the driver. He was more and more bewildered, and ashamed of his visible incompetence.

'Where are we going?' he faltered.

'For tea—there's plenty of time, I do assure you, and I'm faint-ing for a little food.'

'So am I,' he admitted; adding to himself: 'I'll feed the poor thing, and then we'll see what's to be done.'

How he wished he hadn't given away all but his last handful of shillings! His poverty had never been so humiliating to him. What right had he to be pretending to help a refugee? It was as much as he could do to pay the hansom and give her her tea. And then—? A dampness of fear broke over him, and he cursed his cowardice in not having told her at once to make another choice.

'But supposing nobody else had taken her?' he thought, steal-ing a look at her small pointed profile and the pale wisps of hair under her draggled veil. Her insignificance was complete, and he decided that he had probably been her last expedient.

It would be odd if it proved that she was also his. He remem-bered hearing that some of the rich refugees had been able to bring their money with them, and his mind strayed away to the whimsical possibility of being offered a post with emoluments by the frightened creature who was so determined not to let him go.

'If only I knew London,' he thought regretfully, 'I might be worth a good salary to her. The queer thing is that she seems to know it herself...'

Both sat silent, absorbed in their emotions.

It was certainly an odd way to be seeing London for the first time; but he was glad to be travelling at horse-pace, instead of whirling through his thronged sensations in a taxi.

'Trafalgar Square—yes. How clever of you! *Les lions de milord Nelsonne!*' she explained.

They drove on, past palaces and parks.

'Maison du grand Duc ... Arc de triomphe de marbre,' she successively enlightened him, sounding like a gnat in a mega-phone. He leaned and gazed, forgetting her and himself in an ecstasy of assimilation. In the golden autumn haze London loomed mightier and richer than his best dreams of it...

II

The hansom stopped, and they entered a modest tea-room which was not too densely crowded.

'I wanted to get away from that awful mob,' she explained, pushing back her veil as they seated themselves at a table with red and white napkins and a britannia sugar-bowl.

'Crumpets—lots of crumpets and jam,' she instructed a

disdainful girl in a butterfly cap, who languished away with the order to the back of the shop.

Durand sat speechless, overwhelmed by his predicament. Tea and crumpets were all very well—but afterward? He felt that his silence was becoming boorish, and leaned forward over the metal tea-pot. At the same instant, his protégée leaned too, and simultaneously they brought out the question:

{ 'Where were *you* when it broke out?'
{ 'Where were *you* when it broke out?'

'At Louvain,' he answered; and she shuddered.

'Louvain—how terrible!'

'And you, Madame?'

'I? At Brussels...'

'How terrible!' he echoed.

'Yes.' Her eyes filled with tears. 'I had such kind friends there.'

'Ah—of course. Naturally.'

She poured the tea, and pushed his cup to him. The haughty girl reappeared with sodden crumpets, which looked to him like manna steeped in nectar. He tossed off his tea as if it had been champagne, and courage began to flow through his veins. Never would he desert the simple creature who had trusted him! Let no one tell him that an able-bodied man with brains and education could not earn enough, in the greatest city in the world, to support himself and this poor sparrow.

The sparrow had emptied her cup, too, and a soft pink suffused her cheeks, effacing the wrinkles, which had perhaps been only lines of worry. He began to wonder if, after all, she were much more than forty... Rather absurd for a man of his age to have been calling a woman of forty an 'old lady'!

Suddenly he saw that the sense of security, combined with the hot tea and the crumpets, was beginning to act on her famished system like a dangerous intoxicant, and that she was going to tell him everything—or nearly everything. She bent forward, her elbows on the table, the cotton gloves drawn off her thin hands, which were nervously clenched under her chin. He noticed a large sapphire on one of them.

'I can't tell you ... I can't tell you how happy I am,' she faltered with swimming eyes.

He remained silent, through sheer embarrassment, and she went on: 'You see, I'd so completely lost hope—so completely. I thought no one would ever want me... They all told me at home that no one would—my nieces did, and everybody. They taunted me with it.' She broke off, and glanced at him appealingly. 'You *do* understand England, don't you?'

He assented, still more bewildered, and she went on: 'Oh, then it's so much easier—then we can really talk. (No—our train doesn't leave for nearly two hours.) You don't mind my talking, do you? You'll let me make a clean breast of it? I *must!*'

She touched with a claw-like finger the narrow interval between her shoulders, and added: 'For weeks I've been simply suffocating with longing...'

An uncomfortable redness rose to Charlie Durand's forehead. With these foreign women you could never tell: his brief continental experiences had taught him that. After all, he was not a monster, and several ladies had already attempted to prove it to him. There had been one adventure—on the way home to his hotel at Louvain, after dining with the curator of Prehistoric Antiquities—one adventure of which he could not think even now without feeling as if he were in a Turkish bath, with no marble slab to cool off on.

But this poor lady—! Of course he was mistaken. He blushed anew at his mistake...

'They all laughed at me—jeered at me—Caroline and my nieces and all of them. They said it was no use trying—they'd failed, and how was *I* going to succeed? Even Caroline has failed hitherto—and she's so dreadfully determined. And of course for a married woman it's always easier, isn't it?'

She appealed to him with anxious eyes, and his own sank behind his protecting spectacles. Easier for a married woman—! After all, perhaps he hadn't been mistaken. He had heard, of course, that in the highest society the laxity was even worse...

'It's true enough,' (she seemed to be answering him), 'that the young good-looking women got everything away from us. There's nothing new in that: they always have. I don't know how they manage it; but I'm told they were on hand when the very first boat-load of refugees arrived. I understand the young Duchess of Bolchester and Lady Ivy Trantham were down at Folkestone with all the Trantham motors—and from that day to this, though we've all had our names down on the government list, not one of us— not one human being at Lingerfield—has had so much as an application from the Committee. And when I couldn't stand it any longer, and said I was going up to town myself, to wait at the station and seize one of the poor things before any of those unscrupulous women had got him, they said it was just like me to make a show of myself for nothing... But, after all, you see Caroline sneaked off after me without saying anything, and was making a show of herself, too. And when I saw her she evidently hadn't succeeded, for she was running about all alone, looking as

wild as she does on sales days at Harrod's. Caroline is very extravagant, and doesn't mind what she spends; but she never can make
up her mind between bargains, and rushes about like a
madwoman till it's too late.—But, oh, how humiliating for her to
go back to the Hall without a single refugee!' The speaker broke
off with a laugh of triumph, and wiped away her tears.

Charlie Durand sat speechless. The crumpet had fallen from
his fork, and his tea was turning gray; but he was unconscious of
such minor misfortunes.

'I don't … I don't understand …' he began; but as he spoke he
perceived that he did.

It was as clear as daylight: he and his companion had recipro-
cally taken each other for refugees, and she was pressing upon
him the assistance he had been wondering how on earth he
should manage to offer her!

'Of course you don't… I explain so badly … they've always told
me that …' she went on eagerly. 'Fancy my asking you if you'd
brought your mattress, for instance—what you must have
thought! But the fact is, I'd made up my mind you were going to
be one of those poor old women in caps, who take snuff and spill
things, and who have always come away with nothing but their
beds and a saucepan. They all said at Lingerfield: "If you get even
a deaf old woman you're lucky"—and so I arranged to give you—
I mean her—one of the rooms in the postmistress's cottage,
where I've put an old bedstead that the vicar's coachman's
mother died in, but the mattress had to be burnt … whereas of
course now you're coming to *me*—to the Cottage, I mean … and I
haven't even told you where it is, or who I am… Oh, dear, it's so
stupid of me; but you see Kathleen and Agatha and my sister-in-
law all said: "Of course poor Audrey'll never get anybody"; and
I've had the room standing ready for three weeks—all *but* the
mattress; till even the vicar's wife had begun to joke about it with
my brother—oh, my brother's Lord Beausedge—didn't I tell
you?'

She paused breathless, and then added with embarrassment: 'I
don't think I ever made such a long speech in my life.'

He was sure she hadn't, for as she poured out her confession it
had been borne in on him that he was listening not to an habitual
babbler, but to the uncontrollable outburst of a shy woman
grown inarticulate through want of listeners. It was harrowing,
the arrears of self-confession that one guessed behind her torrent
of broken phrases.

'I can't tell you,' she began again, as if she had perceived his
sympathy, 'the difference it's going to make for me at home: my

bringing back the first refugee, and it's being ... well, some one like *you*...'

Her blushes deepened, and she lost herself again in the abasing sense of her inability to explain.

'Well, my name at any rate,' she burst out, 'is Audrey Rushworth ... and I'm not married.'

'Neither am I,' said her guest, smiling. American-fashion, he was groping to produce a card. It would really not be decent in him to keep up the pretence a moment longer, and here was an easy way to let her know of her mistake. He pushed the card toward her, and as he did so his eye fell on it, and he saw, too late, that it was one of those he had rather fatuously had engraved in French for his continental travels.

CHARLES DURAND

PROFESSEUR DES LANGUES ROMANES
À L'UNIVERSITÉ DE LA SALLE
DOCTEUR DES LETTRES DE L'UNIVERSITÉ DE LOUVAIN

She scanned the inscription and raised a reverent glance to him. '*Monsieur le Professeur*—? I'd no idea ... though I suppose I ought to have known at once... Oh, I do hope,' she cied, 'you won't find Lingerfield too unbearably dull!' She added, as if it were wrung from her: 'Some people think my nieces rather clever.'

The Professor of Romance Languages sat fascinated by the consequences of his last blunder. That card seemed to have been dealt out by the finger of fate. Supposing he went to Lingerfield with her—just to see what it was like? He had always pined to see what an English country-seat was like; and Lingerfield was apparently important. He shook off the mad notion with an effort. 'I'll drive with her to the station,' he thought, 'and just lose myself in the crowd. That will be the easiest way.'

'There are three of them—Agatha, Kathleen and Clio... But you'll find us all hopelessly dull,' he heard her repeating.

'I shall—I certainly shan't... I mean, of course, how could I?' he stammered.

It was so much like her own syntax that it appeared to satisfy her.

'No—*I* pay!' she cried, darting between him and the advancing waitress. 'Shall we walk? It's only two steps—' and, seeing him look about for the vanished hansom, 'Oh, I sent the luggage on at once by the cab-driver. You see, there's a good deal of it, and there's such a hideous rush at the booking-office at this hour. He'll have given it to a porter—so please don't worry!'

Firm and elastic as a girl she sprang through the doorway, while, limping at her side, he stared at the decisive fact that his luggage was once more out of his keeping.

III

Charlie Durand (his shaving glass told him) was forty-five, decid-edly bald, with an awkward limp, scant-lashed blue eyes blinking behind gold spectacles, a brow that he believed to be thoughtful and a chin that he knew to be weak.

His height was medium, his figure sedentary, with the hollows and prominences in the wrong places; and he wore ready-made clothes in protective colours, and square-toed boots with side-elastics, and stammered whenever it was all-important to speak fluently.

But his sister Mabel, who knew him better than the others, had once taken one of his cards and run a pen through the word 'Languages,' leaving simply 'Professor of Romance'; and in his secret soul Charlie Durand knew that she was right.

He had, in truth, a dramatic imagination without the power of expression; instead of writing novels, he read them; instead of living adventures, he dreamed them. Being naturally modest he had long since discovered his limitations, and decided that all his imagination would ever do for him was to give him a greater freedom of judgment than his neighbours. Even that was some-thing to be thankful for; but now he began to ask himself if it were enough...

Professor Durand had read 'L'Abbesse de Jouarre', and knew that, in moments of extreme social peril, superior persons often felt themselves justified in casting conventional morality to the winds. He had no thought of proceeding to such extremes; but he did wonder if, at the hour when civilization was shaken to its base, he, Charlie Durand, might not at last permit himself forty-eight hours of romance...

His audacity was fortified by the fact that his luggage was out of his control, for he could hardly picture any situation more subversive than that of being separated from his tooth-brush and his reading-glasses. But the difficulty of explaining himself if he

went any farther in the adventure loomed larger as they
approached the station; and as they crossed its crowded threshold, and Miss Rushworth said: 'Now we'll see about your things',
he saw a fresh possibility of escape, and cried out: 'No—no;
please find places—I'll look for my luggage.'

He felt on his arm the same inexorable grasp that had steered
him through the labyrinth of Charing Cross.

'You're quite right. We'll get our seats first; in such a crowd it's
safer!' she answered gaily, and guided him toward a second-class
compartment (he had always heard the aristocracy travelled
second class in England). 'Besides,' she continued, as she
pounced on two corner seats, 'the luggage is sure to be in the van
already. Or, if it isn't, you'd never find it. All the refugees in
England seem to be travelling by this train!'

They did indeed—and how tell her that there was one less in
the number than she imagined? A new difficulty had only just
occurred to him. It was easy enough to explain to her that she had
been mistaken; but if he did, how justify the hours he had already
spent in her company? Could he tell the sister of Lord Beausedge
that he had taken her for a refugee?

Desperation nerved him to unconsidered action. The train was
not leaving yet—there was still time for the confession.

He scrambled to the seat opposite his captor's and rashly
spoke. 'I ought to tell you... I must apologize—apologize
abjectly—for not explaining sooner...'

Miss Rushworth turned pale, and leaning forward caught him
by the wrist.

'Ah, don't go on—' she gasped.

He lost his last hold on self-possession.

'Not go on—?'

'Don't you suppose I know—didn't you guess that I knew all
along?'

He paled too, and then crimsoned, all his old suspicions
rushing back on him.

'How could I not,' she pursued, 'when I saw all those heaps of
luggage? Of course I knew at once that you were rich, and didn't
need ...' her wistful eyes were wet ... 'need anything *I* could do for
you. but you looked so lonely ... and your lameness, and the
moral anguish... I don't see, after all, why we should open our
houses *only* to pauper refugees; and it's not my fault, is it, if the
Committee simply wouldn't send me any?'

'But ... but ...' he desperately began; and then all at once his
stammer caught him, and an endless succession of b-b-b- issued
from his helpless throat.

With exquisite tact Miss Rushworth smiled away his confusion.
'I won't listen to another word ... not one!—Oh, duck your
head—*quick!*' she shrieked in another voice, flattening herself
back into her corner.

Durand recognized the same note of terror with which she had
hailed her sister-in-law's approach at Charing Cross. It was needless for her to add faintly: 'Caroline.'

As she did so, a plumed and determined head surged up into
the window-frame, and an astonished voice exclaimed: 'Audrey!'

A moment later four ladies, a maid laden with parcels, and two
bushy Chow dogs, had possessed themselves of all that remained
of the compartment; and Durand, as he squeezed himself into his
corner, was feeling the relief which comes with the cessation of
virtuous effort. He had seen at a glance that there was nothing
more to be done.

The young ladies with Lady Beausedge were visibly her daughters. They were of graduated heights, beginning with a very tall
one, and were all thin, conspicuous and queerly dressed, suggesting to the bewildered Professor bad copies of originals he had
never seen. None of them took any notice of him, and the dogs,
after smelling his ankles, contemptuously followed their example.

It would indeed have been difficult, during the first moments,
for any personality less masterful than Lady Beausedge's to assert
itself in her presence. So prevalent was she that Durand found
himself viewing her daughters, dogs and attendant as her mere
fringes and attributes, and thinking with terror: 'She's going to
choose the seat next to me,' when in reality it was only the
youngest and thinnest of the girls who was settling herself at his
side with a play of parcels as sharp as elbows.

Lady Beausedge was already assailing her sister-in-law.

'I'd no idea you were going up to town today, Audrey. You said
nothing of it when you dined with us last night.'

Miss Rushworth's eyes fluttered apprehensively from Lady
Beausedge's awful countenance to the timorous face of the
Professor of Romance Languages, who had bought a newspaper
and was deep in its inner pages.

'Neither did you, Caroline,' Miss Rushworth began with unexpected energy; and the thin girl next to Durand laughed.

'Neither did I what?—What are you laughing at, Clio?'

'Neither did you say *you* were coming up to town, mother.'

Lady Beausedge glared, and the other girls giggled. Even the
maid stooped over the dogs to conceal an appreciative smile. It
was evident that baiting Lady Beausedge was a popular if dangerous amusement.

'As it happens,' said the lady of Lingerfield, 'the Committee telephoned only this morning...'

Miss Rushworth's eyes brightened. She grew almost arch. 'Ah—then you came up about refugees?'

'Naturally.' Lady Beausedge shook out her boa and opened the *Pall Mall Gazette.*

'Such a fight!' groaned the tallest girl, who was also the largest, vividest and most expensively dressed.

'Yes ... it was hardly worth while... Anything so grotesquely mismanaged...'

The young lady called Clio remarked in a quiet undertone: 'Five people and two dogs to fetch down one old woman with a pipe...'

'Ah ... you *have* got one?' murmured Miss Rushworth, with what seemed to Durand a malicious simulation of envy.

'Yes,' her sister-in-law grudgingly admitted. 'But, as Clio says, it's almost an insult to have dragged us all up to town... They'd promised us a large family, with a prima donna from the Brussels Opera (so useful for Agatha's music); and two orphans besides... I suppose Ivy Trantham got them all as usual...' She paused, and aded more condescendingly: 'After all, Audrey, you were right not to try to do anything through the Committee.'

'Yes; I think one does better without,' Miss Rushworth replied with extreme gentleness.

'One does better without refugees, you mean? I daresay we shall find it so. I've no doubt the Bolchester set has taken all but the utterly impossible ones.'

'Not *all*,' said Miss Rushworth.

Something in her tone caused her nieces to exchange a glance, and Lady Beausedge to rear her head from the *Pall Mall Gazette.*

'Not *all*,' repeated Miss Rushworth.

The eldest girls broke into an excited laugh. 'Aunt Audrey— you don't mean *you've* got an old woman with a pipe too?'

'No. Not an old woman.' She paused, and waved her hand in Durand's direction. 'Monsieur le Professeur Durand, de l'Université de Louvain... My sister-in-law, my nieces... (*He speaks English*),' she added in a whisper.

IV

Charlie Durand's window was very low and wide, and quaintly trellised. There was no mistaking it: it was a 'lattice'—a real one, with old bluish panes set in black mouldings, not the stage variety

made of plate-glass and *papier maché* that he had seen in the sham
'Cottage' of æsthetic suburbs at home.

When he pushed the window open a branch of yellow roses
brushed his face, and a dewy clematis gazed in at him with purple
eyes. Below lay a garden, incredibly velvety, flower-filled, and
enclosed in yew-hedges so high that it seemed, under the low
twilight sky, as intimate and shut in as Miss Rushworth's low-
ceilinged drawing-room, which, in its turn, was as open to the air,
and as full of flowers, as the garden.

But all England, that afternoon, as his train traversed it, had
seemed like some great rich garden roofed in from storm and
dust and disorder. What a wonderful place, and what a miracle to
have been thus carried into the very heart of it! All his scruples
vanished in the enchantment of this first encounter with the
English country.

When he had bathed and dressed, and descended the black oak
stairs, he found his hostess waiting in the garden. She was hatless,
with a pale scarf over her head, and a pink spot of excitement on
each faded cheek.

'I should have preferred a quiet evening here; but since Caroline made such a point of our dining at the Hall—' she began.

'Of course, of course ... it's all so lovely...' said her guest reck-
lessly. He would have dined at Windsor Castle with composure.
After the compact and quintessential magic of the Cottage
nothing could surprise or overwhelm him.

They left the garden by a dark green door in a wall of old
peach-coloured brick, and walked in the deepening twilight
across a field and over a stile. A stile! He remembered pictures
and ballads about helping girls over stiles, and lowered his eyes
respectfully as Miss Rushworth's hand rested on his in the
descent.

The next moment they were in the spacious shade of a sort of
forest of Arden, with great groups of bossy trees standing apart,
and deer flashing by at the end of ferny glades.

'Is it—are we—?'

'Oh, yes. This is Lingerfield. The Cottage is on the edge of the
park. It's not a long walk, if we go by the chapel and through the
cloisters.'

The very words oppressed him with their too-crowding suggestions. There was a chapel in the park—there were cloisters!
Lingerfield had an ecclesiastical past—had been an abbey, no
doubt. But even such associations paled in the light of the reality.
As they came out of the shadow of the trees they recovered a last
glow of daylight. In it lay a gray chapel, delicately laced and

pinnacled; and beyond the chapel the arcade of the cloister, a
lawn with one domed cedar, and a long Tudor house, its bricks
still rosy in the dusk, and a gleam of sunset caught in its windows.

'How—how long the daylight lasts in England!' said Professor
Durand, choking with emotion.

The drawing-room into which he had followed Miss Rushworth seemed full of people and full of silence. Professor Durand
had never had, on a social occasion, such an impression of effort-
less quiet. The ladies about the big stone chimney-piece and
between the lamp-lit tables, if they had not been so modern in
dress and attitude, might have been a part of the shadowy past.

Only Lady Beausedge, strongly corseted, many necklaced, her
boa standing out from her bare shoulders like an Elizabethan
ruff, seemed to Durand majestic enough for her background. She
managed a composite image of Bloody Mary and the late Queen.

He was just recovering from the exchange of silences that had
greeted his entrance when he discovered another figure worthy of
the scene. It was Lord Beausedge, standing in the window, and
glancing disgustedly over the evening paper.

Lord Beausedge was as much in character as his wife; only he
belonged to a later period. He suggested stocks and nankeen
trousers, a Lawrence portrait, port wine, fox-hunting, the Penin-
sular campaign, the Indian mutiny, every Englishman doing his
duty, and resistance to the Reform Bill. It was portentous that
one person, in modern clothes and reading a newspaper, should
so epitomize a vanished age.

He made a step or two toward his guest, took him for granted,
and returned to the newspaper.

'Why—why do we all fidget so in America?' Professor Durand
wondered.

'Gwen and Ivy are always late,' said Lady Beausedge, as though
answering a silence.

Miss Rushworth looked agitated.

'Are they coming from Trantham?'

'Not him. Only Gwen and Ivy. Agatha telephoned, and Gwen
asked if they might.'

After that everyone sat silent again for a long time, without any
air or impatience or surprise. Durand had the feeling that they
all—except perhaps Lord Beausedge—had a great deal to say to
him, but that it would be very slow in coming to the surface.
Well—so much the better; time was no consideration, and he was
glad not to crowd his sensations.

'Do you know the Duchess?' asked Lady Beausedge suddenly.

'The Duchess—?'

'Gwen Bolchester. She's coming. She wants to see you.'

'To see *me?*'

'When Agatha telephoned that you were here she chucked a dinner somewhere else, and she's rushing over from Trantham with her sister-in-law.'

Durand looked helplessly at Miss Rushworth and saw that her cheeks were pink with triumph. The Duchess of Bolchester was coming to see her refugee!

'Do people here just chuck dinners like that?' he asked, with a faint facetiousness.

'When they want to,' said Lady Beausedge simply. The conversation again came to a natural end.

It revived with feverish vivacity on the entrance of two tall and emaciated young women, who drifted in after Lord Beausedge had decided to ring for dinner, and who wasted none of their volubility in excusing their late arrival.

The newcomers, who had a kind of limp loveliness totally unknown to the Professor of Romance Languages, he guessed to be the Duchess of Bolchester and Lady Ivy Trantham, the most successful refugee-raiders of the district. They were dressed in pale frail garments and hung with barbaric beads and bangles, and as soon as he saw them he understood why he had thought the daughters of the house looked like bad copies—all except the youngest, whom he was beginning to single out from her sisters.

He was not sure if, during the murmur of talk that followed, some one breathed his name to the newcomers; but certainly no one told him which of the two ladies was which, or indeed made any effort to draw him into the conversation. It was only when the slightly less tall addressed the tallest as 'Gwen' that he remembered this name was the Duchess's.

She had swept him with a smiling glance of her large sweet vacant eyes, and he had the impression that she too had things to say to him, but that the least strain on her attention was too great an effort, and that each time she was about to remember who he was something else distracted her.

The thought that a Duchess had chucked a dinner to see him had made him slightly giddy; and the humiliation of finding that, once they were confronted, she had forgotten what she had come for, was painful even to his disciplined humility.

But Professor Durand was not without his modest perspicacity, and little by little he began to guess that this absence of concentration and insistence was part of a sort of leisurely holiday spirit unlike anything he had ever known. Under the low-voiced volubility and restless animation of these young women (whom the daughters of the house intensely imitated), he felt a great central inattention. Their strenuousness was not fatiguing because it did not insist, but blew about like thistledown from topic to topic. He saw that his safety lay in this, and reassurance began to steal over him as he understood that the last danger he was exposed to was that of being too closely scrutinized or interrogated.

'If I'm an imposter,' he thought, 'at least no one here will find it out.'

And, then, just as he had drawn this sage conclusion, he felt the sudden pounce of the Duchess's eye. Dinner was over, and the party had re-grouped itself in a great book-panelled room, before the carved chimney-piece of which she stood lighting her cigarette, like a Duchess on the cover of a novel.

'You know I'm going to carry you off presently,' she said.

Miss Audrey Rushworth was sitting in a sofa corner beside her youngest niece, whom she evidently found less intimidating than the others. Durand, instinctively glancing toward them, saw the elder lady turn pale, while Miss Clio Rushworth's swinging foot seemed to twinkle with malice.

He bowed as he supposed one ought to bow when addressed by a Duchess.

'Off for a talk?' he hazarded playfully.

'Off to Trantham. Didn't they tell you? I'm giving a big garden-party for the Refugee Relief Fund, and I'm looking for somebody to give us a lecture on Atrocities. That's what I came for,' she added ingenuously.

There was a profound silence, which Lord Beausedge, lifting his head from the *Times*, suddenly broke.

'Damned bad taste, all that sort of thing,' he remarked, and continued his reading.

'But, Gwen, dear,' Miss Rushworth faltered, 'your garden-party isn't till the twentieth.'

The Duchess looked surprised. She evidently had no head for dates. 'Isn't it, Aunt Audrey? Well, it doesn't matter, does it? I want him all the same—we want him awfully, Ivy, don't we?' She shone on Durand. 'You'll see such lots of your own people at Trantham. The Belgian Minister and the French Ambassador are coming down for the lecture. You'll feel less lonely there.'

Lady Beausedge intervened with authority. 'I think I have a prior claim, my dear Gwen. Of course Audrey was not expecting any one—any one like Professor Durand; and at the Cottage he might ... he might ... but *here*, with your uncle, and the girls all speaking French...' She turned to Durand with a hospitable smile.

'Your room's quite ready; and of course my husband will be delighted if you like to use the library to prepare your lecture in. We'll send the governess-cart for your traps tomorrow.' She fixed her firm eyes on the Duchess. 'You see, dear, it was all quite settled before you came.'

Lady Ivy Trantham spoke up. 'It's not a bit of use, Aunt Carry. Gwen can't give him up.' (Being apparently unable to master the Professor's name, the sister-in-law continued to designate him by the personal pronoun). 'The Committee has given us a prima donna from the Brussels Opera to sing the Marseillaise, and the what d'ye-call-it Belgian anthem, but there are lots of people coming just for the Atrocities.'

'Oh, we must have the Atrocities,' the Duchess echoed. She looked musingly at Durand's pink troubled face. 'He'll do them awfully well,' she concluded, talking about him as if he were deaf.

'We must have somebody who's accustomed to lecturing. People won't put up with amateurs,' Lady Ivy reinforced her.

Lady Beausedge's countenance was dark with rage.

'A prima donna from the Brussels Opera! But the Committee telephoned me this morning to come up and meet a prima donna... It's all a mistake *her* being at Trantham, Gwen.'

'Well,' said the Duchess serenely, 'I daresay it's all a mistake *his* being here.' She looked more and more tenderly on the Professor.

'But he's not here; he's with me at the Cottage!' cried Miss Rushworth, springing up with sudden resolution. 'It's too absurd and undignified, this ... squabbling...'

'Yes; don't let's squabble. Come along,' said the Duchess, slipping her long arm through Durand's as Miss Rushworth's had been slipped through it at Charing Cross.

The subject of this flattering but agitating discussion had been struggling, ever since it began, with a nervous contraction of the throat. When at length his lips opened only a torrent of consonants rushed from them, finally followed by the cryptic monosyllables: '—I'm *not!*'

'Not a professional? Oh, but you're a Professor—that'll do,' cried Lady Ivy Trantham briskly; while the Duchess, hugging his arm closer, added in a voice of persuasion: 'You see, we've got one at Trantham already, and we're so awfully afraid of him that we want you to come and talk to him. You *must.*'

'I mean, n-n-not a r-r-ref—' gasped out the desperate Durand.

Suddenly he felt his other arm caught by Miss Clio Rushworth, who gave it a deep and eloquent pinch. At the same time their eyes met, and he read in hers entreaty, command, and the passionate injunction to follow her lead.

'Poor Professor Durand— you'll take us for Red Indians on the war-trail! Come to the dining-room with me and I'll give you a glass of Perrier. I saw the curry was too strong for you,' this young lady insinuatingly declared.

Durand, with one of his rare flashes of self-possession, had converted his stammer into a strangling cough, and, released by the Duchess, made haste to follow his rescuer out of the room. He kept up his cough while they crossed the hall, and by the time they reached the dining-room tears of congestion were running down behind his spectacles, and he sank into a chair and rested his elbows despairingly on a corner of the great mahogany table.

Miss Clio Rushworth disappeared behind a screen and returned with a glass of Perrier. 'Anything in it?' she enquired pleasantly, and smiled at his doleful gesture of negation.

He emptied his glass and cleared his throat; but before he could speak she held up a silencing hand.

'Don't—don't!' she said.

He was startled by this odd echo of her aunt's entreaty, and a little tired of being hurled from one cryptic injunction to another.

'Don't what?' he asked sharply.

'Make a clean breast of it. Not yet. Pretend you *are*, just a little longer, please.'

'Pretend I am—?'

'A refugee.' She sat down opposite him, her sharp chin supported on crossed hands. 'I'll tell you why—'

But Professor Durand was not listening. A momentary rapture of relief at being found out had been succeeded by a sick dread of the consequences. He tried to read the girl's thin ironic face, but her eyes and smile were inscrutable.

'Miss Rushworth, at least let me tell you—'

She shook her head kindly but firmly. 'That you're not a German spy in disguise? Bless you, don't you suppose I can guess what's happened? I saw it the moment we got into the railway carriage. I suppose you came over from Boulogne in the refugee train, and when poor dear Aunt Audrey pounced on you, you began to stammer and couldn't explain...'

Oh, the blessed balm of her understanding! He drew a deep breath of gratitude, and faltered, smiling back at her smile: 'It was worse than that ... much worse... I took *her* for a refugee too: we rescued each other!'

A peal of youthful mirth shook the mighty rafters of the Lingerfield dining-room. Miss Clio Rushworth buried her face and sobbed.

'Oh, I see—I see—I see it all!'

'No you don't—not quite—not yet—' he gurgled back at her.

'Tell me, then; tell me everything!'

And he told her; told her quietly, succinctly and without a stammer, because under her cool kindly gaze he felt himself at last in an atmosphere of boundless comprehension.

'You see ... the adventure fascinated me... I won't deny that,' he ended, laying bare the last fold of his duplicity.

This, for the first time, seemed to stagger her.

'The adventure—an adventure with Aunt Audrey?'

They smiled at each other a little 'I meant, the adventure of England—I've never been in England before—and of a baronial hall: it *is* baronial? In short, of just exactly what's been happening to me. The novelty, you see—but how should you see?—was irresistible. The novelty, and all the old historic associations. England's in our blood, after all.' He looked about him at the big dusky tapestried room. 'Fancy having seen this kind of thing only on the stage! ...Yes, I was drawn on by everything—by everything I saw and heard, from the moment I set foot in London. Of course, if I hadn't been I should have found an opportunity of explaining—or I could have bolted away from her at the station.'

'I'm so glad you didn't. That's what I'm coming to,' said the girl. 'You see, it's been—how shall I explain?—more than an adventure for Aunt Audrey. It's literally the first thing that's ever happened to her.'

Professor Durand blushed to the roots of his hair.

'I don't understand,' he said feebly.

'No. Of course not. Any more, I suppose, than *I* really understand what Lingerfield represents to an American. And you would have had to live at Lingerfield for generations and generations to understand Aunt Audrey. You see, nothing much ever happened to the unmarried women of her time. Most of them were just put away in cottages covered with clematis and forgotten. Aunt Audrey has always been forgotten—even the Refugee Committee forgot her. And my father and mother, and her other brothers and sisters, and my brother and sisters and I—I'm afraid we've always forgotten her too—'

'Not you,' said Professor Durand with sudden temerity.

Miss Clio Rushworth smiled. 'I'm very fond of her; and then I've been a little bit forgotten myself.' She paused a moment, and continued: 'All this would take too long to explain. But what I want to beg of you is this—let her have her adventure, give her her innings, keep up the pretence a little longer. None of the others have guessed, and I promise to get you away safely before they do. Just let Aunt Audrey have her refugee for a bit, and triumph over

Lingerfield and Trantham.—The Duchess? Oh, I'll arrange that too. Slip back to the Cottage now—this way, across the lawn, by the chapel—and I'll say your cough was so troublesome that you rushed off to put on a mustard plaster. I'll tell Gwen you'll be delighted to give the lecture—'

Durand raised his hands in protest, but she went on: 'Why, don't you see that the more you hold out the more she'll want you? Whereas, if you accept at once, and even let her think you're going over to stop at Trantham as soon as your cold is better, she'll forget she's ever asked you.—Insincere, you say? Yes, of course; a *little*. But have you considered what would have happened if you hadn't choked just now, and had succeeded in shouting out before everybody that you were an impostor?'

A cold chill ran down Charlie Durand's spine as his masterful adviser set forth this aspect of the case.

'Yes—I do see... I see it's for the best...' he stammered.

'Well—rather!' She pushed him toward a glass door opening on the lawn. 'Be off now—and do play up, won't you? I'll promise to stick by you and see you out of it, if only you'll do as I ask.'

Their hands met in a merry grasp of complicity, and as he fled away through the moonlight he carried with him the vision of her ugly vivid face, and wondered how such a girl could ever think she could be forgotten.

V

A good many things had happened before he stood again on the pier at Boulogue.

It was in April 1918, and he was buttoned into a too-tight uniform, on which he secretly hoped the Y.M.C.A. initials were not always the first things to strike the eye of the admiring spectator.

It was not that he was ungrateful to the great organization which had found a task for him in its ranks; but that he could never quite console himself for the accident of having been born a few years too soon to be wearing the real uniform of his country. That would indeed have been Romance beyond his dreams; but he had long ago discovered that he was never to get beyond the second-best in such matters. None of his adventures would ever be written with a capital.

Still, he was very content; and never more so than now that he was actually in France again, in touch and in sound of the mighty struggle that had once been more than his nerves could bear, but that they could bear now with perfect serenity because he and his country, for all they were individually worth, had a stake in the affair, and were no longer mere sentimental spectators.

The scene, novel as it was because of the throngs of England and American troops that animated it, was still, in some of its details, pathetically familiar. For the German advance in the north had set in movement the native populations of that region, and among the fugitives some forlorn groups had reached Boulogne and were gathered on the pier, much as he had seen them four years earlier. Only in this case, they were in dozens instead of hundreds, and the sight of them was harrowing more because of what they symbolized than from their actual numbers.

Professor Durand was no more in quest of refugees than he had been formerly. He had been despatched to Boulogne to look after the library of a Y.M.C.A. canteen, and was standing on the pier looking about him for a guide with the familiar initials on his collar.

In the general confusion he could discover no one who took the least interest in his problem, and he was waiting resignedly in the sheltered angle formed by two stacks of packing-cases when he abruptly remembered that he had always known the face he was looking at was not one to forget.

It was that of a dark thin girl in khaki, with a slouch hat and leggings, and her own unintelligible initials on her shoulder, who was giving firm directions to a large orderly in a British army motor.

As Durand looked at her she looked at him. Their eyes met, and she burst out laughing.

'Well, you do have the queerest looking tunics in your army!' she exclaimed as their hands clasped.

'I know we do—and I'm too fat. But you knew me?' he cried triumphantly.

'Why, of course! I should know your spectacles anywhere,' said Miss Clio Rushworth gaily. She finished what she was saying to the orderly, and then came back to the Professor.

'What a lark! What are you? Oh, Y.M.C.A., of course. With the British, I suppose?' They perched on the boxes and exchanged confidences, while Durand inwardly hoped that the man who ought to be looking for him was otherwise engaged.

Apparently he was, for their talk continued to ramble on through a happy labyrinth of reminiscences punctuated with laughter.

'And when your people found out—weren't they too awfully horrified?' he asked at last, blushing at the mere remembrance.

She shook her head with a smile. 'They never did—nobody

found out but father, and he laughed for a week. I wouldn't have had any one else know for the world. It would have spoilt all Aunt Audrey's fun if Lingerfield had known you weren't a refugee. To this day you're her great Adventure.'

'But how did you manage it? I don't see yet.'

'Come in to our canteen tonight and I'll tell you.' She stood up and shoved her cigarette case into the pocket of the tunic that fitted so much better than his.

'I tell you what—as your man hasn't turned up, come over to the canteen now, and see Aunt Audrey.'

Professor Durand paled in an unmartial manner.

'Oh, is Miss Rushworth here?'

'Rather! She's my chief. Come along.'

'Your chief—?' He wavered again, his heart failing him.

'Really—won't it be better for me not to? Suppose—suppose she should remember me?'

Miss Rushworth's niece laughed. 'I don't believe she will, she's so blind. Besides, what if she did? She's seen a good many refugees since your day. You see they've become rather a drug in the market, poor dears. And Aunt Audrey's got her head full of other things now.'

She had started off at her long swift stride and he was hurrying obediently after her.

The big brown canteen was crowded with soldiers who were being variously refreshed by young ladies in trig khaki. At the other end of the main room, Miss Clio Rushworth turned a corner and entered an office. Durand followed her.

At the office desk sat a lady with eye-glasses on a sharp nose. She wore a Colonel's uniform, with several decorations, and was bending over the desk busily writing.

A young girl in a nurse's dress stood beside her, as if waiting for an order, and flattened against the wall of the room sat a row of limp and desolate beings—too evidently refugees.

The Colonel lifted her head quickly and glanced at her niece with a resolute and almost forbidding eye.

'Not another refugee, Clio—not *one!* I absolutely refuse. We've not a hole left to put them in, and the last family you sent me went off with my mackintosh and my electric lamp.'

She bent again sternly to her writing. As she looked up her glance strayed carelessly over Professor Durand's congested countenance, and then dropped to the desk without a sign of recognition.

'Oh, Aunt Audrey—not one, not just *one?*' the Colonel's niece pleaded.

'It's no use, my dear.—Now don't interrupt, please.—Here are the bulletins, Nurse.'

Colonel Audrey Rushworth shut her lips with a snap and her pen drove on steadily over the sheets of official letter paper.

When Professor Durand and Clio Rushworth stood outside of the canteen again in the spring sunshine they looked long at each other without speaking. Charlie Durand, under his momentary sense of relief, was aware of a distinct humiliation.

'I see I needn't have been afraid!' he said, forcing a laugh.

'I told you so. The fact is, Aunt Audrey has a lot of other things to think about nowadays. There's no danger of *her* being forgotten—it's she who does the forgetting now.' She laid a commiserating hand on his arm. 'I'm sorry—but you must excuse her. She's just been promoted again, and she's going to marry the Bishop of the Macaroon Islands next month.'

▼▼

Red Tape

I

THEY WERE GOING. Mr Starkey had made up his mind from the moment of England's ultimatum to Germany. And Miss Delacheroy had made up hers from the moment when he had faced her with it: 'I am going to the front.'

There was nowhere else, he said, he *could* go. To which Miss Delacheroy had replied, 'If you go I go too.'

Nothing in all their long association had drawn such a poignant note from her. But Mr Starkey was visibly uplifted; so, even more visibly, was Miss Delacheroy.

Uplifted or not uplifted, they knew that there could be no two opinions about their going. It was the only way Mr Starkey could serve his country. And it was the only way Miss Delacheroy could serve Mr Starkey. She had to confess that, satisfying as her friendship with Mr Starkey was, it had lacked hitherto its supreme opportunity.

Of course there had been pretexts and occasions. She found them every day in the office of the Kilburn branch of the United Charities, the scene of their associated labours. But none of them appealed to her imagination; none, in her uplifted moods, gave her sanction and absolution; none counted as supreme. Except (she reminded herself) the first occasion of their meeting, which occurred in the office of the United Charities (Kilburn branch). If it came to that, every hour of their association counted, every minute counted, since the day when Mr Starkey, as organising secretary, took over the office and its fittings and Miss Delacheroy.

He had a genius for organisation, and he had begun by organising Miss Delacheroy. She had a genius for being organised. It was his boast that he had trained her; it was hers that she had been trained by him.

More than trained. He took her over as an inconsiderable part of the office furniture—a little machine, shoved aside into its corner, rather the worse for wear and working badly. Under his hands she became a living thing.

That was ten years ago.

He had not always been an organising secretary. Once, in his youth, he had been a medical student. He would have been a medical practitioner now if he had not had the bad luck to fail in his final. Nobody but Mr Starkey knew how long that was ago. And before Miss Delacheroy became a piece of office furniture she had been a lady of leisure, living in her father the General's house, on his income and his pension. Afterwards she lived in the house on her own pension, the General's income having departed with him. That was in Miss Delacheroy's youth, and nobody knew how long ago that was either.

Certainly Mr Starkey did not know. Once, when he had taken her over, he had wondered. The little machine had been going then, by its own confession, seven years. Even now, glancing over his glasses at the live woman working competently in her corner, he wondered still. Gazing at the delicate, wistful thing over the cup of tea that she gave him every Sunday afternoon, he wondered more than ever. For every Sunday afternoon towards four o'clock, wistfully, delicately, she bloomed. He repressed his wonderings as unchivalrous; for every Sunday afternoon she gave him tea.

Every Sunday afternoon he went to see her, walking from his rooms in Bayswater to her house in Maida Vale. In ten years he had formed the habit.

Sometimes they took a motor bus to Regent's Park or Primrose Hill and walked there together. Sometimes they walked in the Zoological Gardens and looked at the animals. (They were fond of animals.) Mr Starkey knew a fellow who knew one of the Fellows, and he could get from him as many Sunday tickets as he wanted, so that they could look at the animals for nothing and with a sense of privilege and intimacy unknown to people who have to plank down their shillings at the gate. From his air of knowing all about it, from his important conversations with the keepers, and from the liberties he took with the King Penguin, Miss Delacheroy thought for some time that Mr Starkey was a Fellow himself.

She liked to be seen walking with him. He was tall, and, in spite of his deplorably lean flanks, impressive. She knew that he had been young once, and it did not seem to her that it could have been so very long ago. He had one of those lean, white faces that wear well. Pale gold hairs glinted among the others in his eyebrows. His top hat, pressed down and tilted backwards, covered the bleak hinterland above the pale gold fringe. Thick-rimmed glasses accentuated his distinguished scheme of pallor and gold.

Sometimes, when it was fine and warm, they sat in Miss Delacheroy's garden and talked. When it was wet they sat in the drawing-room and talked. They talked about their work. They were up to their necks in it. Long ago the United Charities had opened up and swallowed them up. They were in it for life. Even on a Sunday they had difficulty in emerging. The great thing was that they were in it together. Between them they had brought their organisation to such a pitch that the Kilburn branch surpassed all other branches of the United Charities.

She would say, 'It couldn't have been done without you.'

And he, 'It couldn't have been done without *you*, Miss Delacheroy.'

He was necessary to her and she was necessary to him, and they were both necessary to the United Charities. They were in it, they agreed, for life.

There were other things he might have done, other people he might have gone to see, younger women whom he might have known, if he had cared. But Mr Starkey did not care. He did not get on well with other people, for he was much more serious and earnest than other people were. He was much more serious and earnest than it is good for any man to be. He did not get on very well with young women, for young women made him feel not quite so young. He had not formed the habit of them; whereas he *had* formed the habit of Miss Delacheroy. It was not a dangerous habit; and if sometimes a certain fear came over him, a sneaking and unmanly fear, his chivalry suppressed it as it suppressed his wonder. In his secret heart he knew that he was safe. And so every Sunday of his life he walked from his unspeakably depressing rooms in Bayswater to Miss Delacheroy's little house hidden in a side street off Maida Vale. For it was always peaceful there. And the one thing that Mr Starkey loved more than his own earnestness was peace.

Their communion was interrupted three times a year by the holidays. Whatever else they did together, they never went away together for the holidays. Mr Starkey was not prepared to go so far as that, and Miss Delacheroy had not yet been stirred to her depths; therefore she was still unaware how far she was prepared to go. In the year nineteen-fourteen their holidays were fixed for Friday, Aug. 7.

On Tuesday, Aug. 4, Germany declared war on England, and an extraordinary thing happened to Mr Starkey and Miss Delacheroy. It happened to them on the morning of the ultimatum. It happened to them together. It was the beginning of still more extraordinary things.

They lost all interest in the United Charities. Together, suddenly and unanimously, they lost it.

At first you would not have known it. The work of the United Charities went on as usual. Cases were registered, Miss Delacheroy was seen dictating letters to her typist. Beyond rushing out bareheaded into Kilburn High-road and buying the special edition of five newspapers whose politics he disapproved of, Mr Starkey betrayed no sign of aberration. But for all that they were in it the Kilburn branch of the United Charities might have been closed liked the Stock Exchange. They, in their innermost essential being, were not there. They were submerged in the ultimatum. They could talk of nothing else, they could think of nothing else. There was nothing beyond the ultimatum that they saw or heard or felt. And yet they were not suffering, like the Stock Exchange, from panic. They were ready for the war. They had expected it any time within the last five years. They had both seen through the Kaiser's protestations. Mr Starkey had had private information from the War Office. (He was always having private information from important places.) They knew that Germany would not accept the ultimatum.

So it is transparent that they had not lost their heads.

It was the ultimatum. It exalted and possessed them. It filled them—it filled Mr Starkey and Miss Delacheroy—with the power and glory of the world. All day long the ultimatum sounded in their ears like an incantation. It sank into their nerves and worked there like an exquisite poison; it soared into their brains like a magic and almighty wine.

It made them do things, vehement and orgastic things, that they had never done before. It drove them forth together at six o'clock into England's Bohemia. It compelled them to dine together, feverishly, in a low restaurant in Soho. It flung them out under the lamplight on to the surge of the crowd in Trafalgar-square. It swept them with the crowd down Whitehall to Westminster and back again, up the avenue of the Mall, between the solemn ranks of the plane trees and the long processional lights; it thrust them, wedged in the crowd, through the gilded gates, and held them motionless before the golden white façade of Buckingham Palace.

After that it was the mounted police that kept them moving.

The water had ceased playing in the fountain. She wondered why. It was then that he asked her where she was going for her holiday.

She said, 'I am not going anywhere. I shall stay in London to protect my cat.'

He looked down at the water in the basin. It was green as sea water. The jetsam of the crowd floated there. A miniature Union Jack, dropped from a girl's breast, drifted to the stone curb. He looked at it and smiled. He could still smile.

'And you?' She said it for the sake of saying something, for she knew he was going to Llandudno.

He stared at her.

'I? I am going to the front.'

A policeman moved them on. It gave her time to recover.

'Oh, no!' she protested. 'No; not to the front.'

'Where else,' he put it to her, 'can I go?'

He reminded her that he had been a medical student. She had forgotten that.

'Well, then—' He left it to her. He laid it down before her and left it there. He couldn't not go.

And she took it up and gave it back to him. 'If you go I shall go too.'

He said nothing to that, nothing at all. But it stirred in him again, that fear of his, that little creeping and ignoble fear.

It was ten o'clock.

They turned back to the Palace. The crowd had thinned now and was scattered. It moved up and down without rest; it reeled, two-thirds intoxicated; it drifted and returned; it circled round and round the fountain. In the open spaces intoxicated motor-cars and taxicabs darted and tore, with the folly of moths and the fury of destroyers. They stung the air with their hooting. Flags, intoxicated flags, hung from their engines. They came flying drunkenly out of the dark, like a trumpeting swarm of enormous insects, irresistibly, incessantly drawn to the lights of the Palace, hypnotised by the golden white façade.

The two stood together, apart, on the edge of the light. They turned their backs on the Palace. They looked into each other's serious, earnest faces. They were disgusted at the folly of the crowd. They were utterly calm, utterly courageous. They were going to the front.

All night long they lay sleepless with ecstasy, he in Bayswater and she in Maida Vale, surrendered to the embraces of their dream. Each tried to think what it would be like. She saw it as one immense, encompassing sheet of shells and bullets that converged on Mr Starkey in the middle of it. It was there, in the middle of it, that she desired to be. Mr Starkey saw nothing, absolutely nothing. He felt nothing but the will to go.

II

It was all very well to talk about going to the front. The thing, Mr Starkey said, was to get there. They would have to take steps.

The first step they took was to notify the United Charities that, having volunteered for active service, they must resign their posts. The United Charities admired and deplored their resolution; it would be difficult to fill their places. Meanwhile, pending the final arrangements, their places would be kept open for them.

The next step was to let everybody know that they were going. They knew it in the office. Mr Starkey's typist said, 'Mr Starkey is going to the front,' and Miss Delacheroy's typist retorted, 'And Miss Delacheroy is going, too.' All Miss Delacheroy's friends knew. And Mr Starkey's banker knew it, and his doctor and his solicitor.

A few formalities remained, but the send-off had practically begun. Everybody in the office had congratulated them and bidden them God-speed. Mr Starkey's banker told him that England had need of men like him. His doctor slapped him on the back, and said he was a lucky fellow to be going. He also overhauled him and passed him medically for nothing. His solicitor gripped him by the hand, and said that Mr Starkey could rely on him to carry out his instructions to the letter, and that, yes, all legal expenses would be charged to the estate, and that he would await further news with anxiety.

Then Mr Starkey took the final steps. He called at the War Office, he called at the Admiralty, he called at the headquarters of the White Cross Association, and at the headquarters of the St George's Ambulance Society. He called at the offices of all their local branches within a radius of five miles. He called at the War Office and the Admiralty a second time. Then, in consequence of certain very serious statements that were made to him there, he found it necessary to call at Scotland Yard. Acting on the advice of Constable D of the Metropolitan Police, he went on to the Home Office. At the instigation of the Home Secretary, he pursued the secretary of the American White Cross Association down Piccadilly and down the Haymarket and down the Strand. And finally ran him to earth in the basement of the Hotel Cecil. Owing mainly to the tense but clear representations of the secretary, he returned up the Strand and up the Haymarket and up Piccadilly to Park-lane, where he looked in at the American Embassy.

After that he called at the Belgian Embassy and the French Embassy and the Japanese Embassy in succession, which, he said, he had very much better have done first as last. For, from the moment of his entrance at the Belgian Embassy, Mr Starkey's progress became a triumph, an ovation. Nothing could exceed the courtesy and enthusiasm of the foreign officials.

It was Mr Starkey's reception at the Japanese Embassy that encouraged him to go back, as he did, to the War Office and the Admiralty.

That was the incredible sum of his activities, not counting various minor operations at the centres of the White Cross Association and twenty-seven letters that he wrote, chiefly to the heads of departments.

'And when shall you go?' said Miss Delacheroy.

(They were at Sunday, the 9th.)

'I can't tell you,' he said. 'It may be to-morrow.'

'Oh-h!' she breathed. It was her first sign of dismay. She could not possibly be ready, she said, till the day after.

She had one fear, and one fear only, that he might get there first.

'It's no good my going,' she said, 'if we can't go together.'

He stared at her as he had stared that night when they stood beside the fountain. Then he smiled as a man smiles in fear.

'You don't *go* to the front,' he said; 'you're sent.'

'You mean that you'll be sent and I shan't be?'

'Well—' He broke it to her gently. He had taken steps. So vast was the machinery that he had put in motion, it was impossible that he should not be sent.

She agreed that it was, of course, impossible. But she had taken steps, too; small steps but rapid. The day after war was declared she had had herself inoculated for typhoid. She hoped that he had done the same.

He had not. He had never thought of it.

'You should have thought of it,' she said. 'They won't look at you if you aren't done.'

His attentive face told her she had scored a point.

She followed up her advantage. 'You must see about it first thing to-morrow. It takes eight days.'

He made a note of it in his memorandum book.

(That gave her five days' start of him.)

And she had ordered in all her medical stores, from quinine to tooth brushes. Her chemist had recommended bone. A celluloid toothbrush, he said, would be almost certain to ignite if it should happen to come in contact with a bomb.

Had he thought of *that*?

He had not. He made another note, and enquired gently if Miss Delacheroy had got her White Cross certificate?

'Because'—he answered her agonised eyes—'they won't look at *you* without it.'

'Oh!' (she reproached him) 'why didn't you tell me? You knew.'

He was shamefaced before her. Of course he knew. And if he had not told her, why, indeed, was it?

He evaded the conscience that accused him.

'I'm telling you now,' he pleaded.

And he told her. After all, it was quite simple. She had only got to attend one of the emergency classes round the corner at the Blankmore Institute. There was a course of six lectures with demonstrations. Oh, yes; she would get through all right. Anybody could get through.

She made a calculation. If she got through, it would take her six days.

He would still be a day ahead of her.

If up till now he had not played quite fair—he had not, considering the marches he had stolen on her—there was no doubt of his readiness to redeem his error.

For the large hall of the Blankmore Institute was crammed and running over, and it was owing solely to Mr Starkey's influence at headquarters that she was pushed and squeezed through some invisible loophole into a non-existing vacancy in the supplementary class in the basement.

In the basement, from 10.30 to 12.30, and from two to four, and from 7.30 to nine, Miss Delacheroy struggled with the secret intricacies of the human frame, with the infinite vagaries and complications of the Esmarch triangular bandage, and the appalling mysteries of first aid.

The White Cross demonstrator destroyed her *morale* at the very beginning. He told her that there was one spot, and one spot only, where digital pressure should be applied to arrest haemorrhage from the subclavian artery, and that if Miss Delacheroy did not find that spot, if she did not put her finger on it, if she put it a hairsbreadth to one side, that artery would go, he said, on its way rejoicing, and she, Miss Delacheroy, would have killed her man more surely than if she had fired a bullet at him. The Germans, said the demonstrator, would *pay* Miss Delacheroy to do what she was doing.

And when it came to bandaging, she had not a chance; for, by a system most just and admirable in itself, the students practised on each other, and the woman next to Miss Delacheroy, whether because she was taller and stronger and more determined, or for some other reason, invariably succeeded in bandaging Miss Delacheroy first, and by the time she had finished with her the demonstrator had gone on to another bandage, so that Miss Delacheroy was always at least three bandages behind.

The struggle lasted till the end of August. Three times Miss Delacheroy went in for her exam, and failed. The first time it was the human frame that dished her; the second time it was the subclavian artery; the third time it was the bandages—there were too many of them.

And all the time Miss Delacheroy's brain was paralysed with anxiety.

For three weeks the movements of Mr Starkey, like the movements of the Allied Armies, were enveloped in mystery. He had not been to see her for two Sundays. And when she wrote and asked him to tea on the third Sunday, he replied that it was impossible; he was under orders; at any moment he might be sent to the front. Of his whereabouts and of his operations in the meanwhile he gave no account.

She felt that he was keeping something back from her. There followed a brief period of separation, of evasion, of mutual suspicion and hostility. All this was unspeakably painful to Miss Delacheroy.

It was on a Monday that, going late for the first time to her daily bandaging, she came upon him in a place where of all places she had least expected him—in the Blankmore Institute itself. The doors of the large hall were open, and, standing within the towering centre of a dense ring of women, she saw him. He had an Esmarch triangular bandage round his neck, and with another bandage he was doing things to a young woman who had pushed forward (she knew how they *could* push).

And when Mr Starkey left the large hall at 12.30 he found Miss Delacheroy waiting for him in the vestibule.

'What are you doing *here?*' she said.

He was serious and earnest. 'Marking time.'

'We seem to be doing the same thing.'

He admitted that it did seem so, except that he was giving instruction and she was receiving it.

'Oh—for all I receive! I'm plucked again. It's the third time.'

They were walking down Maida Vale together now.

His face was inscrutable, and a terrible suspicion came to her. He was one of them. He did not want her to go with him, and he had kept her back.

They had come to her gate. With the pain of parting madness entered into Miss Delacheroy. She drew him into the garden. The walls sheltered her.

'Were you one of the examiners?'

He was silent.

'I see. You were. It was you who dished me.'

He was cold and correct and kind. He paused before he answered her.

'I might have. But I didn't. You must go up again.'

'Forgive me.'

'There is nothing to forgive.'

'You see how it's getting on my nerves. It's all so terrible and mysterious. I know nothing.'

She meant that she knew he was keeping something back from her.

'You know,' he said, 'as much as I do.'

'I would, perhaps, if you'd tell me. What are you *doing?* Have you been to the War Office again?'

He had. He owned it.

She was sharp and eager. 'Well, what did they say *this* time?'

He looked her squarely in the face. '*This* time I am not at liberty to tell you.'

Then she knew that what he was keeping from her was the imminence of his departure.

'What's the use of hiding it?' she said. 'They *have* sent for you.'

'They will; they will. I'm waiting to hear from Belgium. But it'll be another week.'

'Ten days?'

It was more than probable that it would be ten days.

That gave her just time to go up again and wait for the result. There were women who had been up four times, who went again and again till they had got through.

Now, examinations in the Blankmore Institute are held in two rooms on the top floor, and once every ten days the names of successful candidates are posted there.

The building, unfortunately, has no lift.

But four flights of stone stairs were nothing to Miss Delacheroy when she found that she had passed ninth on an interminable list. She would be just in time if she was quick.

She was very quick.

She ran down the first two flights with a clatter of her little heels; she slid, dramatically, down the third; she was hurled down the fourth from the top to the bottom.

Through the well of the staircase on the third landing she had caught sight of Mr Starkey coming out of the large hall. He had an Esmarch triangular bandage round his neck.

'I'm glad,' said Mr Starkey; 'it's a sprained ankle. That's the one I've got all right. You're the fourth I've had a shot at this week.'

III

He took her home in a taxicab, and the next evening he went to enquire for her.

She stirred on her couch and gave a little cry when she saw him.

'You haven't gone, then?'

'Not yet.'

He said it gently as if to spare her.

She looked at him with humble eyes, a humility incomprehensible to Mr Starkey.

'This is pretty hard lines,' he said, 'after you've passed so well.'

'Yes. But I couldn't have gone in any case.'

'Why not?'

There was a long pause. Then it came from her with the brevity of a supreme confession:

'They won't have me. I'm too old.'

He lowered his eyes before it, as if to the very last he spared her.

'It all goes through the War Office, and they won't look at you if you're over forty. That's what they've told me.'

'It's what they've told *me*.'

'I didn't know,' she said, 'until this morning.'

'I,' said Mr Starkey, 'have known it all the time.'

And he added something about 'the system' and 'red tape.'

JOSEPH CONRAD

▼▼

The Tale

OUTSIDE THE LARGE single window the crepuscular light was dying out slowly in a great square gleam without colour, framed rigidly in the gathering shades of the room.

It was a long room. The irresistible tide of the night ran into the most distant part of it, where the whispering of a man's voice, passionately interrupted and passionately renewed, seemed to plead against the answering murmurs of infinite sadness.

At last no answering murmur came. His movement when he rose slowly from his knees by the side of the deep, shadowy couch holding the shadowy suggestion of a reclining woman revealed him tall under the low ceiling, and sombre all over except for the crude discord of the white collar under the shape of his head and the faint, minute spark of a brass button here and there on his uniform.

He stood over her a moment, masculine and mysterious in his immobility, before he sat down on a chair near by. He could see only the faint oval of her upturned face and, extended on her black dress, her pale hands, a moment before abandoned to his kisses and now as if too weary to move.

He dared not make a sound, shrinking as a man would do from the prosaic necessities of existence. As usual, it was the woman who had the courage. Her voice was heard first—almost conventional while her being vibrated yet with conflicting emotions.

'Tell me something,' she said.

The darkness hid his surprise and then his smile. Had he not just said to her everything worth saying in the world—and that not for the first time!

'What am I to tell you?' he asked, in a voice creditably steady. He was beginning to feel grateful to her for that something final in her tone which had eased the strain.

'Why not tell me a tale?'

'A tale!' He was really amazed.

'Yes. Why not?'

These words came with a slight petulance, the hint of a loved woman's capricious will, which is capricious only because it feels itself to be a law, embarrassing sometimes and always difficult to elude.

'Why not?' he repeated, with a slightly mocking accent, as though he had been asked to give her the moon. But now he was feeling a little angry with her for that feminine mobility that slips out of an emotion as easily as out of a splendid gown.

He heard her say, a little unsteadily with a sort of fluttering intonation which made him think suddenly of a butterfly's flight:

'You used to tell—your—your simple and—and professional—tales very well at one time. Or well enough to interest me. You had a—a sort of art—in the days—the days before the war.'

'Really?' he said, with involuntary gloom. 'But now, you see, the war is going on,' he continued in such a dead, equable tone that she felt a slight chill fall over her shoulders. And yet she persisted. For there's nothing more unswerving in the world than a woman's caprice.

'It could be a tale not of this world,' she explained.

'You want a tale of the other, the better world?' he asked, with a matter-of-fact surprise. 'You must evoke for that task those who have already gone there.'

'No. I don't mean that. I mean another—some other—world. In the universe—not in heaven.'

'I am relieved. But you forget that I have only five days' leave.'

'Yes. And I've also taken a five days' leave from—from my duties.'

'I like that word.'

'What word?'

'Duty.'

'It is horrible—sometimes.'

'Oh, that's because you think it's narrow. But it isn't. It contains infinities, and—and so—'

'What is this jargon?'

He disregarded the interjected scorn. 'An infinity of absolution, for instance,' he continued. 'But as to this "another world"—who's going to look for it and for the tale that is in it?'

'You,' she said, with a strange, almost rough, sweetness of assertion.

He made a shadowy movement of assent in his chair, the irony of which not even the gathered darkness could render mysterious.

'As you will. In that world, then, there was once upon a time a Commanding Officer and a Northman. Put in the capitals, please, because they had no other names. It was a world of seas and continents and islands—'

'Like the earth,' she murmured, bitterly.

'Yes. What else could you expect from sending a man made of our common, tormented clay on a voyage of discovery? What else could he find? What else could you understand or care for, or feel the existence of even? There was comedy in it, and slaughter.'

'Always like the earth,' she murmured.

'Always. And since I could find in the universe only what was deeply rooted in the fibres of my being there was love in it, too. But we won't talk of that.'

'No. We won't,' she said, in a neutral tone which concealed perfectly her relief—or her disappointment. Then after a pause she added: 'It's going to be a comic story.'

'Well—' he paused, too. 'Yes. In a way. In a very grim way. It will be human, and, as you know, comedy is but a matter of the visual angle. And it won't be a noisy story. All the long guns in it will be dumb—as dumb as so many telescopes.'

'Ah, there are guns in it, then! And may I ask—where?'

'Afloat. You remember that the world of which we speak had its seas. A war was going on in it. It was a funny world and terribly in earnest. Its war was being carried on over the land, over the water, under the water, up in the air, and even under the ground. And many young men in it, mostly in wardrooms and messrooms, used to say to each other—pardon the unparliamentary word— they used to say, "It's a damned bad war, but it's better than no war at all." Sounds flippant, doesn't it?'

He heard a nervous, impatient sigh in the depths of the couch while he went on without a pause.

'And yet there is more in it than meets the eye. I mean more wisdom. Flippancy, like comedy, is but a matter of visual first-impression. That world was not very wise. But there was in it a certain amount of common working sagacity. That, however, was mostly worked by the neutrals in diverse ways, public and private, which had to be watched; watched by acute minds and also by actual sharp eyes. They had to be very sharp indeed, too, I assure you.'

'I can imagine,' she murmured, appreciatively.

'What is there that you can't imagine?' he pronounced, soberly. 'You have the world in you. But let us go back to our command-ing officer, who, of course, commanded a ship of a sort. My tales if often professional (as you remarked just now) have never been technical. So I'll just tell you that the ship was of a very ornamen-tal sort once, with lots of grace and elegance and luxury about her. Yes, once! She was like a pretty woman who had suddenly put on a suit of sackcloth and stuck revolvers in her belt. But she floated lightly, she moved nimbly, she was quite good enough.'

'That was the opinion of the commanding officer?' said the voice from the couch.

'It was. He used to be sent out with her along certain coasts to see—what he could see. Just that. And sometimes he had some preliminary information to help him, and sometimes he had not. And it was all one, really. It was about as useful as information trying to convey the locality and intentions of a cloud, of a phantom taking shape here and there and impossible to seize, would have been.

'It was in the early days of the war. What at first used to amaze the commanding officer was the unchanged face of the waters, with its familiar expression, neither more friendly nor more hostile. On fine days the sun strikes sparks upon the blue; here and there a peaceful smudge of smoke hangs in the distance, and it is impossible to believe that the familiar clear horizon traces the limit of one great circular ambush.

'Yes, it is impossible to believe, till some day you see a ship not your own ship (that isn't so impressive), but some ship in company, blow up all of a sudden and plop under almost before you know what has happened to her. Then you begin to believe. Henceforth you go out for the work to see—what you can see, and you keep on at it with the conviction that some day you will die from something you have not seen. One envies the soldiers at the end of the day, wiping the sweat and blood from their faces, counting the dead fallen to their hands, looking at the devastated fields, the torn earth that seems to suffer and bleed with them. One does, really. The final brutality of it—the taste of primitive passion—the ferocious frankness of the blow struck with one's hand—the direct call and the straight response. Well, the sea gave you nothing of that, and seemed to pretend that there was nothing the matter with the world.'

She interrupted, stirring a little.

'Oh, yes. Sincerity—frankness—passion—three words of your gospel. Don't I know them!'

'Think! Isn't it ours—believed in common?' he asked, anxiously, yet without expecting an answer, and went on at once: 'Such were the feelings of the commanding officer. When the night came trailing over the sea, hiding what looked like the hypocrisy of an old friend, it was a relief. The night blinds you frankly—and there are circumstances when the sunlight may grow as odious to one as falsehood itself. Night is all right.

'At night the commanding officer could let his thoughts get away—I won't tell you where. Somewhere where there was no choice but between truth and death. But thick weather, though it blinded one, brought no such relief. Mist is deceitful, the dead luminosity of the fog is irritating. It seems that you *ought* to see.

'One gloomy, nasty day the ship was steaming along her beat in sight of a rocky, dangerous coast that stood out intensely black like an India-ink drawing on gray paper. Presently the second in command spoke to his chief. He thought he saw something on the water, to seaward. Small wreckage, perhaps.

'"But there shouldn't be any wreckage here, sir," he remarked.

'"No," said the commanding officer. "The last reported submarined ships were sunk a long way to the westward. But one never knows. There may have been others since then not reported nor seen. Gone with all hands."

'That was how it began. The ship's course was altered to pass the object close; for it was necessary to have a good look at what one could see. Close, but without touching; for it was not advisable to come in contact with objects of any form whatever floating casually about. Close, but without stopping or even diminishing speed; for in those times it was not prudent to linger on any particular spot, even for a moment. I may tell you at once that the object was not dangerous in itself. No use in describing it. It may have been nothing more remarkable than, say, a barrel of a certain shape and colour. But it was significant.

'The smooth bow-wave hove it up as if for a closer inspection, and then the ship, brought again to her course, turned her back on it with indifference, while twenty pairs of eyes on her deck stared in all directions trying to see—what they could see.

'The commanding officer and his second in command discussed the object with understanding. It appeared to them to be not so much a proof of the sagacity as of the activity of certain neutrals. This activity had in many cases taken the form of replenishing the stores of certain submarines at sea. This was generally believed, if not absolutely known. But the very nature of things in those early days pointed that way. The object, looked at closely and turned away from with apparent indifference, put it beyond doubt that something of the sort had been done somewhere in the neighbourhood.

'The object in itself was more than suspect. But the fact of its being left in evidence roused other suspicions. Was it the result of some deep and devilish purpose? As to that all speculation soon appeared to be a vain thing. Finally the two officers came to the conclusion that it was left there most likely by accident, complicated possibly by some unforeseen necessity; such, perhaps, as the sudden need to get away quickly from the spot, or something of that kind.

'Their discussion had been carried on in curt, weighty phrases, separated by long, thoughtful silences. And all the time their eyes roamed about the horizon in an everlasting, almost mechanical effort of vigilance. The younger man summed up grimly:

' "Well, it's evidence. That's what this is. Evidence of what we were pretty certain of before. And plain, too."

' "And much good it will do to us," retorted the commanding officer. "The parties are miles away; the submarine, devil only knows where, ready to kill; and the noble neutral slipping away to the eastward, ready to lie!"

'The second in command laughed a little at the tone. But he guessed that the neutral wouldn't even have to lie very much. Fellows like that, unless caught in the very act, felt themselves pretty safe. They could afford to chuckle. That fellow was probably chuckling to himself. It's very possible he had been before at the game and didn't care a rap for the bit of evidence left behind. It was a game in which practice made one bold and successful, too.

'And again he laughed faintly. But his commanding officer was in revolt against the murderous stealthiness of methods and the atrocious callousness of complicities that seemed to taint the very source of men's deep emotions and noblest activities; to corrupt their imagination which builds up the final conceptions of life and death. He suffered—'

The voice from the sofa interrupted the narrator.

'How well I can understand that in him!'

He bent forward slightly.

'Yes. I, too. Everything should be open in love and war. Open as the day, since both are the call of an ideal which it is so easy, so terribly easy, to degrade in the name of Victory.'

He paused; then went on:

'I don't know that the commanding officer delved so deep as that into his feelings. But he did suffer from them—a sort of disenchanted sadness. It is possible, even, that he suspected himself of folly. Man is various. But he had no time for much introspection, because from the southwest a wall of fog had advanced upon his ship. Great convolutions of vapours flew over, swirling about masts and funnel, which looked as if they were beginning to melt. Then they vanished.

'The ship was stopped, all sounds ceased, and the very fog became motionless, growing denser and as if solid in its amazing dumb immobility. The men at their stations lost sight of each other. Footsteps sounded stealthy; rare voices, impersonal and remote, died out without resonance. A blind white stillness took possession of the world.

'It looked, too, as if it would last for days. I don't mean to say that the fog did not vary a little in its density. Now and then it would thin out mysteriously, revealing to the men a more or less ghostly presentment of their ship. Several times the shadow of the coast itself swam darkly before their eyes through the fluctuating opaque brightness of the great white cloud clinging to the water.

'Taking advantage of these moments, the ship had been moved cautiously nearer the shore. It was useless to remain out in such thick weather. Her officers knew every nook and cranny of the coast along their beat. They thought that she would be much better in a certain cove. It wasn't a large place, just ample room for a ship to swing at her anchor. She would have an easier time of it till the fog lifted up.

'Slowly, with infinite caution and patience, they crept closer and closer, seeing no more of the cliffs than an evanescent dark loom with a narrow border of angry foam at its foot. At the moment of anchoring the fog was so thick that for all they could see they might have been a thousand miles out in the open sea. Yet the shelter of the land could be felt. There was a peculiar quality in the stillness of the air. Very faint, very elusive, the wash of the ripple against the encircling land reached their ears, with mysterious sudden pauses.

'The anchor dropped, the leads were laid in. The commanding officer went below into his cabin. But he had not been there very long when a voice outside his door requested his presence on deck. He thought to himself: "What is it now?" He felt some impatience at being called out again to face the wearisome fog.

'He found that it had thinned again a little and had taken on a gloomy hue from the dark cliffs which had no form, no outline, but asserted themselves as a curtain of shadows all round the ship, except in one bright spot, which was the entrance from the open sea. Several officers were looking that way from the bridge. The second in command met him with the breathlessly whispered information that there was another ship in the cove.

'She had been made out by several pairs of eyes only a couple of minutes before. She was lying at anchor very near the entrance—a mere vague blot on the fog's brightness. And the commanding officer by staring in the direction pointed out to him by eager hands ended by distinguishing it at last himself. Indubitably a vessel of some sort.

'"It's a wonder we didn't run slap into her when coming in," observed the second in command.

'"Send a boat on board before she vanishes," said the commanding officer. He surmised that this was a coaster. It could hardly be anything else. But another thought came into his head suddenly. "It is a wonder," he said to his second in command, who had rejoined him after sending the boat away.

'By that time both of them had been struck by the fact that the ship so suddenly discovered had not manifested her presence by ringing her bell.

'"We came in very quietly, that's true," concluded the younger officer. "But they must have heard our leadsmen at least. We couldn't have passed her more than fifty yards off. The closest shave! They may even have made us out, since they were aware of something coming in. And the strange thing is that we never heard a sound from her. The fellows on board must have been holding their breath."

'"Aye," said the commanding officer, thoughtfully.

'In due course the boarding-boat returned, appearing suddenly alongside, as though she had burrowed her way under the fog. The officer in charge came up to make his report, but the commanding officer didn't give him time to begin. He cried from a distance:

'"Coaster, isn't she?"

'"No, sir. A stranger—a neutral," was the answer.

'"No. Really! Well, tell us all about it. What is she doing here?'

'The young man stated then that he had been told a long and complicated story of engine troubles. But it was plausible enough from a strictly professional point of view and it had the usual features: disablement, dangerous drifting along the shore, weather more or less thick for days, fear of a gale, ultimately a resolve to go in and anchor anywhere on the coast, and so on. Fairly plausible.

'"Engines still disabled?" inquired the commanding officer.

'"No, sir. She has steam on them."

'The commanding officer took his second aside. "By Jove!" he said, "you were right! They were holding their breaths as we passed them. They were."

'But the second in command had his doubts now.

'"A fog like this does muffle small sounds, sir," he remarked. "And what could his object be, after all?"

'"To sneak out unnoticed," answered the commanding officer.

'"Then why didn't he? He might have done it, you know. Not exactly unnoticed, perhaps. I don't suppose he could have slipped his cable without making some noise. Still, in a minute or so he would have been lost to view—clean gone before we had made him out fairly. Yet he didn't."

'They looked at each other. The commanding officer shook his head. Such supicions as the one which had entered his head are not defended easily. He did not even state it openly. The boarding officer finished his report. The cargo of the ship was of a harmless and useful character. She was bound to an English port. Papers and everything in perfect order. Nothing suspicious to be detected anywhere.

'Then passing to the men, he reported the crew on deck as the usual lot. Engineers of the well-known type, and very full of their achievement in repairing the engines. The mate surly. The master rather a fine specimen of a Northman, civil enough, but appeared to have been drinking. Seemed to be recovering from a regular bout of it.

'"I told him I couldn't give him permission to proceed. He said he wouldn't dare to move his ship her own length out in such weather as this, permission or no permission. I left a man on board, though."

'"Quite right."

'The commanding officer, after communing with his suspicions for a time, called his second aside.

'"What if she were the very ship which had been feeding some infernal submarine or other?" he said in an undertone.

'The other started. Then, with conviction:

'"She would get off scot-free. You couldn't prove it, sir."

'"I want to look into it myself."

'"From the report we've heard I am afraid you couldn't even make a case for reasonable suspicion, sir."

'"I'll go on board all the same."

'He had made up his mind. Curiosity is the great motive power of hatred and love. What did he expect to find? He could not have told anybody—not even himself.

'What he really expected to find there was the atmosphere, the atmosphere of gratuitous treachery, which in his view nothing could excuse; for he thought that even a passion of unrighteousness for its own sake could not excuse that. But could he detect it? Sniff it? Taste it? Receive some mysterious communication which would turn his invincible suspicions into a certitude strong enough to provoke action with all its risks?

'The master met him on the after-deck, looming up in the fog amongst the blurred shapes of the usual ship's fittings. He was a robust Northman, bearded, and in the force of his age. A round leather cap fitted his head closely. His hands were rammed deep into the pockets of his short leather jacket. He kept them there while he explained that at sea he lived in the chart-room, and led the way there, striding carelessly. Just before reaching the door under the bridge he staggered a little, recovered himself, flung it open, and stood aside, leaning his shoulder as if involuntarily against the side of the house, and staring vaguely into the fog-filled space. But he followed the commanding officer at once, flung the door to, snapped on the electric light, and hastened to thrust his hands back into his pockets, as though afraid of being seized by them either in friendship or in hostility.

'The place was stuffy and hot. The usual chart-rack overhead was full, and the chart on the table was kept unrolled by an empty cup standing on a saucer half-full of some spilt dark liquid. A slightly nibbled biscuit reposed on the chronometer-case. There were two settees, and one of them had been made up into a bed with a pillow and some blankets, which were now very much tumbled. The Northman let himself fall on it, his hands still in his pockets.

' "Well, here I am," he said, with a curious air of being surprised at the sound of his own voice.

'The commanding officer from the other settee observed the handsome, flushed face. Drops of fog hung on the yellow beard and moustaches of the Northman. The much darker eyebrows ran together in a puzzled frown, and suddenly he jumped up.

' "What I mean is that I don't know where I am. I really don't," he burst out, with extreme earnestness. "Hang it all! I got turned around somehow. The fog has been after me for a week. More than a week. And then my engines broke down. I will tell you how it was."

'He burst out into loquacity. It was not hurried, but it was insistent. It was not continuous for all that. It was broken by the most queer, thoughtful pauses. Each of these pauses lasted no more than a couple of seconds, and each had the profundity of an endless meditation. When he began again nothing betrayed in him the slightest consciousness of these intervals. There was the same fixed glance, the same unchanged earnestness of tone. He didn't know. Indeed, more than one of these pauses occurred in the middle of a sentence.

'The commanding officer listened to the tale. It struck him as more plausible than simple truth is in the habit of being. But that, perhaps, was prejudice. All the time the Northman was speaking the commanding officer had been aware of an inward voice, a grave murmur in the depth of his very own self, telling another tale, as if on purpose to keep alive in him his indignation and his anger with that baseness of greed or of mere outlook which lies often at the root of simple ideas.

'It was the story that had been already told to the boarding officer an hour or so before. The commanding officer nodded slightly at the Northman from time to time. The latter came to an end and turned his eyes away. He added, as an afterthought:

'"Wasn't it enough to drive a man out of his mind with worry? And it's my first voyage to this part, too. And the ship's my own. Your officer has seen the papers. She isn't much, as you can see for yourself. Just an old cargo-boat. Bare living for my family."

'He raised a big arm to point at a row of photographs plastering the bulkhead. The movement was ponderous, as if the arm had been made of lead. The commanding officer said, carelessly:

'"You will be making a fortune yet for your family with this old ship."

'"Yes, if I don't lose her," said the Northman, gloomily.

'"I mean—out of this war," added the commanding officer.

'The Northman stared at him in a curiously unseeing and at the same time interested manner, as only eyes of a particular blue shade can stare.

'"And you wouldn't be angry at it," he said, "would you? You are too much of a gentleman. We didn't bring this on you. And suppose we sat down and cried. What good would that be? Let those cry who made the trouble," he concluded, with energy. "Time's money, you say. Well—*this* time *is* money. Oh! isn't it!"

'The commanding officer tried to keep under the feeling of immense disgust. He said to himself that it was unreasonable. Men were like that—moral cannibals feeding on each other's misfortunes. He said aloud:

'"You have made it perfectly plain how it is that you are here. Your log-book confirms you very minutely. Of course, a log-book may be cooked. Nothing easier."

'The Northman never moved a muscle. He was gazing at the floor; he seemed not to have heard. He raised his head after a while.

'"But you can't suspect me of anything," he muttered, negligently.

'The commanding officer thought: "Why should he say this?"

'Immediately afterwards the man before him added: "My cargo is for an English port."

'His voice had turned husky for the moment. The commanding officer reflected: "That's true. There can be nothing. I can't suspect him. Yet why was he lying with steam up in this fog—and then, hearing us come in, why didn't he give some sign of life? Why? Could it be anything else but a guilty conscience? He could tell by the leadsmen that this was a man-of-war."

'Yes—why? The commanding officer went on thinking: "Suppose I ask him and then watch his face. He will betray himself in some way. It's perfectly plain that the fellow *has* been drinking. Yes, he has been drinking; but he will have a lie ready all the same." The commanding officer was one of those men who are made morally and almost physically uncomfortable by the mere thought of having to beat down a lie. He shrank from the act in scorn and disgust, which were invincible because more temperamental than moral.

'So he went out on deck instead and had the crew mustered formally for his inspection. He found them very much what the report of the boarding officer had led him to expect. And from their answers to his questions he could discover no flaw in the log-book story.

'He dismissed them. His impression of them was—a picked lot; have been promised a fistful of money each if this came off; all slightly anxious, but not frightened. Not a single one of them likely to give the show away. They don't feel in danger of their life. They know England and English ways too well!

'He felt alarmed at catching himself thinking as if his vaguest suspicions were turning into a certitude. For, indeed, there was no shadow of reason for his inferences. There was nothing to give away.

'He returned to the chart-room. The Northman had lingered behind there; and something subtly different in his bearing, more bold in his blue, glassy stare, induced the commanding officer to conclude that the fellow had snatched at the opportunity take another swig at the bottle he must have had concealed somewhere.

'He noticed, too, that the Northman on meeting his eyes put on an elaborately surprised expression. At least, it seemed elaborated. Nothing could be trusted. And the Englishman felt himself with astonishing conviction faced by an enormous lie, solid like a wall, with no way round to get at the truth, whose ugly murderous face he seemed to see peeping over at him with a cynical grin.

'"I dare say," he began, suddenly, "you are wondering at my proceedings, though I am not detaining you, am I? You wouldn't dare to move in this fog?"

'"I don't know where I am," the Northman ejaculated, earnestly. "I really don't."

'He looked around as if the very chart-room fittings were

strange to him. The commanding officer asked him whether he had not seen any unusual objects floating about while he was at sea.

'"Objects! What objects? We were groping blind in the fog for days."

'"We had a few clear intervals," said the commanding officer. "And I'll tell you what we have seen and the conclusion I've come to about it."

'He told him in a few words. He heard the sound of a sharp breath indrawn through closed teeth. The Northman with his hand on the table stood absolutely motionless and dumb. He stood as if thunderstruck. Then he produced a fatuous smile.

'Or at least so it appeared to the commanding officer. Was this significant, or of no meaning whatever? He didn't know, he couldn't tell. All the truth had departed out of the world as if drawn in, absorbed in this monstrous villainy this man was—or was not—guilty of.

'"Shooting's too good for people that conceive neutrality in this pretty way," remarked the commanding officer, after a silence.

'"Yes, yes, yes," the Northman assented, hurriedly—then added an unexpected and dreamy-voiced "Perhaps."

'Was he pretending to be drunk, or only trying to appear sober? His glance was straight, but it was somewhat glazed. His lips outlined themselves firmly under his yellow moustache. But they twitched. Did they twitch? And why was he drooping like this in his attitude?

'"There's no perhaps about it," pronounced the commanding officer sternly.

'The Northman had straightened himself. And unexpectedly he looked stern, too.

'"No. But what about the tempters? Better kill that lot off. There's about four, five, six million of them," he said, grimly; but in a moment changed into a whining key. "But I had better hold my tongue. You have some suspicions."

' "No, I've no suspicions," declared the commanding officer.

'He never faltered. At that moment he had the certitude. The air of the chart-room was thick with guilt and falsehood braving the discovery, defying simple right, common decency, all humanity of feeling, every scruple of conduct.

'The Northman drew a long breath. "Well, we know that you English are gentlemen. But let us speak the truth. Why should we love you so very much? You haven't done anything to be loved. We don't love the other people, of course. They haven't done anything for that either. A fellow comes along with a bag of gold ... I haven't been in Rotterdam my last voyage for nothing."

'"You may be able to tell something interesting, then, to our people when you come into port," interjected the officer.

'"I might. But you keep some people in your pay at Rotterdam. Let them report. I am a neutral—am I not? ... Have you ever seen a poor man on one side and a bag of gold on the other? Of course, I couldn't be tempted. I haven't the nerve for it. Really I haven't. It's nothing to me. I am just talking openly for once."

'"Yes. And I am listening to you," said the commanding officer, quietly.

'The Northman leaned forward over the table. "Now that I know you have no suspicions, I talk. You don't know what a poor man is. I do. I am poor myself. This old ship, she isn't much, and she is mortgaged, too. Bare living, no more. Of course, I wouldn't have the nerve. But a man who has nerve! See. The stuff he takes aboard looks like any other cargo—packages, barrels, tins, copper tubes—what not. He doesn't see it work. It isn't real to him. But he sees the gold. That's real. Of course, nothing could induce me. I suffer from an internal disease. I would either go crazy from anxiety—or—or—take to drink or something. The risk is too great. Why—ruin!"

'"It should be death." The commanding officer got up, after this curt declaration, which the other received with a hard stare oddly combined with an uncertain smile. The officer's gorge rose at the atmosphere of murderous complicity which surrounded him, denser, more impenetrable, more acrid than the fog outside.

'"It's nothing to me," murmured the Northman, swaying visibly.

'"Of course not," assented the commanding officer, with a great effort to keep his voice calm and low. The certitude was strong within him. "But I am going to clear all you fellows off this coast at once. And I will begin with you. You must leave in half an hour."

'By that time the officer was walking along the deck with the Northman at his elbow.

'"What! In this fog?" the latter cried out, huskily.

'"Yes, you will have to go in this fog."

'"But I don't know where I am. I really don't."

'The commanding officer turned round. A sort of fury possessed him. The eyes of the two men met. Those of the Northman expressed a profound amazement.

'"Oh, you don't know how to get out." The commanding officer spoke with composure, but his heart was beating with anger and dread. "I will give you your course. Steer south-by-east-half-east for about four miles and then you will be clear to haul to the eastward for your port. The weather will clear up before very long."

'"Must I? What could induce me? I haven't the nerve."

'"And yet you must go. Unless you want to—"

'"I don't want to," panted the Northman. "I've enough of it."

'The commanding officer got over the side. The Northman remained still as if rooted to the deck. Before his boat reached his ship the commanding officer heard the steamer beginning to pick up her anchor. Then, shadowy in the fog, she steamed out on the given course.

'"Yes," he said to his officers, "I let him go." '

The narrator bent forward towards the couch, where no movement betrayed the presence of a living person.

'Listen,' he said, forcibly. 'That course would lead the Northman straight on a deadly ledge of rock. And the commanding officer gave it to him. He steamed out—ran on it—and went down. So he had spoken the truth. He did not know where he was. But it proves nothing. Nothing either way. It may have been the only truth in all his story. And yet ... He seems to have been driven out by a menacing stare—nothing more.'

He abandoned all pretence.

'Yes, I gave that course to him. It seemed to me a supreme test. I believe—no, I don't believe. I don't know. At the time I was certain. They all went down; and I don't know whether I have done stern retribution—or murder; whether I have added to the corpses that litter the bed of the unreadable sea the bodies of men completely innocent or basely guilty. I don't know. I shall never know.'

He rose. The woman on the couch got up and threw her arms round his neck. Her eyes put two gleams in the deep shadow of the room. She knew his passion for truth, his horror of deceit, his humanity.

'Oh, my poor, poor—'

'I shall never know,' he repeated, sternly, disengaged himself, pressed her hands to his lips, and went out.

J. M. BARRIE

▼▼▼

The New Word

ANY ROOM nowadays must be the scene, for any father and any son are the *dramatis personæ*. We could pick them up in Mayfair, in Tooting, on the Veldt, in rectories or in grocers' back parlours, dump them down on our toy stage and tell them to begin. It is a great gathering to choose from, but our needs are small. Let the company shake hands, and all go away but two.

The two who have remained (it is discovered on inquiry) are Mr. Torrance and his boy; so let us make use of them. Torrance did not linger in order to be chosen, he was anxious, like all of them, to be off; but we recognised him, and sternly signed to him to stay. Not that we knew him personally, but the fact is, we remembered him (we never forget a face) as the legal person who reads out the names of the jury before the court opens, and who brushes aside your reasons for wanting to be let off. It pleases our humour to tell Mr. Torrance that we cannot let him off.

He does not look so formidable as when last we saw him, and this is perhaps owing to our no longer being hunched with others on those unfeeling benches. It is not because he is without a wig, for we saw him, on the occasion to which we are so guardedly referring, both in a wig and out of it; he passed behind a screen without it, and immediately (as quickly as we write) popped out in it, giving it a finishing touch rather like the butler's wriggle to his coat as he goes to the door. There are the two kinds of learned brothers, those who use the screen, and those who (so far as the jury knows) sleep in their wigs. The latter are the swells, and include the judges; whom, however, we have seen in the public thoroughfares without their wigs, a horrible sight that has doubtless led many an onlooker to crime.

Mr. Torrance, then, is no great luminary; indeed, when we accompany him to his house, as we must, in order to set our scene properly, we find that it is quite a suburban affair, only one servant kept, and her niece engaged twice a week to crawl about the floors. There is no fire in the drawing-room, so the family remain on after dinner in the dining-room, which rather gives them away. There is really no one in the room but Roger. That is the truth of it, though to the unseeing eye all the family are there except Roger. They consist of Mr., Mrs., and Miss Torrance. Mr. Torrance is enjoying his evening paper and a cigar, and every line of him is insisting stubbornly that nothing unusual is happening in the house. In the home circle (and now that we think of it, even in court) he has the reputation of being a somewhat sarcastic gentleman; he must be dogged, too, otherwise he would have ceased long ago to be sarcastic to his wife, on whom wit falls like pellets on sandbags; all the dents they make are dimples.

Mrs. Torrance is at present exquisitely employed; she is listening to Roger's step overhead. You know what a delightful step the boy has. And what is more remarkable is that Emma is listening to it too, Emma who is seventeen, and who has been trying to keep Roger in his place ever since he first compelled her to bowl to him. Things have come to a pass when a sister so openly admits that she is only number two in the house.

Remarks well worthy of being recorded fall from these two ladies as they gaze upward. 'I think—didn't I, Emma?' is the mother's contribution, while it is Emma who replies in a whisper, 'No, not yet!'

Mr. Torrance calmly reads, or seems to read, for it is not possible that there can be anything in the paper as good as this. Indeed he occasionally casts a humorous glance at his womenfolk. Perhaps he is trying to steady them. Let us hope he has some such good reason for breaking in from time to time on their entrancing occupation.

'Listen to this, dear. It is very important. The paper says, upon apparently good authority, that love laughs at locksmiths.'

His wife answers without lowering her eyes. 'Did you speak, John? I am listening.'

'Yes, I was telling you that the Hidden Hand has at last been discovered in a tub in Russell Square.'

'I hear, John. How thoughtful.'

'And so they must have been made of margarine, my love.'

'I shouldn't wonder, John.'

'Hence the name Petrograd.'

'Oh, was that the reason?'

'You will be pleased to hear, Ellen, that the honourable gentleman then resumed his seat.'

'That was nice of him.'

'As I,' good-naturedly, 'now resume mine, having made my usual impression.'

'Yes, John.'

Emma slips upstairs to peep through a keyhole, and it strikes her mother that John has been saying something. They are on too good terms to make an apology necessary. She observes blandly, 'John, I haven't heard a word you said.'

'I'm sure you haven't, woman.'

'I can't help being like this, John.'

'Go on being like yourself, dear.'

'Am I foolish?'

'Um.'

'Oh, but, John, how can you be so calm—with him up there?'

'He has been up there a good deal, you know, since we presented him to an astounded world nineteen years ago.'

'But he—he is not going to be up there much longer, John.' She sits on the arm of his chair, so openly to wheedle him that it is not worth his while to smile. Her voice is tremulous; she is a woman who can conceal nothing. 'You will be nice to him—to-night—won't you, John?'

Mr. Torrance is a little pained. 'Do I just begin to-night, Ellen?'

'Oh no, no; but I think he is rather—shy of you at times.'

'That,' he says a little wryly, 'is because he is my son, Ellen.'

'Yes—it's strange; but—yes.'

With a twinkle that is not all humorous, 'Did it ever strike you, Ellen, that I am a bit—shy of him?'

She is indeed surprised. 'Of Rogie!'

'I suppose it is because I am his father.'

She presumes that this is his sarcasm again, and lets it pass at that. It reminds her of what she wants to say.

'You are so sarcastic,' she has never quite got the meaning of this word, 'to Rogie at times. Boys don't like that, John.'

'Is that so, Ellen?'

'Of course I don't mind your being sarcastic to *me*—'

'Much good,' groaning, 'my being sarcastic to you! You are so seldom aware of it.'

'I am not asking you to be a mother to him, John.'

'Thank you, my dear.'

She does not know that he is sarcastic again. 'I quite understand that a man can't think all the time about his son as a mother does.'

'Can't he, Ellen? What makes you so sure of that?'

'I mean that a boy naturally goes to his mother with his troubles rather than to his father. Rogie tells me everything.'

Mr. Torrance is stung. 'I daresay he might tell me things he wouldn't tell you.'

She smiles at this. It is very probably sarcasm.

'I want you to be serious just now. Why not show more warmth to him, John?'

With an unspoken sigh, 'It would terrify him, Ellen. Two men show warmth to each other! Shame, woman!'

'Two men!' indignantly. 'John, he is only nineteen.'

'That's all,' patting her hand. 'Ellen, it is the great age to be to-day, nineteen.'

Emma darts in.

'Mother, he has unlocked the door! He is taking a last look at himself in the mirror before coming down!'

Having made the great announcment, she is off again.

'You won't be sarcastic, John?'

'I give you my word—if you promise not to break down.'

Rashly, 'I promise.' She hurries to the door and back again. 'John, I'll contrive to leave you and him alone together for a little.'

Mr. Torrance is as alarmed as if the judge had looked over the bench and asked where he was. 'For God's sake, woman, don't do that! Father and son! He'll bolt; or if he doesn't, I will.'

Emma Torrance flings open the door grandly, and we learn what all the to-do is about.

EMMA. 'Allow me to introduce 2nd Lieutenant Torrance of the Royal Sussex. Father—your son; 2nd Lieutenant Torrance—your father. Mother—your little Rogie.'

Roger, in uniform, walks in, strung up for the occasion. Or the uniform comes forward with Roger inside it. He has been a very ordinary nice boy up to now, dull at his 'books'; by an effort Mr. Torrance had sent him to an obscure boarding-school, but at sixteen it was evident that an office was the proper place for Roger. Before the war broke out he was treasurer of the local lawn tennis club, and his golf handicap was seven; he carried his little bag daily to and from the city, and his highest relaxation was giggling with girls or about them. Socially he had fallen from the standards of the home; even now that he is in his uniform the hasty might say something clever about 'temporary gentlemen.' But there are great ideas buzzing in Roger's head, which would never have been there save for the war. At present he is chiefly conscious of his clothes. His mother embraces him with cries of rapture, while Mr. Torrance surveys him quizzically over the paper; and Emma, rushing to the piano, which is of such an old-fashioned kind that it can also be used as a sideboard, plays 'See the Conquering Hero Comes.'

ROGER, *in an agony,* 'Mater, do stop that chit making an ass of me.'

He must be excused for his 'mater.' That was the sort of school; and his mother is rather proud of the phrase, though it sometimes makes his father wince.

MRS. TORRANCE. 'Emma, please, don't. But I'm sure you deserve it, my darling. Doesn't he, John?'

MR. TORRANCE, *missing his chance*, 'Hardly yet, you know. Can't be exactly a conquering hero the first night you put them on, can you, Roger?'

ROGER, *hotly*, 'Did I say I was?'

MRS. TORRANCE. 'Oh, John! Do turn round, Rogie. I never did—I never did!'

EMMA. 'Isn't he a pet!'

ROGER. 'Shut up, Emma.'

MRS. TORRANCE, *challenging the world*, 'Though I say it who shouldn't—and yet, why shouldn't I?'

MR. TORRANCE. 'In any case you will—so go ahead, "mater."'

MRS. TORRANCE. 'I knew he would look splendid; but I–of course I couldn't know that he would look quite so splendid as this.'

ROGER. 'I know I look a bally ass. That is why I was such a time in coming down.'

MR. TORRANCE. 'We thought we heard you upstairs strutting about.'

MRS. TORRANCE. 'John! Don't mind him, Rogie.'

ROGER, *haughtily*, 'I don't.'

MR. TORRANCE. 'Oh!'

ROGER. 'But I wasn't strutting.'

MRS. TORRANCE. 'That dreadful sword! No, I would prefer you not to draw it, dear—not till necessity makes you.'

MR. TORRANCE. 'Come, come, Ellen; that's rather hard lines on the boy. If he isn't to draw it here, where is he to draw it?'

EMMA, *with pride*, 'At the Front, father.'

MR. TORRANCE. 'I thought they left them at home nowadays, Roger?'

ROGER. 'Yes, mater; you see, they are a bit in the way.'

MRS. TORRANCE, *foolishly*, 'Not when you have got used to them.'

MR. TORRANCE. 'That isn't what Roger means.'

(*His son glares.*)

EMMA, *who, though she has not formerly thought much of Roger, is now proud to trot by his side and will henceforth count the salutes*, 'I know what he means. If you carry a sword the snipers know you are an officer, and they try to pick you off.'

MRS. TORRANCE. 'It's no wonder they are called Huns. Fancy a

British sniper doing that! Roger, you will be very careful, won't you, in the trenches?'

ROGER. 'Honour bright, mater.'

MRS. TORRANCE. 'Above all, don't look up.'

MR. TORRANCE. 'The trenches ought to be so deep that they can't look up.'

MRS. TORRANCE. 'What a good idea, John.'

ROGER. 'He's making game of you, mater.'

MRS. TORRANCE, *unruffled*, 'Is he, my own?—very likely. Now about the question of provisions—'

ROGER. 'Oh, lummy, you talk as if I was going off to-night! I mayn't go for months and months.'

MRS. TORRANCE. 'I know—and, of course, there is a chance that you may not be needed at all.'

ROGER, *poor boy*, 'None of that, mater.'

MRS. TORRANCE. 'There is something I want to ask you, John—How long do you think the war is likely to last?' *Here John resumes his paper.* 'Rogie, I know you will laugh at me, but there are some things that I could not help getting for you.'

ROGER. 'You know, you have knitted enough things already to fit up my whole platoon.'

MRS. TORRANCE, *proud almost to tears*, 'His platoon.'

EMMA. 'Have you noticed how fine all the words in -oon are? Platoon! Dragoon!'

MR. TORRANCE. 'Spitoon!'

EMMA. 'Colonel is good, but rather papaish; Major is nosey; Admiral of the Fleet is scrumptious, but Maréchal de France—that is the best of all.'

MRS. TORRANCE. 'I think there is nothing so nice as 2nd Lieutenant.' *Gulping*, 'Lot of little boys.'

ROGER. 'Mater!'

MRS. TORRANCE. 'I mean, just think of their cold feet.' *She produces many parcels and displays their strange contents.* 'Those are for putting inside your socks. Those are for outside your socks. I am told that it is also advisable to have straw in your boots.'

MR. TORRANCE. 'Have you got him some straw?'

MRS. TORRANCE. 'I thought, John, he could get it there. But if you think—'

ROGER. 'He's making fun of you again, mater.'

MRS. TORRANCE. 'I shouldn't wonder. Here are some overalls. One is leather and one fur, and this one is waterproof. The worst of it is that they are from different shops, and each says that the others keep the damp in, or draw the feet. They have such odd names, too. There are new names for everything nowadays. Vests are called cuirasses. Are you laughing at me, Rogie?'

MR. TORRANCE, *sharply*, 'If he is laughing, he ought to be ashamed of himself.'

ROGER, *barking*, 'Who was laughing?'

MRS. TORRANCE. 'John!'

Emma cuffs her father playfully.

MR. TORRANCE. 'All very well, Emma, but it's past your bedtime.'

EMMA, *indignantly*, 'You can't expect me to sleep on a night like this.'

MR. TORRANCE. 'You can try.'

MRS. TORRANCE. '2nd Lieutenant! 2nd Lieutenant!'

MR. TORRANCE, *alarmed*, 'Ellen, don't break down. You promised.'

MRS. TORRANCE. 'I am not going to break down; but—but there is a photograph of Rogie when he was very small—'

MR. TORRANCE. 'Go to bed!'

MRS. TORRANCE. 'I happen—to have it in my pocket—'

ROGER. 'Don't bring it out, mater.'

MRS. TORRANCE. 'If I break down, John, it won't be owing to the picture itself so much as because of what is written on the back.'

She produces it dolefully.

MR. TORRANCE. 'Then don't look at the back.'

He takes it from her.

MRS. TORRANCE, *not very hopeful of herself*, 'But I know what is written on the back, "Roger John Torrance, aged two years four months, and thirty-three pounds." '

MR. TORRANCE. 'Correct.' *She weeps softly.* 'There, there, woman.' *He signs imploringly to Emma.*

EMMA, *kissing him*, 'I'm going to by-by. 'Night, mummy. 'Night, Roge.' *She is about to offer him her cheek, then salutes instead, and rushes off, with Roger in pursuit.*

MRS. TORRANCE. 'I shall leave you together, John.'

MR. TORRANCE, *half liking it, but nervous*, 'Do you think it's wise?' *With a groan*, 'You know what I am.'

MRS. TORRANCE. 'Do be nice to him, dear.' *Roger's return finds her very artful indeed.* 'I wonder where I put my glasses?'

ROGER. 'I'll look for them.'

MRS. TORRANCE. 'No, I remember now. They are upstairs in such a funny place that I must go myself. Do you remember, Rogie, that I hoped they would reject you on account of your eyes?'

ROGER. 'I suppose you couldn't help it.'

MRS. TORRANCE, *beaming on her husband*, 'Did you believe I really meant it, John?'

MR. TORRANCE, *curious*, 'Did *you*, Roger?'

ROGER. 'Of course. Didn't you, father?'

MR. TORRANCE. 'No! I knew the old lady better.'

He takes her hand.

MRS. TORRANCE, *sweetly*, 'I shouldn't have liked it, Rogie dear. I'll tell you something. You know your brother Harry died when he was seven. To you, I suppose, it is as if he had never been. You were barely five.'

ROGER. 'I don't remember him, mater.'

MRS. TORRANCE. 'No—no. But I do, Rogie. He would be twenty-one now; but though you and Emma grew up I have always gone on seeing him as just seven. Always till the war broke out. And now I see him a man of twenty-one, dressed in khaki, fighting for his country, same as you. I wouldn't have had one of you stay at home, though I had had a dozen. That is, if it is the noble war they all say it is. I'm not clever, Rogie, I have to take it on trust. Surely they wouldn't deceive mothers. I'll get my glasses.'

She goes away, leaving the father and son somewhat moved. It is Mr. Torrance who speaks first, gruffly.

'Like to change your mother, Roger?'

The answer is also gruff. 'What do *you* think?'

Then silence falls. These two are very conscious of being together, without so much as the tick of a clock to help them. The father clings to his cigar, sticks his knife into it, studies the leaf, tries crossing his legs another way. The son examines the pictures on the walls as if he had never seen them before, and is all the time edging toward the door.

Mr. Torrance wets his lips; it must be now or never, 'Not going, Roger?'

Roger counts the chairs. 'Yes, I thought—'

'Won't you—sit down and—have a chat?'

Roger is bowled over. 'A what? You and me!'

'Why not?' rather truculently.

'Oh—oh, all right,' sitting uncomfortably.

The cigar gets several more stabs.

'I suppose you catch an early train tomorrow?'

'The 5.20. I have flag-signalling at half-past six.'

'Phew! Hours before I shall be up.'

'I suppose so.'

'Well, you needn't dwell on it, Roger.'

Indignantly, 'I didn't.' He starts up. 'Good-night, father.'

'Good-night. Damn. Come back. My fault. Didn't I say I wanted to have a chat with you?'

'I thought we had had it.'

Gloomily, 'No such luck.'

There is another pause. A frightened ember in the fire makes an appeal to some one to say something. Mr. Torrance rises. It is now he who is casting eyes at the door. He sits again, ashamed of himself.

'I like your uniform, Roger,' he says pleasantly.

Roger wriggles. 'Haven't you made fun of me enough?'

Sharply, 'I'm not making fun of you. Don't you see I'm trying to tell you that I'm proud of you?'

Roger is at last aware of it, with a sinking. He appeals, 'Good lord, father, *you* are not going to begin now.'

The father restrains himself.

'Do you remember, Roger, my saying that I didn't want you to smoke till you were twenty?'

'Oh, it's that, is it?' Shutting his mouth tight, 'I never promised.'

Almost with a shout, 'It's not that.' Then kindly, 'Have a cigar, my boy?'

'Me?'

A rather shaky hand passes him a cigar case. Roger selects from it and lights up nervously. He is now prepared for the worst.

'Have you ever wondered, Roger, what sort of a fellow I am?'

Guardedly, 'Often.'

Mr. Torrance casts all sense of decency to the winds; such is one of the effects of war.

'I have often wondered what sort of fellow you are, Roger. We have both been at it on the sly. I suppose that is what makes a father and son so uncomfortable in each other's presence.

Roger is not yet prepared to meet him half-way, but he casts a line.

'Do you feel the creeps when you are left alone with me?'

'Mortally, Roger. My first instinct is to slip away.'

'So is mine,' with deep feeling.

'You don't say so!' with such surprise that the father undoubtedly goes up a step in the son's estimation. 'I always seem to know what you are thinking, Roger.'

'Do you? Same here.'

'As a consequence it is better, it is right, it is only decent that you and I should be very chary of confidences with each other.'

Roger is relieved. 'I'm dashed glad you see it in that way.'

'Oh, quite. And yet, Roger, if you had to answer this question on oath, "Whom do you think you are most like in this world?" I don't mean superficially, but deep down in your vitals, what would you say? Your mother, your uncle, one of your friends on the golf links?'

'No.'

'Who?'

Darkly, 'You.'

'Just how I feel.'

There is such true sympathy in the manly avowal that Roger cannot but be brought closer to his father.

'It's pretty ghastly, father.'

'It is. I don't know which it is worse for.'

They consider each other without bitterness.

'You are a bit of a wag at times, Roger.'

'You soon shut me up.'

'I have heard that you sparkle more freely in my absence.'

'They say the same about you.'

'And now that you mention it, I believe it is true; and yet, isn't it a bigger satisfaction to you to catch me relishing your jokes than any other person?'

Roger's eyes open wide. 'How did you know that?'

'Because I am so bucked if I see you relishing mine.'

'*Are* you?' Roger's hold on the certain things in life are slipping. 'You don't show it.'

'That is because of our awkward relationship.'

Roger lapses into gloom. 'We have got to go through with it.'

His father kicks the coals. 'There's no way out.'

'No.'

'We have, as it were, signed a compact, Roger, never to let on that we care for each other. As gentlemen we must stick to it.'

'Yes. What are you getting at, father?'

'There is a war on, Roger.'

'That needn't make any difference.'

'Yes, it does. Roger, be ready; I hate to hit you without warning. I'm going to cast a grenade into the middle of you. It's this, I'm fond of you, my boy.'

Roger squirms. 'Father, if any one were to hear you!'

'They won't. The door is shut, Amy is gone to bed, and all is quiet in our street. Won't you—won't you say something civil to me in return, Roger?'

Rogers looks at him and away from him. 'I sometimes—bragged about you at school.'

Mr. Torrance is absurdly pleased. 'Did you? What sort of things, Roger?'

'I—I forget.'

'Come on, Roger.'

'Is this fair, father?'

'No, I suppose it isn't.' Mr. Torrance attacks the coals again. 'You and your mother have lots of confidences, haven't you?'

'I tell her a good deal. Somehow—'

'Yes, somehow one can.' With the artfulness that comes of years, 'I'm glad you tell her everything.'

Roger looks down his cigar. 'Not everything, father. There are things—about oneself—'

'Aren't there, Roger!'

'Best not to tell her.'

'Yes—yes. If there are any of them you would care to tell me instead—just if you want to, mind—just if you are in a hole or anything?'

'No thanks,' very stiffly.

'Any little debts, for instance?'

That's all right now. Mother—'

'She did?'

Roger is ready to jump at him. 'I was willing to speak to you about them, but—'

'She said, "Not worth while bothering father." '

'How did you know?'

'Oh, I have met your mother before, you see. Nothing else?'

'No.'

'Haven't been an ass about a girl or anything of that sort?'

'Good lord, father!'

'I shouldn't have said it. In my young days we sometimes—It's all different now.'

'I don't know. I could tell you things that would surprise you.'

'No! Not about yourself?'

'No. At least—'

'Just as you like, Roger.'

'It blew over long ago.'

'Then there's no need?'

'No—oh no. It was just—you know—the old, old story.'

He eyes his father suspiciously, but not a muscle in Mr. Torrance's countenance is out of place.

'I see. It hasn't—left you bitter about the sex, Roger, I hope?'

'Not now. She—you know what women are.'

'Yes, yes.'

'You needn't mention it to mother.'

'I won't.' Mr. Torrance is elated to share a secret with Roger about which mother is not to know. 'Think your mother and I are an aged pair, Roger?'

'I never—of course you are not young.'

'How long have you known that? I mean, it's true—but I didn't know it till quite lately.'

'That you're old?'

'Hang it, Roger, not so bad as that—elderly. This will stagger you; but I assure you that until the other day I jogged along thinking of myself as on the whole still one of the juveniles.' He makes a wry face. 'I crossed the bridge, Roger, without knowing it.'

'What made you know?'

'What makes us know all the new things, Roger?—the war. I'll tell you a secret. When we realised in August of 1914 that myriads of us were to be needed, my first thought wasn't that I had a son, but that I must get fit myself.'

'You!'

'Funny, isn't it?' says Mr. Torrance quite nastily. 'But, as I tell you, I didn't know I had ceased to be young. I went into Regent's Park and tried to run a mile.'

'Lummy, you might have killed yourself.'

'I nearly did—especially as I had put a weight on my shoulders to represent my kit. I kept at it for a week, but I knew the game was up. The discovery was pretty grim, Roger.'

'Don't you bother about that part of it. You are doing your share, taking care of mother and Emma.'

Mr. Torrance emits a laugh of self-contempt. 'I am not taking care of them. It is you who are taking care of them. My friend, you are the head of the house now.'

'Father!'

'Yes, we have come back to hard facts, and the defender of the house is the head of it.'

'Me? Fudge.'

'It's true. The thing that makes me wince most is that some of my contemporaries have managed to squeeze back: back into youth, Roger, though I guess they were a pretty tight fit in the turnstile. There is Coxon; he is in khaki now, with his hair dyed, and when he and I meet at the club we know that we belong to different generations. I'm a decent old fellow, but I don't really count any more, while Coxon, lucky dog, is being damned daily on parade.'

'I hate your feeling it in that way, father.'

'I don't say it is a palatable draught, but when the war is over we shall all shake down to the new conditions. No fear of my being sarcastic to you then, Roger. I'll have to be jolly respectful.'

'Shut up, father!'

'You've begun, you see. Don't worry, Roger. Any rawness I might feel in having missed the chance of seeing whether I was a man—like Coxon, confound him!—is swallowed up in the pride of giving the chance to you. I'm in a shiver about you, but— It's all true, Roger, what your mother said about 2nd Lieutenants. Till the other day we were so little of a military nation that most of us didn't know there *were* 2nd Lieutenants. And now, in thousands of homes we feel that there is nothing else. 2nd Lieutenant! It is like a new word to us—one, I daresay, of many that the war will add to our language. We have taken to it, Roger. If a son of mine were to tarnish it—'

'I'll try not to,' Roger growls.

'If you did, I should just know that there had been something wrong about me.'

Gruffly, 'You're all right.'

'If I am, you are.' It is a winning face that Mr. Torrance turns on his son. 'I suppose you have been asking yourself of late, what if you were to turn out to be a funk!'

'Father, how did you know?'

'I know because you are me. Because ever since there was talk of this commission I have been thinking and thinking what were you thinking—so as to help you.'

This itself is a help. Roger's hand—but he withdraws it hurriedly.

'They all seem to be so frightfully brave, father,' he says wistfully.

'I expect, Roger, that the best of them had the same qualms as you before their first engagement.'

'I—I kind of think, father, that I won't be a funk.'

'I kind of think so too, Roger.' Mr Torrance forgets himself. 'Mind you don't be rash, my boy; and for God's sake, keep your head down in the trenches.'

Roger has caught him out. He points a gay finger at his anxious father.

'You know you laughed at mother for saying that!'

'Did I? Roger, your mother thinks that I have an unfortunate manner with you.'

The magnanimous Roger says, 'Oh, I don't know. It's just the father-and-son complication.'

'That is really all it is. But she thinks I should show my affection for you more openly.'

Roger wriggles again. Earnestly, 'I wouldn't do that.' Nicely, 'Of course for this once—but in a general way I wouldn't do that. *We* know, you and I.'

'As long as we know, it's no one else's affair, is it?'

'That's the ticket, father.'

'Still—' It is to be feared that Mr. Torrance is now taking advantage of his superior slyness. 'Still, before your mother—to please her—eh?'

Faltering, 'I suppose it would.'

'Well, what do you say?'

'I know she would like it.'

'Of course you and I know that display of that sort is all bunkum—repellant even to our natures.'

'Lord, yes!'

'But to gratify her.'

'I should be so conscious.'

Mr. Torrance is here quite as sincere as his son. 'So should I.'

Roger considers it. 'How far would you go?'

'Oh, not far. Suppose I called you "Old Rogie"? There's not much in that.'

'It all depends on the way one says these things.'

'I should be quite casual.'

'Hum. What would you like me to call you?'

Severely, 'It isn't what would *I* like. But I daresay your mother would beam if you called me "dear father." '

'I don't think so.'

'You know quite well that you think so, Roger.'

'It's so effeminate.'

'Not if you say it casually.'

With something very like a snort Roger asks, 'How does one say a thing like that casually?'

'Well, for instance, you could whistle while you said it—or anything of that sort.'

'Hum. Of course you—if we were to—be like that, you wouldn't *do* anything.'

'How do you mean?'

'You wouldn't paw me?'

'Roger,' with some natural indignation, 'you forget yourself.' But apparently it is for him to continue. 'That reminds me of a story I heard the other day of a French general. He had asked for volunteers from his airmen for some specially dangerous job— and they all stepped forward. Pretty good that. Then three were chosen and got their orders and saluted, and were starting off when he stopped them. "Since when," he said, "have brave boys departing to the post of danger omitted to embrace their father?" They did it then. Good story?'

Roger lowers. 'They were French.'

'Yes, I said so. Don't you think it's good?'

'Why do you tell it to me?'

'Because it's a good story.'

'You are sure, father,' sternly, 'that there is no other reason?' Mr. Torrance tries to brazen it out, but he looks guilty. 'You know, father, that is barred.'

Just because he knows that he has been playing it low, Mr. Torrance snaps angrily, 'What is barred?'

'You know,' says his monitor.

Mr. Torrance shouts.

'I know that you are a young ass.'

'Really, father—'

'Hold your tongue.'

Roger can shout also.

'I must say, father—'

'Be quiet, I tell you.'

It is in the middle of this competition that the lady who dotes on them both chooses to come back, still without her spectacles.

'Oh dear! And I had hoped— Oh, John!'

Mr. Torrance would like to kick himself. 'My fault,' he says with a groan.

'But whatever is the matter?'

'Nothing, mater.' The war is already making Roger quite smart. 'Only father wouldn't do as I told him.'

Mr. Torrance cannot keep pace with his son's growth. He raps out, 'Why the dickens should I?'

Roger is imperturbable; this will be useful in France. 'You see, mater, he said I was the head of the house.'

'You, Rogie!' She goes to her husband's side. 'What nonsense!'

Roger grins. 'Do you like my joke, father?'

The father smiles upon him and is at once uproariously happy. He digs his boy boldly in the ribs.

'Roger, you scoundrel!'

'That's better,' says Mrs. Torrance at a venture.

Roger feels that things have perhaps gone far enough. 'I think I'll go to my room now. You will come up, mater?'

'Yes, dear. I shan't be five minutes, John.'

'More like half an hour.'

She hesitates. 'There is nothing wrong, is there? I thought I noticed a—a—'

'A certain liveliness, my dear. No, we were only having a good talk.'

'What about, John?' wistfully.

'About the war,' Roger breaks in hurriedly.

'About tactics and strategy, wasn't it, Roger?'

'Yes.'

'The fact is, Ellen, I have been helping Roger to take his first trench.' With a big breath, 'And we took it too, together, didn't we, Roger?'

'You bet,' says Roger valiantly.

'Though I suppose,' sighing, 'it is one of those trenches that the enemy retake during the night.'

'Oh, I—I don't know, father.'

The lady asks, 'Whatever are you two talking about?'

'Aha,' says Mr. Torrance in high feather, patting her, but unable to resist a slight boast, 'it is very private. *We* don't tell you everything, you know, Ellen.'

She beams, though she does not understand.

'Come on, mater, it's only his beastly sarcasm again. 'Night, father; I won't see you in the morning.

''Night,' says Mr. Torrance.

But Roger has not gone yet. He seems to be looking for something—a book, perhaps. Then he begins to whistle—casually.

'Good-night, dear father.'

Mr. John Torrance is left alone, rubbing his hands.

▼▼

Spud Trevor of the Red Hussars

IT WOULD BE but a small exaggeration to say that in every God-forsaken hole and corner of the world, where soldiers lived and moved and had their being, before Nemesis overtook Europe, the name of Spud Trevor of the Red Hussars was known. From Simla to Singapore, from Khartoum to the Curragh his name was symbolical of all that a regimental office should be. Senior subalterns guiding the erring feet of the young and frivolous from the tempting paths of night clubs and fair ladies, to the infinitely better ones of hunting and sport, were apt to quote him. Adjutants had been known to hold him up as an example to those of their flock who needed chastening for any of the hundred and one things that adjutants do not like—if they have their regiment at heart. And he deserved it all.

I, who knew him, as well perhaps as anyone; I, who was privileged to call him friend, and yet in the hour of his greatest need failed him; I, to whose lot it has fallen to remove the slur from his name, state this in no half-hearted way. He deserved it, and a thousand times as much again. He was the type of man beside whom the ordinary English gentleman—the so-called white man—looked dirty-grey in comparison. And yet there came a day when men who had openly fawned on him left the room when he came in, when whispers of an unsuspected yellow streak in him began to circulate, when senior subalterns no longer held him up as a model. Now he is dead: and it has been left to me to vindicate him. Perchance by so doing I may wipe out a little of the stain of guilt that lies so heavy on my heart; perchance I may atone, in some small degree, for my doubts and suspicions; and, perchance too, the whitest man that ever lived may of his understanding and knowledge, perfected now in the Great Silence to which he has gone, accept my tardy reparation, and forgive. It is only yesterday that the document, which explained everything, came into my hands. It was sent to me sealed, and with it a short covering letter from a firm of solicitors stating that their client was dead—killed in France—and that according to his instructions they were forwarding the enclosed, with the request that I should make such use of it as I saw fit.

To all those others, who, like myself, doubted, I address these words. Many have gone under: to them I venture to think everything is now clear. Maybe they have already met Spud, in the great vast gulfs where the mists of illusion are rolled away. For those who still live, he has no abuse—that incomparable sportsman and sahib; no recriminations for us who ruined his life. He goes farther, and finds excuses for us; God knows we need them. Here is what he has written. The document is reproduced exactly as I received it—saving only that I have altered all names. The man, whom I have called Ginger Bathurst, and everyone else concerned, will, I think, recognise themselves. And, pour les autres—let them guess.

In two days, old friend, my battalion sails for France; and, now with the intention full formed and fixed in my mind, that I shall not return, I have determined to put down on paper the true facts of what happened three years ago: or rather, the true motives that impelled me to do what I did. I put it that way, because you already know the facts. You know that I was accused of saving my life at the expense of a woman's when the *Astoria* foundered in mid-Atlantic; you know that I was accused of having thrust her aside and taken her place in the boat. That accusation is true. I did save my life at a woman's expense. But the motives that impelled my action you do not know, nor the identity of the woman concerned. I hope and trust that when you have read what I shall write you will exonerate me from the charge of a cowardice, vile and abominable beyond words, and at the most only find me guilty of a mistaken sense of duty. These words will only reach you in the event of my death; do with them what you will. I should like to think that the old name was once again washed clean of the dirty blot it has on it now; so do your best for me, old pal, do your best.

You remember Ginger Bathurst—of course you do. Is he still a budding Staff Officer at the War Office, I wonder, or is he over the water? I'm out of touch with the fellows in these days—(*the pathos of it: Spud out of touch, Spud of all men, whose soul was in the Army*)—one doesn't live in the back of beyond for three years and find Army lists and gazettes growing on the trees. You remember also, I suppose, that I was best man at his wedding when he married the Comtesse de Grecin. I told you at the time that I was not particularly enamoured of his choice, but it was *his* funeral; and with the old boy asking me to steer him through, I had no possible reason for refusing. Not that I had anything against the woman: she was charming, fascinating, and had a pretty useful share of this world's boodle. Moreover, she seemed extraordinarily in love with Ginger, and was just the sort of woman to push an ambitious fellow like him right up to the top of the tree. He, of course, was simply idiotic: he was stark, raving mad about her; vowed she was the most peerless woman that ever a wretched being like himself had been privileged to look at; loaded her with presents which he couldn't afford, and generally took it a good deal worse than usual. I think, in a way, it was the calm acceptance of those presents that first prejudiced me against her. Naturally I saw a lot of her before they were married, being such a pal of Ginger's, and I did my best for his sake to overcome my dislike. But he wasn't a wealthy man—at the most he had about six hundred a year private means—and the presents of jewellery alone that he gave her must have made a pretty large hole in his capital.

However that is all by the way. They were married, and shortly afterwards I took my leave big game shooting and lost sight of them for a while. When I came back Ginger was at the War Office, and they were living in London. They had a delightful little flat in Hans Crescent, and she was pushing him as only a clever woman can push. Everybody who could be of the slightest use to him sooner or later got roped in to dinner and was duly fascinated.

To an habitual onlooker like myself, the whole thing was clear, and I must quite admit that much of my first instinctive dislike—and dislike is really too strong a word—evaporated. She went out of her way to be charming to me, not that I could be of any use to the old boy, but merely because I was his great friend; and of course she knew that I realised—what he never dreamed of—that she was paving the way to pull some really big strings for him later.

I remember saying good-bye to her one afternoon after a luncheon, at which I had watched with great interest the complete capitulation of two generals and a well-known diplomatist.

'You're a clever man, Mr. Spud,' she murmured, with that charming air of taking one into her confidence, with which a woman of the world routs the most confirmed misogynist. 'If only Ginger—' She broke off and sighed: just the suggestion of a sigh; but sufficient to imply—lots.

'My lady,' I answered, 'keep him fit; make him take exercise: above all things don't let him get fat. Even you would be powerless with a fat husband. But provided you keep him thin, and never let him decide anything for himself, he will live to be a lasting monument and example of what a woman can do. And warriors and statesmen shall bow down and worship, what time they drink tea in your boudoir and eat buns from your hand. Bismillah!'

But time is short, and these details are trifling. Only once again, old pal, I am living in the days when I moved in the pleasant paths of life, and the temptation to linger is strong. Bear with me a moment. I am a sybarite for the moment in spirit: in reality—God! how it hurts.

> 'Gentlemen rankers out on the spree,
> Damned from here to eternity:
> God have mercy on such as we.
>   Bah!   Yah!   Bah!'

I never thought I should live to prove Kipling's lines. But that's what I am—a gentleman ranker; going out to the war of wars—a private. I, and that's the bitterest part of it, I, who had, as you know full well, always, for years, lived for this war, the war against those cursed Germans. I knew it was coming—you'll bear me witness of that fact—and the cruel irony of fate that has made that very knowledge my downfall is not the lightest part of the little bundle fate has thrown on my shoulders. Yes, old man, we're getting near the motives now; but all in good time. Let me lay it out dramatically; don't rob me of my exit—I'm feeling a bit theatrical this evening. It may interest you to know that I saw Lady Delton to-day: she's a V.A.D., and did not recognise me, thank Heaven!

(*Need I say again that Delton is not the name he wrote. Sufficient that she and Spud knew one another very well, in other days. But in some men it would have emphasised the bitterness of spirit.*)

Let's get on with it. A couple of years passed, and the summer of 1912 found me in New York. I was temporarily engaged on a special job which it is unnecessary to specify. It was not a very important one, but, as you know, a gift of tongues and a liking for poking my nose into the affairs of nations had enabled me to get a certain amount of more or less diplomatic work. The job was over, and I was merely marking time in New York waiting for the *Astoria* to sail. Two days before she was due to leave, and just as I was turning into the doors of my hotel, I ran full tilt into von Basel—a very decent fellow in the Prussian Guard—who was seconded and doing military attaché work in America. I'd met him off and on hunting in England—one of the few Germans I know who really went well to hounds.

'Hullo! Trevor,' he said, as we met. 'What are you doing here?'

'Marking time,' I answered. 'Waiting for my boat.'

We strolled to the bar, and over a cocktail he suggested that if I had nothing better to do I might as well come to some official ball that was on that evening. 'I can get you a card,' he remarked. 'You ought to come; your friend, Mrs. Bathurst—Comtesse de Grecin that was—is going to be present.'

'I'd no idea she was this side of the water,' I said, surprised.

'Oh, yes! Come over to see her people or something. Well! will you come?'

I agreed, having nothing else on, and as he left the hotel, he laughed. 'Funny the vagaries of fate. I don't suppose I come into this hotel once in three months. I only came down this evening to tell a man not to come and call as arranged, as my kid has got measles—and promptly ran into you.'

Truly the irony of circumstances! If one went back far enough, one might find that the determining factor of my disgrace was the quarrel of a nurse and her lover which made her take the child another walk than usual and pick up infection. Dash it all! you might even find that it was a spot on her nose that made her do so, as she didn't want to meet him when not looking at her best! But that way madness lies.

Whatever the original cause—I went: and in due course met the Comtesse. She gave me a couple of dances, and I found that she, too, had booked her passage on the *Astoria*. I met very few people I knew, and having found it the usual boring stunt, I decided to get a glass of champagne and a sandwich and then retire to bed. I took them along to a small alcove where I could smoke a cigarette in peace, and sat down. It was as I sat down that I heard from behind a curtain which completely screened me from view, the words 'English Army' spoken in German. And the voice was the voice of the Comtesse.

Nothing very strange in the words you say, seeing that she spoke German, as well as several other languages, fluently. Perhaps not—but you know what my ideas used to be—how I was obsessed with the spy theory: at any rate, I listened. I listened for a quarter of an hour, and then I got my coat and went home— went home to try and see a way through just about the toughest proposition I'd ever been up against. For the Comtesse—Ginger Bathurst's idolised wife—was hand in glove with the German Secret Service. She was a spy, not of the wireless installation up the chimney type, not of the document-stealing type, but of a very much more dangerous type than either, the type it is almost impossible to incriminate.

I can't remember the conversation I overheard exactly, I cannot give it to you word for word, but I will give you the substance of it. Her companion was von Basel's chief—a typical Prussian officer of the most overbearing description.

'How goes it with you, Comtesse?' he asked her, and I heard the scrape of a match as he lit a cigarette.

'Well, Baron, very well.'

'They do not suspect?'

'Not an atom. The question has never been raised even as to my national sympathies, except once, and then the suggestion—not forced or emphasised in any way—that, as the child of a family who had lost everything in the '70 war, my sympathies were not hard to discover, was quite sufficient. That was at the time of the Agadir crisis.'

'And you do not desire revanche?'

'My dear man, I desire money. My husband with his pay and private income has hardly enough to dress me on.'

'But, dear lady, why, if I may ask, did you marry him? With so many others for her choice, surely the Comtesse de Grecin could have commanded the world?'

'Charming as a phrase, but I assure you that the idea of the world at one's feet is as extinct as the dodo. No, Baron, you may take it from me he was the best I could do. A rising junior soldier, employed on a staff job at the War Office, *persona grata* with all the people who really count in London by reason of his family, and moreover infatuated with his charming wife.' Her companion gave a guttural chuckle; I could feel him leering. 'I give the best dinners in London; the majority of his senior officers think I am on the verge of running away with them, and when they become too obstreperous, I allow them to kiss my—fingers.

'Listen to me, Baron,' she spoke rapidly, in a low voice so that I could hardly catch what she said. 'I have already given information about some confidential big howitzer trials which I saw; it was largely on my reports that action was stopped at Agadir; and there are many other things—things intangible, in a certain sense—points of view, the state of feeling in Ireland, the conditions of labour, which I am able to hear the inner side of, in a way quite impossible if I had not the entrée into that particular class of English society which I now possess. Not the so-called smart set, you understand; but the real ruling set—the leading soldiers, the leading diplomats. Of course they are discreet—'

'But you are a woman and a peerless one, chère Comtesse. I think we may leave that cursed country in your hands with perfect safety. And, sooner perhaps than even we realise, we may see der Tag.'

Such then was briefly the conversation I overheard. As I said, it is not given word for word—but that is immaterial. What was I to do? That was the point which drummed through my head as I walked back to my hotel; that was the point which was still drumming through my head as the dawn came stealing in through my window. Put yourself in my place, old man; what would you have done?

I, alone, of everyone who knew her in London, had stumbled by accident on the truth. Bathurst idolised her, and she exaggerated no whit when she boasted that she had the entrée to the most exclusive circle in England. I know; I was one of it myself. And though one realises that it is only in plays and novels that Cabinet Ministers wander about whispering State secrets into the ears of beautiful adventuresses, yet one also knows in real life how devilish dangerous a really pretty and fascinating woman can be—especially when she's bent on finding things out and is clever enough to put two and two together.

Take one thing alone, and it was an aspect of the case that particularly struck me. Supposing diplomatic relations became strained between us and Germany—and I firmly believed, as you know, that sooner or later they would; supposing mobilisation was ordered—a secret one; suppose any of the hundred and one things which would be bound to form a prelude to a European war—and which at all costs must be kept secret—had occurred; think of the incalculable danger a clever woman in her position might have been, however discreet her husband was. And, my dear old boy, you know Ginger!

Supposing the Expeditionary Force were on the point of embarkation. A wife might guess their port of departure and arrival by an artless question or two as to where her husband on the Staff had motored to that day. But why go on? You see what I mean. Only to me, at that time—and now I might almost say that I am glad events have justified me—it appealed even more than it would have, say, to you. For I was so convinced of the danger that threatened us.

But what was I to do? It was only my word against hers. Tell Ginger? The idea made even me laugh. Tell the generals and the diplomatists? They didn't want to kiss *my* hand. Tell some big bug in the Secret Service? Yes—that anyway; but she was such a devilish clever woman, that I had but little faith in such a simple remedy, especially as most of them patronised her dinners themselves.

Still, that was the only thing to be done—that, and to keep a look-out myself, for I was tolerably certain she did not suspect me. Why should she?

And so in due course I found myself sitting next to her at dinner as the *Astoria* started her journey across the water.

I am coming to the climax of the drama, old man; I shall not bore you much longer. But before I actually give you the details of what occurred on that ill-fated vessel's last trip, I want to make sure that you realise the state of mind I was in, and the action that I had decided on. Firstly, I was convinced that my dinner partner—the wife of one of my best friends—was an unscrupulous spy. That the evidence would not have hung a fly in a court of law was not the point; the evidence was my own hearing, which was good enough for me.

Secondly, I was convinced that she occupied a position in society which rendered it easy for her to get hold of the most invaluable information in the event of a war between us and Germany.

Thirdly, I was convinced that there would be a war between us and Germany.

So much for my state of mind; now, for my course of action.

I had decided to keep a watch on her, and, if I could get hold of the slightest incriminating evidence, expose her secretly, but mercilessly, to the Secret Service. If I could not—and if I realised there was danger brewing—to inform the Secret Service of what I had heard, and, sacrificing Ginger's friendship if necessary, and my own reputation for chivalry, swear away her honour, or anything, provided only her capacity for obtaining information temporarily ceased. Once that was done, then face the music, and be accused, if needs be, of false swearing, unrequited love, jealousy, what you will. But to destroy her capacity for harm to my country was my bounden duty, whatever the social or personal results to me.

And there was one other thing—and on this one thing the whole course of the matter was destined to hang: *I alone could do it, for I alone knew the truth.* Let that sink in, old son; grasp it, realise it, and read my future actions by the light of that one simple fact.

I can see you sit back in your chair, and look into the fire with the light of comprehension dawning in your eyes; it does put the matter in a different complexion, doesn't it, my friend? You begin to appreciate the motives that impelled me to sacrifice a woman's life; so far so good. You are even magnanimous: what is one woman compared to the danger of a nation?

Dear old boy, I drink a silent toast to you. Have you no suspicions? What if the woman I sacrificed was the Comtesse herself? Does it surprise you; wasn't it the God-sent solution to everything?

Just as a freak of fate had acquainted me with her secret; so did a freak of fate throw me in her path at the end....

We hit an iceberg, as you may remember, in the middle of the night, and the ship foundered in under twenty minutes.

You can imagine the scene of chaos after we struck, or rather you can't. Men were running wildly about shouting, women were screaming, and the roar of the siren bellowing forth into the night drove people to a perfect frenzy. Then all the lights went out, and darkness settled down like a pall on the ship. I struggled up on deck, which was already tilting up at a perilous angle, and there—in the mass of scurrying figures—I came face to face with the Comtesse. In the panic of the moment I had forgotten all about her. She was quite calm, and smiled at me, for of course our relations were still as before.

Suddenly there came the shout from close at hand, 'Room for one more only.' What happened then, happened in a couple of seconds; it will take me longer to describe.

There flashed into my mind what would occur if I were drowned and the Comtesse was saved. There would be no one to combat her activities in England; she would have a free hand. My plans were null and void if I died; I must get back to England—or England would be in peril. I must pass on my information to someone—for I alone knew.

'Hurry up! one more.' Another shout from near by, and looking round I saw that we were alone. It was she or I.

She moved towards the boat, and as she did so I saw the only possible solution—I saw what I then thought to be my duty; what I still consider—and, God knows, that scene is never long out of my mind—what I still consider to have been my duty. I took her by the arm and twisted her facing me.

'As Ginger's wife, yes,' I muttered; 'as the cursed spy I know you to be, no—a thousand times no.'

'My God!' she whispered. 'My God!'

Without further thought I pushed by her and stepped into the boat, which was actually being lowered into the water. Two minutes later the *Astoria* sank, and she went down with her....

That is what occurred that night in mid-Atlantic. I make no excuses, I offer no palliation; I merely state facts.

Only had I not heard what I did hear in that alcove she would have been just—Ginger's wife. Would the Expeditionary Force have crossed so successfully, I wonder?

As I say, I did what I still consider to have been my duty. If both could have been saved, well and good; but if it was only one, it *had* to be me, or neither. That's the rub; should it have been neither?

Many times since then, old friend, has the white twitching face of that woman haunted me in my dreams and in my waking hours. Many times since then have I thought that—spy or no spy—I had no right to save my life at her expense; I should have gone down with her. Quixotical, perhaps, seeing she was what she was; but she was a woman. One thing and one thing only I can say. When you read these lines, I shall be dead; they will come to you as a voice from the dead. And, as a man who faces his Maker, I tell you, with a calm certainty that I am not deceiving myself, that that night there was no trace of cowardice in my mind. It was not a desire to save my own life that actuated me; it was the fear of danger to England. An error of judgment possibly; an act of cowardice—no. That much I state, and that much I demand that you believe.

And now we come to the last chapter—the chapter that you know. I'd been back about two months when I first realised that there were stories going round about me. There were whispers in the club; men avoided me; women cut me. Then came the dreadful night when a man—half drunk—in the club accused me of cowardice point-blank, and sneeringly contrasted my previous reputation with my conduct on the *Astoria*. And I realised that someone must have seen. I knocked that swine in the club down; but the whispers grew. I knew it. Someone had seen, and it would be sheer hypocrisy on my part to pretend that such a thing didn't matter. It mattered everything: it ended me. The world—our world—judges deeds, not motives; and even had I published at the time this document I am sending to you, our world would have found me guilty. They would have said what you would have said had you spoken the thoughts I saw in your eyes that night I came to you. They would have said that a sudden wave of cowardice had overwhelmed me, and that brought face to face with death I had saved my own life at the expense of a woman's. Many would have gone still further, and said that my black cowardice was rendered blacker still by my hypocrisy in inventing such a story; that first to kill the woman, and then to blacken her reputation as an excuse, showed me as a thing unfit to live. I know the world.

Moreover, as far as I knew then—I am sure of it now—whoever it was who saw my action, did not see who the woman was, and therefore the publication of this document at that time would have involved Ginger, for it would have been futile to publish it without names. Feeling as I did that perhaps I should have sunk with her; feeling as I did that, for good or evil, I had blasted Ginger's life, I simply couldn't do it. You didn't believe in me, old chap; at the bottom of their hearts all my old pals thought I'd shown the yellow streak; and I couldn't stick it. So I went to the Colonel, and told him I was handing in my papers. He was in his quarters, I remember, and started filling his pipe as I was speaking.

'Why, Spud?' he asked, when I told him my intention.

And then I told him something of what I have written to you. I said it to him in confidence, and when I'd finished he sat very silent.

'Good God!' he muttered at length. 'Ginger's wife!'

'You believe me, Colonel?' I asked.

'Spud,' he said, putting his hands on my shoulders, 'that's a damn rotten thing to ask me—after fifteen years. But it's the regiment.' And he fell to staring at the fire.

Aye, that was it. It was the regiment that mattered. For better or for worse I had done what I had done, and it was my show. The Red Hussars must not be made to suffer; and their reputation would have suffered through me. Otherwise I'd have faced it out. As it was, I had to go; I knew it. I'd come to the same decision myself.

Only now, sitting here in camp with the setting sun glinting through the windows of the hut, just a Canadian private under an assumed name, things are a little different. The regiment is safe; I must think now of the old name. The Colonel was killed at Cambrai; therefore you alone will be in possession of the facts. Ginger, if he reads these words, will perhaps forgive me for the pain I have inflicted on him. Let him remember that though I did a dreadful thing to him, a thing which up to now he has been ignorant of, yet I suffered much for his sake after. During my life it was one thing; when I am dead his claims must give way to a greater one—my name.

Wherefore I, Patrick Courtenay Trevor, having the unalterable intention of meeting my Maker during the present war, and therefore feeling in a measure that I am, even as I write, standing at the threshold of His Presence, do swear before Almighty God that what I have written is the truth, the whole truth, and nothing but the truth. So help me, God.

The fall-in is going, old man. Good-bye.

ARTHUR MACHEN

▼▼

The Bowmen

IT WAS DURING the Retreat of the Eighty Thousand, and the authority of the Censorship is sufficient excuse for not being more explicit. But it was on the most awful day of that awful time, on the day when ruin and disaster came so near that their shadow fell over London far away; and, without any certain news, the hearts of men failed within them and grew faint; as if the agony of the army in the battlefield had entered into their souls.

On this dreadful day, then, when three hundred thousand men in arms with all their artillery swelled like a flood against the little English company, there was one point above all other points in our battle line that was for a time in awful danger, not merely of defeat, but of utter annihilation. With the permission of the Censorship and of the military expert, this corner may, perhaps, be described as a salient, and if this angle were crushed and broken, then the English force as a whole would be shattered, the Allied left would be turned, and Sedan would inevitably follow.

All the morning the German guns had thundered and shrieked against this corner, and against the thousand or so of men who held it. The men joked at the shells, and found funny names for them, and had bets about them, and greeted them with scraps of music-hall songs. But the shells came on and burst, and tore good Englishmen limb from limb, and tore brother from brother, and as the heat of the day increased so did the fury of that terrific cannonade. There was no help, it seemed. The English artillery was good, but there was not nearly enough of it; it was being steadily battered into scrap iron.

There comes a moment in a storm at sea when people say to one another, 'It is at its worst; it can blow no harder,' and then there is a blast ten times more fierce than any before it. So it was in these British trenches.

There were no stouter hearts in the whole world than the hearts of these men; but even they were appalled as this seven-times-heated hell of the German cannonade fell upon them and overwhelmed them and destroyed them. And at this very moment they saw from their trenches that a tremendous host was moving against their lines. Five hundred of the thousand remained, and as far as they could see the German infantry was pressing on against them, column upon column, a grey world of men, ten thousand of them, as it appeared afterwards.

There was no hope at all. They shook hands, some of them. One man improvised a new version of the battlesong, 'Good-bye, good-bye to Tipperary,' ending with 'And we shan't get there.' And they all went on firing steadily. The officers pointed out that such an opportunity for high-class, fancy shooting might never occur again; the Germans dropped line after line; the Tipperary humorist asked, 'What price Sidney Street?' And the few machine guns did their best. But everybody knew it was of no use. The dead grey bodies lay in companies and battalions, as others came on and on and on, and they swarmed and stirred and advanced from beyond and beyond.

'World without end. Amen,' said one of the British soldiers with some irrelevance as he took aim and fired. And then he remembered—he says he cannot think why or wherefore—a queer vegetarian restaurant in London where he had once or twice eaten eccentric dishes of cutlets made of lentils and nuts that pretended to be steak. On all the plates in this restaurant there was printed a figure of St. George in blue, with the motto, *Adsit Anglis Sanctus Georgius*—May St. George be a present help to the English. This soldier happened to know Latin and other useless things, and now, as he fired at his man in the grey advancing mass—300 yards away—he uttered the pious vegetarian motto. He went on firing to the end, and at last Bill on his right had to clout him cheerfully over the head to make him stop, pointing out as he did so that the King's ammunition cost money and was not lightly to be wasted in drilling funny patterns into dead Germans.

For as the Latin scholar uttered his invocation he felt something between a shudder and an electric shock pass through his body. The roar of the battle died down in his ears to a gentle murmur; instead of it, he says, he heard a great voice and a shout louder than a thunder-peal crying, 'Array, array, array!'

His heart grew hot as a burning coal, it grew cold as ice within him, as it seemed to him that a tumult of voices answered to his summons. He heard, or seemed to hear, thousands shouting: 'St. George! St. George!'

'Ha! messire; ha! sweet Saint, grant us good deliverance!'

'St. George for merry England!'

'Harow! Harow! Monseigneur St. George, succour us.'

'Ha! St. George! Ha! St. George! a long bow and a strong bow.'

'Heaven's Knight, aid us!'

And as the soldier heard these voices he saw before him, beyond the trench, a long line of shapes, with a shining about them. They were like men who drew the bow, and with another shout their cloud of arrows flew singing and tingling through the air towards the German hosts.

The other men in the trench were firing all the while. They had no hope; but they aimed just as if they had been shooting at Bisley.

Suddenly one of them lifted up his voice in the plainest English.

'Gawd help us!' he bellowed to the man next to him, 'but we're blooming marvels! Look at those grey ... gentlemen, look at them! D'ye see them? They're not going down in dozens, nor in 'undreds; it's thousands, it is. Look! look! there's a regiment gone while I'm talking to ye.'

'Shut it!' the other soldier bellowed, taking aim, 'what are ye gassing about?'

But he gulped with astonishment even as he spoke, for, indeed, the grey men were falling by the thousands. The English could hear the guttural scream of the German officers, the crackle of their revolvers as they shot the reluctant; and still line after line crashed to the earth.

All the while the Latin-bred soldier heard the cry: 'Harow! Harow! Monseigneur, dear saint, quick to our aid! St. George help us!'

'High Chevalier, defend us!'

The singing arrows fled so swift and thick that they darkened the air; the heathen horde melted from before them.

'More machine guns!' Bill yelled to Tom.

'Don't hear them,' Tom yelled back. 'But, thank God, anyway; they've got it in the neck.'

In fact, there were ten thousand dead German soldiers left before that salient of the English army, and consequently there was no Sedan. In Germany, a country ruled by scientific principles, the Great General Staff decided that the contemptible English must have employed shells containing an unknown gas of a poisonous nature, as no wounds were discernible on the bodies of the dead German soldiers. But the man who knew what nuts tasted like when they called themselves steak knew also that St. George had brought his Agincourt Bowmen to help the English.

Rudyard Kipling

▼▼

Mary Postgate

OF MISS MARY POSTGATE, Lady McCausland wrote that she was 'thoroughly conscientious, tidy, companionable, and ladylike. I am very sorry to part with her, and shall always be interested in her welfare'.

Miss Fowler engaged her on this recommendation, and to her surprise, for she had had experience of companions, found that it was true. Miss Fowler was nearer sixty than fifty at the time, but though she needed care she did not exhaust her attendant's vitality. On the contrary, she gave out, stimulatingly and with reminiscences. Her father had been a minor Court official in the days when the Great Exhibition of 1851 had just set its seal on Civilization made perfect. Some of Miss Fowler's tales, none the less, were not always for the young. Mary was not young, and though her speech was as colourless as her eyes or her hair, she was never shocked. She listened unflinchingly to every one; said at the end, 'How interesting!' or 'How shocking!' as the case might be, and never again referred to it, for she prided herself on a trained mind, which 'did not dwell on these things'. She was, too, a treasure at domestic accounts, for which the village tradesmen, with their weekly books, loved her not. Otherwise she had no enemies; provoked no jealousy even among the plainest; neither gossip nor slander had ever been traced to her; she supplied the odd place at the Rector's or the Doctor's table at half an hour's notice; she was a sort of public aunt to very many small children of the village street, whose parents, while accepting everything, would have been swift to resent what they called 'patronage'; she served on the Village Nursing Committee as Miss Fowler's nominee when Miss Fowler was crippled by rheumatoid arthritis, and came out of six months' fortnightly meetings equally respected by all the cliques.

And when Fate threw Miss Fowler's nephew, an unlovely orphan of eleven, on Miss Fowler's hands, Mary Postgate stood to her share of the business of education as practised in private and public schools. She checked printed clothes-lists, and unitemized bills of extras; wrote to Head and House masters, matrons, nurses and doctors, and grieved or rejoiced over half-term reports. Young Wyndham Fowler repaid her in his holidays by calling her 'Gatepost', 'Postey', or 'Packthread', by thumping her between her narrow shoulders, or by chasing her bleating, round the garden, her large mouth open, her large nose high in air, at a stiff-necked shamble very like a camel's. Later on he filled the house with clamour, argument, and harangues as to his personal needs, likes and dislikes, and the limitations of 'you women', reducing Mary to tears of physical fatigue, or, when he chose to be humorous, of helpless laughter. At crises, which multiplied as he grew older, she was his ambassadress and his interpretress to Miss Fowler, who had no large sympathy with the young; a vote in his interest at the councils on his future; his sewing-woman, strictly accountable for mislaid boots and garments; always his butt and his slave.

And when he decided to become a solicitor, and had entered an office in London; when his greeting had changed from 'Hullo, Postey, you old beast', to 'Mornin', Packthread', there came a war which, unlike all wars that Mary could remember, did not stay decently outside England and in the newspapers, but intruded on the lives of people whom she knew. As she said to Miss Fowler, it was 'most vexatious'. It took the Rector's son, who was going into business with his elder brother; it took the Colonel's nephew on the eve of fruit-farming in Canada; it took Mrs Grant's son who, his mother said, was devoted to the ministry; and, very early indeed, it took Wynn Fowler, who announced on a postcard that he had joined the Flying Corps and wanted a cardigan waistcoat.

'He must go, and he must have the waistcoat,' said Miss Fowler. So Mary got the proper-sized needles and wool, while Miss Fowler told the men of her establishment—two gardeners and an odd man, aged sixty—that those who could join the Army had better do so. The gardeners left. Cheape, the odd man, stayed on, and was promoted to the gardener's cottage. The cook, scorning to be limited in luxuries, also left, after a spirited scene with Miss Fowler, and took the housemaid with her. Miss Fowler gazetted Nellie, Cheape's seventeen-year-old daughter, to the vacant post; Mrs Cheape to the rank of cook, with occasional cleaning bouts; and the reduced establishment moved forward smoothly.

Wynn demanded an increase in his allowance. Miss Fowler, who always looked facts in the face, said, 'He must have it. The chances are he won't live long to draw it, and if three hundred makes him happy—'

Wynn was grateful, and came over, in his tight-buttoned uniform, to say so. His training centre was not thirty miles away, and his talk was so technical that it had to be explained by charts of the various types of machines. He gave Mary such a chart.

'And you'd better study it, Postey,' he said. 'You'll be seeing a lot of 'em soon.' So Mary studied the chart, but when Wynn next arrived to swell and exalt himself before his womenfolk, she failed badly in cross-examination, and he rated her as in the old days.

'You *look* more or less like a human being,' he said in his new Service voice. 'You *must* have had a brain at some time in your past. What have you done with it? Where d'you keep it? A sheep would know more than you do, Postey. You're lamentable. You are less use than an empty tin can, you dowey old cassowary.'

'I suppose that's how your superior officer talks to *you*?' said Miss Fowler from her chair.

'But Postey doesn't mind,' Wynn replied. 'Do you, Pack-thread?'

'Why? Was Wynn saying anything? I shall get this right next time you come,' she muttered, and knitted her pale eyebrows again over the diagrams of Taubes, Farmans, and Zeppelins.

In a few weeks the mere land and sea battles which she read to Miss Fowler after breakfast passed her like idle breath. Her heart and her interest were high in the air with Wynn, who had finished 'rolling' (whatever that might be) and had gone on from a 'taxi' to a machine more or less his own. One morning it circled over their very chimneys, alighted on Vegg's Heath, almost outside the garden gate, and Wynn came in, blue with cold, shouting for food. He and she drew Miss Fowler's bath-chair, as they had often done, along the Heath foot-path to look at the biplane. Mary observed that 'it smelt very badly'.

'Postey, I believe you think with your nose,' said Wynn. 'I know you don't with your mind. Now, what type's that?'

'I'll go and get the chart,' said Mary.

'You're hopeless! You haven't the mental capacity of a white mouse,' he cried, and explained the dials and the sockets for bomb-dropping till it was time to mount and ride the wet clouds once more.

'Ah!' said Mary, as the stinking thing flared upward. 'Wait till our Flying Corps gets to work! Wynn says it's much safer than in the trenches.'

'I wonder,' said Miss Fowler. 'Tell Cheape to come and tow me home again.'

'It's all downhill. I can do it,' said Mary, 'if you put the brake on.' She laid her lean self against the pushing-bar and home they trundled.

'Now, be careful you aren't heated and catch a chill,' said over-dressed Miss Fowler.

'Nothing makes me perspire,' said Mary. As she bumped the chair under the porch she straightened her long back. The exertion had given her a colour, and the wind had loosened a wisp of hair across her forehead. Miss Fowler glanced at her.

'What do you ever think of, Mary?' she demanded suddenly.

'Oh, Wynn says he wants another three pairs of stockings—as thick as we can make them.'

'Yes. But I mean the things that women think about. Here you are, more than forty—'

'Forty-four,' said truthful Mary.

'Well?'

'Well?' Mary offered Miss Fowler her shoulder as usual.

'And you've been with me ten years now.'

'Let's see,' said Mary. 'Wynn was eleven when he came. He's twenty now, and I came two years before that. It must be eleven.'

'Eleven! And you've never told me anything that matters in all that while. Looking back, it seems to me that *I've* done all the talking.'

'I'm afraid I'm not much of a conversationalist. As Wynn says, I haven't the mind. Let me take your hat.'

Miss Fowler, moving stiffly from the hip, stamped her rubber-tipped stick on the tiled hall floor. 'Mary, aren't you *anything* except a companion? Would you *ever* have been anything except a companion?'

Mary hung up the garden hat on its proper peg. 'No,' she said after consideration. 'I don't imagine I ever should. But I've no imagination, I'm afraid.'

She fetched Miss Fowler her eleven-o'clock glass of Contrexéville.

That was the wet December when it rained six inches to the month, and the women went abroad as little as might be. Wynn's flying chariot visited them several times, and for two mornings (he had warned her by postcard) Mary heard the thresh of his propellers at dawn. The second time she ran to the window, and stared at the whitening sky. A little blur passed overhead. She lifted her lean arms towards it.

That evening at six o'clock there came an announcement in an official envelope that Second-Lieutenant W. Fowler had been killed during a trial flight. Death was instantaneous. She read it and carried it to Miss Fowler.

'I never expected anything else,' said Miss Fowler; 'but I'm sorry it happened before he had done anything.'

The room was whirling round Mary Postgate, but she found herself quite steady in the midst of it.

'Yes,' she said. 'It's a great pity he didn't die in action after he had killed somebody.'

'He was killed instantly. That's one comfort,' Miss Fowler went on.

'But Wynn says the shock of a fall kills a man at once—whatever happens to the tanks,' quoted Mary.

The room was coming to rest now. She heard Miss Fowler say impatiently, 'But why can't we cry, Mary?' and herself replying, 'There's nothing to cry for. He has done his duty as much as Mrs Grant's son did.'

'And when he died, *she* came and cried all the morning,' said Miss Fowler. 'This only makes me feel tired—terribly tired. Will you help me to bed, please, Mary?—And I think I'd like the hot-water bottle.'

So Mary helped her and sat beside, talking of Wynn in his riotous youth.

'I believe,' said Miss Fowler suddenly, 'that old people and young people slip from under a stroke like this. The middle-aged feel it most.'

'I expect that's true,' said Mary, rising. 'I'm going to put away the things in his room now. Shall we wear mourning?'

'Certainly not,' said Miss Fowler. 'Except, of course, at the funeral. I can't go. You will. I want you to arrange about his being buried here. What a blessing it didn't happen at Salisbury!'

Every one, from the Authorities of the Flying Corps to the Rector, was most kind and sympathetic. Mary found herself for the moment in a world where bodies were in the habit of being despatched by all sorts of conveyances to all sorts of places. And at the funeral two young men in buttoned-up uniforms stood beside the grave and spoke to her afterwards.

'You're Miss Postgate, aren't you?' said one. 'Fowler told me about you. He was a good chap—a first-class fellow—a great loss.'

'Great loss!' growled his companion. 'We're all awfully sorry.'

'How high did he fall from?' Mary whispered.

'Pretty nearly four thousand feet, I should think, didn't he? You were up that day, Monkey?'

'All of that,' the other child replied. 'My bar made three thousand, and I wasn't as high as him by a lot.'

'Then *that*'s all right,' said Mary. 'Thank you very much.'

They moved away as Mrs Grant flung herself weeping on Mary's flat chest, under the lych-gate, and cried, '*I* know how it feels! *I* know how it feels!'

'But both his parents are dead,' Mary returned, as she fended her off. 'Perhaps they've all met by now,' she added vaguely as she escaped towards the coach.

'I've thought of that too,' wailed Mrs Grant; 'but then he'll be practically a stranger to them. Quite embarrassing!'

Mary faithfully reported every detail of the ceremony to Miss Fowler, who, when she described Mrs Grant's outburst, laughed aloud.

'Oh, how Wynn would have enjoyed it! He was always utterly unreliable at funerals. D'you remember—' And they talked of him again, each piecing out the other's gaps. 'And now,' said Miss Fowler, 'we'll pull up the blinds and we'll have a general tidy. That always does us good. Have you seen to Wynn's things?'

'Everything—since he first came,' said Mary. 'He was never destructive—even with his toys.'

They faced that neat room.

'It can't be natural not to cry,' Mary said at last. 'I'm *so* afraid you'll have a reaction.'

'As I told you, we old people slip from under the stroke. It's you I'm afraid for. Have you cried yet?'

'I can't. It only makes me angry with the Germans.'

'That's sheer waste of vitality,' said Miss Fowler. 'We must live till the War's finished.' She opened a full wardrobe. 'Now, I've been thinking things over. This is my plan. All his civilian clothes can be given away—Belgian refugees, and so on.'

Mary nodded. 'Boots, collars, and gloves?'

'Yes. We don't need to keep anything except his cap and belt.'

'They came back yesterday with his Flying Corps clothes'— Mary pointed to a roll on the little iron bed.

'Ah, but keep his Service things. Some one may be glad of them later. Do you remember his sizes?'

'Five feet eight and a half; thirty-six inches round the chest. But he told me he's just put on an inch and a half. I'll mark it on a label and tie it on his sleeping-bag.'

'So that disposes of *that*,' said Miss Fowler, tapping the palm of one hand with the ringed third finger of the other. 'What waste it all is! We'll get his old school trunk to-morrow and pack his civilian clothes.'

'And the rest?' said Mary. 'His books and pictures and the games and the toys—and—and the rest?'

'My plan is to burn every single thing,' said Miss Fowler. 'Then we shall know where they are and no one can handle them afterwards. What do you think?'

'I think that would be much the best,' said Mary. 'But there's such a lot of them.'

'We'll burn them in the destructor,' said Miss Fowler.

This was an open-air furnace for the consumption of refuse; a little circular four-foot tower of pierced brick over an iron grating. Miss Fowler had noticed the design in a gardening journal years ago, and had had it built at the bottom of the garden. It suited her tidy soul, for it saved unsightly rubbish-heaps, and the ashes lightened the stiff clay soil.

Mary considered for a moment, saw her way clear, and nodded again. They spent the evening putting away well-remembered civilian suits, underclothes that Mary had marked, and the regiments of very gaudy socks and ties. A second trunk was needed, and, after that, a little packing-case, and it was late next day when Cheape and the local carrier lifted them to the cart. The Rector luckily knew of a friend's son, about five feet eight and a half inches high, to whom a complete Flying Corps outfit would be most acceptable, and sent his gardener's son down with a barrow to take delivery of it. The cap was hung up in Miss Fowler's bedroom, the belt in Miss Postgate's; for, as Miss Fowler said, they had no desire to make tea-party talk of them.

'That disposes of *that*,' said Miss Fowler. 'I'll leave the rest to you, Mary. *I* can't run up and down the garden. You'd better take the big clothes-basket and get Nellie to help you.'

'I shall take the wheel-barrow and do it myself,' said Mary, and for once in her life closed her mouth.

Miss Fowler, in moments of irritation, had called Mary deadly methodical. She put on her oldest waterproof and gardening-hat and her ever-slipping goloshes, for the weather was on the edge of more rain. She gathered fire-lighters from the kitchen, a half-scuttle of coals, and a faggot of brushwood. These she wheeled in the barrow down the mossed paths to the dank little laurel shrubbery where the destructor stood under the drip of three oaks. She climbed the wire fence into the Rector's glebe just behind, and from his tenant's rick pulled two large armfuls of good hay, which she spread neatly on the fire-bars. Next, journey by journey, passing Miss Fowler's white face at the morning-room window each time, she brought down in the towel-covered clothes-basket, on the wheelbarrow, thumbed and used Hentys, Marryats, Levers, Stevensons, Baroness Orczys, Garvices, school-books, and atlases, unrelated piles of the *Motor Cyclist*, the *Light Car*, and catalogues of Olympia Exhibitions; the remnants of a fleet of sailing-ships from ninepenny cutters to a three-guinea yacht; a prep-school dressing-gown; bats from three-and-sixpence to twenty-four shillings; cricket and tennis balls; disintegrated steam and clockwork locomotives with their twisted rails; a grey-and-red tin model of a submarine; a dumb gramophone and cracked records; golf-clubs that had to be broken across the knee, like his walking-sticks, and an assegai; photographs of private and public school cricket and football elevens, and his O.T.C. on the line of march; kodaks and film-rolls; some pewters, and one real silver cup, for boxing competitions and Junior Hurdles; sheaves of school photographs; Miss Fowler's photograph; her own which he had borne off in fun and (good care she took not to ask!) had never returned; a playbox with a secret drawer; a load of flannels, belts, and jerseys, and a pair of spiked shoes unearthed in the attic; a packet of all the letters that Miss Fowler and she had ever written to him, kept for some absurd reason through all these years; a five-day attempt at a diary; framed pictures of racing motors in full Brooklands career, and load upon load of undistinguishable wreckage of tool-boxes, rabbit-hutches, electric batteries, tin soldiers, fret-saw outfits, and jig-saw puzzles.

Miss Fowler at the window watched her come and go, and said to herself, 'Mary's an old woman. I never realized it before.'

After lunch she recommended her to rest.

'I'm not in the least tired,' said Mary. 'I've got it all arranged. I'm going to the village at two o'clock for some paraffin. Nellie hasn't enough, and the walk will do me good.'

She made one last quest round the house before she started, and found that she had overlooked nothing. It began to mist as soon as she had skirted Vegg's Heath, where Wynn used to descend—it seemed to her that she could almost hear the beat of his propellers overhead, but there was nothing to see. She hoisted her umbrella and lunged into the blind wet till she had reached the shelter of the empty village. As she came out of Mr Kidd's shop with a bottle of paraffin in her string shopping-bag, she met Nurse Eden, the village nurse, and fell into talk with her, as usual, about the village children. They were just parting opposite the 'Royal Oak', when a gun, they fancied, was fired immediately behind the house. It was followed by a child's shriek dying into a wail.

'Accident!' said Nurse Eden promptly, and dashed through the empty bar, followed by Mary. They found Mrs Gerritt, the publican's wife, who could only gasp and point to the yard, where a little cart-lodge was sliding sideways amid a clatter of tiles. Nurse

Eden snatched up a sheet drying before the fire, ran out, lifted something from the ground, and flung the sheet round it. The sheet turned scarlet and half her uniform too, as she bore the load into the kitchen. It was little Edna Gerritt, aged nine, whom Mary had known since her perambulator days.

'Am I hurted bad?' Edna asked, and died between Nurse Eden's dripping hands. The sheet fell aside and for an instant, before she could shut her eyes, Mary saw the ripped and shredded body.

'It's a wonder she spoke at all,' said Nurse Eden. 'What in God's name was it?'

'A bomb,' said Mary.

'One o' the Zeppelins?'

'No. An aeroplane. I thought I heard it on the Heath, but I fancied it was one of ours. It must have shut off its engines as it came down. That's why we didn't notice it.'

'The filthy pigs!' said Nurse Eden, all white and shaken. 'See the pickle I'm in! Go and tell Dr Hennis, Miss Postgate.' Nurse looked at the mother, who had dropped face down on the floor. 'She's only in a fit. Turn her over.'

Mary heaved Mrs Gerritt right side up, and hurried off for the doctor. When she told her tale, he asked her to sit down in the surgery till he got her something.

'But I don't need it, I assure you,' said she. 'I don't think it would be wise to tell Miss Fowler about it, do you? Her heart is so irritable in this weather.'

Dr Hennis looked at her admiringly as he packed up his bag.

'No. Don't tell anybody till we're sure,' he said, and hastened to the 'Royal Oak', while Mary went on with the paraffin. The village behind her was as quiet as usual, for the news had not yet spread. She frowned a little to herself, her large nostrils expanded uglily, and from time to time she muttered a phrase which Wynn, who never restrained himself before his women-folk, had applied to the enemy. 'Bloody pagans! They *are* bloody pagans. But,' she continued, falling back on the teaching that had made her what she was, 'one mustn't let one's mind dwell on these things.'

Before she reached the house Dr Hennis, who was also a special constable, overtook her in his car.

'Oh, Miss Postgate,' he said, 'I wanted to tell you that that accident at the "Royal Oak" was due to Gerritt's stable tumbling down. It's been dangerous for a long time. It ought to have been condemned.'

'I thought I heard an explosion too,' said Mary.

'You might have been misled by the beams snapping. I've been looking at 'em. They were dry-rotted through and through. Of course, as they broke, they would make a noise just like a gun.'

'Yes?' said Mary politely.

'Poor little Edna was playing underneath it,' he went on, still holding her with his eyes, 'and that and the tiles cut her to pieces, you see?'

'I saw it,' said Mary, shaking her head. 'I heard it too.'

'Well, we cannot be sure.' Dr Hennis changed his tone completely. 'I know both you and Nurse Eden (I've been speaking to her) are perfectly trustworthy, and I can rely on you not to say anything—yet, at least. It is no good to stir up people unless—'

'Oh, I never do—anyhow,' said Mary, and Dr Hennis went on to the county town.

After all, she told herself, it might, just possibly, have been the collapse of the old stable that had done all those things to poor little Edna. She was sorry she had even hinted at other things, but Nurse Eden was discretion itself. By the time she reached home the affair seemed increasingly remote by its very monstrosity. As she came in, Miss Fowler told her that a couple of aeroplanes had passed half an hour ago.

'I thought I heard them,' she replied, 'I'm going down to the garden now. I've got the paraffin.'

'Yes, but—what *have* you got on your boots? They're soaking wet. Change them at once.'

Not only did Mary obey but she wrapped the boots in newspaper, and put them into the string bag with the bottle. So, armed with the longest kitchen poker, she left.

'It's raining again,' was Miss Fowler's last word, 'but—I know you won't be happy till that's disposed of.'

'It won't take long. I've got everything down there, and I've put the lid on the destructor to keep the wet out.'

The shrubbery was filling with twilight by the time she had completed her arrangements and sprinkled the sacrificial oil. As she lit the match that would burn her heart to ashes, she heard a groan or a grunt behind the dense Portugal laurels.

'Cheape?' she called impatiently, but Cheape, with his ancient lumbago, in his comfortable cottage would be the last man to profane the sanctuary. 'Sheep,' she concluded, and threw in the match. The pyre went up in a roar, and the immediate flames hastened night around her.

'How Wynn would have loved this!' she thought, stepping back from the blaze.

By its light she saw, half hidden behind a laurel not five paces away, a bareheaded man sitting very stiffly at the foot of one of the oaks. A broken branch lay across his lap—one booted leg protruding from beneath it. His head moved ceaselessly from side to side, but his body was as still as the tree's trunk. He was dressed—she moved sideways to look more closely—in a uniform something like Wynn's, with a flap buttoned across the chest. For an instant, she had some idea that it might be one of the young flying men she had met at the funeral. But their heads were dark and glossy. This man's was as pale as a baby's, and so closely cropped that she could see the disgusting pinky skin beneath. His lips moved.

'What do you say?' Mary moved towards him and stooped.

'Laty! Laty! Laty!' he muttered, while his hands picked at the dead wet leaves. There was no doubt as to his nationality. It made her so angry that she strode back to the destructor, though it was still too hot to use the poker there. Wynn's books seemed to be catching well. She looked up at the oak behind the man; several of the light upper and two or three rotten lower branches had broken and scattered their rubbish on the shrubbery path. On the lowest fork a helmet, with dependent strings, showed like a bird's-nest in the light of a long-tongued flame. Evidently this person had fallen through the tree. Wynn had told her that it was quite possible for people to fall out of aeroplanes. Wynn told her, too, that trees were useful things to break an aviator's fall, but in this case the aviator must have been broken or he would have moved from his queer position. He seemed helpless except for his horrible rolling head. On the other hand, she could see a pistol-case at his belt—and Mary loathed pistols. Months ago, after reading certain Belgian reports together, she and Miss Fowler had had dealings with one—a huge revolver with flat-nosed bullets, which latter, Wynn said, were forbidden by the rules of war to be used against civilized enemies. 'They're good enough for us,' Miss Fowler had replied. 'Show Mary how it works.' And Wynn, laughing at the mere possibility of any such need, had led the craven winking Mary into the Rector's disused quarry, and had shown her how to fire the terrible machine. It lay now in the top left-hand drawer of her toilet-table—a memento not included in the burning. Wynn would be pleased to see how she was not afraid.

She slipped up to the house to get it. When she came through the rain, the eyes in the head were alive with expectation. The mouth even tried to smile. But at sight of the revolver its corners went down just like Edna Gerritt's. A tear trickled from one eye, and the head rolled from shoulder to shoulder as though trying to point out something.

'Cassée. Tout cassée,' it whimpered.

'What do you say?' said Mary disgustedly, keeping well to one side, though only the head moved.

'Cassée,' it repeated. 'Che me rends. Le médecin! Toctor!'

'Nein!' said she, bringing all her small German to bear with the big pistol. 'Ich haben der todt Kinder gesehn.'

The head was still. Mary's hand dropped. She had been careful to keep her finger off the trigger for fear of accidents. After a few moments' waiting, she returned to the destructor, where the flames were falling, and churned up Wynn's charring books with the poker. Again the head groaned for the doctor.

'Stop that!' said Mary, and stamped her foot. 'Stop that, you bloody pagan!'

The words came quite smoothly and naturally. They were Wynn's own words, and Wynn was a gentleman who for no consideration on earth would have torn little Edna into those vividly coloured strips and strings. But this thing hunched under the oak-tree had done that thing. It was no question of reading horrors out of newspapers to Miss Fowler. Mary had seen it with her own eyes on the 'Royal Oak' kitchen table. She must not allow her mind to dwell upon it. Now Wynn was dead, and everything connected with him was lumping and rustling and tinkling under her busy poker into red-black dust and grey leaves of ash. The thing beneath the oak would die too. Mary had seen death more than once. She came of a family that had a knack of dying under, as she told Miss Fowler, 'most distressing circumstances'. She would stay where she was till she was entirely satisfied that It was dead—dead as dear papa in the late 'eighties; aunt Mary in 'eighty-nine; mamma in 'ninety-one; cousin Dick in 'ninety-five; Lady McCausland's housemaid in 'ninety-nine; Lady McCausland's sister in nineteen hundred and one; Wynn buried five days ago; and Edna Gerritt still waiting for decent earth to hide her. As she thought—her underlip caught up by one faded canine, brows knit and nostrils wide—she wielded the poker with lunges that jarred the grating at the bottom, and careful scrapes round the brick-work above. She looked at her wrist-watch. It was getting on to half-past four, and the rain was coming down in earnest. Tea would be at five. If It did not die before that time, she would be soaked and would have to change. Meantime, and this occupied her, Wynn's things were burning well in spite of the hissing wet, though now and again a book-back with a quite distinguishable title would be heaved up out of the mass. The exercise of stoking had given her a glow which seemed to reach to the marrow of her bones. She hummed—Mary never had a voice—to herself. She had never believed in all those advanced views—though Miss

Fowler herself leaned a little that way—of woman's work in the world; but now she saw there was much to be said for them. This, for instance, was *her* work—work which no man, least of all Dr Hennis, would ever have done. A man, at such a crisis, would be what Wynn called a 'sportsman'; would leave everything to fetch help, and would certainly bring It into the house. Now a woman's business was to make a happy home for—for a husband and children. Failing these—it was not a thing one should allow one's mind to dwell upon—but—

'Stop it!' Mary cried once more across the shadows. 'Nein, I tell you! Ich haben der todt Kinder gesehn.'

But it was a fact. A woman who had missed these things could still be useful—more useful than a man in certain respects. She thumped like a pavior through the settling ashes at the secret thrill of it. The rain was damping the fire, but she could feel—it was too dark to see—that her work was done. There was a dull red glow at the bottom of the destructor, not enough to char the wooden lid if she slipped it half over against the driving wet. This arranged, she leaned on the poker and waited, while an increasing rapture laid hold on her. She ceased to think. She gave herself up to feel. Her long pleasure was broken by a sound that she had waited for in agony several times in her life. She leaned forward and listened, smiling. There could be no mistake. She closed her eyes and drank it in. Once it ceased abruptly.

'Go on,' she murmured, half aloud. 'That isn't the end.'

Then the end came very distinctly in a lull between two rain-gusts. Mary Postgate drew her breath short between her teeth and shivered from head to foot. '*That*'s all right,' said she contentedly, and went up to the house, where she scandalized the whole routine by taking a luxurious hot bath before tea, and came down looking, as Miss Fowler said when she saw her lying all relaxed on the sofa, 'quite handsome!'

Ford Madox Ford

▼▼▼

The Scaremonger

A Tale of the War Times

'HE OUGHT TO BE HANGED,' the Lieutenant in command of the troops said. 'You think that this collection of bungalows and bathing places is of no importance. And, of course, it isn't. But I tell you, old Blue Funk has done definite mischief. It isn't only that he frightens half the little girls in the village into fits by telling them that the enemy is going to land to-night and cut all their throats. And it isn't only that he spends every night on the beach in a rough-rider's uniform with three revolvers—which is as much as to say that my sentinels go to sleep. But I tell you, General, I have actually traced the rumour about the sinking of three battleships off Chatham to this ridiculous....'

'Well, we won't hang him this afternoon,' the Inspecting General said, 'more particularly since I am dining with him this evening. But I admit that he ought not to have frightened your little Ina, and I don't see why you should not frighten him out of the place, if you can. Only it must be done officially, as a surprise attack, for my inspection. There must not be any warning your shore unit before the attack. Let's see how quickly the Squire and the scouts and the sentries can get them out. I'll sanction that.'

The Squire of Bleakham—old Blue Funk, as he almost liked to be called—had been a member of an exceedingly opulent city firm, and had retired from business much too early for his soul's health to the marine village of Bleakham, whose lordship of the manor, along with the manor house, he had purchased about fifteen years before. Thus he was an indubitable squire, though few squires could have been less squire-like, since the whole of his time had been devoted to so serious a study of the works of Horace and the mediaeval Latinists that he found never a minute, even, to devote to the study of the newspapers. Indeed he was accustomed to boast that, such was the dilettante elegance of his remote existence, not once in the last fifteen years had he perused the day's news. His appointments, his furniture, his electric light-ing, his motors, his billiard-room, and his kitchen were, nevertheless, of the most modern and the most sought-after. His port was beyond praise.

Thus the General inspecting the district took pleasure in dining with the Squire when he was in the neighbourhood, and that evening there were at table Lord and Lady Treffries, the General, Sir Thomas Larne, the lung specialist, and a Scholar of Trinity College, Cambridge.

The Squire made no secret of his terror—of his terror, personal, immediate, and frantic. The enemy, he was certain, would land in Bleakham, and in no other place than Bleakham, that night, the next night, or the night after next. They would come in one of the new, great submarines. A hundred cyclists would land, burning, executing, pillaging the neighbourhood during the hours of darkness; then they would disappear again into the black depths of the sea. And the first house that they would visit would be the manor house, because it was the resi-dence of himself, old Blue Funk.

But, as old Lord Treffries amiably put it, 'the White Terror' would have been the more fitting epithet, since sheer terror had rendered the Squire absolutely white. Ever since the first days of the hostilities the Squire's features had fallen away; colour had deserted them till they had the dull opacity of alabaster; his grey hair had, in the four months of war, grown absolutely white— paper-white. His mouth dragged over to one side; only his eyes had any sign of life. These even sparkled when he spread panic in the village. That night he was in a singular state of agitation.

At the opening of the war the papers had struck him with a wave of panic. You have to imagine how a daily paper of the first days of war must appear to a dilettante Latinist who had not looked at such a sheet for fifteen years. In the last fifteen years the papers have, you know, made much progress in the conveying of excitements. And the Squire had had to read them then. They had revenged themselves amply for his neglect of them.

Every bush, every barn, every bridge, concealed for him an armed spy; behind every cloud there was a dirigible bearing two tons of great, explosive, and poisonous projectiles. The words 'national degeneration' were continually on his lips. When an old cruiser was sunk by a mine he would say: 'There! We used to believe that we could trust the Navy. But even that faint hope deserts us!' And his most peculiar personal terror attached itself to the figure of his once most intimate friend, Professor Eitel-Scharnhorst, of the University of Berlin. Professor Scharnhorst was the brother of Heinrich von Scharnhorst-Fosterdingen, the redoubtable director of submarines of the enemy's navy—and Professor Eitel-Scharnhorst had been in Bleakham again and again as the guest of the Squire. Indeed, it would not be untrue to say that the Squire had learned to believe in the degeneracy of his countrymen from the Professor, whose department had been Latin-classical philology and whose contempt for British philologists had been notorious. It had come finally to an almost ensanguined row, early that summer, between the Professor and the Squire—over the proper punctuation of the ode 'Planco Consule.' For incautiously the Professor had let slip the fact that he had inwardly as great a contempt for the Latinity of the Squire as for that of the Squire's countrymen. And, since that date, the Squire had launched an exceedingly venomous pamphlet against the Professor's edition of the 'Satyrikon' of Petronius. Immediately afterwards the war had broken out.

In the intervening four months the Squire had received only one communication from Professor Scharnhorst—and that was not of a nature to quiet his fears. It was written with all the almost incredible hatred for this country that distinguishes the Prussian professoriate; it gave fifteen scientific reasons for believing that the inhabitants of this country are physically, eugenically, and mentally degenerate; it demolished the Squire's objections to the Professor's notes upon the 'Satyrikon,' and it stated that the Professor had begged his brother, Heinrich von Scharnhorst-Fosterdingen, to pay particular submarine attention to the marine hamlet of Bleakham.

The General, eating his dinner in silence, for the most part listened more or less attentively to the Squire's description of the Scharnhorst letter, for the Squire went over it again and again, most of the time to an accompaniment of laughter. The laughter, indeed, was uncontrollable, and the Squire accepted it almost as a tribute—as if he were a Jeremiah, a true prophet of real disaster, preaching to degenerate fools and Society idiots. It appeared to the General that there might, after all, be something in the famous letter. Certainly the Squire knew something about the enemy's submarines—he had learned several things with accuracy and practical knowledge. No doubt the Professor, who was the brother of the director of submarines, had talked about his brother's activities. He might even have talked a little incautiously; boastful professors sometimes do talk incautiously in the midst of patriotic out-pourings. And suddenly the General asked:

'How often did the Professor stop with you? Every other year or so? Was he—now—interested in, say, fossils?'

But the Professor had not been interested in fossils. He had liked to walk on the sands or sail about the shallows in a small boat, discussing the 'Satyrikon.' It had amused him to go shrimping. But even, the Squire said, if the Professor had been trying to get soundings of the sands off Bleakham they would now be useless. The great storm of September 29 had completely changed the lie of the large sand-banks off the end of Bleakham Bill. What knowledge he had of the position before would be harmful rather than of any use to a landing-party.

That, however, was the only crumb of comfort that the Squire could get into his conversation. Otherwise he was certain that the enemy would land on the Bill that night, or next night, or on the night after next. And he began to talk of the run of the mid-winter tides in the channel, and of the strong motives that the enemy would have for making a dash on Bleakham—it was only about nine miles from Dover. They could destroy an infinite number of telephone wires in half an hour; they could sack half a dozen country seats, including that of Lord Treffries; and, above all, they could hang the Squire, the enemy of Professor Scharnhorst.

It was one of those marvellously still, marvellously warm nights that sometimes visit the neighbourhoods of the Channel waters in mid-December, and, after dinner, most of the Squire's guests sat out on his sheltered verandah, watching the beams of the restless searchlights from Dover as they played upon loose flakes of cloud in a sky brilliant with stars. They had dined uncommonly well, and mostly were sleepily and comfortably silent. Once the General said:

'I should imagine that a lot of chaps landing out of a submarine would be pretty stupid for half an hour or so. I understand the interior air is pretty hellish with stinks, and if there were a hundred it would make it all the worse, wouldn't it?'

The Squire answered that only the most desperate, trained fellows would come.

'Still,' the General said, 'it would make a difference to their shooting, don't you think?' He was the only one of the guests who appeared to pay any deference to the opinion of the host.

'Oh, they'll shoot well enough to get me,' the Squire said; 'right through the forehead, they'll go. It's a consolation to think that they will not hang me.'

There fell on that dark verandah a suspicion of discomfort; the man ought not to talk like that, and for quite two seconds there was a silence.

'Right through the forehead,' the Squire said again. 'I betrayed my country and this place by inviting that fellow here. It's my deserts to get shot, but not to be hanged.'

There was great creaking of chairs; it was getting more than the guests could stand—the sorrowing and the heavy fatalism of the fellow's voice. They all left the verandah except the General and the Scholar of Trinity, who was stopping in the house. The General was waiting for the Squire, who went indoors to arm himself for the vigil that he passed each night on the shore at the end of the Bill. They were quite silent, both of them, until the Scholar said:

'That must be a large liner going down the Channel. Don't you hear the screw? It must be unusually close in.' The thudding of a large vessel's screw was very plainly audible.

The Lieutenant in command of the troops billetted in the empty bungalows of Bleakham had called half of them out, and had gone off towards the east. He had previously warned his little daughter Ina that she was not to be afraid if she heard firing. That would only be himself, making a surprise attack on the bungalows in order to demonstrate to the General that his men were prepared. Incidentally, they were going to frighten or to laugh out of the place the unholy blighter who had given his little Ina such a scare the night before by saying that the enemy were going to land and burn the bungalows and cut her throat. He would, he said, get right out on the sands at low tide, fire a volley of blank cartridge, shout commands in German, rouse all the other troops in a hurry, and, if possible, take the Squire prisoner in the midst of ten or twenty of his men who spoke German or something like it—for many of them were chemist's assistants or city clerks with a smattering of language. Ina was not to mind however much firing she heard; it would only be her father having some fun....

The resulting ten minutes—for it did not take more—was a most unholy mix up. The Lieutenant—he is now senior Captain of the Mid-Kent 57th Cyclist Corps—says that, cycling gently along in the dark, at the very edge of the low-tide, about a quarter of a mile from the beach, he actually ran, at right angles, into the cycle of another man, who cursed him vigorously for a clumsy fool, in German. He had impressed on his own men the absolute necessity for silence, so that the men behind him halted themselves with the merest whispers. Then he dimly made out, to seawards, a black and, as it were, a domed blot. From its top rim, in the merest glimmer of light thrown from below, he perceived to emerge against the stars, four bicycles, twisting slowly round, and painted everywhere a dull grey. Then he had a sense that there were other men walking about and whispering, in the sea itself. He had not the least idea what he did after that—or no clear idea. It was, he said, a most fearful jam up of fists, gun-barrels, bicycles getting between your legs, whispers going into shouts. He got landed fearfully hard with something on the side of the jaw. A long light came out of the top of the black dome; there came into existence in the light the absurd thatches and cupolas of the bungalows of Bleakham, the figure of the Squire in a black rough-rider uniform, the figure of a man in khaki beside him. It struck him as being like an absurd cinematograph effect. There was a figure dimly visible behind the searchlight, crouching down.

A voice said in his ear:

'There's a ladder up the side, sir. We could get up and pot into the inside if your revolver's loaded. The men have only got blank cartridge.'

Suddenly, as he ran into the shallow sea, he shot the man behind the searchlight. That was how it presented itself to him in after years. What he saw at the moment was that the long beam travelled swiftly up the sands, lit for the last moment the roofs of the bungalows, and then, as if contentedly, illuminated the road to the North Star. The man he had shot must have fallen on to a lever. The last illuminated object that he saw by its light was an imp-like Boy Scout with a puff of smoke at his feet, high up the beach. And there was a report like that of two fifteen point sevens. The Boy Scout had fired a maroon. A revolver began to crackle from the sands; a bugle called with the hurry of panic from among the bungalows. Then he was being guided up to the foot of an iron ladder by a man with a cool voice. Jenks was the owner of that voice—Staff-Sergeant Jenks, lately of the Coldstreams.

It was obviously Jenks who got the commander of the U 174, who was just coming out of the hatch, with the butt of a rifle he had snatched from somebody. But the Lieutenant in command was anxious to impress upon you, when he talked about the matter, that there was not any plan, or any heroism either, though that may have been only his modesty. He and the sergeant sat on the lid, as he called it, of the submarine whilst, in and about the surrounding sea, ninety-eight men of the Mid-Kent Cyclist Corps used fists and rifle-butts on forty-two surprised men from East Prussia who were falling over bicycles. But the cyclists captured that submarine with its crew and the fifty-eight men who had not yet emerged, and the newspapers could comment *ad libitum* on a contest between a whale and foxes, or on the ineffectuality of submarines considered as naval units when directed against bungalows. The casualties of the mid-Kents amounted to three men wounded, and they were wounded by the revolver of the Squire who had advanced alone against the submarine, firing twelve shots from two revolvers. He was found by a Boy Scout at the edge of the tide next morning, with a nasty hole in the middle of his alabaster forehead. He had turned the last shot against himself.

In a letter accompanying his testamentary dispositions, which were complicated and very arbitrary, he expressed the hope that, owing to his having written a pamphlet confuting the views of Professor Eitel-Scharnhorst on the subject of Petronius Arbiter, and by his exertions in the cause of averting national degeneracy, he might be said to have deserved well of his country. No doubt he had, if you think it out.

▼▼▼

Gustav

WHEN ASHENDEN, given charge of a number of spies working from Switzerland, was first sent there, R., wishing him to see the sort of reports that he would be required to obtain, handed him the communications, a sheaf of typewritten documents, or a man known in the secret service as Gustav.

'He's the best fellow we've got,' said R. 'His information is always very full and circumstantial. I want you to give his reports your very best attention. Of course Gustav is a clever little chap, but there's no reason why we shouldn't get just as good reports from the other agents. It's merely a question of explaining exactly what we want.'

Gustav, who lived at Basle, represented a Swiss firm with branches at Frankfurt, Mannheim and Cologne, and by virtue of his business was able to go in and out of Germany without risk. He travelled up and down the Rhine, and gathered material about the movement of troops, the manufacture of munitions, the state of mind of the country (a point on which R. laid stress) and other matters upon which the Allies desired information. His frequent letters to his wife hid an ingenious code and the moment she received them in Basle she sent them to Ashenden in Geneva, who extracted from them the important facts and communicated these in the proper quarter. Every two months Gustav came home and prepared one of the reports that served as models to the other spies in this particular section of the secret service.

His employers were pleased with Gustav and Gustav had reason to be pleased with his employers. His services were so useful that he was not only paid more highly than the others, but for particular scoops had received from time to time a handsome bonus.

This went on for more than a year. Then something aroused R.'s quick suspicions; he was a man of an amazing alertness, not so much of mind, as of instinct, and he had suddenly a feeling that some hanky-panky was going on. He said nothing definite to Ashenden (whatever R. surmised he was disposed to keep to himself), but told him to go to Basle, Gustav being then in Germany, and have a talk with Gustav's wife. He left it to Ashenden to decide the tenor of the conversation.

Having arrived at Basle, and leaving his bag at the station, for he did not yet know whether he would have to stay or not, he took a tram to the corner of the street in which Gustav lived and, with a quick look to see that he was not followed, walked along to the house he sought. It was a block of flats that gave you the impression of decent poverty and Ashenden conjectured that they were inhabited by clerks and small tradespeople. Just inside the door was a cobbler's shop and Ashenden stopped.

'Does Herr Grabow live here?' he asked in his none too fluent German.

'Yes, I saw him go up a few minutes ago. You'll find him in.'

Ashenden was startled, for he had but the day before received through Gustav's wife a letter addressed from Mannheim in which Gustav by means of his code gave the numbers of certain regiments that had just crossed the Rhine. Ashenden thought it unwise to ask the cobbler the question that rose to his lips, so thanked him and went up to the third floor on which he knew already that Gustav lived. He rang the bell and heard it tinkle within. In a moment the door was opened by a dapper little man with a close-shaven round head and spectacles. He wore carpet slippers.

'Herr Grabow?' asked Ashenden.

'At your service,' said Gustav.

'May I come in?'

Gustav was standing with his back to the light and Ashenden could not see the look on his face. He felt a momentary hesitation and gave the name under which he received Gustav's letters from Germany.

'Come in, come in. I am very glad to see you.'

Gustav led the way into a stuffy little room, heavy with carved oak furniture, and on the large table covered with a table-cloth of green velveteen was a typewriter. Gustav was apparently engaged in composing one of his invaluable reports. A woman was sitting at the open window darning socks, but at a word from Gustav rose, gathered up her things and left. Ashenden had disturbed a pretty picture of connubial bliss.

'Sit down, please. How very fortunate that I was in Basle! I have long wanted to make your acquaintance. I have only just this minute returned from Germany.' He pointed to the sheets of paper by the typewriter. 'I think you will be pleased with the news I bring. I have some very valuable information.' He chuckled. 'One is never sorry to earn a bonus.'

He was very cordial, but to Ashenden his cordiality rang false. Gustav kept his eyes, smiling behind the glasses, fixed watchfully on Ashenden, and it was possible that they held a trace of nervousness.

'You must have travelled quickly to get here only a few hours after your letter, sent here and then sent on by your wife, reached me in Geneva.'

'That is very probable. One of the things I had to tell you is that the Germans suspect that information is getting through by means of commercial letters and so they have decided to hold up all mail at the frontier for eight-and-forty hours.'

'I see,' said Ashenden amiably. 'And was it on that account that you took the precaution of dating your letter forty-eight hours after you sent it?'

'Did I do that? That was very stupid of me. I must have mistaken the day of the month.'

Ashenden looked at Gustav with a smile. That was very thin; Gustav, a business man, knew too well how important in his particular job was the exactness of a date. The circuitous routes by which it was necessary to get information from Germany made it difficult to transmit news quickly and it was essential to know precisely on what days certain events had taken place.

'Let me look at your passport a minute,' said Ashenden.

'What do you want with my passport?'

'I want to see when you went into Germany and when you came out.'

'But you do not imagine that my comings and goings are marked on my passport? I have methods of crossing the frontier.'

Ashenden knew a good deal of this matter. He knew that both the Germans and the Swiss guarded the frontier with severity.

'Oh? Why should you not cross in the ordinary way? You were engaged because your connection with a Swiss firm supplying necessary goods to Germany made it easy for you to travel backwards and forwards without suspicion. I can understand that you might get past the German sentries with the connivance of the Germans, but what about the Swiss?'

Gustav assumed a look of indignation.

'I do not understand you. Do you mean to suggest that I am in the service of the Germans? I give you my word of honour ... I will not allow my straightforwardness to be impugned.'

'You would not be the only one to take money from both sides and provide information of value to neither.'

'Do you pretend that my information is of no value? Why then have you given me more bonuses than any other agent has received? The Colonel has repeatedly expressed the highest satisfaction with my services.'

It was Ashenden's turn now to be cordial.

'Come, come, my dear fellow, do not try to ride the high horse. You do not wish to show me your passport and I will not insist. You are not under the impression that we leave the statements of our agents without corroboration or that we are so foolish as not to keep track of their movements? Even the best of jokes cannot bear an indefinite repetition. I am in peace-time a humorist by profession and I tell you that from bitter experience.' Now Ashenden thought the moment had arrived to attempt his bluff; he knew something of the excellent but difficult game of poker. 'We have information that you have not been to Germany now, nor since you were engaged by us, but have sat here quietly in Basle, and all your reports are merely due to your fertile imagination.'

Gustav looked at Ashenden and saw a face expressive of nothing but tolerance and good humour. A smile slowly broke on his lips and he gave his shoulders a little shrug.

'Did you think I was such a fool as to risk my life for fifty pounds a month? I love my wife.'

Ashenden laughed outright.

'I congratulate you. It is not everyone who can flatter himself that he has made a fool of our secret service for a year.'

'I had the chance of earning money without any difficulty. My firm stopped sending me into Germany at the beginning of the war, but I learned what I could from the other travellers. I kept my ears open in restaurants and beer-cellars, and I read the German papers. I got a lot of amusement out of sending you reports and letters.'

'I don't wonder,' said Ashenden.

'What are you going to do?'

'Nothing. What can we do? You are not under the impression that we shall continue to pay you a salary?'

'No, I cannot expect that.'

'By the way, if it is not indiscreet, may I ask if you have been playing the same game with the Germans?'

'Oh, no,' Gustav cried vehemently. 'How can you think it? My sympathies are absolutely pro-ally. My heart is entirely with you.'

'Well, why not?' asked Ashenden. 'The Germans have all the money in the world and there is no reason why you should not get some of it. We could give you information from time to time that the Germans would be prepared to pay for.'

Gustav drummed his fingers on the table. He took up a sheet of the now useless report.

'The Germans are dangerous people to meddle with.'

'You are a very intelligent man. And after all, even if your salary is stopped, you can always earn a bonus by bringing us news that can be useful to us. But it will have to be substantiated; in future we pay only by results.'

'I will think of it.'

For a moment or two Ashenden left Gustav to his reflections. He lit a cigarette and watched the smoke he had inhaled fade into the air. He thought too.

'Is there anything particular you want to know?' asked Gustav suddenly.

Ashenden smiled.

'It would be worth a couple of thousand Swiss francs to you if you could tell me what the Germans are doing with a spy of theirs in Lucerne. He is an Englishman and his name is Grantley Caypor.'

'I have heard the name,' said Gustav. He paused a moment. 'How long are you staying here?'

'As long as necessary. I will take a room at the hotel and let you know the number. If you have anything to say to me you can be sure of finding me in my room at nine every morning and at seven every night.'

'I should not risk coming to the hotel. But I can write.'

'Very well.'

Ashenden rose to go and Gustav accompanied him to the door.

'We part without ill-feeling then?' he asked.

'Of course. Your reports will remain in our archives as models of what a report should be.'

Ashenden spent two or three days visiting Basle. It did not much amuse him. He passed a good deal of time in the book-shops turning over the pages of books that would have been worth reading if life were a thousand years long. Once he saw Gustav in the street. On the fourth morning a letter was brought up with his coffee. The envelope was that of a commercial firm unknown to him and inside it was a typewritten sheet. There was no address and no signature. Ashenden wondered if Gustav was aware that a typewriter could betray its owner as certainly as a handwriting. Having twice carefully read the letter, he held the paper up to the light to see the watermark (he had no reason for doing this except that the sleuths of detective novels always did it), then struck a match and watched it burn. He scrunched up the charred fragments in his hand.

He got up, for he had taken advantage of his situation to breakfast in bed, packed his bag and took the next train to Berne. From there he was able to send a code telegram to R. His instructions were given to him verbally two days later, in the bedroom of his hotel at an hour when no one was likely to be seen walking along a corridor, and within twenty-four hours, though by a circuitous route, he arrived at Lucerne.

▼▼

Count Lothar's Heart

I

ELSA was twenty-four the year the Count went off to war, and the Count was twenty-two. She remembered very well how he looked the day he left: the light hair brushed back from the point of his forehead, and color high on his cheeks because he had come fast through the chill of the September afternoon. All the manly, bodily things came alive in his blood when he walked and rang aloud until the echo was heard in every woman's heart that he passed. He had broken the black branches from the trees as they walked that day and carried them back to dress up the *Schloss* before he went away. On the other side of the Traunsee stood the mountains Elsa and Count Lothar had climbed all their childhood together, rising almost straight from the water and the crests, unwooded and faintly blue with height.

The *Schloss* had no beauty or comfort to offer, belonging as it did to other centuries and people with a grimness no woman or season could subdue. The flagstones in the entryway were wide enough to mark a grave, and the carpets Count Lothar's mother had set down in the halls and the reception rooms were as good as nothing. There was nothing strong enough to defeat the hard, cold living of the ancestors: their cellars and their earth beneath the house were present in every room, imbuing, invading, destroying with a damp, chill, deathly breath.

The old Countess was sitting with her velvet boots on by the fire, and the old Count reading his newspaper there. It was nearly dark, but the lamps were still unlighted. Everything that came into the house and everything that went out of it was counted so there would never be any want for the people who came after. There was only a little wood in the chimney, burning slowly, scarcely enough to give a heart of warmth to the tall, gray-windowed, sepulchral room.

Elsa and Count Lothar came in through the arch of the door and put down their branches of leaves on the piano. The leaves hung yellow and thin as silk from the ebony stems of the boughs. The old Countess looked up at once at Elsa, and took her hand from the pocket of her gown. It might have been that she had been waiting for them, her thoughts going sharp and lean with venom, gathering her bitterness close to give it to them when they came through the door.

'Here's the ring, Elsa,' she said. Her face was set in dry and violent old age against the blast of evening they brought in. 'You may as well have it now as long as Lothar has taken it into his head to die.'

Lothar stepped toward the fire, smiling, rubbing his fair, strong hands over and over before the wan, fluttering wings of flame.

'I'm not going to die, Mother,' he said with patience.

No one said anything about the war, except these other things that were said of it, but in a little while he would be on a train going toward it with a quiver of exaltation in his blood. He was so young that he was in haste to make for himself an unconquerable, a manly past, and come back with the power of that as well in the look that he gave a woman on the street. He squatted there on the hearth on his fine, strong thighs, reaching out with his hands for the fire that was nearer to death than life. And Elsa sat down near the old Count, and opened her coat at the neck.

'There's your engagement ring,' said the old Countess sharply, and she leaned forward from the other side and tossed the ring into Elsa's lap.

'Whom am I engaged to?' said Elsa, and she picked it up from her dress and laughed. She sat in her dark suit in the chair, looking with laughter in her eyes at the two old people, and at their son, who did not turn from the flame.

'If Lothar hasn't asked you yet,' said the old Countess, lighting a cigarette, 'then I'm sorry for you. Love and courtship, thank God, were entirely different when I was young. My husband fought two duels for me in the afternoon and we waltzed the whole night together after he had won me.'

The old Count started up gently, as if from sleep, folded his newspaper over, and smoothed out his white soft mustaches with his delicate, shaking hand.

'I forgot about it,' said Lothar, without turning on his heels. 'It's all right with you, isn't it, Elsa?'

They had known each other so long, the same mountains and lakes, heard the same music, the same words over and over, all since they were children, but there had been no talk of love. But somehow, and without passion, it had been known between them;

it had been understood, and Elsa's face was warm and brimming now as she held the fine ring closed inside her hand.

'Yes, Lothar. Yes, it is all right,' she said softly, but the old woman cried out: 'Kiss her! Kiss her!'

Count Lothar stood up and turned his back to the fireplace and walked to the chair where Elsa sat. She saw his face, clear and youthful, coming closer, bending to her, his eyes confused, his color rising. And suddenly she leaped up laughing.

'No, no, Lothar, not now!' she said. 'It's really silly to do it now, isn't it? It doesn't matter! We'll do it some other time,' she said.

'I never met "another time" coming toward me,' said the old Countess, and she snapped the end of her cigarette into the scarcely flickering fire. 'They were always going the other way and they always will be.'

The old Count cleared his throat and took out his watch in the palm of his hand.

'The train goes in half an hour,' he said, peering into the face of it in the gathering dark.

'I'm going to the station with you,' said Elsa softly, and Count Lothar said: 'I'm going to drive the horses myself,' and his eyes were glowing.

The old Countess watched her son sharply a moment, and then she stood up and faced him, holding fast to the back of her chair.

'If you come back,' she said, 'I hope you have some of the rot licked out of you. War has nothing to do with courage. You won't hear me out when I try to tell you. You and your father here, you take every word from the papers. Neither one or the other of you has ever had a thought of his own. When I was a girl there weren't any politics, the men were too good for it. But you were born too late in my life, and you're the worse for it. You kept hemming and hawing around and taking your time, and when I was near forty you made up your mind to appear. War has nothing to do with gentlemen!' she cried out. 'Anyone with good blood in him and some sense has better things to do!'

Her hand was shaking on the high, carved head of her chair, and her face was lifted, white and strongly boned, with the skin drawn over it like lace.

'Lothar will be going in five minutes now,' said the old Count as if in apology to them all.

'Upstarts!' said the old lady fiercely. 'Pot-wallopers like Napoleon! War was good enough for them, just as harlots were good enough for them to marry.' She stood with her two hands clasping the head of the chair, the empty folds of her soft cheeks quivering, the beak of her high nose thin as a blade. Her lids were stretched across her marble eyes, like curtains fallen, and she looking mightily and brazenly up from under their frayed hems. And suddenly Lothar crossed the space between them, dropped his head, and with his lips embraced her hands which did not falter. She stood holding to the strong, elaborate carving while Lothar followed the old Count from the room.

'You mustn't worry. It will be all right,' said Elsa softly.

And 'Worry?' cried out the old lady. The sound of the horses and the carriage could be heard on the drive. 'My dear girl,' said the old Countess, 'you have my sympathy.' She stood tall and immobile, staring without emotion beyond the sight of Elsa buttoning her warm coat over. 'Your fiancé is a man of no particular talents, neither studious nor musical, gifted nor ambitious. He could never keep a single date of history in his head. He is stubborn as a mule, and I frequently wonder where he gets it from.' Elsa pulled on her gloves, and from the hall they could hear the sound of his box being carried down. The old Countess drew her mouth in, close and bloodless in her sagging face. 'He has no more idea why he is going to war than those horses out there, tearing the ground up with their feet, know why they're being driven to the station.'

Elsa went quickly to the old lady and touched her hand. Her eyes had filled with tears before the old lady's dry, unswerving gaze.

'Say good-by to him then,' she said softly. 'Say good-by to him before he goes.'

'Good-by won't enlighten him,' said the old Countess tartly. She stood quite motionless, her hands holding fast to the chair back as Elsa too went out into the hall. The dark was gathering in the window behind her and blotting out entirely the day.

II

Count Lothar had been gone six years, and now it was the end of the summer again and the war a long time over. The old Countess was dead, and the old Count lived to himself, alone in the castle among the ravaged trees. In the spring of each year since Count Lothar had been gone, the trees had been cut down for fuel, and the *Schloss* was no longer now a place of mystery and darkness. It could be seen clearly from the road and from the water, towering in solitude over the gaps and the destruction where the bitten trunks stood.

No one had thought to see him again, for everything that had to do with his youth had dwindled and dimmed and it was almost

certain that he had died as well. The whole country had fallen
into poverty, and if he were alive somewhere, why should he
return? Elsa wore the ring on her finger still, but she wore it in
dignity and resignation, as an old lady might who had known the
things of love and sorrow as they came: year after year the births
and deaths and the altering of the spirit, the despair and the
renunciation. If he comes back, was written in Elsa's face but she
never spoke it out, he will come back because there is nowhere
else to go.

There had been letters from him from Siberia, where he
worked in the prison camp, and letters from China when they
wrote him that his mother had died. But no one ever thought to
see him back again, for so many of the prisoners had stayed and
made a new life where they were, or else they had perished; but
Count Lothar came back one day at the tail end of summer. He
had only a rucksack to carry on his shoulders, so when he came
through the gate at the station he started at once down the road.
His boots were heavy and caked with earth and his topcoat was
graying with a mist of use and age. He was still a thick-set fairish
man with a small nose, fresh color running under his skin, and a
look of gravity and willfulness in his eyes. His face was marked
with weariness, and in weariness he took the first path into the
woods, packed thick with the rotting leaves as it was under foot,
and followed it as if from habit.

At the side of the water he halted and watched the boats
curving out under their single canvas wings. He thought of his
own sloop lying, still belly-up doubtless, as he had left it in the
boat shed near the mouth of the stream. The swift, lovely boats
were blowing across the Traunsee's shining breast, and he
remembered the leap of his own boat's perilous giving and the
rope running quick as water through his hands. He stood there a
little, watching the single petals of the masts unfurling, now to the
right in the wind and now to the left. The mountains on the other
side had looked mighty and barren to him when he went away,
and he saw with surprise now what had happened to them in his
sight: they seemed to have lost their wildness and their power,
and they were as pretty and mild as any pastureland.

Near to the town where the moored boats and the little white
steamer rode on the water, the swans were floating still as they
had floated every summer of his life. He had put his rucksack
down on the gravel and with his arms crossed on the railing he
watched these things, dimly, dimly, as a man in a dream might see
profoundly, yet scarcely see. And, watching so, he saw the swans
rise suddenly and of one accord from the water where they drifted

and fly in great, strong, eager flight above the lake. Their necks were stretched out hungering and thirsting before them as they went, and the mighty flap of their wings was as good as a clear wind blowing. The blood ran up into Count Lothar's face, and he cried aloud:

'My God, I'd forgotten the swans flying!'

They were not near to him, but still he could feel on his flesh the strength of the pure white pinions stroking the quiet air. They might have passed close to him, so well could he feel the power and love of their bodies as they went. They were not like birds in flight, for the masterful wings seemed to raise strong, stallionlike, white bodies from their natural place and fling them headlong in egression into space. White horses might have flown like this, their vulnerable, soft breasts pressed sweet with flesh upon the current. The sight of the swans in flight across the Traunsee was a thing that made Count Lothar's heart rouse suddenly in anguish.

The birds had settled again on the water, and Count Lothar was standing so by the rail when Elsa came down the walk. Her head was lowered, her face ageless, colorless, and she was walking toward the streets of Gmunden with her shopping bag over her arm. There was nothing of youth left to her, nothing there that he might remember. She went past him in her high-laced, black shoes, and he looked back at the swans which were drifting at ease far out on the water. How ugly and shabby this woman and all the other women were, he thought, going down the walk past the lake and into the town.

'Your mother was very sorry to go without seeing you again,' said the old Count after they had eaten together. He looked from Lothar's face to Elsa's, apologizing because the old Countess had died. 'She was very sorry at the end.'

'What did she say?' asked Count Lothar, sitting with his legs stretched out and his eye and his heart quite dry.

'She didn't say anything,' said the old Count, smoothing in his fingers what was left of his mustaches. 'But she turned your photograph around so that it faced her. She had turned it to the wall the day you went away.'

In a little while the old Count went out of the room, leaving Count Lothar and Elsa together, and the afternoon light came through the windows and fell on the dust on the floor and the ashes in the fireplace. There was white in Elsa's hair: it ran back from her brow in a dull, wide avenue of resignation, and Count Lothar turned his face from one side to the other. He looked at the rug worn thin on the floor, and at the light in the window. He did not want to see her face or to hear what she would say.

'You'll take a rest for a while, won't you, Lothar?' she said at last.

'What's that?' he said, and he started at the sound of her voice.

'You'll take a rest here,' she repeated, 'and then I suppose you'll go to Vienna?'

'To Vienna?' said Count Lothar in true surprise.

'There isn't anywhere else to make a living, is there?' said Elsa, and she opened her hands out quietly in her lap.

'Oh, no,' said Lothar. 'I forgot. That's true.'

'What do you think you want to do?' said Elsa gently after a moment.

'Do?' asked Count Lothar, and the look in his face might easily have been taken for stupidity. He had no sharpness and no subterfuge, but all that he felt in his flesh he felt so deeply that it moved him one way or the other of its own accord. All the years were put away behind him in confusion, and he was back amongst his people in confusion. He sat quite still, looking at the rug at his feet and the dust that had gathered on it, his gaze threshing from the table to the window, away from Elsa in despair.

After tea they walked down to the lake and past it out over the pathway of wooden bridges that followed the overflow of the Traunsee where it fell in a fast-running stream. Here the water poured out of the lake and went off down the mountains, and here where they walked above it, it was dammed in a staircase of smooth sliding falls. On the edge of these the swans had gathered; they were standing clear of the falling water on the brink, their webbed feet spread in the fernlike slime that rippled with the current, their legs as black as leather in the startling clarity of the quivering stream.

Count Lothar and Elsa stopped on the bridge, and the birds below them were preening their immaculate breasts and opening their wings out one by one, stretching them stark white against the water.

'How wonderful their necks are!' Count Lothar said, and suddenly a tremor of wonder ran through his blood and he had to steady himself by taking the wooden rail of the bridgeway in his hands.

'Do you remember?' said Elsa softly, holding his arm in hers. 'We used to come here so often—'

He saw her face beside him, distasteful as a stranger's face, the lip of it trembling, and the bar of gray like a warning in her hair. And he turned his eyes back, slowly, in dumb confusion to the sight of the birds on the edge of slipping water. Some of them had thrust the long stalks of their throats down into the deeper places

before the falls and were seeking for refuse along the bottom.
Nothing remained but the soft, flickering, short peaks of their
clean rumps and their leathery black elbows with the down
blowing soft at the ebony bone. In such ecstasies of beauty were
they seeking in the filth of lemon rinds and shells and garbage
that had drifted from the town, prodding the leaves and branches
apart with their dark, lustful mouths.

'Lothar,' said Elsa, and then she stopped speaking. 'I thought—'
she began again, and suddenly she slipped the ring off her finger
and put it in his hand. 'I don't want you to feel bound to me,
Lothar,' she said. 'It's been so long. I don't want to hold you to
anything you don't want. I know there may be someone else, I
understand that very well.'

Count Lothar looked at the ring lying in the palm of his hand,
and then he gave it back to her.

'No,' he said. 'There is nobody else. I'll make some money, I'm
sure I shall find something to do, and then we can get married.'

And then he burst out laughing at what was left of the swans
above the water: the white, beautiful rumps wagging and flickering and seeming to hark to the sudden burst of sound. Elsa put
the ring back upon her finger and she spoke his name softly, but
he was laughing aloud in delight and he did not hear her. He
scarcely knew she was there, for he was watching the strong,
greedy beaks and the weaving of the swans' necks under water.

So he took the habit of coming to see the swans every afternoon, no matter what the weather. He would come down past the
Traunsee and stand on the bridgeway, watching the swans. When
the fine mountain rain of the autumn was falling, the great birds
would go under the beams, under the rotting pillars of the pier,
and he could see them interwinding the long, white vines of their
throats, one with the other. He could stand so on the boards over
the shallow stream, leaning with his arms crossed on the railing,
and watch the swans forever. They were a deep caress to his
wandering spirit, they were a soft call in the darkness to his heart.
He did not know what he thought of them, but there he stood
hour after hour, watching the writhing necks of the white birds
uncoiling and bridling suavely in embrace.

'I hope the snow doesn't come early this year,' Count Lothar
said to his father one afternoon, for he was thinking of what might
become of the birds once the cold of the winter set in.

But the old Count said: 'Perhaps you'll be in Salzburg by that
time.'

Count Lothar was thinking of the swans, and for a moment he
did not seem to hear. He could not remember well the things of

his youth and he did not know any more if the birds stayed here or if they went to warmer places. But suddenly he lifted his head.

'Why should I be in Salzburg?' he said.

The old man had begun to tremble as if in fear of some echo of his dead wife's wrath which might now sound out of his son's mouth. He raised his failing, gentlemanly hand and from where they walked on the road he pointed back through the mutilated trees.

'There's the *Schloss*,' he said, and his voice was shaking. 'I would like to give it to you when you marry. I would like to see you and Elsa live in it together, while I am still here. Elsa and I have been trying here and there, and there's a bank in Salzburg where they've offered you a place. You could come back here with your wife to the *Schloss* for the summers. It would be nice for your children to grow up here,' he said.

'That's true,' said Count Lothar, but he spoke as if he had scarcely heard. 'Do the swans migrate or do they stay the winter here?' he asked after a little while.

In the night the moon was out and Count Lothar put his coat on after supper. The old Count woke up in his chair where he had been sleeping by the fire, and looked with his small, pink eyes at his son.

'Are you going to see Elsa?' he asked, and his voice was faint with hope on his lips. Count Lothar nodded, and at once the tears sprang from the old man's eyes.

But Count Lothar's heart was as dry as a dead leaf blowing down the driveway. He went past the gleaming edge of the lake, and walked through the town, and so out over the bridges that carried the wooden pathway down the shining stream. The moon was high and perfect in the sky, and the swarming light of it gave the land a single dimension of cold, exalted purity. The waters below him were slipping down the stony bed, warbling and calling softly to each other, hollow and sweet as flute notes sounding. Count Lothar stopped on the bridgeway and looked back at the lake that lay behind: the moon's light was riding, white as ice, on the dark waves that murmured in through the stones.

As the Count stood watching the nightly, muted world, a stirring of life sounded out across the water: it began at the end of the lake that was far from him, and it moved like a wind on the water. It came as strong as a foehn wind over the lake, gathering throb by throb until the sky and the land were filled with the sound of passage. Count Lothar held fast to the rail of the bridge, and the blood was shaking in his body, and his ears and his mouth were filled with music like those of a drowning man. There was no longer any earth on which to stand, no air to breathe, no human sound to hear. The elements had become one in the great wind that filled the rushing heavens, drawing with it, long and slow and mighty, the power of spread, gigantic wings.

'Is it the swans? Is it the swans indeed?' Count Lothar cried out in madness, for it seemed to him that a thousand birds had risen on the current and were passing above him, their necks outstretched, their rich, majestic bodies flowing with the deep, ardent pulsing of their monstrous wings. 'Is it the swans?' he cried into the thunder of their flight, and the air itself was passing, lashed fast as pinion feathers to the curved and reaching bone.

As he listened now, he could hear the young Cossacks coming, riding six abreast, the sound of their horses as they galloped. He could see their young faces, as beautiful as women's, and he could hear them singing in wild, high, boyish voices, galloping, with their coats gone white as swans under the falling snow, galloping, galloping, galloping as they crossed the heavens. Elsa had come onto the bridgeway and was standing there beside him, and he seized her arm in his fingers and began calling out to her of what he saw. He could hear the young Cossacks coming, he could see them riding six abreast, coming into the camp as young and rich as stallions.

'Listen to me now, Elsa,' he said. 'Listen to me.'

He saw the women well who came to the prison camp, and were given to the men as rations were given, with no youth or beauty or gusto left in their flesh. He saw their hard, long, riddled faces, and the look of greed they had under the scars left there by hunger and pox and cold. He held Elsa's arm like a man gone mad, and he told her what he saw, telling her these things, talking fast. There were the women offered them, and over the snow rode the Cossacks, galloping, galloping six abreast. They came into the camp, elegant in their good furs, stamping and chattering and dancing like lively women as they warmed their fingers by the stove.

'In some men and women there are conflicting cells,' said Count Lothar, talking wildly as they walked. 'There are the male and the female cells. We're near the beginning of life still and there is still the conflict of the two physical demands in us. We're near to the worms and the snails, and they are both male and female in themselves.'

He saw them laying their coats off, the wide bear coats that went down to their heels. He heard them asking that wine be brought, and the youth in their bodies was thundering, thundering, like the blood that thunders aloud in the ears.

'They never looked at the women,' he said. 'Some of the women were so strong that they carried wounded men for miles on their backs. And some of the strongest, youngest men turned in loneliness to one another.'

He could see their faces clearly, and their eyes turned up like Oriental women's, tilted with lust under their silky brows.

'In some men,' Count Lothar was saying wildly, 'there are more of the female cells, and only in need they discover this.... And in need we turned to one another....'

They had suddenly come to the road, and Elsa was holding fast to him, looking up into his face. At last, at last, was her silence saying softly, at last. He is speaking, and I am to know a little of what became of his youth and what became of the things he had in the years he has been away. At last, at last....

'In Siberia,' Count Lothar said, and then his throat seemed to close in despair and he could say no more. Elsa pressed his arm in gentleness.

'Tell me, tell me,' she said. 'It is very beautiful ... it is friendship ... tell me, do.'

Count Lothar saw that the road lights were burning at intervals beneath the hanging boughs along the road, and that people were walking back from the *Kino* that was just over in the town.

'There is nothing to tell,' he said in a low voice. 'No, I have said it all. There is nothing more to tell,' he said, and they never spoke of it again, neither in Salzburg, where he worked in the bank in the winter, or in the *Schloss*, where they came every summertime.

Biographical information

COMPILED BY JASON EDWARDS AND TRUDI TATE

▼▼▼

RICHARD ALDINGTON (1892–1962). Novelist, poet, translator and biographer, Aldington worked as secretary to Ford Madox Ford and as literary editor of *The Egoist*. He served in the Great War from 1916 to 1918 and suffered later from shell-shock and depression. His war writings include the novel *Death of a Hero* (1929), poetry in *Reverie* (1917) and *Images of War* (1919), as well as short stories in *Roads to Glory* (1930), from which 'The Case of Lieutenant Hall' is taken. Aldington wrote biographies of D. H. Lawrence and Lawrence of Arabia. He married the American modernist writer H.D. (Hilda Doolittle); their marriage ended during the Great War.

MULK RAJ ANAND was born in 1905 in Peshawar, in the North-West Frontier Province of pre-independence India. Educated at the Universities of the Punjab and London, Anand was involved in Gandhi's independence movement in 1921; in the 1930s and 1940s he divided his time between London and India. His father served in the Great War. As a young man, Anand worked on T. S. Eliot's *Criterion* magazine. A highly successful writer, from his earliest works *Untouchable* (1935) and *Coolie* (1936) Anand demonstrates a strong concern with political issues in his writing. His novel *Across the Black Waters* (1940) deals with the experience of an Indian soldier in the Great War. 'The Maharaja and the Tortoise' comes from *The Barber's Trade Union and Other Stories*, published in 1944.

J. M. BARRIE (1860–1937). Playwright and novelist Barrie was born in Kirriemuir and educated at the University of Edinburgh. Best known for his play *Peter Pan* (1904), Barrie also wrote a biography of his mother, *Margaret Ogilvy* (1896), a trilogy of Scottish novels (1888–91), and the plays *Quality Street* (1901) and *The Admirable Crichton* (1902). In 1914 Barrie made an unsuccessful propaganda trip to the United States; he also wrote a number of propaganda pieces, including *Der Tag* (1914), which invokes the myth of the Angels of Mons, and the sketches collected in *Echoes of the War* (1918), from which 'The New Word' is taken.

GWENDOLYN BENNETT (d.1981) Artist, writer and university teacher, Bennett was born in Texas and studied at Columbia University and the Pratt Institute. She taught at Howard University before travelling to Paris to study art on a scholarship. In 1926 she returned to the United States to teach fine arts at Howard. Bennett was involved with a group of young African-American artists and intellectuals after the Great War;

other members included Zora Neale Hurston, Aaron Douglas, Langston Hughes and Wallace Thurman. Seven writers contributed to a new journal called *FIRE!!*, from which 'Wedding Day' is taken. Only one issue appeared, in 1926; fire and insolvency caused the journal to fold. Bennett wrote for other journals, however, including *Opportunity*, and was actively involved in a number of African-American community and federal art projects.

KAY BOYLE (1902–93). Novelist, essayist and short-story writer Boyle was born in Minnesota but lived for much of her life, and through two world wars, in Europe. Boyle was involved in obtaining American visas for European Jews in the 1930s, and worked as a foreign correspondent for *The New Yorker* in the 1940s and 1950s. She was later arrested during protests against the Vietnam War, and worked as a writer for Amnesty International. Her novels include *Plagued by the Nightingale* (1931), *The Year Before Last* (1932), *My Next Bride* (1934) and *Avalanche* (1944). A prolific writer of short stories, Boyle twice received the O. Henry Award for short fiction. 'Count Lothar's Heart' is taken from the collection *Thirty Stories*, published in 1946.

MARY BUTTS (1890–1937). Novelist and short-story writer Butts was born in Dorset. During the Great War she worked in London, where she knew Ezra Pound, H.D., May Sinclair and Rebecca West. For a while she was married to the translator John Rodker. She spent the 1920s in Paris, where she was well known both for her writing and for her interest in drugs and the occult. Her first book was a collection of stories, *Speed the Plough* (1923), from which the title story is taken. Her other works include a war novel, *Ashe of Rings* (1926), the novel *Armed with Madness* (1928) and short story collections, *Several Occasions* (1932) and *Last Stories* (1938). A number of her stories deal with the Great War, and especially with the problem of war trauma.

JOSEPH CONRAD (1857–1924). Novelist and short-story writer Conrad was born to Polish parents, activists for Polish independence, but was orphaned early in his life. Escaping compulsory service in the Russian army, Conrad went to Marseilles in 1874; later he joined the British merchant navy, working at sea for twenty years. He took British nationality in 1886, then settled in England in 1894 and started a second career as an English novelist, though English was his third language. His major works include *The Nigger of the 'Narcissus'* (1897), *Lord Jim* (1900), *Heart of Darkness* (1899), *Nostromo* (1904), *The Secret Agent* (1907) and *Under Western Eyes* (1911). His son Borys served in the Great War and was gassed and shell-shocked. 'The Tale' is taken from *Tales of Hearsay*, published posthumously in 1925.

H.D. (HILDA DOOLITTLE) (1886–1961). Poet and novelist H.D. was born in Pennsylvania and educated for a short time at Bryn Mawr. She moved to London in 1911 and was a key figure in the Imagist movement in poetry. Her first collection of poems, *Sea Garden*, was published in 1916, and can be read as a book of modernist war poetry. Her novel *Bid Me to Live* (1960) is based on her experiences during the war, including the break-up of her marriage to Richard Aldington after he enlisted. *Asphodel*, published posthumously, also deals with this period. After the war, H.D. became involved with Bryher, the woman who was to become her lifelong companion. A prolific writer of poetry, including the Second World War sequence, *Trilogy*, H.D. also wrote a number of prose works, including an autobiographical novel, *Her* (1981) and a striking story about war neurosis, 'Kora and Ka' (1930, reprinted in *That Kind of Woman*, edited by Bronte Adams and Trudi Tate, London, Virago, 1991). 'Ear-Ring' was published in *Life and Letters Today* in 1936.

WILLIAM FAULKNER (1897–1962). Novelist, short-story writer and screenwriter Faulkner was born in Mississippi. In 1918 he enlisted in the Royal Air Force in Canada, but the war ended while he was still in training. For many years he claimed to have fought in the war, and to have sustained a number of injuries. Faulkner travelled to Europe in 1925 and visited some of the battlefields. His first novel, *Soldiers' Pay* (1926), is about an American soldier who is injured in the Great War. His other novels include *The Sound and the Fury* (1929), *As I Lay Dying* (1930), and *Absalom, Absalom!* (1936). *The Fable* (1954) is a fantasy about the Great War; a number of his short stories also deal with the war. 'All the Dead Pilots' is taken from *These Thirteen*, published in 1931.

FORD MADOX FORD (1873–1939). Novelist, critic and poet Ford Hermann Hueffer changed his name to Ford Madox Ford in 1919. He served in the British Army from 1915 to 1917; the experience of being blown up caused him to lose his memory and left him with war-neurotic symptoms which lasted into the 1920s. Ford's best known work is *The Good Soldier*, written just before the war, but published in 1915. Also published in 1915 was *Zeppelin Nights*, co-written with Violet Hunt. In the early part of the war, Ford wrote propaganda, including *When Blood is their Argument* (1915), which he dictated to his secretary, Richard Aldington. Ford's major war novel, *Parade's End*, was published in 1924–28. 'The Scaremonger' was published in *The Bystander* in 1914.

RADCLYFFE HALL (1886–1943). Novelist, poet and short-story writer Marguerite Radclyffe Hall is best known for her lesbian novel *The Well of Loneliness* (1928), which was the subject of a famous obscenity trial. The novel is set partly during the Great War, when the central character joins an ambulance corps and meets the woman who will become her lover. Hall supported the war, and wanted to join an ambulance unit, but was unable to leave her partner, who was ill. Instead, she encouraged others to enlist, and wrote recruitment leaflets. Her other works include *The Unlit Lamp* (1924) and *Adam's Breed* (1926). 'Miss Ogilvy Finds Herself' is the title piece of a collection of stories, several of which are set in the Great War, published in 1934.

ERNEST HEMINGWAY (1899–1961). Novelist, journalist and short-story writer Hemingway was born in Illinois and volunteered as a Red Cross ambulance driver in Italy in 1918. He was severely wounded after only three weeks at the Front, and spent several months recuperating in hospital. Later he claimed he had joined the Italian army, but recent research suggests that this was not true. In the 1920s Hemingway lived among the American expatriates in Paris, where he knew Pound and Stein. He worked as a war journalist in the Greek–Turkish war in 1922 and as a war correspondent in the Spanish Civil War between 1937 and 1938. His writing about the Great War includes *The Sun Also Rises* (1926) and *A Farewell to Arms* (1929). Many of his short stories deal with the Great War, including some of those collected in *Men Without Women* (1927), from which 'In Another Country' is taken. Other works include *For Whom the Bell Tolls* (1940) and *The Old Man and the Sea* (1952). In 1942 Hemingway edited and introduced a collection of war stories entitled *Men at War*.

WINIFRED HOLTBY (1898–1935). Novelist, lecturer, feminist, journalist and short-story writer Holtby was born in Yorkshire. After a year at Somerville College, Oxford, she joined Queen Mary's Auxiliary Army Corps in the Great War. After the war she returned to Oxford, where she met Vera Brittain; the two women became committed peace campaigners. Later Brittain wrote about their relationship and their work in *Testament of Friendship* (1940). A prolific journalist, Holtby travelled throughout Europe, lecturing for the League of Nations Union. She died prematurely, partly from overwork, in 1935. Her writings include *The Land of Green Ginger* (1927), *South Riding* (1936) and a study of Virginia Woolf (1932), as well as the stories collected in *Truth is Not Sober* (1934), from which 'So Handy for the Fun Fair' is taken.

RUDYARD KIPLING (1865–1936). Poet, novelist and short-story writer Kipling was born in India and educated in England. Perhaps the most popular writer in English between 1890 and 1920, Kipling wrote a good deal about war: imperial wars, the Boer War and the Great War. In 1915 his son John went missing on his first day in action; his body was never found. In 1917 Kipling became an Imperial War Graves Commissioner; for the rest of his life he felt highly ambivalent about the Great War and about his own role in supporting it. His Great War writings include a history of the Irish Guards in the war (1923), poetry collected in *The Years Between* (1919), stories in *A Diversity of Creatures* (1917), from which 'Mary Postgate' is taken, and stories and poems in *Debits and Credits* (1926). A range of Kipling's war writings over several decades is collected in *War Stories and Poems*, edited by Andrew Rutherford (Oxford University Press, 1990).

D. H. LAWRENCE (1885–1930). Novelist, poet, critic and short-story writer Lawrence was born in Nottinghamshire where his father was a coalminer. He worked as a teacher until forced to resign because of ill health. Like many of his circle, Lawrence was bitterly opposed to the war, though he was also hostile to pacifists; he and Bertrand Russell fell out over the issue in 1915. In 1917 he and his German wife Frieda were accused of being spies and evicted from Cornwall. Many of Lawrence's writings deal with the war, including stories in *England, My England* (1922), from which 'Monkey Nuts' is taken, as well as the novels *Aaron's Rod* (1922), *Kangaroo* (1923), *The Ladybird* (1923) and *The Fox* (1923). Other important works include *Sons and Lovers* (1913), *The Rainbow* (1915) and *Women in Love* (1920); in his preface to *Women in Love*, Lawrence stated that the bitterness of the Great War could be felt throughout the novel, although it is never mentioned explicitly. A detailed account of Lawrence's war experiences can be found in Paul Delany, *D. H. Lawrence's Nightmare* (Hassocks, Harvester, 1979).

WYNDHAM LEWIS (1882–1957). Artist, novelist and critic Percy Wyndham Lewis was born in Canada but grew up in England. He edited *Blast* magazine during 1914 and 1915, and led the Vorticist movement in painting. Lewis enlisted in the war in 1916 and served as a gunner. In 1917 he became an official war artist for the Canadian government; his war paintings are collected in *Wyndham Lewis: Art and War*, edited by Paul Edwards (London, Lund Humphries, 1992). His war writings include the autobiographies *Blasting and Bombadiering* (1937, revised edition 1967) and *Rude Assignment* (1950), as well as some of the stories in the posthumous collection *Unlucky for Pringle* (1973). Highly critical of many of his contemporaries, Lewis wrote attacks and satires against Eliot, Faulkner, Hemingway, Joyce, Lawrence, Pound and Woolf. 'The French Poodle' was published in *The Egoist* in 1916.

ARTHUR MACHEN (1863–1947). Novelist, translator and journalist Machen was born in Caerlon-on-Usk. He moved to London in 1880 and worked as a cataloguer of books about the occult. Later he became involved in cabbalism, theosophy and the Order of the Golden Dawn. He worked in London as a journalist for the *Evening News*, the paper in which 'The Bowmen' first appeared, in September 1914. Other works include Gothic and supernatural tales in the 1890s, critical essays in *Hieroglyphics* (1902), *Dreads and Drolls* (1926), the war fantasy *The Terror* (1917) and two volumes of autobiography: *Far Off Things* (1922) and *Things Near and Far* (1923).

KATHERINE MANSFIELD (1888–1923). Short-story writer and critic Katherine Mansfield was born in New Zealand, educated in London between 1903 and 1906, and came to live in London in 1908. In 1912 she met John Middleton Murry, with whom she edited the journal *Signature*, and whom she married in 1918. Her brother Leslie Beauchamp was killed in the war in 1915. Mansfield visited the war zone in 1915; 'An Indiscreet Journey' is based on this visit. She moved to France during the war and lived there during 1918 and 1919; she died of tuberculosis at the age of 34. Collections of her stories include *In a German Pension* (1911),

Bliss (1920), *The Garden Party* (1922) and *The Dove's Nest* (1923), from which 'The Fly', written in 1922, is taken.

W. SOMERSET MAUGHAM (1874–1965). Novelist, short-story writer and playwright Maugham was orphaned at a young age. He trained in London as a doctor, then settled in Paris in 1898. Maugham travelled widely and volunteered for an ambulance unit in Flanders in 1914; he also worked for the Intelligence Department during the war, and was sent to Russia in 1917 as part of Britain's effort to prevent the revolution and keep Russia in the Great War. The stories in *Ashenden* (1928) are based on these experiences; 'Gustav' comes from this collection. He also wrote a popular anti-war play *For Services Rendered* (1932). Other works include the novels *Of Human Bondage* (1915), *The Moon and Sixpence* (1919), *The Painted Veil* (1925) and *The Razor's Edge* (1945), and the plays *The Tenth Man* (1910) and *Our Betters* (1917).

SAPPER (1888–1937). 'Sapper' H. C. McNeile was born in Cornwall and educated at the Royal Military Academy at Woolwich. He joined the Royal Engineers, serving from 1907 to 1919. Sapper is best remembered now for his stories about Hugh 'Bulldog' Drummond, starting with *Bulldog Drummond* (1920), subtitled *The Adventures of a Demobilized Officer who found Peace Dull*, a work which was very popular with ex-servicemen. The Bulldog Drummond works appeared in several volumes until 1935; after McNeile's death, they were continued by G. T. Fairlie under the same pseudonym. Sapper also wrote other collections of war stories including *Men, Women and Guns* (1916), from which 'Spud Trevor of the Red Hussars' is taken.

MAY SINCLAIR (1863–1946). Novelist, critic and short-story writer Sinclair was born in Cheshire. A campaigner for women's suffrage as well as a successful and popular writer, Sinclair supported the war and went to the war zone in September 1914 as the member of an ambulance corps. She was then 51. Her war writings include *Journal of Impressions in Belgium* (1915), *The Tree of Heaven* (1917), *The Romantic* (1920), *Anne Severn and the Fieldings* (1922), *Far End* (1926) and *Tales Told by Simpson* (1930). Other works include *Mary Olivier: A Life* (1919) and *Life and Death of Harriet Frean* (1922). 'Red Tape' was published in *The Queen: The Lady's Newspaper* in November 1914.

GERTRUDE STEIN (1874–1946). Poet, novelist and short-story writer Gertrude Stein was born in Pennsylvania. In 1902 she left the United States after studying at Harvard Annexe and the Johns Hopkins School of Medicine; in 1903 she settled in Paris and from 1907 lived the rest of her life with her lover, Alice B. Toklas. Stein spent the early part of the war in England and in Spain, then she and Toklas volunteered for the American Fund for French Wounded, transporting supplies for wounded soldiers in a car named Auntie. Stein engages with the Great War in many of her writings, including *The Autobiography of Alice B. Toklas*

(1933) and *Wars I Have Seen* (1945), as well as some of the shorter pieces collected in *Look At Me Now and Here I Am* (1967) and in *Geography and Plays* (1922), from which 'Tourty or Tourtebattre', written in 1919, is taken.

SYLVIA TOWNSEND WARNER (1893–1978). Novelist, poet and short-story writer Warner was born in Harrow. As a young woman, she worked extensively on fifteenth- and sixteenth-century music, co-editing the ten volume *Tudor Church Music*. During the Great War Warner worked in a munitions factory. In the 1930s she was on the executive committee of the Association of Writers for Intellectual Liberty, and she went to Spain during the Civil War. Her novels include *Lolly Willowes* (1926), *Mr Fortune's Maggot* (1927), *The True Heart* (1929) and *Summer Will Show* (1936). She also wrote a large number of short stories, publishing regularly in *New Yorker* magazine. 'A Love Match' was first published in *A Stranger with a Bag* (1961) and reprinted in *Collected Stories* (1989).

EDITH WHARTON (1862–1937). Novelist and short-story writer Wharton was born in New York and moved to Paris in 1907. During the Great War Wharton was involved in setting up and administering a number of American relief organizations, including the American Hostels for Refugees, medical clinics and an employment agency for refugees in France. She visited the war zone in 1915. Her war writing includes war journalism collected in *Fighting France* (1915), novels *The Marne* (1918) and *A Son at the Front* (1923), as well as *The Book of the Homeless* (1915), a volume Wharton edited to raise money for refugees. 'The Refugees' was published in *Certain People* (1930). Other works include the novels *The House of Mirth* (1905), *Ethan Frome* (1911), *The Reef* (1912), *The Age of Innocence* (1920), *The Children* (1928) and *Hudson River Bracketed* (1929), as well as an autobiographical work, *A Backward Glance* (1934).

VIRGINIA WOOLF (1882–1941). Novelist, critic and short-story writer Woolf was born in London and educated at home. Recognized as one of the foremost practitioners of modernist fiction, Woolf produced nine novels and several collections of short stories, as well as essays and reviews. Her concern with the relationship between culture and politics, including war, is explored in two non-fictional works, *A Room of One's Own* (1929) and *Three Guineas* (1938). Woolf's engagement with the Great War is complex and often difficult to pin down, but it is a key issue in many of her novels including *Jacob's Room* (1922), *Mrs Dalloway* (1925), *To the Lighthouse* (1927), *The Years* (1937) and *Between the Acts* (1941). 'The Mark on the Wall' (1917) was one of the first works to be published by Virginia Woolf and her husband Leonard at the Hogarth Press.